MODELS IN MICROECONOMIC THEORY

MODELS IN MICROECONOMIC THEORY
Expanded Second Edition

Martin J. Osborne
University of Toronto

Ariel Rubinstein
Tel Aviv University
New York University

https://www.openbookpublishers.com

© 2020, 2023 (expanded second edition) Martin J. Osborne and Ariel Rubinstein

ISBN Paperback: 978-1-80511-124-5
ISBN Hardback: 978-1-80511-125-2
ISBN Digital (PDF): 978-1-80511-126-9
DOI: 10.11647/OBP.0362

This book is available in two versions, one that uses feminine pronouns and one that uses masculine pronouns. This version uses masculine pronouns.

Version: 2023.5.30 (h)

Contents

Part II   Equilibrium   103

Personal note

In 1981 I joined the Department of Economics at the Hebrew University of Jerusalem and started teaching a course in "Price Theory". In those days, I battled colleagues to bring some game theory into the course — a step that was frowned upon. In 1986, I stopped teaching undergraduate microeconomics (with exceptions in one or two years). But, as my retirement from my Israeli university approached, I felt an urge to return to the subject. For five years (2012–2017), I taught a course in intermediate microeconomics at Tel Aviv University. This time I tried to put less game theory in the course and focus more on concepts of market equilibrium. One can view this trajectory as part of a cycle of life. But a principle also links my strivings during these two periods: I don't see anything holy in economic models. I don't view a model as right or wrong. I find some models interesting and others less so. I prefer to teach a course that contains a variety of models and not to be dogmatic regarding one particular approach. And I don't have any respect for what is considered to be fashionable by the academic community.

The lecture notes (in Hebrew) from my course in Tel Aviv were the basis of this book. I thank my Teaching Assistants in that course for their help.

In 2016, I joined forces with my old friend and coauthor Martin Osborne. The collaboration reshaped my original sloppy lecture notes in both style and degree of precision.

I don't consider the current version to be the end of the journey. We have made some progress, but, to my mind, some chapters (chiefly 4–7, 11–12, and 15–16) are insufficiently innovative. So I hope we will revise the book significantly in the coming years.

As for all my other books, the electronic version of this book is freely available. I invite you to download my books at http://arielrubinstein.tau.ac.il/books.html.

Ariel Rubinstein
Tel Aviv University and New York University
http://arielrubinstein.tau.ac.il

Preface

The book contains material for a year-long undergraduate course in what is often called "Intermediate microeconomics". It covers basic concepts and models of current microeconomics theory. Our main aim is to give the reader an understanding of the *concepts* of model and equilibrium in microeconomic theory.

The connection between models in microeconomics and the world is subtle, and microeconomic theorists differ in their views about the purpose of their work. Ariel has expressed his views about the meaning of models in economic theory frequently, especially in his book *Economic fables* (Rubinstein 2012). Although we do not discuss applications and implications of the theory for policy, we strongly believe that economic models should be connected to the world; they should concern concepts we use in the real world when thinking about economic interactions.

A main principle that guides us is that concepts, models and results should be stated precisely. Nevertheless, the mathematics we use is elementary, and in particular we use almost no calculus. We also have tried to avoid involved computations, both in the text and the exercises. However, many of the proofs involve sustained logical arguments.

Contents

Part I (Chapters 1–7) presents basic models of an economic agent. We start with an abstract discussion of preferences (Chapter 1), choice (Chapter 2), and decision making under uncertainty (Chapter 3) and then discuss the consumer (Chapters 4 and 5), the producer (Chapter 6) and monopoly (Chapter 7). The chapter on the producer is unconventional in not assuming that a producer necessarily wants to maximize profit.

The core of the book is Part II (Chapters 8–14), which introduces the concept of equilibrium in economic models. Chapters 8 and 9 provide an unconventional introduction to the topic through the models of the jungle (Chapter 8) and an economy with indivisible goods (Chapter 9). The subsequent chapters cover the more conventional model of an exchange economy (Chapters 10 and 11), introducing production (Chapter 12), rational expectations (Chapter 13), and asymmetric information (Chapter 14).

Part III (Chapters 15–16) provides a short introduction to game theory and its applications in economics. We discuss only the concepts of Nash equilibrium

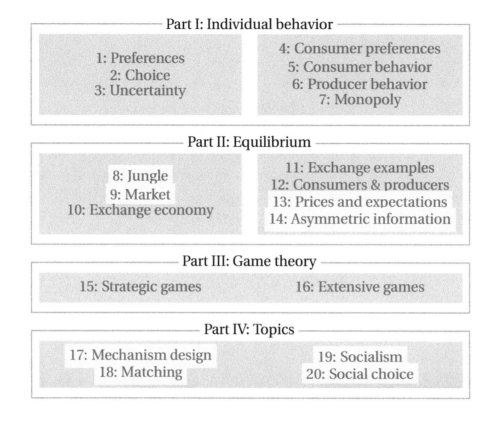

and subgame perfect equilibrium, and treat equilibria only as steady states; we do not discuss epistemic interpretations of the solution concepts.

Part IV (Chapters 17–20) gives the reader a taste of the topics of mechanism design (Chapter 17), matching (Chapter 18), the axiomatic analysis of economic systems (Chapter 19) and social choice (Chapter 20).

Some chapters (for example, 8, 9, 13, 14, and 17–20) could be used as a basis for advanced undergraduate or graduate courses in microeconomics.

We intend to revise the book occasionally. See our personal websites for information about revisions.

Exercises

The book contains about 150 exercises. A solution manual is available for instructors. To request it, please visit the page about the book on either of our websites.

Hyperlinks

Every term with a technical meaning in each definition is hyperlinked to its definition. After clicking on such a term, click the "Back" button in your pdf viewer to return to the definition; if your viewer does not have such a button, the key combination `alt+left arrow` may have the same effect.

Personal pronouns

During our thirty years of collaboration we have often debated the use of gendered pronouns in academic material. In our book *A course in game theory* (1994) we expressed our opinions, which remain unchanged. Martin prefers to use feminine pronouns and Ariel insists on using masculine pronouns. We do not repeat our positions in detail here. In one sentence, Ariel argues: "I am a strong believer in the need to repair gender injustice but the cure is in other frontiers, which require much more than language gestures". Martin's position is elaborated in his book *An introduction to game theory* (2004, xv–xvi), where he cites evidence that the use of male-focussed language reinforces sexist stereotypes and ways of thought, and argues that while the use of feminine pronouns is obviously not sex-neutral, it can only help to address the existing bias.

In our 1994 book we adopted a compromise that neither of us liked. Here we adopt a different solution: this book has two editions, one that uses feminine pronouns and one that uses masculine pronouns. We leave it to you to make your choice.

Acknowledgments

We are grateful to Minghao Zou, who read the entire book and alerted us to many errors and confusions.

We thank all the members of the Open Book Publishers team for their very efficient handling of the book. Working with them has been a pleasure.

Martin J. Osborne
University of Toronto
https://economics.utoronto.ca/osborne

Ariel Rubinstein
Tel Aviv University and New York University
http://arielrubinstein.tau.ac.il

MODELS IN MICROECONOMIC THEORY

Individual behavior

1 Preferences and utility

1.1 Preferences

In the first part of the book we discuss models of individuals. These models are of interest in their own right, but we discuss them mainly to prepare for the study of interactions between individuals, which occupies the remaining parts of the book.

Our goal is to study an individual's choice from a set of alternatives in an economic environment. We can imagine building models in which the individual's characteristics are, for example, his social status or ethnic identity, his experience in the environment we are studying, or even the structure of his brain. However, we follow the approach of almost all economic theory and characterize an individual by his preferences among the alternatives, without considering the origin of these preferences.

Before we study choice, we discuss in this chapter a model of preferences over a set of alternatives. We regard an individual's preferences as a description of his mental attitude, outside the context of any choice. You may have preferences regarding the works of art shown in a local museum even though you are not going to see them; you might have preferences about what you would have done had you lived 3,000 years ago although you cannot travel in time; you might have preferences about the actions of others and the features of the natural world, like the weather, although you cannot affect these actions and features.

When we express preferences, we make statements like "I prefer a to b", "I like a much better than b", "I slightly prefer a to b", and "I love a and hate b". In this book, as in much of economic theory, the model of preferences captures only statements of the first type. That is, it contains information only about an individual's ranking of the alternatives, not about the intensity of his feelings.

> At this point we suggest that you spend a few minutes completing the questionnaire at http://arielrubinstein.org/gt/exp11/.

We can think of an individual's preferences over a set of alternatives as encoding the answers to a questionnaire. For every pair (x, y) of alternatives in the set,

Chapter of *Models in Microeconomic Theory* by Martin J. Osborne and Ariel Rubinstein. Version 2023.5.30 (h).

the questionnaire asks the individual which of the following three statements fits best his attitude to the alternatives.

1. I prefer x to y.
2. I prefer y to x.
3. I regard x and y as equally desirable.

The individual's mental attitude to the alternatives determines his answers to the questionnaire. We do not assume that the individual thinks explicitly about such a questionnaire; rather, his preferences reflect the answers he would give to such a questionnaire if he had to answer it.

One way to encode the individual's answers to the questionnaire is to assign a symbol "1", "-1", or "0" to (x, y) according to whether the answer is "I prefer x to y", "I prefer y to x", or "I regard x and y as equally desirable". However, we follow the convention in economics and describe the answers by means of a binary relation.

A binary relation on a set X specifies, for each ordered pair (x, y) of members of X, whether or not x relates to y in a certain way. For example, "acquaintance" is a binary relation on a set of people. For some pairs (x, y) of people, the statement "x is acquainted with y" is true, and for some pairs it is false. Another example of a binary relation is "smaller than" on the set of numbers. For some pairs (x, y) of numbers, x is smaller than y, and for some it is not. For a binary relation R, the expression $x \, R \, y$ means that x is related to y according to R. For any pair (x, y) of members of X, the statement $x \, R y$ either holds or does not hold. For example, for the binary relation $<$ on the set of numbers, we have $3 < 5$, but not $7 < 1$.

Now return to the questionnaire. One way to encode the answers to it by a binary relation is to say that x is *at least as desirable as* y, denoted $x \succeq y$, if the individual's answer to the question regarding x and y is either "I prefer x to y" or "I regard x and y as equally desirable". In this way we encode the three possible answers to the question regarding x and y, as illustrated in Figure 1.1. The answer "I prefer x to y" is encoded as $x \succeq y$ but not $y \succeq x$; the answer "I prefer y to x" is encoded as $y \succeq x$ but not $x \succeq y$; and the answer "I regard x and y as equally desirable" is encoded as $x \succeq y$ and $y \succeq x$.

From the binary relation $\succeq$ we deduce two other binary relations, $\sim$ and $\succ$, defined by

$$x \sim y \text{ if both } x \succeq y \text{ and } y \succeq x$$
$$x \succ y \text{ if } x \succeq y \text{ but not } y \succeq x.$$

We interpret the relation $\sim$ as "indifference" and the relation $\succ$ as "strict preference". These interpretations are consistent with the derivation of $\succeq$ from the

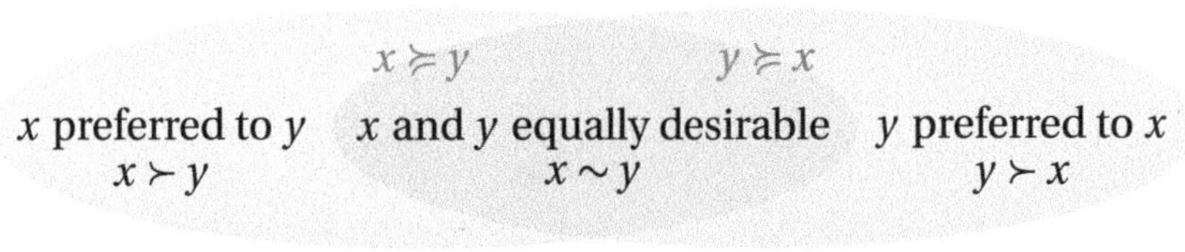

$$x \succcurlyeq y \qquad\qquad y \succcurlyeq x$$

x preferred to y   x and y equally desirable   y preferred to x
$$x \succ y \qquad\qquad x \sim y \qquad\qquad y \succ x$$

Figure 1.1 An individual's preference between x and y.

individual's answers to the questionnaire: if $x \sim y$ then $x \succcurlyeq y$ and $y \succcurlyeq x$, so that the individual's answer to the questionnaire is "I regard x and y as equally desirable", and if $x \succ y$ then the individual's answer is "I prefer x to y".

We assume that the individual answers all the questions on the questionnaire. Given our interpretation of the binary relation $\succcurlyeq$ as a description of responses to the questionnaire, this assumption means that for all distinct alternatives x and y either $x \succcurlyeq y$ or $y \succcurlyeq x$. We assume in addition that the same is true if x and y are the *same* alternative. That is, we assume that $x \succcurlyeq x$ for every alternative x, a property called reflexivity. The questionnaire does not ask "how do you compare x and x?", so the reflexivity of an individual's preferences cannot be deduced from his answers. We assume it because it fits the interpretation of the binary relation: it says that the individual regards every alternative to be at least as desirable as itself.

The property that for all alternatives x and y, distinct or not, either $x \succcurlyeq y$ or $y \succcurlyeq x$, is called completeness.

> **Definition 1.1: Complete binary relation**
>
> A binary relation R on the set X is *complete* if for all members x and y of X, either $x\,R\,y$ or $y\,R\,x$ (or both). A complete binary relation is, in particular, *reflexive*: for every $x \in X$ we have $x\,R\,x$.

For a binary relation $\succcurlyeq$ to correspond to a preference relation, we require not only that it be complete, but also that it be consistent in the sense that if $x \succcurlyeq y$ and $y \succcurlyeq z$ then $x \succcurlyeq z$. This property is called transitivity.

> **Definition 1.2: Transitive binary relation**
>
> A binary relation R on the set X is *transitive* if for any members x, y, and z of X for which $x\,R\,y$ and $y\,R\,z$, we have $x\,R\,z$.

In requiring that a preference relation be transitive, we are restricting the permitted answers to the questionnaire. If the individual's response to the question regarding x and y is either "I prefer x to y" or "I am indifferent between x and y", and if his response to the question regarding y and z is "I prefer y to z" or "I am indifferent between y and z", then his answer to the question regarding x and z must be either "I prefer x to z" or "I am indifferent between x and z".

To conclude, we model an individual's preferences by a complete and transitive binary relation.

Definition 1.3: Preference relation

A *preference relation* on the set X is a complete and transitive binary relation on X.

Note that the binary relations $\sim$ (indifference) and $\succ$ (strict preference) derived from a preference relation $\succeq$ are both transitive. To show the transitivity of $\sim$, note that if $x \sim y$ and $y \sim z$ then $x \succeq y$, $y \succeq x$, $y \succeq z$, and $z \succeq y$, so by the transitivity of $\succeq$ we have $x \succeq z$ and $z \succeq x$, and hence $x \sim z$. You are asked to show the transitivity of $\succ$ in Problem 1a. Note also that if $x \succeq y$ and $y \succ z$ (or $x \succ y$ and $y \succeq z$) then $x \succ z$ (Problem 1b).

We sometimes refer to the following additional properties of binary relations.

Definition 1.4: Symmetric and antisymmetric binary relations

A binary relation R on the set X is *symmetric* if for any members x and y of X for which $x R y$ we have $y R x$, and is *antisymmetric* if for any members x and y of X for which $x \neq y$ and $x R y$, it is not the case that $y R x$.

An example of a symmetric binary relation is "is a neighbor of" (a relation that in general is not transitive) and an example of an antisymmetric binary relation is "is older than". Note that the property of antisymmetry differs from that of asymmetry, which requires that for every x and y, including $x = y$, if $x R y$ then it is not the case that $y R x$.

The binary relation $\sim$ derived from a preference relation $\succeq$ is reflexive, symmetric, and, as we have just argued, transitive. Binary relations with these properties are called equivalence relations.

Definition 1.5: Equivalence relation

A binary relation is an *equivalence relation* if it is reflexive, symmetric, and transitive.

Problem 4 concerns the properties of equivalence relations. In particular, it asks you to show that any equivalence relation R on a set X divides X into disjoint subsets such that two alternatives x and y belong to the same subset if and only if $x R y$. Each of these subsets is called an equivalence class. For the indifference relation, the equivalence classes are referred to also as *indifference sets*;

the individual regards all alternatives in an indifference set as equally desirable and alternatives in different indifference sets as not equally desirable.

1.2   Preference formation

When we model individuals, we endow them with preference relations, which we take as given; we do not derive these preference relations from any more basic considerations. We now briefly describe a few such considerations, some of which result in preference relations and some of which do not.

Value function   The individual has in mind a function v that attaches to each alternative a number, interpreted as his subjective "value" of the alternative; the higher the value, the better the individual likes the alternative. Formally, the individual's preference relation $\succeq$ is defined by $x \succeq y$ if and only if $v(x) \geq v(y)$. The binary relation $\succeq$ derived in this way is indeed a preference relation: it is complete because we can compare any two numbers (for any two numbers a and b either $a \geq b$ or $b \geq a$ (or both)) and it is transitive because the binary relation $\geq$ is transitive (if $x \succeq y$ and $y \succeq z$ then $v(x) \geq v(y)$ and $v(y) \geq v(z)$, and hence $v(x) \geq v(z)$, so that $x \succeq z$).

Distance function   One alternative is "ideal" for the individual; how much he likes every other alternative is determined by the distance of that alternative from the ideal, as given by a function d. That is, the individual's preference relation $\succeq$ is defined by $x \succeq y$ if and only if $d(x) \leq d(y)$. This scheme is an example of a value function, with $v(x) = -d(x)$.

Lexicographic preferences   An individual has in mind two complete and transitive binary relations, $\succeq_1$ and $\succeq_2$, each of which relates to one feature of the alternatives. For example, if X is a set of computers, the features might be the size of the memory and the resolution of the screen. The individual gives priority to the first feature, breaking ties by the second feature. Formally, the individual's preference relation $\succeq$ is defined by $x \succeq y$ if (*i*) $x \succ_1 y$ or (*ii*) $x \sim_1 y$ and $x \succeq_2 y$.

   The binary relation $\succeq$ defined in this way is a preference relation. Its completeness follows from the completeness of $\succeq_1$ and $\succeq_2$. Now consider its transitivity. Suppose that $x \succeq y$ and $y \succeq z$. There are two cases. (*i*) The first feature is decisive when comparing x and y: $x \succ_1 y$. Given $y \succeq z$ we have $y \succeq_1 z$, so by the transitivity of $\succeq_1$ we obtain $x \succ_1 z$ (see Problem 1b) and thus $x \succeq z$. (*ii*) The first feature is not decisive when comparing x and y: $x \sim_1 y$ and $x \succeq_2 y$. If the first feature is decisive for y and z, namely $y \succ_1 z$, then from the transitivity of $\succ_1$ we obtain $x \succ_1 z$ and therefore $x \succeq z$. If the first feature is not decisive for y and z, then $y \sim_1 z$ and $y \succeq_2 z$. By the transitivity of $\sim_1$ we obtain $x \sim_1 z$ and by the transitivity of $\succeq_2$ we obtain $x \succeq_2 z$. Thus $x \succeq z$.

Unanimity rule   The individual has in mind n considerations, represented by the complete and transitive binary relations $\succcurlyeq_1, \succcurlyeq_2, \ldots, \succcurlyeq_n$. For example, a parent may take into account the preferences of his n children. Define the binary relation $\succcurlyeq$ by $x \succcurlyeq y$ if $x \succcurlyeq_i y$ for $i = 1, \ldots, n$. This binary relation is transitive but not necessarily complete. Specifically, if two of the relations $\succcurlyeq_i$ disagree ($x \succcurlyeq_j y$ and $y \succ_k x$), then $\succcurlyeq$ is not complete.

Majority rule   The individual uses three criteria to evaluate the alternatives, each of which is expressed by a complete, transitive, and antisymmetric binary relation $\succcurlyeq_i$. (The antisymmetry of the relations implies that no two alternatives are indifferent according to any relation.) Define the binary relation $\succcurlyeq$ by $x \succcurlyeq y$ if and only if a majority (at least two) of the binary relations $\succcurlyeq_i$ rank x above y. Then $\succcurlyeq$ is complete: for all alternatives x and y either $x \succcurlyeq_i y$ for at least two criteria or $y \succcurlyeq_i x$ for at least two criteria. But the relation is not necessarily transitive, as an example known as the Condorcet paradox shows. Let $X = \{a, b, c\}$ and suppose that $a \succ_1 b \succ_1 c$, $b \succ_2 c \succ_2 a$, and $c \succ_3 a \succ_3 b$. Then $a \succ b$ (a majority of the criteria rank a above b) and $b \succ c$ (a majority rank b above c), but $c \succ a$ (a minority rank a above c).

1.3   An experiment

The assumption that preferences are transitive seems natural. When people are alerted to intransitivities in their preferences they tend to be embarrassed and change their evaluations. However, it is not difficult to design an environment in which most of us exhibit some degree of intransitivity. In Section 1.1 we suggested you respond to a long and exhausting questionnaire, with 36 questions, each asking you to compare a pair of alternatives taken from a set of nine alternatives. Each alternative is a description of a vacation package with four parameters: the city, hotel quality, food quality, and price.

As of April 2018, only 15% of the approximately 1,300 responses to the questionnaire do not exhibit any violation of transitivity. We count a set of three alternatives as a violation of transitivity if the answers to the three questions comparing pairs of alternatives from the set are inconsistent with transitivity. Among participants, the median number of triples that violate transitivity is 6 and the average is 9.5. (As a matter of curiosity, the highest number of intransitivities for any participant is 66. There are 84 sets of three alternatives, but the highest possible number of intransitivities is less than 84.)

A quarter of the participants' expressed preferences violate transitivity among the following alternatives.

1. A weekend in Paris, with 4 star hotel, food quality 17, for $574.
2. A weekend in Paris, for $574, food quality 17, with 4 star hotel.
3. A weekend in Paris, food quality 20, with 3–4 star hotel, for $560.

Notice that options 1 and 2 describe the same package; the descriptions differ only in the order of the characteristics. Almost all participants say they are indifferent between these two alternatives, so the intransitivity is a result of differences in the expressed preferences between options 1 and 3 and options 2 and 3. That is, the order in which the features of the package are listed has an effect on the expressed preferences.

Many responses consistent with transitivity are consistent with a simple principle, like focussing on one feature, like the price, and ignoring the others, or giving priority to one feature, like the city, and breaking ties using a second feature, like the food quality (as in lexicographic preferences). Principles like these may be easier to apply consistently than more complex criteria.

1.4   Utility functions

In many economic models, an individual is described not by his preferences but by a value function. This formulation does not imply that the individual explicitly derives his preferences from a value function, but only that his preferences *can* be derived from such a function. Preferences with this property are said to be *represented by* the value function. We refer to a value function that represents preferences as a *utility function.*

Definition 1.6: Utility function

For any set X and preference relation $\succsim$ on X, the function $u : X \to \mathbb{R}$ *represents* $\succsim$ if

$$x \succsim y \text{ if and only if } u(x) \geq u(y).$$

We say that u is a *utility function for* $\succsim$.

Example 1.1

Consider the preference relation $\succsim$ on the set $\{a, b, c, d\}$ for which $a \succ b \sim c \succ d$. The function u for which $u(a) = 5$, $u(b) = u(c) = -1$, and $u(d) = -17$ is a utility function for $\succsim$.

Under what conditions can a preference relation be represented by a utility function? To answer this question, we need another definition.

Definition 1.7: Minimal and maximal alternatives

For any set X and preference relation $\succsim$ on X, the alternative $x \in X$ is *minimal with respect to* $\succsim$ *in X* if $y \succsim x$ for all $y \in X$ and is *maximal with respect to* $\succsim$ *in X* if $x \succsim y$ for all $y \in X$.

The next result shows that every preference relation on a finite set has minimal and maximal members.

Lemma 1.1: Existence of minimal and maximal alternatives

Let X be a nonempty finite set and let $\succsim$ be a preference relation on X. At least one member of X is minimal with respect to $\succsim$ in X and at least one member is maximal.

Proof

We prove the result for minimality; the argument for maximality is analogous. We use induction on the number n of members of X. If $n = 1$ the single member of X is minimal with respect to $\succsim$ in X. Assume the result is true for $n - 1$; we prove it is true for n. Let y be an arbitrary member of X and let x be minimal with respect to $\succsim$ in $X \backslash \{y\}$ (a set with $n - 1$ members). If $y \succsim x$ then x is minimal in X. If not, then $x \succsim y$. In this case, take any $z \in X \backslash \{y\}$. Because x is minimal in $X \backslash \{y\}$, we have $z \succsim x$, so by transitivity $z \succsim y$. Thus y is minimal in X.

Problem 2b asks you to give an example of a preference relation on an infinite set for which there is no minimal or maximal member.

We can now show that any preference relation on a finite set can be represented by a utility function.

Proposition 1.1: Representing preference relation by utility function

Every preference relation on a finite set can be represented by a utility function.

Proof

Let X be a finite set and let $\succsim$ be a preference relation on X. Let $Y_0 = X$ and define M_1 to be the set of alternatives minimal with respect to $\succsim$ in Y_0. By Lemma 1.1, Y_0 is not empty. For $k \geq 1$ inductively define $Y_k = Y_{k-1} \backslash M_k$ as long as Y_{k-1} is nonempty, and let M_{k+1} be the (nonempty) set of alternatives minimal with respect to $\succsim$ in Y_k. In other words, at every stage

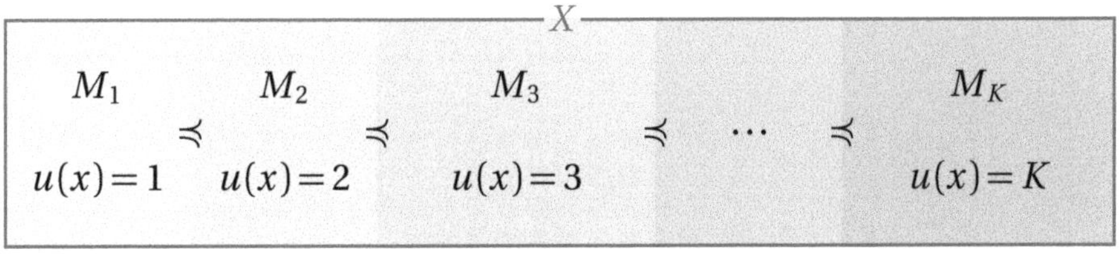

Figure 1.2 An illustration of the construction in the proof of Proposition 1.1.

remove from the set of remaining alternatives the alternatives minimal with respect to $\succeq$. (Figure 1.2 illustrates the construction.)

As long as Y_k is not empty, by Lemma 1.1 the set M_{k+1} is not empty. Because X is finite, there exists a number K such that the set Y_K is empty (but the set Y_{K-1} is nonempty). Thus every $x \in X$ is a member of some set M_k for some k, $1 \leq k \leq K$.

Define the function $u : X \to \mathbb{R}$ by $u(x) = k$ for all $x \in M_k$, $k = 1, \ldots, K$. That is, attach to every alternative the number of the stage at which it is removed from X.

We argue that u is a utility function for $\succeq$. That is, for any alternatives a and b we have $a \succeq b$ if and only if $u(a) \geq u(b)$.

We have $u(a) = u(b)$ if and only if a and b are both minimal with respect to $\succeq$ in $Y_{u(a)-1}$, so that $b \succeq a$ and $a \succeq b$, and hence $a \sim b$.

We have $u(b) > u(a)$ if and only if a is minimal with respect to $\succeq$ in $Y_{u(a)-1}$, so that $b \succeq a$, and $b \in Y_{u(a)-1}$ but is not minimal with respect to $\succeq$ in $Y_{u(a)-1}$, so that it is not the case that $a \succeq b$. Hence $b \succ a$.

Example 1.2: Cinema seats

A cinema has 2,000 seats, arranged in 40 rows and 50 columns. The rows are numbered starting at the screen from 1 to 40 and the columns are numbered from left to right from 1 to 50. An individual has a lexicographic preference relation over the set of seats. His first priority is to sit as far back as possible. Comparing seats in the same row, he prefers to sit as far to the left as possible (close to the exit, which is on the left, in case he wants to leave before the end of the screening).

In the construction in the proof of Proposition 1.1, the set M_1 consists of the single seat in row 1, column 50, so this seat is assigned the utility 1; the set M_2 consists of the single seat in row 1, column 49, so this seat is assigned the utility 2; ...; the set M_{2000} consists of the single seat in row 40, column 1, so this seat is assigned the utility 2,000. (A cinema with ten rows

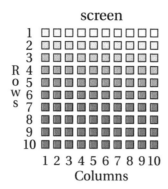

Figure 1.3 A cinema like the one in Example 1.2, with ten rows of ten seats. For the individual, no two seats are indifferent. He prefers seat x to seat y if x is shaded with a darker blue than y.

> of ten seats is illustrated in Figure 1.3.) The individual's preference relation is represented by the utility function u defined by $u(x) = 50r(x) - c(x) + 1$, where $r(x)$ is the row number of the seat and $c(x)$ is its column number.

Many preference relations on *infinite* sets can also be represented by utility functions. A simple example is the preference relation $\succcurlyeq$ on the set of nonnegative real numbers defined by $x \succcurlyeq y$ if and only if $x \geq y$, which is represented by the utility function u defined by $u(x) = x$. However, not all preference relations on infinite sets can be represented by utility functions. An example is the lexicographic preference relation over the unit square $X = \{(x_1, x_2) : x_1, x_2 \in [0,1]\}$ for which the first priority is the first coordinate and the second priority is the second coordinate (so that, for example, $(0.3, 0.1) \succ (0.2, 0.9) \succ (0.2, 0.8)$). (Figure 1.4 shows the set of alternatives preferred to a given alternative.)

Proposition 1.2: Preference relation not represented by utility function

The (lexicographic) preference relation $\succcurlyeq$ on $\{(x_1, x_2) : x_1, x_2 \in [0,1]\}$ defined by $(x_1, x_2) \succ (y_1, y_2)$ if and only if either (*i*) $x_1 > y_1$ or (*ii*) $x_1 = y_1$ and $x_2 > y_2$ is not represented by any utility function.

The proof of this result requires more mathematical knowledge than the other arguments in the book.

Proof

Assume, contrary to the claim, that the function u represents $\succcurlyeq$. For each $x \in [0,1]$, we have $(x, 1) \succ (x, 0)$, so that $u(x, 1) > u(x, 0)$. Define a function f that assigns to every number $x \in [0,1]$ a rational number in the

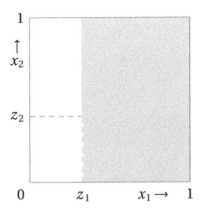

Figure 1.4 The set of alternatives preferred to (z_1, z_2) according to the lexicographic preference relation described in the text is the area shaded blue, excluding the part of the boundary indicated by a dashed line.

interval $(u(x, 0), u(x, 1))$. Such a number exists because between any two real numbers there is a rational number. The function f is one-to-one since if $a > b$ then $(a, 0) \succ (b, 1)$, so that $u(a, 0) > u(b, 1)$, and hence the interval $(u(a, 0), u(a, 1))$ from which $f(a)$ is selected does not intersect the interval $(u(b, 0), u(b, 1))$ from which $f(b)$ is selected. The contradiction now follows from Cantor's diagonal argument, which shows that there is no one-to-one function from the set $[0, 1]$ into a countable set (like the set of rational numbers).

If a utility function represents a given preference relation, then many other utility functions do so too. For example, if the function u represents a given preference relation then so does the function $3u - 7$ or any other function of the form $au + b$ where a is a positive number. Generally, we have the following result. Note that we define a function f to be increasing if $f(x) > f(y)$ whenever $x > y$ (and nondecreasing if $f(x) \geq f(y)$ whenever $x > y$).

Proposition 1.3: Increasing function of utility function is utility function

Let $f : \mathbb{R} \to \mathbb{R}$ be an increasing function. If u represents the preference relation $\succeq$ on X, then so does the function w defined by $w(x) = f(u(x))$ for all $x \in X$.

Proof

We have $w(x) \geq w(y)$ if and only if $f(u(x)) \geq f(u(y))$ if and only if $u(x) \geq u(y)$ (given that f is increasing), which is true if and only if $x \succeq y$.

Problems

1. *Properties of binary relations.* Assume that $\succeq$ is a preference relation.

   a. Show that the binary relation $\succ$ defined by $x \succ y$ if $x \succeq y$ and not $y \succeq x$ is transitive and antisymmetric.

   b. Show that if $x \succeq y$ and $y \succ z$ (or $x \succ y$ and $y \succeq z$) then $x \succ z$.

2. *Minimal element.* Let $\succeq$ be a preference relation over a finite set X.

   a. Show that a is minimal with respect to $\succeq$ in X if and only if there is no $x \in X$ such that $a \succ x$.

   b. Give an example to show that if X is not finite then a preference relation may have no minimal and maximal elements in X.

3. *Similarity relations.* Consider the following preference formation scheme. An individual has in mind a function $v : X \to \mathbb{R}$ that attaches to each alternative a number, but is sensitive only to significant differences in the value of the function; he is indifferent between alternatives that are "similar". Specifically, the individual prefers x to y if $v(x) - v(y) > 1$ and is indifferent between x and y if $-1 \leq v(x) - v(y) \leq 1$. Is the individual's preference relation necessarily transitive?

4. *Equivalence relations.*

   a. Give two examples of equivalence relations on different sets.

   b. Show that the binary relation R on the set of positive integers defined by $x R y$ if $x + y$ is even is an equivalence relation.

   c. A partition of the set X is a set of nonempty subsets of X such that every member of X is a member of one and only one subset. For example, the set of sets $\{\{1,3,5\}, \{2,4,6\}\}$ is a partition of the set $\{1,2,3,4,5,6\}$. Show that every equivalence relation R on X induces a partition of the set X in which x and y are in the same member of the partition if and only if $x R y$.

5. *Independence of properties.* Find an example of a binary relation that is complete and transitive but not symmetric. Find also an example of a binary relation that is reflexive, transitive, and symmetric but not complete.

6. *Shepard scale and Escher.* Listen to the Shepard scale and look at a picture of Penrose stairs. (The video at `http://techchannel.att.com/play-video.cfm/2011/10/10/AT&T-Archives-A-Pair-of-Paradoxes` combines them.

The lithograph *Ascending and descending* by M. C. Escher is a rendering of Penrose stairs.) Explain the connection between these two examples and the concept of transitivity.

7. *Utility representation.* Let X be the set of all positive integers.

   a. An individual prefers the number 8 to all other numbers. Comparing a pair of numbers different from 8 he prefers the higher number. Construct a utility function that represents these preferences.

   b. An individual prefers the number 8 to all other numbers. Comparing a pair of numbers different from 8 he prefers the number that is closer to 8. Construct a utility function that represents these preferences.

8. *Utility representation.* Consider the preference relation on the positive integers in which x is preferred to y if *either* (*i*) x is even and y is odd, *or* (*ii*) x and y are even and $x > y$, *or* (*iii*) x and y are odd and $x > y$.

   a. Show that no utility function with integer values represents this preference relation.

   b. Define a utility function the values of which are real numbers that represents the preference relation.

9. *Representations with additive utility.* An individual has preferences over the set of units in an apartment building. He prefers a unit with 5 rooms on floor 12 to one with 4 rooms on floor 20, one with 4 rooms on floor 5 to one with 2 rooms on floor 12, and one with 2 rooms on floor 20 to one with 5 rooms on floor 5.

   a. Show that the individual's preferences are consistent with a preference relation.

   b. Show that the individual's preference relation cannot be represented by a function u with $u(x) = f(r(x)) + g(l(x))$ for functions f and g, where $r(x)$ is the number of rooms and $l(x)$ is the floor for any unit x.

Notes

The formalization of the notion of a preference relation appears to be due to Frisch, in 1926 (see Frisch 1957), and the first analysis of the problem of representing a preference relation by a utility function appears to be Wold (1943). Proposition 1.2 is due to Debreu (1954, footnote 1, 164). The exposition of the chapter draws on Rubinstein (2006a, Lecture 1).

2 Choice

2.1 Choice and rational choice

In the previous chapter we discuss an individual's preference relation, a formal concept that describes his mental attitude to all relevant alternatives. We now develop a formal tool to describe an individual's behavior. The two concepts, preferences and choice, are building blocks of the economic models we develop later.

Recall that the notion of a preference relation refers only to the individual's mental attitude, not to the choices he may make. In this chapter, we describe a concept of choice, independently of preferences. This description specifies his decision in any possible choice problem he may confront within the context we are modeling. Suppose, for example, that we want to model a worker who is applying for a job. Then a complete description of his behavior specifies not only which job he chooses if all jobs in the world are open to him, but also his choice from any subset of jobs that he might be offered.

Formally, let X be the set of all the alternatives an individual might face. A choice problem is a nonempty subset A of X, from which the individual chooses an alternative. A choice function describes the individual's choice for every possible choice problem.

Definition 2.1: Choice problem and choice function

Given a set X, a *choice problem for X* is a nonempty subset of X and a *choice function for X* associates with every choice problem $A \subseteq X$ a single member of A (the member chosen).

Usually in economics we connect the individual's behavior and his mental attitude by assuming that the individual is *rational* in the sense that

- he has a preference relation over X
- whenever he has to make a choice, he is aware of the set of possible alternatives
- he chooses an alternative that is best according to his preference relation over the set of possible alternatives.

Chapter of *Models in Microeconomic Theory* by Martin J. Osborne and Ariel Rubinstein. Version 2023.5.30 (h).
© 2023 Martin J. Osborne and Ariel Rubinstein CC BY-NC-ND 4.0.   https://doi.org/10.11647/OBP.0362.02

Note that this model of rationality does not make any assumptions about the content of the individual's preferences. His preferences might be "irrational" in the everyday sense of the word and be inconsistent with what he, or we, would consider to be his well-being. For example, an individual who chooses an alternative that causes him the greatest pain (measured in some way) is rational in the sense we have defined.

If the preference relation of an individual is represented by the utility function u, then the individual acts as if he maximizes the function u under the constraint that $x \in A$. Formally we write his problem as

$$\max\{u(x) : x \in A\}.$$

Note that if two individuals have two different strict preference relations and, given any set A choose alternatives in A that are best according to these preference relations, then their corresponding choice functions differ. That is, if for two alternatives x and y one individual prefers x to y and the other prefers y to x, then the choice function of the first individual assigns x to the problem $\{x, y\}$ and the choice function of the second individual assigns y to this set.

2.2   Rationalizing choice

Human beings usually do not consciously maximize a preference relation when they make decisions. The standard justification for modeling individuals as rational is that although individuals rarely explicitly choose the best alternatives according to their preference relations, their behavior can often be described *as if* they make choices in this way. Individuals do not have to be aware of their preference relations. The assumption that they maximize some preference relation is appropriate as long as we can describe them as if they behave in this way. Accordingly, we make the following definition.

> **Definition 2.2: Rationalizable choice function**
>
> A choice function is *rationalizable* if there is a preference relation such that for every choice problem the alternative specified by the choice function is the best alternative according to the preference relation.

Notice that this definition requires that the alternative chosen from any set is *the unique* best alternative. If we were to require only that it is a best alternative, then every choice function would be rationalizable by the preference relation in which all alternatives are indifferent. We return to the issue in Section 5.5.

Example 2.1

Let $X = \{a,b,c\}$. The choice function that assigns a to $\{a,b,c\}$, a to $\{a,b\}$, a to $\{a,c\}$, and b to $\{b,c\}$ is rationalized by the preference relation $\succeq$ for which $a \succ b \succ c$. That is, we can describe the behavior of an individual with this choice function *as if* he always chooses the best available alternative according to $\succeq$.

On the other hand, any choice function that assigns a to $\{a,b\}$, c to $\{a,c\}$, and b to $\{b,c\}$ is not rationalizable. If this choice function could be rationalized by a preference relation $\succeq$, then $a \succ b$, $b \succ c$, and $c \succ a$, which contradicts transitivity.

Of the 24 possible choice functions for the case in which X contains three alternatives, only six are rationalizable.

We now give some examples of choice procedures and examine whether the resulting choice functions are rationalizable.

Example 2.2: The median

An individual has in mind an ordering of the alternatives in the set X from left to right. For example, X could be a set of political candidates and the ordering might reflect their position from left to right. From any set A of available alternatives, the individual chooses a median alternative. Precisely, if the number of available alternatives is odd, with $a_1 < a_2 < \cdots < a_{2k+1}$ for some integer k, the individual chooses the single median a_{k+1}, and if the number of alternatives is even, with $a_1 < a_2 < \cdots < a_{2k}$, then the individual chooses a_k, the leftmost of the two medians.

No preference relation rationalizes this choice function. Assume that A contains five alternatives, $a_1 < a_2 < a_3 < a_4 < a_5$. From this set, he chooses a_3. If he has to choose from $\{a_3, a_4, a_5\}$, he chooses a_4. If a preference relation $\succeq$ rationalizes this choice function then $a_3 \succ a_4$ from his first choice and $a_4 \succ a_3$ from his second choice, a contradiction.

Note that the individual's behavior has a rationale of a different type: he always prefers the central option. But this rationale cannot be described in terms of choosing the best alternative according to a preference relation over the set of available alternatives. The behavior can be rationalized if we view the set of alternatives to be the positions $Y = \{$median, one left of median, one right of median, two left of median, two right of median$\}$. Then the first choice problem is Y and the second choice problem is $\{$one left of median, median, one right of median$\}$. The preference relation $\succeq$ given by

$$\text{median} \succ \text{one left of median} \succ \text{one right of median} \succ \ldots$$

rationalizes the choice function.

Example 2.3: Steak and salmon

Luce and Raiffa (1957, 288) give an example of a person entering a restaurant in a strange city.

> The waiter informs him that there is no menu, but that this evening he may have either broiled salmon at $2.50 or steak at $4.00. In a first-rate restaurant his choice would have been steak, but considering his unknown surroundings and the different prices he elects the salmon. Soon after the waiter returns from the kitchen, apologizes profusely, blaming the uncommunicative chef for omitting to tell him that fried snails and frog's legs are also on the bill of fare at $4.50 each. It so happens that our hero detests them both and would always select salmon in preference to either, yet his response is "Splendid, I'll change my order to steak".

Consider a set X that consists of the four main courses, salmon, steak, snails, and frog's legs. No preference relation over X rationalizes the person's behavior, because such a preference relation would have to rank salmon above steak by his choice from {salmon, steak} and steak above salmon by his choice from X.

A reasonable explanation for the person's behavior is that although steak appears in both choice problems, he does not regard it to be the same dish. The availability of snails and frog's legs tells him that the steak is likely to be of high quality. Without this information, he views steak as low quality and chooses salmon.

No preference relation on X rationalizes the person's behavior, but a preference relation on {salmon, low quality steak, high quality steak, snails, frog's legs} does so:

$$\text{high quality steak} \succ \text{salmon} \succ \text{low quality steak} \succ \text{snails} \succ \text{frog's legs}.$$

An underlying assumption behind the concept of a choice function is that an alternative is the same in every choice set in which it appears. The choice function in the example cannot be rationalized because the example identifies two different options as the same alternative.

Example 2.4: Partygoer

Each of the people in the set $X = \{A, B_1, B_2\}$ organizes a party. A person might be invited to a subset of those parties and can attend only one party. Individuals B_1 and B_2 are both good friends of the partygoer but the relations between B_1 and B_2 are tense. The person's behavior is as follows. If he is invited by A and B_1, he accepts B_1's invitation. If he is invited by all three individuals, he accepts A's invitation. He does so because he is worried that accepting the invitation of B_1 or B_2 will be interpreted negatively by the other individual. Obviously such behavior is not rationalizable by a preference relation over X. As in the previous example, the meaning of choosing one alternative (B_1) is affected by the presence or absence of another alternative (B_2).

2.3 Property α

We say that a choice function satisfies property α if whenever the choice from A is in a subset B then the alternative chosen from A is chosen also from B. We show that (i) any choice function that selects the best alternative according to a preference relation satisfies this property and (ii) any choice function that satisfies the property is rationalizable.

Definition 2.3: Property α

Given a set X, a choice function c for X *satisfies property* α if for any sets A and B with $B \subset A \subseteq X$ and $c(A) \in B$ we have $c(B) = c(A)$.

Notice that property α is not satisfied by the choice functions in Examples 2.2, 2.3, and 2.4.

Proposition 2.1: Rationalizable choice function satisfies property α

Every rationalizable choice function satisfies property α.

Proof

Let c be a rationalizable choice function for X and let $\succcurlyeq$ be a preference relation such that for every set $A \subseteq X$, $c(A)$ is the best alternative according to $\succcurlyeq$ in A. Assume that $B \subset A$ and $c(A) \in B$. Since $c(A) \succcurlyeq y$ for all $y \in A$ we have $c(A) \succcurlyeq y$ for all $y \in B$ and thus $c(B) = c(A)$.

> **Proposition 2.2: Choice function satisfying property α is rationalizable**
>
> If X is a finite set then any choice function for X satisfying property α is rationalizable.

> **Proof**
>
> Let c be a choice function for X satisfying property α. Denote by n the number of elements in X. We construct a preference relation that rationalizes c as follows. Denote $c(X) = a_1$, $c(X \setminus \{a_1\}) = a_2$, $c(X \setminus \{a_1, a_2\}) = a_3$, and so on. That is, a_k is the choice from the set X after removing the elements $a_1, \ldots, a_{k-1}$.
>
> Consider the preference relation $\succeq$ defined by $a_1 \succ a_2 \succ \cdots \succ a_n$. Let A be a choice problem. The best alternative in A according to $\succeq$ is the first member of A in the sequence $a_1, a_2, \ldots, a_n$, say a_m. By construction, $c(\{a_m, a_{m+1}, \ldots, a_n\}) = a_m$ and since $A \subseteq \{a_m, a_{m+1}, \ldots, a_n\}$ and $a_m \in A$, from property α we have $c(A) = a_m$.

2.4 Satisficing

Imagine an employer who must hire a worker. He interviews the candidates in alphabetical order until he reaches a candidate whom he considers to be good enough, and then stops. If no candidate is good enough, he chooses the last candidate to be interviewed.

Formally, denote the set of candidates by X. The employer has in mind a function $v : X \to \mathbb{R}$ that measures the candidates' qualities. He has in mind also a number v^*, an *aspiration level*. Let O be an ordering of the set X (for example, alphabetical order), which describes the sequence in which the employer interviews candidates. Given a set A of alternatives, the employer chooses the first alternative $a \in A$ in the ordering O for which $v(a) \geq v^*$ if such an alternative exists, and otherwise chooses the last element in A according to O.

> **Definition 2.4: Satisficing choice function**
>
> Let X be a finite set. Given a function $v : X \to \mathbb{R}$ (the *valuation function*), a number v^* (the *aspiration level*), and an ordering O of X, the *satisficing choice function* c is defined as follows. Let $A = \{a_1, \ldots, a_K\}$ where $a_1 O a_2 O \cdots O a_K$. Then
> $$c(A) = \begin{cases} a_k & \text{if } v(a_k) \geq v^* \text{ and } v(a_l) < v^* \text{ for } l = 1, \ldots, k-1 \\ a_K & \text{if } v(a_l) < v^* \text{ for } l = 1, \ldots, K. \end{cases}$$

Every alternative x for which $v(x) \geq v^*$ is *satisfactory* and every other alternative is *unsatisfactory*.

Proposition 2.3: Satisficing choice function is rationalizable

A satisficing choice function is rationalizable.

This result can be proved by showing that any satisficing choice function satisfies property α (see Problem 3). Here we provide a direct proof.

Proof

Let c be the satisficing choice function for valuation function v, aspiration level v^*, and ordering O. We construct a preference relation $\succeq$ that rationalizes c. At the top of the preference relation we put the satisfactory alternatives, $X^+ = \{x \in X : v(x) \geq v^*\}$, in the order given by O. Then we put all the unsatisfactory alternatives, $X^- = \{x \in X : v(x) < v^*\}$, in the order given by the *reverse* of O. (If, for example, $X = \{a, b, c, d\}$, O is alphabetical order, $v^* = 0$, and the valuation function is defined by $v(a) = -1$, $v(b) = -2$, $v(c) = 1$, and $v(d) = 3$, then the preference relation we construct is $c \succ d \succ b \succ a$.)

We now show that this preference relation rationalizes c. Let $A \subseteq X$. If A contains a member of X^+ then the best alternative in A according to $\succeq$ is the first alternative, according to O, in $A \cap X^+$, which is $c(A)$. If A does not contain a member of X^+ then $A \subseteq X^-$ and the best alternative in A according to $\succeq$ is the last element in A according to O, which is $c(A)$.

2.5   The money pump argument

The assumption that a choice function is rationalizable is sometimes defended on the ground that behavior that is inconsistent with rationality could produce choices that harm the individual.

Suppose that X consists of three alternatives, a, b, and c, interpreted as objects, and that an individual's choice function assigns a to $\{a, b\}$, b to $\{b, c\}$, and c to $\{a, c\}$. An implication of this choice function is that for any object x, if the individual holds x then there is an object y such that the individual is willing to exchange x for y; given that he prefers y to x, he is willing to pay some (possibly small) amount of money to make the exchange. Assume that for each such exchange, this amount of money is at least \$1. In this case, a manipulator could first give a to the individual, then offer to replace a with c in return for \$1, then offer to replace c with b in return for another \$1, and then offer to replace b with a for yet another \$1. After these three exchanges, the individual holds a, as he did initially, and is \$3 poorer. The manipulator can repeat the exercise, taking as much money from the individual as he likes. Such a mechanism is known as a money pump.

In fact, for any choice function c that does not satisfy condition α, such manipulation is possible. Assume that there are sets A and B with $B \subset A \subseteq X$ and $c(A) \in B$ and $c(B) \neq c(A)$. The manipulation goes as follows.

Take $c(A)$. (i) Are you willing to replace $c(A)$ with any element in $B \setminus \{c(A)\}$ for some amount of money? The individual can now choose from the set B and will agree and choose $c(B)$. (ii) Are you willing to replace $c(B)$ with an alternative in $A \setminus \{c(B)\}$ for some amount of money? The individual can now choose from the entire set A and will agree and choose $c(A)$. The manipulator can repeat the two steps as many times as he wishes.

The effectiveness of the manipulation depends on the inability of the manipulated individual to notice the exploitation. We leave it to you to judge whether the argument is a persuasive justification of the assumption that choice is rationalizable.

2.6   Evidence of choices inconsistent with rationality

Ample research demonstrates that human behavior is sometimes not rational in the sense we have defined. From the multitude of examples, we select three experiments that demonstrate this point; for each example, we identify features of behavior that are inconsistent with the assumption of rational behavior. The first experiment involves a situation in which some subjects' choices conflict with property α. The second and third experiments challenge the assumption that an individual chooses an alternative from a set, independently of the way the set is described. The experiments were first conducted many years ago (see the Notes at the end of the chapter). Here we report results of online experiments (using the website http://arielrubinstein.org/gt) in which the subjects were a large number of students around the world with similar academic backgrounds to those of the potential readers of this book.

2.6.1   Attention effect

Which of the following cameras do you choose?

Camera A   Average rating 9.1, 6 megapixels
Camera B   Average rating 8.3, 9 megapixels

Now make another choice.

> Which of the following cameras do you choose?
>
> *Camera A* Average rating 9.1, 6 megapixels
> *Camera B* Average rating 8.3, 9 megapixels
> *Camera C* Average rating 8.1, 7 megapixels

Each question was answered by about 1,300 participants on the website `http://arielrubinstein.org/gt`. The results are given in the following tables.

Choice between *A* and *B*	
Camera A	48%
Camera B	52%

Choice between *A*, *B*, and *C*	
Camera A	30%
Camera B	68%
Camera C	2%

Thus the appearance of *C* does not lead people to choose *C*, but rather causes a significant fraction of participants to choose *B*, which dominates *C*, even though in a choice between *A* and *B* they choose *A*. One explanation of this result is that the availability of *C* directs the participants' focus to *B*, the alternative that dominates it. An alternative explanation is that the dominance of *B* over *C* provides a reason to choose *B*, a reason that does not apply to *A*.

2.6.2 Framing effects

Sometimes individuals' choices depend on the way in which the alternatives are described.

> You have to spin either roulette *A* or roulette *B*. The outcomes of spinning each roulette are given in the following table.
>
> | | White | Red | Green | Yellow |
> | --- | --- | --- | --- | --- |
> | roulette *A* | 90% | 6% | 1% | 3% |
> | | $0 | $45 | $30 | −$15 |
> | roulette *B* | 90% | 7% | 1% | 2% |
> | | $0 | $45 | −$10 | −$15 |
>
> Which roulette do you choose?

Subjects' choices in this experiment are generally split more or less equally between the two roulettes. About 51% of around 4,000 participants at the website `http://arielrubinstein.org/gt` have chosen *A*.

A common explanation for the choice of A is that the problem is complicated and participants simplify it by "canceling" similar parameters. The outcomes of White in the two roulettes are identical and the outcomes of Red and Yellow are very similar; ignoring these colors leaves Green, which yields a much better outcome for roulette A.

Here is another choice problem.

> You have to spin either roulette C or roulette D. The outcomes of spinning each roulette are given in the following table.
>
> | | White | Red | Black | Green | Yellow |
> |------------|-------|------|-------|-------|--------|
> | roulette C | 90% | 6% | 1% | 1% | 2% |
> | | $0 | $45 | $30 | −$15 | −$15 |
> | roulette D | 90% | 6% | 1% | 1% | 2% |
> | | $0 | $45 | $45 | −$10 | −$15 |
>
> Which roulette do you choose?

It is clear that D dominates C, and indeed almost all participants (93%) at `http://arielrubinstein.org/gt` have chosen D.

Now notice that A and C differ only in their presentation (the color Yellow in A is split in C into two contingencies). The same is true of B and D (the color Red in B is split in D into two contingencies). The different presentations seem to cause at least half of the participants to apply different choice procedures: they reduce the complicated problem to a simpler one in the choice between A and B and apply a domination criterion in the choice between C and D.

2.6.3 Mental accounting

> Imagine that you have bought a ticket for a show for $40. When you reach the theatre you discover that you have lost the ticket. You can buy another ticket at the same price. Will you do so?

Now think about another situation.

> Imagine that you intend to go to a show. When you take your wallet out of your pocket to pay for the $40 ticket, you discover that you have lost $40, but you still have enough cash to buy a ticket. Will you do so?

In both of these situations, you face a choice between

1. having $80 less than you did before departing home and seeing the performance
2. having $40 less than you did before departing home and not seeing the performance.

Although in both situations you face these same options, more people choose to buy the ticket in the second situation than in the first situation. About 65% of the 1,200 participants at http://arielrubinstein.org/gt have stated that they would buy a new ticket in the first situation, in which they discover they have lost a ticket they purchased previously. Among a similar number of different participants, 79% have stated they would buy a ticket after discovering that they had lost $40. The reason for the difference seems to be that in the first case people follow a mental accounting process that counts the price of a ticket as $80, and they regard that price as too high. In the second case, some people appear to think about the loss of the $40 as unrelated to the issue of ticket purchase and count the price of a ticket as only $40.

Problems

1. *Five choice procedures.* Determine whether each of the following five choice functions over a set X is rationalizable. If the answer is positive, find a preference relation that rationalizes the choice function. Otherwise, prove that the choice function is not rationalizable.

   a. The set X consists of candidates for a job. An individual has a complete ranking of the candidates. When he has to choose from a set A, he first orders the candidates in A alphabetically, and then examines the list from the beginning. He goes down the list as long as the new candidate is better than the previous one. If the nth candidate is the first who is better than the $(n+1)$th candidate, he stops and chooses the nth candidate. If in his journey he never gets to a candidate who is inferior to the previous one, he chooses the last candidate.

   b. The set X consists of n basketball teams, indexed 1 to n. The teams participate in a round robin tournament. That is, every team plays against every other team. An individual knows, for every pair of teams, which one wins. When he chooses a team from a set A, he chooses the one with the largest number of wins among the games between teams in A. If more than one team has the largest number of wins, he chooses the team with the lowest index among the tied teams.

    c. The set X consists of pictures. An individual has in mind L binary criteria, each of which takes the value 0 (the criterion is not met) or 1 (the criterion is met). Examples of such criteria are whether the painting is modern, whether the painter is famous, and whether the price is above \$1,000. The criteria are ordered: criterion$_1$, criterion$_2$, …, criterion$_L$. When the individual chooses a picture from a subset of X, he rejects those that do not satisfy the first criterion. Then, from those that satisfy the first criterion, he rejects those that do not satisfy the second criterion. And so on, until only one picture remains. Assume that any two alternatives have a criterion by which they differ, so that the procedure always yields a unique choice.

    d. An individual has in mind two numerical functions, u and v, on the set X. For any set $A \subseteq X$, he first looks for the u-maximal alternative in A. If its u value is at least 10, he selects it. If not, he selects the v-maximal alternative in A.

    e. An individual has in mind a preference relation on the set X. Each alternative is either red or blue. Given a set $A \subseteq X$, he chooses the best alternative among those with the color that is more common in A. In the case of a tie, he chooses among the red alternatives.

2. *Property of a choice function satisfying property α.* An individual has a choice function that satisfies property α. Consider two sets, A and B, such that $c(A) \in B$ and $c(B) \in A$. Prove that $c(A) = c(B)$.

3. *Alternative proof of Proposition 2.3.* Prove Proposition 2.3 by showing that any satisficing choice function satisfies property α.

4. *Variant of satisficing.* An individual follows a procedure that differs from the satisficing procedure only in that if he does not find any satisfactory alternative then he goes back and examines all the alternatives and chooses the one for which $v(x)$ is highest. Show that the individual's choice function satisfies property α and construct a preference relation that rationalizes it.

5. *Path independence.* Consider the following property of a choice function, called *path independence*:

$$c(A \cup B) = c(\{c(A), c(B)\}) \text{ whenever } A \cap B = \varnothing.$$

That is, if the individual splits a choice set into two disjoint subsets, makes a choice from each subset, and then chooses between those two alternatives, he chooses the same alternative as he does when he chooses from the entire set.

a. Let c be a choice function that assigns to each set the best alternative according to some preference relation. Show that c is path independent.

b. Show that any choice function that is path independent is rationalizable (by showing it satisfies property α).

6. *Caring up to a limit.* An individual has in mind two numerical functions u and v defined on the set X. Given a choice problem A, he first looks for the u-maximal element x in A. If $v(x) \geq v^*$ he chooses x. Otherwise, he chooses the v-maximal element in A. (Notice that this choice function differs from the one in Problem 1d.)

a. Interpret the choice function in the case that u is a measure of the well-being of a friend and v is a measure of the wellbeing of the individual.

b. Show that for some X, u, and v the procedure is not rationalizable.

7. *Extension of Proposition 2.2.* Let X be an infinite set and c a choice function on X. Show, using the following two steps, that if c satisfies property α then it can be rationalized.

a. Define a binary relation $\succsim$ by $x \succsim y$ if $c(\{x,y\}) = x$. Show that this relation is a preference relation.

b. Show that for every choice problem A, $c(A) \succsim a$ for every $a \in A$.

8. *Money pump.* Can a trader who thinks that $2 + 3 = 6$ survive in our cruel world?

Notes

Property α was formulated by Chernoff (1954, Postulate 4, 429). The notion of satisficing is due to Simon (1956). The idea of a money pump appears to be due to Davidson et al. (1955, 145–146). Example 2.3 is taken from Luce and Raiffa (1957, 288). The experiment in Section 2.6.1 is based on the idea in Huber et al. (1982). The experiment in Section 2.6.2 was suggested by Tversky and Kahneman (1986, S263–S265). Section 2.6.3 is taken from Kahneman and Tversky (1984, 347–348). The exposition of the chapter draws on Rubinstein (2006a, Lecture 3).

3 Preferences under uncertainty

3.1 Lotteries

In Chapter 1 we discuss a model of preferences over an arbitrary set of alternatives. In this chapter we study an instance of the model in which an alternative in the set involves randomness regarding the consequence it yields. We refer to these alternatives as *lotteries*. For example, a raffle ticket that yields a car with probability 0.001 and nothing otherwise is a lottery. A vacation on which you will experience grey weather with probability 0.3 and sunshine with probability 0.7 can be thought of as a lottery as well.

The set X in the model we now discuss is constructed from a set Z of objects called prizes. A lottery specifies the probability with which each prize is realized. For simplicity, we study only lotteries for which the number of prizes that can be realized is finite.

Definition 3.1: Lotteries

Let Z be a set (of *prizes*). A *lottery over Z* is a function $p : Z \to \mathbb{R}$ that assigns a positive number (probability) $p(z)$ to a finite number of members of Z and 0 to all other members, with $\sum_{z \in Z} p(z) = 1$. The *support* of the lottery p, denoted supp(p), is the set of all prizes to which p assigns positive probability, $\{z \in Z : p(z) > 0\}$.

We denote the set of all lotteries over Z by $L(Z)$, the lottery that yields the prize z with probability 1 by $[z]$, and the lottery that yields the prize z_k with probability α_k for $k = 1, \ldots, K$ by $\alpha_1 \cdot z_1 \oplus \alpha_2 \cdot z_2 \oplus \cdots \oplus \alpha_K \cdot z_K$.

If Z consists of two prizes, z_1 and z_2, then each member p of $L(Z)$ is specified by a pair (p_1, p_2) of nonnegative numbers with sum 1, where $p_1 = p(z_1)$ and $p_2 = p(z_2)$ are the probabilities of the prizes. Thus in this case $L(Z)$ can be identified with the blue line segment in Figure 3.1a. If Z includes three options, $L(Z)$ can similarly be identified with the triangle in Figure 3.1b.

3.2 Preferences over lotteries

We are interested in preference relations over $L(Z)$. In terms of the model in Chapter 1, the set X is equal to $L(Z)$. Here are some examples.

Chapter of *Models in Microeconomic Theory* by Martin J. Osborne and Ariel Rubinstein. Version 2023.5.30 (h).

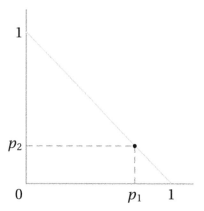

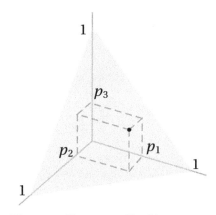

(a) The set $L(\{z_1, z_2\})$ of lotteries. The point (p_1, p_2) on the line segment represents the lottery p for which $p(z_1) = p_1$ and $p(z_2) = p_2$.

(b) The set $L(\{z_1, z_2, z_3\})$ of lotteries. The point (p_1, p_2, p_3) in the triangle represents the lottery p for which $p(z_1) = p_1$, $p(z_2) = p_2$, and $p(z_3) = p_3$.

Figure 3.1

Example 3.1: A pessimist

An individual has a strict preference relation $\succ^*$ over the set Z of prizes and (pessimistically) evaluates lotteries by the worst prize, according to the preference relation, that occurs with positive probability. That is, he prefers the lottery $p \in L(Z)$ to the lottery $q \in L(Z)$ if he prefers the worst prize that occurs with positive probability in p to the worst prize that occurs with positive probability in q. Formally, define $w(p)$ to be a prize in $\text{supp}(p)$ such that $y \succ^* w(p)$ for all $y \in \text{supp}(p)$. Then the individual's preference relation $\succsim$ over $L(Z)$ is defined by $p \succsim q$ if $w(p) \succsim^* w(q)$.

Note that there are many pessimistic preference relations, one for each preference relation over the set of prizes.

For any such preferences, the individual is indifferent between two lotteries whenever he is indifferent between the worst prizes that occur with positive probability in the lotteries. In one variant of the preferences that breaks this tie, if two lotteries share the same worst possible prize then the one for which the probability of the worst prize is lower is preferred.

Example 3.2: Good and bad

An individual divides the set Z of prizes into two subsets, *good* and *bad*. For any lottery $p \in L(Z)$, let $G(p) = \sum_{z \in good} p(z)$ be the total probability that a prize in *good* occurs. The individual prefers the lottery $p \in L(Z)$ to the lottery $q \in L(Z)$ if the probability of a prize in *good* occurring is at least as high for p as it is for q. Formally, $p \succcurlyeq q$ if $G(p) \geq G(q)$.

Different partitions of Z into *good* and *bad* generate different preference relations.

Example 3.3: Minimizing options

An individual wants the number of prizes that might be realized (the number of prizes in the support of the lottery) to be as small as possible. Formally, $p \succcurlyeq q$ if $|\mathrm{supp}(p)| \leq |\mathrm{supp}(q)|$. This preference relation makes sense for an individual who does not care about the realization of the lottery but wants to be as prepared as possible (physically or mentally) for all possible outcomes.

Preference relations over lotteries can take an unlimited number of other forms. To help us organize this large set, we now describe two plausible properties of preference relations and identify the set of all preference relations that satisfy the properties.

3.2.1 Properties of preferences

Continuity Suppose that for the prizes a, b, and c we have $[a] \succ [b] \succ [c]$, and consider lotteries of the form $\alpha \cdot a \oplus (1 - \alpha) \cdot c$ (with $0 \leq \alpha \leq 1$). The continuity property requires that as we move continuously from $\alpha = 1$ (the degenerate lottery $[a]$, which is preferred to $[b]$) to $\alpha = 0$ (the degenerate lottery $[c]$, which is worse than $[b]$) we pass (at least once) some value of α such that the lottery $\alpha \cdot a \oplus (1 - \alpha) \cdot c$ is indifferent to $[b]$.

Definition 3.2: Continuity

For any set Z of prizes, a preference relation $\succcurlyeq$ over $L(Z)$ is *continuous* if for any three prizes a, b, and c in Z such that $[a] \succ [b] \succ [c]$ there is a number α with $0 < \alpha < 1$ such that $[b] \sim \alpha \cdot a \oplus (1 - \alpha) \cdot c$.

When Z includes at least three prizes, pessimistic preferences are not continuous: if $[a] \succ [b] \succ [c]$ then $[b] \succ \alpha \cdot a \oplus (1 - \alpha) \cdot c$, for every number $\alpha < 1$. Good and bad preferences and minimizing options preferences satisfy the continuity condition vacuously because in each case there are no prizes a, b and c for which $[a] \succ [b] \succ [c]$.

Independence To define the second property, we need to first define the notion of a compound lottery. Suppose that uncertainty is realized in two stages. First the lottery p_k is drawn with probability α_k, for $k = 1, \ldots, K$, and then each prize z is realized with probability $p_k(z)$. In this case, the probability that each prize z is ultimately realized is $\sum_{k=1,\ldots,K} \alpha_k p_k(z)$. Note that $\sum_{k=1,\ldots,K} \alpha_k p_k(z) \geq 0$ for each z and the sum of these expressions over all prizes z is equal to 1. We refer to the lottery in which each prize z occurs with probability $\sum_{k=1,\ldots,K} \alpha_k p_k(z)$ as a compound lottery, and denote it by $\alpha_1 \cdot p_1 \oplus \cdots \oplus \alpha_K \cdot p_K$. For example, let $Z = \{W, D, L\}$, and define the lotteries $p = 0.6 \cdot W \oplus 0.4 \cdot L$ and $q = 0.2 \cdot W \oplus 0.3 \cdot D \oplus 0.5 \cdot L$. Then the compound lottery $\alpha \cdot p \oplus (1-\alpha) \cdot q$ is the lottery

$$(\alpha 0.6 + (1-\alpha)0.2) \cdot W \oplus ((1-\alpha)0.3) \cdot D \oplus (\alpha 0.4 + (1-\alpha)0.5) \cdot L.$$

Definition 3.3: Compound lottery

Let Z be a set of prizes, let $p_1, \ldots, p_K$ be lotteries in $L(Z)$, and let $\alpha_1, \ldots, \alpha_K$ be nonnegative numbers with sum 1. The *compound lottery* $\alpha_1 \cdot p_1 \oplus \cdots \oplus \alpha_K \cdot p_K$ is the lottery that yields each prize $z \in Z$ with probability $\sum_{k=1,\ldots,K} \alpha_k p_k(z)$.

We can now state the second property of preference relations over lotteries.

Definition 3.4: Independence

Let Z be a set of prizes. A preference relation $\succcurlyeq$ over $L(Z)$ satisfies the *independence property* if for any lotteries $\alpha_1 \cdot z_1 \oplus \cdots \oplus \alpha_k \cdot z_k \oplus \cdots \oplus \alpha_K \cdot z_K$ and $\beta \cdot a \oplus (1-\beta) \cdot b$ we have

$$[z_k] \succcurlyeq \beta \cdot a \oplus (1-\beta) \cdot b$$

$$\Leftrightarrow$$

$$\alpha_1 \cdot z_1 \oplus \cdots \oplus \alpha_k \cdot z_k \oplus \cdots \oplus \alpha_K \cdot z_K$$
$$\succcurlyeq \alpha_1 \cdot z_1 \oplus \cdots \oplus \alpha_k \cdot (\beta \cdot a \oplus (1-\beta) \cdot b) \oplus \cdots \oplus \alpha_K \cdot z_K.$$

The logic of the property is procedural: the only difference between the lottery $\alpha_1 \cdot z_1 \oplus \cdots \oplus \alpha_k \cdot z_k \oplus \cdots \oplus \alpha_K \cdot z_K$ and the compound lottery $\alpha_1 \cdot z_1 \oplus \cdots \oplus \alpha_k \cdot (\beta a \oplus (1-\beta)b) \oplus \cdots \oplus \alpha_K \cdot z_K$ is in the kth term, which is z_k in the first case and $\beta \cdot a \oplus (1-\beta) \cdot b$ in the second case. Consequently it is natural to compare the two lotteries by comparing $[z_k]$ and $\beta \cdot a \oplus (1-\beta) \cdot b$.

Pessimistic preferences do not satisfy this property. Let $[a] \succ [b]$ and consider, for example, the lotteries

$$p = 0.6 \cdot a \oplus 0.4 \cdot b \quad \text{and} \quad q = 0.6 \cdot b \oplus 0.4 \cdot b = [b].$$

These lotteries differ only in the prize that is realized with probability 0.6. Given that $[a] \succ [b]$, the independence property requires that $p \succ q$. However, for a pessimist the two lotteries are indifferent since the worst prize in the lotteries is the same (b).

Minimizing options preferences also violate the independence property: for any prizes a and b, the lotteries $[a]$ and $[b]$ are indifferent, but $0.5 \cdot a \oplus 0.5 \cdot b \prec 0.5 \cdot b \oplus 0.5 \cdot b$.

Good and bad preferences satisfy the independence property. Let p be the lottery $\alpha_1 \cdot z_1 \oplus \cdots \oplus \alpha_k \cdot z_k \oplus \cdots \oplus \alpha_K \cdot z_K$ and let q be the compound lottery

$$\alpha_1 \cdot z_1 \oplus \cdots \oplus \alpha_k \cdot (\beta \cdot a \oplus (1 - \beta) \cdot b) \oplus \cdots \oplus \alpha_K \cdot z_K.$$

Note that $G(p) - G(q) = \alpha_k G([z_k]) - \alpha_k G(\beta \cdot a \oplus (1 - \beta) \cdot b)$, so that since $\alpha_k > 0$, the sign of $G(p) - G(q)$ is the same as the sign of $G([z_k]) - G(\beta \cdot a \oplus (1 - \beta) \cdot b)$. Thus the preferences compare p and q in the same way that they compare $[z_k]$ and $\beta \cdot a \oplus (1 - \beta) \cdot b$.

Monotonicity Consider lotteries that assign positive probability to only two prizes a and b, with $[a] \succ [b]$. We say that a preference relation over $L(Z)$ is monotonic if it ranks such lotteries by the probability that a occurs. That is, monotonic preferences rank lotteries of the type $\alpha \cdot a \oplus (1 - \alpha) \cdot b$ according to the value of α.

The next result says that any preference relation over $L(Z)$ that satisfies the independence property is monotonic.

Lemma 3.1: Independence implies monotonicity

Let Z be a set of prizes. Assume that $\succcurlyeq$, a preference relation over $L(Z)$, satisfies the independence property. Let a and b be two prizes with $[a] \succ [b]$, and let α and β be two probabilities. Then

$$\alpha > \beta \quad \Leftrightarrow \quad \alpha \cdot a \oplus (1 - \alpha) \cdot b \succ \beta \cdot a \oplus (1 - \beta) \cdot b.$$

Proof

Let $p_\alpha = \alpha \cdot a \oplus (1 - \alpha) \cdot b$. Because $\succcurlyeq$ satisfies the independence property, $p_\alpha \succ \alpha \cdot b \oplus (1 - \alpha) \cdot b = [b]$. Using the independence property again we get

$$p_\alpha = (\beta/\alpha) \cdot p_\alpha \oplus (1 - \beta/\alpha) \cdot p_\alpha \succ (\beta/\alpha) \cdot p_\alpha \oplus (1 - \beta/\alpha) \cdot b = \beta \cdot a \oplus (1 - \beta) \cdot b.$$

3.3 Expected utility

We now introduce the type of preferences most commonly assumed in economic theory. These preferences emerge when an individual uses the following scheme to compare lotteries. He attaches to each prize z a number, which we refer to as the value of the prize (or the Bernoulli number) and denote $v(z)$; when evaluating a lottery p, he calculates the expected value of the lottery, $\sum_{z\in Z} p(z)v(z)$. The individual's preferences are then defined by

$$p \succeq q \quad \text{if} \quad \sum_{z\in Z} p(z)v(z) \geq \sum_{z\in Z} q(z)v(z).$$

Definition 3.5: Expected utility

For any set Z of prizes, a preference relation $\succeq$ on the set $L(Z)$ of lotteries is *consistent with expected utility* if there is a function $v : Z \to \mathbb{R}$ such that $\succeq$ is represented by the utility function U defined by $U(p) = \sum_{z\in Z} p(z)v(z)$ for each $p \in L(Z)$. The function v is called the *Bernoulli function* for the representation.

We first show that a preference relation consistent with expected utility is continuous and satisfies the independence property.

Proposition 3.1: Expected utility is continuous and independent

A preference relation on a set of lotteries that is consistent with expected utility satisfies the continuity and independence properties.

Proof

Let Z be a set of prizes, let $\succeq$ be a preference relation over $L(Z)$, and let $v : Z \to \mathbb{R}$ be a function such that the function U defined by $U(p) = \sum_{z\in Z} p(z)v(z)$ for each $p \in L(Z)$ represents $\succeq$.

Continuity Let a, b, and $c \in Z$ satisfy $[a] \succ [b] \succ [c]$. For every $z \in Z$, $U([z]) = v(z)$. Thus $v(a) > v(b) > v(c)$. Let α satisfy $\alpha v(a) + (1-\alpha)v(c) = v(b)$ (that is, $0 < \alpha = (v(b)-v(c))/(v(a)-v(c)) < 1$). Then $\alpha \cdot a \oplus (1-\alpha) \cdot c \sim [b]$.

Independence Consider lotteries $\alpha_1 \cdot z_1 \oplus \cdots \oplus \alpha_K \cdot z_K$ and $\beta \cdot a \oplus (1-\beta) \cdot b$. We have

$$\alpha_1 \cdot z_1 \oplus \cdots \oplus \alpha_k \cdot z_k \oplus \cdots \oplus \alpha_K \cdot z_K$$
$$\succeq \alpha_1 \cdot z_1 \oplus \cdots \oplus \alpha_k \cdot (\beta \cdot a \oplus (1-\beta) \cdot b) \oplus \cdots \oplus \alpha_K \cdot z_K$$
$$\Leftrightarrow \text{(by the formula for } U \text{, which represents } \succeq \text{)}$$

$$\alpha_1 v(z_1) + \cdots + \alpha_k v(z_k) + \cdots + \alpha_K v(z_K)$$
$$\geq \alpha_1 v(z_1) + \cdots + \alpha_k \beta v(a) + \alpha_k (1-\beta) v(b) + \cdots + \alpha_K v(z_K)$$
$$\Leftrightarrow \text{(by algebra)}$$
$$\alpha_k v(z_k) \geq \alpha_k \beta v(a) + \alpha_k (1-\beta) v(b)$$
$$\Leftrightarrow \text{(since } \alpha_k > 0)$$
$$v(z_k) \geq \beta v(a) + (1-\beta) v(b)$$
$$\Leftrightarrow \text{(by the formula for } U, \text{ which represents } \succcurlyeq)$$
$$[z_k] \succcurlyeq \beta \cdot a \oplus (1-\beta) \cdot b.$$

The next result, the main one of this chapter, shows that any preference relation that satisfies continuity and independence is consistent with expected utility. That is, we can attach values to the prizes such that the comparison of the expected values of any two lotteries is equivalent to the comparison of the lotteries according to the preference relation.

Proposition 3.2: Continuity and independence implies expected utility

A preference relation on a set of lotteries with a finite set of prizes that satisfies the continuity and independence properties is consistent with expected utility.

Proof

Let Z be a finite set of prizes and let $\succcurlyeq$ be a preference relation on $L(Z)$ satisfying continuity and independence. Label the members of Z so that $[z_1] \succcurlyeq \cdots \succcurlyeq [z_K]$. Let $z_1 = M$ (the best prize) and $z_K = m$ (the worst prize).

First suppose that $[M] \succ [m]$. Then by continuity, for every prize z there is a number $v(z)$ such that $[z] \sim v(z) \cdot M \oplus (1-v(z)) \cdot m$. In fact, by monotonicity this number is unique. Consider a lottery $p(z_1) \cdot z_1 \oplus \cdots \oplus p(z_K) \cdot z_K$. By applying independence K times, the individual is indifferent between this lottery and the compound lottery

$$p(z_1) \cdot \big(v(z_1) \cdot M \oplus (1-v(z_1)) \cdot m \big) \oplus \cdots \oplus p(z_K) \cdot \big(v(z_K) \cdot M \oplus (1-v(z_K)) \cdot m \big).$$

This compound lottery is equal to the lottery

$$\left(\sum_{k=1,\ldots,K} p(z_k) v(z_k) \right) \cdot M \oplus \left(1 - \sum_{k=1,\ldots,K} p(z_k) v(z_k) \right) \cdot m.$$

Given $[M] \succ [m]$, Lemma 3.1 implies that the comparison between the lotteries p and q is equivalent to the comparison between the numbers $\sum_{k=1,\ldots,K} p(z_k)v(z_k)$ and $\sum_{k=1,\ldots,K} q(z_k)v(z_k)$.

Now suppose that $[M] \sim [m]$. Then by independence, $p \sim [M]$ for any lottery p. That is, the individual is indifferent between all lotteries. In this case, choose $v(z_k) = 0$ for all k. Then the function U defined by $U(p) = \sum_{z \in Z} p(z)v(z) = 0$ for each $p \in L(Z)$ represents the preference relation.

Comment

Note that if the function $v : Z \to \mathbb{R}$ is the Bernoulli function for an expected utility representation of a certain preference relation over $L(Z)$ then for any numbers $\alpha > 0$ and β so too is the function w given by $w(z) = \alpha v(z) + \beta$ for all $z \in Z$. In fact the converse is true also (we omit a proof): if $v : Z \to \mathbb{R}$ and $w : Z \to \mathbb{R}$ are Bernoulli functions for representations of a certain preference relation then for some numbers $\alpha > 0$ and β we have $w(z) = \alpha v(z) + \beta$ for all $z \in Z$.

3.4   Theory and experiments

We now briefly discuss the connection (and disconnection) between the model of expected utility and human behavior. The following well-known pair of questions demonstrates a tension between the two.

Imagine that you have to choose between the following two lotteries.

L_1:   you receive \$4,000 with probability 0.2 and zero otherwise.
R_1:   you receive \$3,000 with probability 0.25 and zero otherwise.

Which lottery do you choose?

Imagine that you have to choose between the following two lotteries.

L_2:   you receive \$4,000 with probability 0.8 and zero otherwise.
R_2:   you receive \$3,000 with certainty.

Which lottery do you choose?

The responses of 7,932 students at http://arielrubinstein.org/gt are summarized in the following table.

	L_2	R_2
L_1	20%	44%
R_1	5%	31%

In our notation, the lotteries are

$$L_1 = 0.2 \cdot [\$4000] \oplus 0.8 \cdot [\$0] \quad \text{and} \quad R_1 = 0.25 \cdot [\$3000] \oplus 0.75 \cdot [\$0]$$
$$L_2 = 0.8 \cdot [\$4000] \oplus 0.2 \cdot [\$0] \quad \text{and} \quad R_2 = [\$3000].$$

Note that $L_1 = 0.25 \cdot L_2 \oplus 0.75 \cdot [0]$ and $R_1 = 0.25 \cdot R_2 \oplus 0.75 \cdot [0]$. Thus if a preference relation on $L(Z)$ satisfies the independence property, it should rank L_1 relative to R_1 in the same way that it ranks L_2 relative to R_2. So among individuals who have a strict preference between the lotteries, only those whose answers are (*i*) L_1 and L_2 or (*ii*) R_1 and R_2 have preferences that can be represented by expected utility. About 51% of the participants are in this category.

Of the rest, very few (5%) choose R_1 and L_2. The most popular pair of answers is L_1 and R_2, chosen by 44% of the participants. Nothing is wrong with those subjects (which include the authors of this book). But such a pair of choices conflicts with expected utility theory; the conflict is known as the Allais paradox.

One explanation for choosing R_2 over L_2 is that the chance of getting an extra $1,000 is not worth the risk of losing the certainty of getting $3,000. The idea involves risk aversion, which we discuss in the next section.

Many of us use a different consideration when we compare L_1 and R_1. There, we face a dilemma: increasing the probability of winning versus a significant loss in the prize. The probabilities 0.25 and 0.2 seem similar whereas the prizes $4,000 and $3,000 are not. Therefore, we ignore the difference in the probabilities and focus on the difference in the prizes, a consideration that pushes us to choose L_1.

Experimentalists usually present the two questions to different groups of people, randomly assigning each participant to one of the questions. They do so to avoid participants guessing the object of the experiment, in which case a participant's answer to the second question might be affected by his answer to the first one. However, even when the two questions are given to the same people, we get similar results.

Findings like the ones we have described have led to many suggestions for alternative forms of preferences over the set of lotteries. In experiments, the behavior of many people is inconsistent with any of these alternatives; each theory seems at best to fit some people's behavior in some contexts.

3.5 Risk aversion

We close the chapter by considering attitudes to risk. We assume that the set Z of prizes is the set of nonnegative real numbers, and think of the prize z as

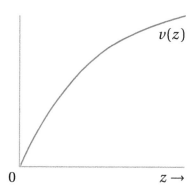

Figure 3.2 A concave Bernoulli function.

the monetary reward of $\$z$. We denote the expected value of any lottery p by $E(p) = \sum_{z \in \text{supp}(Z)} p(z)z$.

An individual is risk-neutral if he cares only about the expectation of a lottery, so that his preferences over lotteries are represented by $E(p)$. Such preferences are consistent with expected utility—take $v(z) = z$. An individual is risk-averse if for every lottery p he finds the prize equal to the expectation of p at least as good as p. That is, an individual with preference relation $\succsim$ is risk-averse if $[E(p)] \succsim p$ for every p. If for every lottery p that involves more than one prize, the individual strictly prefers $[E(p)]$ to p, he is strictly risk-averse.

> **Definition 3.6: Risk aversion and risk neutrality**
>
> If $Z = \mathbb{R}_+$, a preference relation $\succsim$ on the set $L(Z)$ of lotteries over Z is *risk-averse* if $[E(p)] \succsim p$ for every lottery $p \in L(Z)$, is *strictly risk-averse* if $[E(p)] \succ p$ for every lottery $p \in L(Z)$ that involves more than one prize, and is *risk-neutral* if $[E(p)] \sim p$ for every lottery $p \in L(Z)$, where $E(p) = \sum_{z \in Z} p(z)z$.

A strictly risk-averse individual is willing to pay a positive amount of money to replace a lottery with its expected value, so that the fact that an individual buys insurance (which typically reduces but does not eliminate risk) suggests that his preferences are strictly risk-averse. On the other hand, the fact that an individual gambles, paying money to replace a certain amount of money with a lottery with a lower expected value, suggests that his preferences are not risk-averse.

The property of risk aversion applies to any preference relation, whether or not it is consistent with expected utility. We now show that if an individual's preference relation is consistent with expected utility, it is risk-averse if and only if it has a representation for which the Bernoulli function is concave. (Refer to Figure 3.2.)

> ## Proposition 3.3: Risk aversion and concavity of Bernoulli function
>
> Let $Z = \mathbb{R}_+$, assume $\succcurlyeq$ is a preference relation over $L(Z)$ that is consistent with expected utility, and let v be the Bernoulli function for the representation. Then $\succcurlyeq$ is risk-averse if and only if v is concave.

> ## Proof
>
> Let x and y be any prizes and let $\alpha \in [0,1]$. If $\succcurlyeq$ is risk-averse then $[\alpha x + (1-\alpha)y] \succcurlyeq \alpha \cdot x \oplus (1-\alpha) \cdot y$, so that $v(\alpha x + (1-\alpha)y) \geq \alpha v(x) + (1-\alpha)v(y)$. That is, v is concave.
>
> Now assume that v is concave. Then Jensen's inequality implies that $v\left(\sum_{z \in Z} p(z)z\right) \geq \sum_{z \in Z} p(z)v(z)$, so that $\left[\sum_{z \in Z} p(z)z\right] \succcurlyeq p$. Thus the individual is risk-averse.

Problems

1. *Most likely prize.* An individual evaluates a lottery by the probability that the most likely prize is realized (independently of the identity of the prize). That is, for any lotteries p and q we have $p \succcurlyeq q$ if $\max_z p(z) \geq \max_z q(z)$. Such a preference relation is reasonable in a situation where the individual is indifferent between all prizes (e.g., the prizes are similar vacation destinations) and he can prepare himself for only one of the options (in contrast to Example 3.3, where he wants to prepare himself for all options and prefers a lottery with a smaller support).

   Show that if Z contains at least three elements, this preference relation is continuous but does not satisfy independence.

2. *A parent.* A parent has two children, A and B. The parent has in hand only one gift. He is indifferent between giving the gift to either child but prefers to toss a fair coin to determine which child obtains the gift over giving it to either of the children.

   Explain why the parent's preferences are not consistent with expected utility.

3. *Comparing the most likely prize.* An individual has in mind a preference relation $\succcurlyeq^*$ over the set of prizes. Whenever each of two lotteries has a single most likely prize he compares the lotteries by comparing the most likely prizes using $\succcurlyeq^*$. Assume Z contains at least three prizes. Does such a preference relation satisfy continuity or independence?

4. *Two prizes.* Assume that the set Z consists of two prizes, a and b. Show that only three preference relations over $L(Z)$ satisfy independence.

5. *Simple lotteries.* Let Y be a finite set of objects. For any number $\alpha \in [0, 1]$ and object $z \in Y$, the *simple lottery* (α, z) means that z is obtained with probability α and nothing is obtained with probability $1 - \alpha$. Consider preference relations over the set of simple lotteries.

   A preference relation satisfies A1 if for every $x, y \in Y$ with $(1, y) \succ (1, x)$ there is a probability α such that $(\alpha, y) \sim (1, x)$.

   A preference relation satisfies A2 if when $\alpha \geq \beta$ then for any $x, y \in Y$ the comparison between (α, x) and (β, y) is the same as that between $(1, x)$ and $(\beta/\alpha, y)$.

   a. Show that if an individual has in mind a function v that attaches a number $v(z) > 0$ to each object z and his preference relation $\succeq$ is defined by $(\alpha, x) \succeq (\beta, y)$ if $\alpha v(x) \geq \beta v(y)$, then the preference relation satisfies both A1 and A2.

   b. Suggest a preference relation that satisfies A1 but not A2 and one that satisfies A2 but not A1.

   The following questions refer to the model of expected utility with monetary prizes and risk aversion described in Section 3.5. For these questions, consider a risk-averse individual whose preferences are consistent with expected utility. A prize is the total amount of money he holds after he makes a choice and after the realization of the uncertainties. Denote by v a Bernoulli function whose expected value represents the individual's preferences over $L(Z)$ and assume that v has a derivative.

6. *Additional lottery.* An individual faces the monetary lottery p. He is made the offer to replace every z in the support of p with the lottery that yields $z - 1$ and $z + 1$ each with probability $\frac{1}{2}$. Describe the lottery that he faces if he accepts the offer and show that if he is strictly risk-averse he rejects the offer.

7. *Casino.* An individual has wealth w and has to choose an amount x, after which a lottery is conducted in which with probability α he gets $2x$ and with probability $1 - \alpha$ he loses x. Show that the higher is α the higher is the amount x he chooses.

8. *Insurance.* An individual has wealth w and is afraid that an accident will occur with probability p that will cause him a loss of D. The individual has

to choose an amount, x, he will pay for insurance that will pay him λx (for some given λ) if the accident occurs.

a. The insurer's expected profit is $x - \lambda px$. Assume that λ makes this profit zero, so that $\lambda = 1/p$. Show that if the individual is risk-averse he optimally chooses $x = pD$, so that he is fully insured: his net wealth is the same whether or not he has an accident.

b. Assume that $p\lambda < 1$ (that is, the insurer's expected profit is positive). Show that if the individual is strictly risk-averse then he chooses partial insurance: $\lambda x < D$.

Notes

The theory of expected utility was developed by von Neumann and Morgenstern (1947, 15–29 and 617–628). The Allais paradox (Section 3.4) is due to Allais (1953, 527). The notion of risk aversion (Section 3.5) is due to Pratt (1964). The exposition of the chapter draws upon Rubinstein (2006a, Lecture 7).

4 Consumer preferences

In this chapter and the next we study preferences and choice in a context central to standard economic theory: an individual contemplating and choosing quantities of various goods. We refer to such an individual as a consumer. In this chapter, which is parallel to Chapter 1, we discuss preferences, without considering choice. In the next chapter, parallel to Chapter 2, we discuss properties of a consumer's choice function.

4.1 Bundles of goods

We take the set X of all alternatives that a consumer may face to be $\mathbb{R}^2_+$, the set of all pairs of nonnegative numbers. We refer to an element $(x_1, x_2) \in X$ as a bundle and interpret it as a pair of quantities of two goods, called 1 and 2.

Definition 4.1: Set of alternatives (bundles)

The set of alternatives is $X = \mathbb{R}^2_+$. A member of X is a *bundle*.

Goods could be entities like tables, potatoes, money, or leisure time. But, more abstractly, goods can be thought of as considerations the consumer has in mind; his preferences over X reflect his tradeoffs between these considerations. For example, the two goods could be the amounts of attention devoted to two projects or the welfare of the individual and his partner.

The assumption that $X = \mathbb{R}^2_+$ may seem odd, since talking about π tables or $\frac{1}{9}$ of a car has little meaning. We consider the quantities of the goods to be continuous variables for modeling convenience: doing so allows us to easily talk about the tradeoffs consumers face when they want more of each good but are constrained in what they can achieve.

The algebraic operations on the space $X = \mathbb{R}^2_+$ have natural interpretations. Given two bundles x and y, $x + y = (x_1 + x_2, y_1 + y_2)$ is the bundle formed by combining x and y into one bundle. Given a bundle x and a positive number λ, the bundle $\lambda x = (\lambda x_1, \lambda x_2)$ is the λ-multiple of the bundle x. For example, for any integer $m > 1$ the bundle $(1/m)x$ is the bundle obtained by dividing x into m equal parts. Note that given two bundles x and y and a number $\lambda \in (0, 1)$, the bundle $\lambda x + (1 - \lambda)y$ lies on the line segment in $\mathbb{R}^2_+$ that connects the two bundles.

Chapter of *Models in Microeconomic Theory* by Martin J. Osborne and Ariel Rubinstein. Version 2023.5.30 (h).

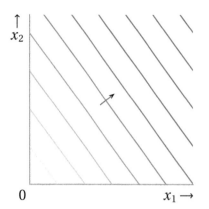 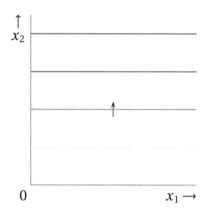

(a) Some indifference sets for the prefer-
ence relation in Example 4.1 for $v_1/v_2 = \frac{4}{3}$.

(b) Some indifference sets for the preference relation in Example 4.2.

Figure 4.1

4.2   Preferences over bundles

We now give some examples of preference relations over bundles. Many preference relations may helpfully be illustrated by diagrams that show a few indifference sets (sometimes called indifference curves). The indifference set for the
preference relation $\succeq$ and bundle a is $\{y \in X : y \sim a\}$, the set of all bundles indifferent to a. The collection of all indifferent sets is the partition induced by the
equivalence relation $\sim$. If $\succeq$ is represented by a utility function u, the indifference set for the bundle a can alternatively be expressed as $\{y \in X : u(y) = u(a)\}$,
the contour of u for the bundle a.

Example 4.1: Constant tradeoff

The consumer has in mind two numbers v_1 and v_2, where v_i is the value
he assigns to a unit of good i. His preference relation $\succeq$ is defined by the
condition that $x \succeq y$ if $v_1 x_1 + v_2 x_2 \geq v_1 y_1 + v_2 y_2$. Thus $\succeq$ is represented
by the utility function $v_1 x_1 + v_2 x_2$. The indifference set for the bundle
(a_1, a_2) is $\{(x_1, x_2) : v_1 x_1 + v_2 x_2 = v_1 a_1 + v_2 a_2\}$, a line with slope $-v_1/v_2$.
Figure 4.1a shows some indifference sets for $v_1/v_2 = \frac{4}{3}$. The arrow in the
figure indicates the direction in which bundles are preferred.

Example 4.2: Only good 2 is valued

The consumer cares only about good 2, which he likes. His preference relation is represented by the utility function x_2. For this preference relation,
every indifference set is a horizontal line; see Figure 4.1b.

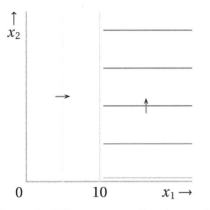

(a) Some indifference sets for the preference relation in Example 4.3.

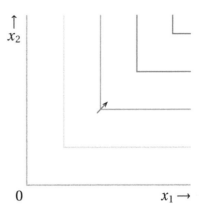

(b) Some indifference sets for the preference relation in Example 4.4.

Figure 4.2

Example 4.3: Minimal amount of good 1 and then good 2

The consumer cares only about increasing the quantity of good 1 until this quantity exceeds 10, and then he cares only about increasing the quantity of good 2. Precisely, $(x_1, x_2) \succsim (y_1, y_2)$ if (*i*) $y_1 \leq 10$ and $x_1 \geq y_1$ or (*ii*) $x_1 > 10$, $y_1 > 10$, and $x_2 \geq y_2$.

These preferences are represented by the utility function

$$\begin{cases} x_1 & \text{if } x_1 \leq 10 \\ 11 + x_2 & \text{if } x_1 > 10. \end{cases}$$

See Figure 4.2a. Notice that the indifference sets for utility levels above 10 are horizontal half lines that are open on the left.

Example 4.4: Complementary goods

The consumer wants the same amount of each good and prefers larger quantities. That is, he prefers a bundle x to a bundle y if and only if $\min\{x_1, x_2\} > \min\{y_1, y_2\}$. (Think of the goods as right and left shoes). Thus $\min\{x_1, x_2\}$ is a utility function that represents his preference relation (see Figure 4.2b).

Example 4.5: Ideal bundle

The consumer has in mind an ideal bundle x^*. He prefers a bundle x to a bundle y if and only if x is closer to x^* than is y according to some measure

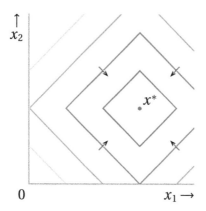

Figure 4.3 Some indifference sets for the preference relation in Example 4.5.

of distance. An example of a distance measure is the sum of the absolute differences of the components, in which case $x \succcurlyeq y$ if $|x_1 - x_1^*| + |x_2 - x_2^*| \leq |y_1 - x_1^*| + |y_2 - x_2^*|$. A utility function that represents this preference relation is $-(|x_1 - x_1^*| + |x_2 - x_2^*|)$. See Figure 4.3.

Example 4.6: Lexicographic preferences

The consumer cares primarily about the quantity of good 1; if this quantity is the same in two bundles, then he prefers the bundle with the larger quantity of good 2. Formally, $x \succcurlyeq y$ if either (*i*) $x_1 > y_1$ or (*ii*) $x_1 = y_1$ and $x_2 \geq y_2$. For this preference relation, for any two bundles x and y we have $x \succ y$ or $y \succ x$, so that each indifference set consists of a single point. The preference relation has no utility representation (Proposition 1.2).

In the rest of the chapter we discuss several properties of consumers' preferences that are often assumed in economic models.

4.3   Monotonicity

Monotonicity is a property of a consumer's preference relation that expresses the assumption that goods are desirable.

Definition 4.2: Monotone preference relation

The preference relation $\succcurlyeq$ on $\mathbb{R}_+^2$ is *monotone* if

$$x_1 \geq y_1 \text{ and } x_2 \geq y_2 \quad \Rightarrow \quad (x_1, x_2) \succcurlyeq (y_1, y_2)$$

and

$$x_1 > y_1 \text{ and } x_2 > y_2 \quad \Rightarrow \quad (x_1, x_2) \succ (y_1, y_2).$$

Thus if the bundle y is obtained from the bundle x by adding a positive amount of one of the goods then for a monotone preference relation $\succeq$ we have $y \succeq x$, and if y is obtained from x by adding positive amounts of both goods then $y \succ x$. For example, the bundle $(3,7)$ is preferred to the bundle $(2,6)$ and it may be preferred to $(3,5)$ or indifferent to it, but cannot be inferior.

The following property is a stronger version of monotonicity. If the bundle x has more of one good than the bundle y and not less of the other good then for a strongly monotone preference relation $\succeq$ we have $x \succ y$.

Definition 4.3: Strongly monotone preference relation

The preference relation $\succeq$ on $\mathbb{R}_+^2$ is *strongly monotone* if

$$x_1 \geq y_1,\ x_2 \geq y_2,\ \text{and}\ (x_1, x_2) \neq (y_1, y_2) \quad \Rightarrow \quad (x_1, x_2) \succ (y_1, y_2).$$

The following table indicates, for each example in the previous section, whether the preference relation is monotone or strongly monotone.

Example	Monotonicity	Strong monotonicity
4.1: Constant tradeoff	✓	if $v_1 > 0$ and $v_2 > 0$
4.2: Only good 2 is valued	✓	✗
4.3: Minimal amount of 1, then 2	✓	✗
4.4: Complementary goods	✓	✗
4.5: Ideal bundle	✗	✗
4.6: Lexicographic	✓	✓

4.4 Continuity

Continuity is a property of a consumer's preference relation that captures the idea that if a bundle x is preferred to a bundle y then bundles close to x are preferred to bundles close to y.

Definition 4.4: Continuous preference relation

The preference relation $\succeq$ on $\mathbb{R}_+^2$ is *continuous* if whenever $x \succ y$ there exists a number $\varepsilon > 0$ such that for every bundle a for which the distance to x is less than ε and every bundle b for which the distance to y is less than ε we have $a \succ b$ (where the distance between any bundles (w_1, w_2) and (z_1, z_2) is $\sqrt{|w_1 - z_1|^2 + |w_2 - z_2|^2}$).

Note that a lexicographic preference relation is not continuous. We have $x = (1,2) \succ y = (1,0)$, but for every $\varepsilon > 0$ the distance of the bundle $a_\varepsilon = (1 - \varepsilon/2, 2)$ from x is less than ε but nevertheless $a_\varepsilon \prec y$.

> **Proposition 4.1: Continuous preference relation and continuous utility**
>
> A preference relation on $\mathbb{R}_+^2$ that can be represented by a continuous utility function is continuous.

> **Proof**
>
> Let $\succeq$ be a preference relation and let u be a continuous function that represents it. Let $x \succ y$. Then $u(x) > u(y)$. Let $\varepsilon = \frac{1}{3}(u(x) - u(y))$. By the continuity of u there exists $\delta > 0$ small enough such that for every bundle a within the distance δ of x and every bundle b within the distance δ of y we have $u(a) > u(x) - \varepsilon$ and $u(y) + \varepsilon > u(b)$. Thus for all such bundles a and b we have $u(a) > u(x) - \varepsilon > u(y) + \varepsilon > u(b)$ and thus $a \succ b$.

Comments

1. The converse result holds also: every continuous preference relation can be represented by a continuous utility function. A proof of this result is above the mathematical level of this book.

2. One can show that if $\succeq$ is a continuous preference relation on X and $a \succ b \succ c$ then on the line between the bundles a and c there is a bundle that is indifferent to b. That is, there is a number $0 < \lambda < 1$ such that $\lambda a + (1 - \lambda)c \sim b$. This property is analogous to the property of continuity of preferences over the space of lotteries in the previous chapter.

4.5   Convexity

Consider a world in which five candidates for a political job have positions commonly recognized to be ordered along the left-right political line as follows:

$$ \text{---}\, D \text{---} A \text{-----} C \text{---------} B \text{------} E \text{---} $$

Assume that a person tells you that he cares only about the candidates' positions on this dimension and says that he prefers A to B. What additional conclusions are you likely to make about his preferences?

You would probably conclude that he prefers C to B. If moving from B to A is an improvement, then going part of the way should also be an improvement. As to the comparison between A and C you would probably be unsure: you might think that he prefers A (if you believe that he is inclined to the left) or you might think that he prefers C (if you think that C is his favorite position among those adopted by the candidates). Thus our intuition is asymmetric: if a change makes

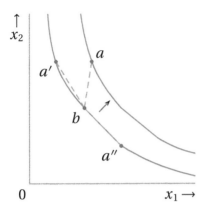

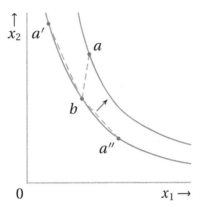

(a) Some indifference sets for a convex preference relation. Each bundle a, a', and a'' is at least as good as b, and all the bundles on each line segment from b to any one of these bundles are also at least as good as b, though bundles between a'' and b are not strictly better.

(b) Some indifference sets for a strictly convex preference relation. Each bundle a, a', and a'' is at least as good as b, and all the bundles on each line segment from b to any one of these bundles, excluding the endpoints, are better than b.

Figure 4.4

the person better off then a partial change probably does so too, but if a change makes him worse off then a partial change may make him better off.

Another natural conclusion is that a person who prefers A to B prefers also B to E, because it does not make sense that he considers candidates both to the left and to the right of B to be improvements over B. But D might be preferred to A (if D is the person's favorite candidate) or inferior to A (if A is the person's favorite candidate).

This example leads us to define a property of preferences called convexity, which is often assumed in economic theory.

Definition 4.5: Convex preference relation

The preference relation $\succcurlyeq$ on $\mathbb{R}^2_+$ is *convex* if

$$a \succcurlyeq b \quad \Rightarrow \quad \lambda a + (1-\lambda)b \succcurlyeq b \text{ for all } \lambda \in (0,1)$$

and is *strictly convex* if

$$a \succcurlyeq b \text{ and } a \neq b \quad \Rightarrow \quad \lambda a + (1-\lambda)b \succ b \text{ for all } \lambda \in (0,1).$$

Geometrically, $\lambda a + (1-\lambda)b$ is a bundle on the line segment from a to b, so the condition for a convex preference relation says that if a is at least as good as b then every bundle on the line segment from a to b is at least as good as b. For a strictly convex preference relation, all the bundles on the line segment, excluding the end points, are better than b. See Figures 4.4a and 4.4b.

Example 4.7: Convexity of lexicographic preferences

Lexicographic preferences are convex by the following argument. Assume $(a_1, a_2) \succeq (b_1, b_2)$. If $a_1 > b_1$ then for every $\lambda \in (0, 1)$ we have $\lambda a_1 + (1-\lambda)b_1 > b_1$ and thus $\lambda a + (1-\lambda)b \succ b$. If $a_1 = b_1$ then $\lambda a_1 + (1-\lambda)b_1 = b_1$. In this case $a_2 \geq b_2$ and hence $\lambda a_2 + (1-\lambda)b_2 \geq b_2$, so that $\lambda a + (1-\lambda)b \succeq b$.

Proposition 4.2: Characterization of convex preference relation

The preference relation $\succeq$ on $\mathbb{R}_+^2$ is convex if and only if for all $x^* \in X$ the set $\{x \in X : x \succeq x^*\}$ (containing all bundles at least as good as x^*) is convex.

Proof

Assume that $\succeq$ is convex. Let $a, b \in \{x \in X : x \succeq x^*\}$. Without loss of generality assume that $a \succeq b$. Then for $\lambda \in (0, 1)$, by the convexity of $\succeq$ we have $\lambda a + (1-\lambda)b \succeq b$ and by its transitivity we have $\lambda a + (1-\lambda)b \succeq x^*$, so that $\lambda a + (1-\lambda)b \in \{x : x \succeq x^*\}$. Thus this set is convex.

Now assume that $\{x \in X : x \succeq x^*\}$ is convex for all $x^* \in X$. If $a \succeq b$ then we have $a \in \{x \in X : x \succeq b\}$. Given that b is also in $\{x \in X : x \succeq b\}$, the convexity of this set implies that $\lambda a + (1-\lambda)b$ is in the set. Thus $\lambda a + (1-\lambda)b \succeq b$.

The next result involves the notion of a concave function. A function $u : X \to \mathbb{R}$ is concave if for all $a, b \in X$, $u(\lambda a + (1-\lambda)b) \geq \lambda u(a) + (1-\lambda)u(b)$ for all $\lambda \in (0, 1)$.

Proposition 4.3: Preferences with concave representation are convex

A preference relation on $\mathbb{R}_+^2$ that is represented by a concave function is convex.

Proof

Let $\succeq$ be a preference relation that is represented by a concave function u. Assume that $a \succeq b$, so that $u(a) \geq u(b)$. By the concavity of u,

$$u(\lambda a + (1-\lambda)b) \geq \lambda u(a) + (1-\lambda)u(b) \geq u(b).$$

Thus $\lambda a + (1-\lambda)b \succeq b$, so that $\succeq$ is convex.

Note that convex preferences may be represented also by utility functions that are not concave. For example, the convex preference relation represented by the concave function $\min\{x_1, x_2\}$ is represented also by the function $(\min\{x_1, x_2\})^2$, which is not concave.

The convexity of a strongly monotone preference relation is connected with the property known as decreasing marginal rate of substitution. Consider three bundles $a = (10, 10)$, $b = (11, 10 - \beta)$, and $c = (12, 10 - \beta - \gamma)$ for which $a \sim b \sim c$. When the amount of good 1 increases from 10 to 11, the consumer is kept indifferent by reducing the amount of good 2 by β, and when the amount of good 1 increases by another unit, he is kept indifferent by further reducing the amount of good 2 by γ. We now argue that if the consumer's preference relation is strongly monotone and convex then $\beta \geq \gamma$. That is, the rate at which good 2 is substituted for good 1 decreases as the amount of good 1 increases. Assume to the contrary that $\beta < \gamma$. Then $\beta < \frac{1}{2}(\beta + \gamma)$, so that by strong monotonicity $(11, 10 - \frac{1}{2}(\beta + \gamma)) \prec b = (11, 10 - \beta)$. But $(11, 10 - \frac{1}{2}(\beta + \gamma)) = \frac{1}{2}a + \frac{1}{2}c$, and the convexity of the preferences implies that $\frac{1}{2}a + \frac{1}{2}c \succeq c$, so that $(11, 10 - \frac{1}{2}(\beta + \gamma)) \succeq c \sim b$, a contradiction.

4.6   Differentiability

Consumers' preferences are commonly assumed to have smooth indifference sets, like the one in Figure 4.5a. The indifference set in Figure 4.5b, by contrast, is not smooth. A formal property of a preference relation that ensures the smoothness of indifference sets is differentiability. We define this property only for monotone and convex preference relations.

Definition 4.6: Differentiable preference relation

A monotone and convex preference relation $\succeq$ on $\mathbb{R}^2_+$ is *differentiable* if for every bundle z there is a pair $(v_1(z), v_2(z)) \neq (0, 0)$ of nonnegative numbers, called the consumer's *local valuations at z*, such that for all numbers δ_1 and δ_2,

$$v_1(z)\delta_1 + v_2(z)\delta_2 > 0 \quad \Leftrightarrow \quad \text{there exists } \varepsilon > 0 \text{ such that } z + (\varepsilon\delta_1, \varepsilon\delta_2) \succ z.$$

Geometrically, this definition says that for any given bundle z there is a line (like the green one in Figure 4.5a) such that (*i*) for any bundle x above the line, every bundle sufficiently close to z on the line segment from z to x (like x' in Figure 4.5a) is preferred to z and (*ii*) any bundle that is preferred to z is above the line.

The numbers $v_1(z)$ and $v_2(z)$ can be interpreted as the consumer's valuations of small changes in the amounts of the goods he consumes away from z. If his

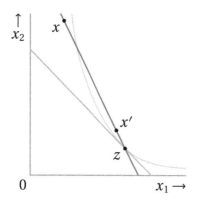

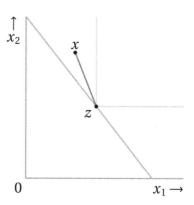

(a) An indifference set for a differentiable preference relation.

(b) An indifference set for a preference relation that is not differentiable.

Figure 4.5

preference relation is differentiable, then for $\varepsilon > 0$ small enough the change from the bundle z to the bundle $z' = (z_1 + \varepsilon \delta_1, z_2 + \varepsilon \delta_2)$ is an improvement for the consumer whenever $v_1(z)\delta_1 + v_2(z)\delta_2 > 0$. (Note that only the ratio $v_1(z)/v_2(z)$ matters; if $(v_1(z), v_2(z))$ is a pair of local valuations, then so is $(\alpha v_1(z), \alpha v_2(z))$ for any number $\alpha > 0$.)

Figure 4.5b gives an example of an indifference set for preferences that are not differentiable. For every line (like the green one) through z such that all bundles preferred to z lie above the line, there are bundles (like x in the figure) such that *no* bundle on the line segment from x to z is preferred to z.

Lexicographic preferences are not differentiable. Suppose that the quantity of the first good has first priority and that of the second good has second priority. For any bundle z, the only vector $(v_1(z), v_2(z))$ such that for all δ_1 and δ_2 the left-hand side of the equivalence in Definition 4.6 implies the right-hand side is $(1, 0)$ (or a positive multiple of $(1, 0)$). However, for this vector the right-hand side of the equivalence does not imply the left-hand side: for $(\delta_1, \delta_2) = (0, 1)$ we have $1 \cdot \delta_1 + 0 \cdot \delta_2 = 0$ although $(z_1 + \varepsilon \delta_1, z_2 + \varepsilon \delta_2) \succ (z_1, z_2)$ for $\varepsilon > 0$.

The following result, a proof of which is beyond the scope of the book, says that a preference relation represented by a utility function with continuous partial derivatives is differentiable and its pair of partial derivatives is one pair of local valuations.

> **Proposition 4.4: Local valuations and partial derivatives**
>
> If a preference relation on $\mathbb{R}_+^2$ is monotone and convex and is represented by a utility function u that has continuous partial derivatives, then it is differentiable and for any bundle z one pair of local valuations is the pair of partial derivatives of u at z.

Thus, for example, the preference relation represented by the utility function u defined by $u(x_1, x_2) = x_1 x_2$ is differentiable and for any bundle z, $(v_1(z), v_2(z)) = (z_2, z_1)$ is a pair of local valuations.

Problems

1. *Three examples.* Describe each of the following three preference relations formally, giving a utility function that represents the preferences wherever possible, draw some representative indifference sets, and determine whether the preferences are monotone, continuous, and convex.

   a. The consumer prefers the bundle (x_1, x_2) to the bundle (y_1, y_2) if and only if (x_1, x_2) is further from $(0,0)$ than is (y_1, y_2), where the distance between the (z_1, z_2) and (z_1', z_2') is $\sqrt{(z_1 - z_1')^2 + (z_2 - z_2')^2}$.

   b. The consumer prefers any balanced bundle, containing the same amount of each good, to any unbalanced bundle. Between balanced bundles, he prefers the one with the largest quantities. Between unbalanced bundles, he prefers the bundle with the largest quantity of good 2.

   c. The consumer cares first about the sum of the amounts of the goods; if the sum is the same in two bundles, he prefers the bundle with more of good 1.

2. *Three more examples.* For the preference relation represented by each of the following utility functions, draw some representative indifference sets and determine (without providing a complete proof) whether the preference relation is monotone, continuous, and convex.

   a. $\max\{x_1, x_2\}$

   b. $x_1 - x_2$

   c. $\log(x_1 + 1) + \log(x_2 + 1)$

3. *Continuous preferences.* The preference relation $\succcurlyeq$ is monotone and continuous and is thus represented by a utility function u that is increasing and continuous. Show that for every bundle x there is a bundle y with $y_1 = y_2$ such that $y \sim x$.

4. *Quasilinear preferences.* A preference relation is represented by a utility function of the form $u(x_1, x_2) = x_2 + g(x_1)$, where g is a continuous increasing function.

   a. How does each indifference set for this preference relation relate geometrically to the other indifference sets?

    b. Show that if g is concave then the preference relation is convex.

5. *Maxmin preferences.* Prove that the preference relation represented by the utility function $\min\{x_1, x_2\}$ is convex.

6. *Ideal bundle.* Show that the preference relation in Example 4.5, in which the consumer has in mind an ideal bundle, is continuous and convex.

7. *One preference relatively favors one good more than another.* We say that the preference relation $\succeq_A$ favors good 1 more than does $\succeq_B$ if for all positive numbers α and β we have

$$(x_1 - \alpha, x_2 + \beta) \succeq_A (x_1, x_2) \quad \Rightarrow \quad (x_1 - \alpha, x_2 + \beta) \succ_B (x_1, x_2).$$

    a. Illustrate by two collections of indifference sets the configuration in which $\succeq_A$ favors good 1 more than does $\succeq_B$.

    b. Explain why the preference relation $\succeq_A$ represented by $2x_1 + x_2$ favors good 1 more than does the preference relation $\succeq_B$ represented by $x_1 + x_2$.

    c. Explain why a lexicographic preference relation (Example 4.6) favors good 1 more than does any strongly monotone preference relation.

Notes

The result mentioned at the end of Section 4.4 that every continuous preference relation can be represented by a continuous utility function is due to Debreu (1954). The exposition of the chapter, and in particular the presentation of differentiability, draws upon Rubinstein (2006a, Lecture 4).

5 Consumer behavior

In this chapter we apply the model of individual choice presented in Chapter 2 to the behavior of a consumer. The set X of all alternatives the consumer may face is $\mathbb{R}^2_+$, the set of bundles, and a choice problem is a subset of X. As we discussed in Chapter 2, to completely describe an individual's behavior we need to specify his choice for every choice problem he may face. Not every subset of X is a choice problem for a consumer. Since we are interested in the connection between prices and the consumer's choices, we focus on the behavior of a consumer who faces a particular type of choice problem, called a budget set.

5.1 Budget sets

A choice problem for a consumer is the set of bundles that he can purchase, given the prices and his wealth. We refer to this set as the consumer's budget set. More precisely, given prices p_1 and p_2 and wealth w, the consumer's budget set is the set of all bundles the consumer can obtain by exchanging w for the goods at the fixed exchange rates of p_1 units of wealth for one unit of good 1 and p_2 units of wealth for one unit of good 2.

Definition 5.1: Budget set

For any positive numbers p_1, p_2, and w, the *budget set* of a consumer with wealth w when the prices are (p_1, p_2) is

$$B((p_1, p_2), w) = \{(x_1, x_2) \in X : p_1 x_1 + p_2 x_2 \leq w\}.$$

The set $\{(x_1, x_2) \in X : p_1 x_1 + p_2 x_2 = w\}$ is the consumer's *budget line*.

Geometrically, a budget set is a triangle like the one in Figure 5.1. Note that multiplying wealth and prices by the same positive number does not change the set: $B((\lambda p_1, \lambda p_2), \lambda w) = B((p_1, p_2), w)$ for any $\lambda > 0$, because the inequalities $\lambda p_1 x_1 + \lambda p_2 x_2 \leq \lambda w$ and $p_1 x_1 + p_2 x_2 \leq w$ that define these sets are equivalent.

Every budget set is convex: if a and b are in $B((p_1, p_2), w)$ then $p_1 a_1 + p_2 a_2 \leq w$ and $p_1 b_1 + p_2 b_2 \leq w$, so that for any $\lambda \in [0, 1]$ we have

$$p_1(\lambda a_1 + (1-\lambda)b_1) + p_2(\lambda a_2 + (1-\lambda)b_2)$$
$$= \lambda(p_1 a_1 + p_2 a_2) + (1-\lambda)(p_1 b_1 + p_2 b_2) \leq w,$$

Chapter of *Models in Microeconomic Theory* by Martin J. Osborne and Ariel Rubinstein. Version 2023.5.30 (h).
© 2023 Martin J. Osborne and Ariel Rubinstein CC BY-NC-ND 4.0.   https://doi.org/10.11647/OBP.0362.05

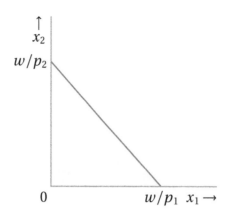

Figure 5.1 The light green triangle is the budget set of a consumer with wealth w when the prices of the goods are p_1 and p_2, $\{(x_1, x_2) \in X : p_1 x_1 + p_2 x_2 \leq w\}$. The dark green line is the budget line.

and hence $(\lambda a_1 + (1 - \lambda)b_1, \lambda a_2 + (1 - \lambda)b_2)$ is in $B((p_1, p_2), w)$.

Figure 5.1 shows also the budget line: the set of all bundles (x_1, x_2) satisfying $p_1 x_1 + p_2 x_2 = w$, a line with negative slope. The equation of this line can be alternatively expressed as $x_2 = (-p_1/p_2)x_1 + w/p_1$. The slope of the line, $-p_1/p_2$, expresses the tradeoff the consumer faces: consuming one more unit of good 1 requires consuming p_1/p_2 fewer units of good 2.

Thus every choice problem of the consumer is a right triangle with two sides on the axes. Every such triangle is generated by some pair $((p_1, p_2), w)$. The same collection of choice problems is generated also in a different model of the consumer's environment. Rather than assuming that the consumer can purchase the goods at given prices using his wealth, assume that he initially owns a bundle e and can exchange goods at the fixed rate of one unit of good 1 for β units of good 2. Then his choice problem is $\{(x_1, x_2) \in X : (e_1 - x_1)\beta \geq x_2 - e_2\}$ or $\{(x_1, x_2) \in X : \beta x_1 + x_2 \leq \beta e_1 + e_2\}$, which is equal to the budget set $B((\beta, 1), \beta e_1 + e_2)$.

5.2 Demand functions

A consumer's choice function, called a demand function, assigns to every budget set one of its members. A budget set here is defined by a pair $((p_1, p_2), w)$ with p_1, p_2, and w positive. (In some later chapters it is specified differently.) Thus, a consumer's behavior can be described as a function of $((p_1, p_2), w)$.

Definition 5.2: Demand function

A *demand function* is a function x that assigns to each budget set one of its members. Define $x((p_1, p_2), w)$ to be the bundle assigned to the budget set $B((p_1, p_2), w)$.

Note that $x((\lambda p_1, \lambda p_2), \lambda w) = x((p_1, p_2), w)$ for all $((p_1, p_2), w)$ and all $\lambda > 0$ because $B((\lambda p_1, \lambda p_2), \lambda w) = B((p_1, p_2), w)$.

The definition does not assume that the demand function is the result of the consumer's maximizing a preference relation. We are interested also in patterns of behavior that are not derived from such optimization.

Here are some examples of demand functions that reflect simple rules of behavior. In each case, the function x satisfies $x((\lambda p_1, \lambda p_2), \lambda w) = x((p_1, p_2), w)$ for all $((p_1, p_2), w)$ and all $\lambda > 0$, as required.

Example 5.1: All wealth spent on the cheaper good

The consumer purchases only the cheaper good; if the prices of the goods are the same, he divides his wealth equally between the two. Formally,

$$x((p_1, p_2), w) = \begin{cases} (w/p_1, 0) & \text{if } p_1 < p_2 \\ (w/(2p_1), w/(2p_2)) & \text{if } p_1 = p_2 \\ (0, w/p_2) & \text{if } p_1 > p_2. \end{cases}$$

Example 5.2: Equal amounts of the goods

The consumer chooses the same quantity of each good and spends all his wealth, so that $x((p_1, p_2), w) = (w/(p_1 + p_2), w/(p_1 + p_2))$.

Example 5.3: Half of wealth spent on each good

The consumer spends half of his wealth on each good, so that $x((p_1, p_2), w) = (w/(2p_1), w/(2p_2))$.

Example 5.4: Purchase one good up to a limit

The consumer buys as much as he can of good 1 up to 7 units and with any wealth remaining buys good 2. That is,

$$x((p_1, p_2), w) = \begin{cases} (w/p_1, 0) & \text{if } w/p_1 \leq 7 \\ (7, (w - 7p_1)/p_2) & \text{otherwise.} \end{cases}$$

5.3 Rational consumer

A rational consumer has a fixed preference relation, and for any budget set chooses the best bundle in the set according to the preference relation. We refer to the problem of finding the best bundle in a budget set according to a given preference relation as the consumer's problem.

> ## Definition 5.3: Consumer's problem
>
> For a preference relation $\succeq$ on $\mathbb{R}^2_+$ and positive numbers p_1, p_2, and w, the *consumer's problem* is the problem of finding the best bundle in the budget set $B((p_1, p_2), w)$ according to $\succeq$. If $\succeq$ is represented by the utility function u, this problem is
>
> $$\max_{(x_1, x_2) \in X} u(x_1, x_2) \text{ subject to } p_1 x_1 + p_2 x_2 \leq w.$$

The following result gives some basic properties of a consumer's problem.

> ## Proposition 5.1: Solution of consumer's problem
>
> Fix a preference relation on $\mathbb{R}^2_+$ and a budget set.
>
> a. If the preference relation is continuous then the consumer's problem has a solution.
>
> b. If the preference relation is strictly convex then the consumer's problem has at most one solution.
>
> c. If the preference relation is monotone then any solution of the consumer's problem is on the budget line.

> ## Proof
>
> a. If the preference relation is continuous then it has a continuous utility representation (see Comment 1 on page 50). Given that both prices are positive, the budget set is compact, so that by a standard mathematical result the continuous utility function has a maximizer in the budget set, which is a solution of the consumer's problem.
>
> b. Assume that distinct bundles a and b are both solutions to a consumer's problem. Then the bundle $(a+b)/2$ is in the budget set (which is convex); by the strict convexity of the preference relation this bundle is strictly preferred to both a and b.
>
> c. Suppose that the bundle (a_1, a_2) is in the consumer's budget set for prices p_1 and p_2 and wealth w, but is not on the budget line. Then

$p_1a_1 + p_2a_2 < w$, so there exists $\varepsilon > 0$ small enough that $p_1(a_1 + \varepsilon) + p_2(a_2 + \varepsilon) < w$, so that $(a_1 + \varepsilon, a_2 + \varepsilon)$ is in the budget set. By the monotonicity of the preference relation, $(a_1 + \varepsilon, a_2 + \varepsilon)$ is preferred to (a_1, a_2), so that (a_1, a_2) is not a solution of the consumer's problem.

The next two examples give explicit solutions of the consumer's problem for specific preference relations.

Example 5.5: Complementary goods

Consider a consumer with a preference relation represented by the utility function $\min\{x_1, x_2\}$ (see Example 4.4). This preference relation is monotone, so a solution (x_1, x_2) of the consumer's problem lies on the budget line: $p_1x_1 + p_2x_2 = w$. Since $p_1 > 0$ and $p_2 > 0$, any solution (x_1, x_2) also has $x_1 = x_2$. If, for example, $x_1 > x_2$, then for $\varepsilon > 0$ small enough the bundle $(x_1 - \varepsilon, x_2 + \varepsilon p_1/p_2)$ is in the budget set and is preferred to x. Thus the consumer's problem has a unique solution $(w/(p_1 + p_2), w/(p_1 + p_2))$. Notice that the consumer's problem has a unique solution even though the preference relation is only convex, not strictly convex.

Example 5.6: Substitutable goods

A consumer wants to maximize the sum of the amounts of the two goods. That is, his preference relation is represented by $x_1 + x_2$ (Example 4.1 with $v_1 = v_2$). Such a preference relation makes sense if the two goods differ only in ways irrelevant to the consumer. When $p_1 \neq p_2$, a unique bundle solves the consumer's problem: $(w/p_1, 0)$ if $p_1 < p_2$ and $(0, w/p_2)$ when $p_1 > p_2$. When $p_1 = p_2$, all bundles on the budget line are solutions of the consumer's problem.

5.4 Differentiable preferences

If a consumer's preference relation is monotone, convex, and differentiable, then for any bundle z the local valuations $v_1(z)$ and $v_2(z)$ represent the value of each good to the consumer at z. Thus a small change in the bundle z is an improvement for the consumer if and only if the change increases the value of the bundle measured by the local valuations at z. The consumer finds it desirable to give up a small amount α of good 1 in return for an additional amount β of good 2 if and only if $-\alpha v_1(z) + \beta v_2(z) > 0$, or $\beta/\alpha > v_1(z)/v_2(z)$. Similarly, he finds it desirable to give up a small amount β of good 2 in return for an additional amount

α of good 1 if and only if $\alpha v_1(z) - \beta v_2(z) > 0$, or $\beta/\alpha < v_1(z)/v_2(z)$. The ratio $v_1(z)/v_2(z)$ is called his marginal rate of substitution at z.

> **Definition 5.4: Marginal rate of substitution**
>
> For a monotone, convex, and differentiable preference relation on $\mathbb{R}^2_+$ and bundle z, the *marginal rate of substitution* at z, denoted $MRS(z)$, is $v_1(z)/v_2(z)$, where $v_1(z)$ and $v_2(z)$ are the consumer's local valuations at z.

The following result characterizes the solution of the consumer's problem if the consumer's preference relation is monotone, convex, and differentiable.

> **Proposition 5.2: Marginal rate of substitution and price ratio**
>
> Assume that a consumer has a monotone, convex, and differentiable preference relation on $\mathbb{R}^2_+$. If x^* is a solution of the consumer's problem for (p_1, p_2, w) then
>
> a. $x_1^* > 0$ and $x_2^* > 0 \Rightarrow MRS(x^*) = p_1/p_2$
>
> b. $x_1^* = 0 \Rightarrow MRS(x^*) \leq p_1/p_2$
>
> c. $x_2^* = 0 \Rightarrow MRS(x^*) \geq p_1/p_2$.

> **Proof**
>
> To show (*a*), denote the local valuations at x^* by $v_1(x^*)$ and $v_2(x^*)$. Suppose that $x_1^* > 0$, $x_2^* > 0$, and $MRS(x^*) = v_1(x^*)/v_2(x^*) < p_1/p_2$. For any $\varepsilon > 0$ let $y(\varepsilon) = x^* + (-\varepsilon, \varepsilon p_1/p_2)$. (Refer to Figure 5.2a.) Then
>
> $$p_1 y_1(\varepsilon) + p_2 y_2(\varepsilon) = p_1(x_1^* - \varepsilon) + p_2(x_2^* + \varepsilon p_1/p_2) = w,$$
>
> so that $y(\varepsilon)$ is on the budget line. Also
>
> $$v_1(x^*)(-\varepsilon) + v_2(x^*)(\varepsilon p_1/p_2) = -\varepsilon[v_1(x^*) - (p_1/p_2)v_2(x^*)] > 0.$$
>
> Thus by the differentiability of the preference relation, there exists $\varepsilon > 0$ such that $y(\varepsilon) \succ x^*$, contradicting the fact that x^* is a solution of the consumer's problem.
>
> Similar arguments establish results (*b*) and (*c*) (refer to Figure 5.2b). Notice that if a bundle x^* with $x_1^* = 0$ is optimal, then the inequality $MRS(x^*) < p_1/p_2$ does not contradict the optimality of x^* because the consumer cannot reduce his consumption of good 1 in exchange for some amount of good 2. Therefore the optimality of x^* implies only the inequality $MRS(x^*) \leq p_1/p_2$ and not the equality $MRS(x^*) = p_1/p_2$.

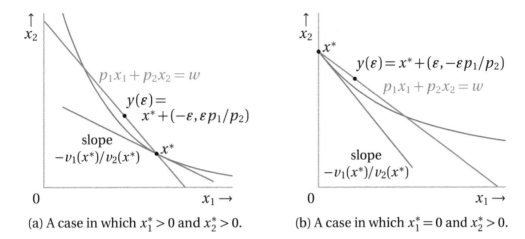

(a) A case in which $x_1^* > 0$ and $x_2^* > 0$.

(b) A case in which $x_1^* = 0$ and $x_2^* > 0$.

Figure 5.2 An illustration of the proof of Proposition 5.2.

Example 5.7

A consumer's preference relation is represented by the utility function $x_1 x_2$. (An indifference curve is shown in Figure 5.3.) Any bundle (x_1, x_2) with $x_1 > 0$ and $x_2 > 0$ is preferred to any bundle with $x_1 = 0$ or $x_2 = 0$, so if x^* is a solution of the consumer's problem then $x_1^* > 0$ and $x_2^* > 0$. The preference relation is monotone, convex, and differentiable, so by Proposition 5.2, $MRS(x^*) = p_1/p_2$. Proposition 4.4 implies that $MRS(x^*)$ is the ratio of the partial derivatives of the utility function at x^*, namely $MRS(x^*) = x_2^*/x_1^*$. Thus $x_2^*/x_1^* = p_1/p_2$, so that $p_1 x_1^* = p_2 x_2^*$. Since the preference relation is monotone, by Proposition 5.1c x^* lies on the budget line: $p_1 x_1^* + p_2 x_2^* = w$. Therefore $(x_1^*, x_2^*) = (w/(2p_1), w/(2p_2))$: the consumer spends half his wealth on each good.

Example 5.8

A consumer's preference relation is represented by the utility function $x_1 + \sqrt{x_2}$. This preference relation is monotone, convex, and differentiable, so that by Proposition 5.1c a solution of the consumer's problem is on the budget line and satisfies the conditions in Proposition 5.2. We have $MRS(x_1, x_2) = 2\sqrt{x_2}$, so as x_1 increases and x_2 decreases along the budget line, $MRS(x_1, x_2)$ decreases from $2\sqrt{w/p_2}$ to 0. (See Figure 5.4.) Hence if $2\sqrt{w/p_2} \geq p_1/p_2$ the unique solution (x_1^*, x_2^*) of the consumer's problem satisfies $MRS(x_1^*, x_2^*) = 2\sqrt{x_2^*} = p_1/p_2$, or $x_2^* = p_1^2/(4p_2^2)$ and $x_1^* = w/p_1 - p_1/(4p_2)$. If $2\sqrt{w/p_2} \leq p_1/p_2$, we have $(x_1^*, x_2^*) = (0, w/p_2)$: the consumer spends all his wealth on the second good.

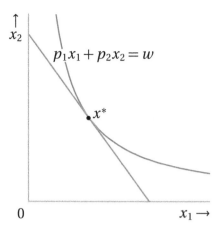

Figure 5.3 An indifference set for the preference relation in Example 5.7.

5.5   Rationalizing a demand function

In the previous two sections, we study the demand function obtained from the maximization of a preference relation. We now study whether a demand function, which could be the outcome of a different procedure, is consistent with the consumer's maximization of a preference relation. That is, rather than deriving a demand function from a preference relation, we go in the opposite direction: for a given demand function, we ask whether there exists a monotone preference relation such that the solutions of the consumer's problem are consistent with the demand function. Or, more compactly, we ask which demand functions are rationalized by preference relations.

> **Definition 5.5: Rationalizable demand function**
>
> A demand function is *rationalizable* if there is a monotone preference relation such that for every budget set the alternative specified by the demand function is a solution of the consumer's problem.

Note that the definition does not require that the alternative specified by the demand function is the *only* solution of the consumer's problem.

In Section 2.2 we show (Propositions 2.1 and 2.2) that a choice function is rationalizable if and only if it satisfies property α. These results have no implications for a consumer's demand function, because property α is vacuous in this context: if the bundle a is chosen from budget set B and is on the frontier of B then no other budget set that contains a is a subset of B.

We now give some examples of demand functions and consider preference relations that rationalize them.

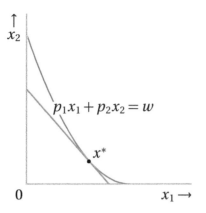
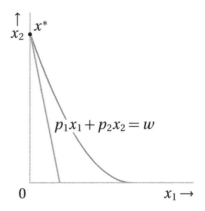

(a) A case in which the solution x^* has $x_1^* > 0$ and $MRS(x_1^*, x_2^*) = p_1/p_2$.

(b) A case in which the solution x^* has $x_1^* = 0$ and $MRS(x_1^*, x_2^*) > p_1/p_2$.

Figure 5.4 Solutions of the consumer's problem in Example 5.8.

Example 5.9: All wealth spent on the cheaper good

Consider the demand function in Example 5.1. That is, if the prices of the good differ, the consumer spends all his wealth on the cheaper good; if the prices are the same, he splits his wealth equally between the two goods. This demand function is rationalized by the preference relation represented by $x_1 + x_2$. It is also rationalized by the preference relations represented by $\max\{x_1, x_2\}$ and by $x_1^2 + x_2^2$.

Example 5.10: Half of wealth spent on each good

Consider the demand function in Example 5.3. That is, the consumer spends half of his wealth on each good, independently of the prices and his wealth. This demand function is rationalized by the preference relation represented by the function $x_1 x_2$ (Example 5.7). Thus although maximizing the product of the quantities of the goods may seem odd, this function rationalizes a natural demand function.

Example 5.11: All wealth spent on the more expensive good

The consumer spends all his wealth on the more expensive good; if the prices are the same, he buys only good 1. That is, $x((p_1, p_2), w) = (w/p_1, 0)$ if $p_1 \geq p_2$ and $(0, w/p_2)$ if $p_1 < p_2$. This demand function *cannot* be rationalized by a monotone preference relation. The consumer chooses the bundle a from $B((1, 2), 2)$ and the bundle b from $B((2, 1), 2)$ (see Figure 5.5).

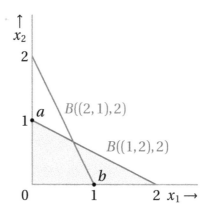

Figure 5.5 An illustration of the demand function in Example 5.11. The light blue triangle is the budget set $B((1,2),2)$ and the light green triangle is the budget set $B((2,1),2)$.

> Since b is in the interior of $B((1,2),2)$, we have $a \succ b$ for any monotone preference relation $\succeq$ that rationalizes the demand function. Similarly, $b \succ a$ because a is in the interior of $B((2,1),2)$, a contradiction.

The demand function in this last example might make sense in environments in which the price of a good reveals information about the quality of the good, or consumers like the prestige of consuming an expensive good. The example highlights a hidden assumption in the model of consumer behavior: prices do not convey information about the quality of the goods, and an individual's preferences are not affected by the prices and his wealth.

The weak axiom of revealed preference

If an individual chooses alternative a when alternative b is available, we might conclude that he finds a to be at least as good as b. If he chooses a when b is available and costs less than a, we might similarly conclude, if the goods are desirable, that he prefers a to b. (See Figure 5.6a.) For example, if an individual purchases the bundle $(2,0)$ when he could have purchased the bundle $(0,2)$, then we conclude that he finds $(2,0)$ at least as good as the bundle $(0,2)$ and prefers $(2,0)$ to $(0,1.9)$.

Definition 5.6: Revealed preference

Given the demand function x, the bundle a is *revealed to be at least as good as the bundle b* if for some prices (p_1, p_2) and wealth w the budget set $B((p_1, p_2), w)$ contains both a and b, and $x((p_1, p_2), w) = a$. The bundle a is *revealed to be better than b* if for some prices (p_1, p_2) and wealth w

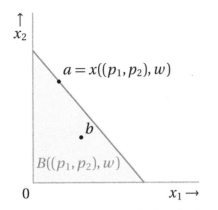

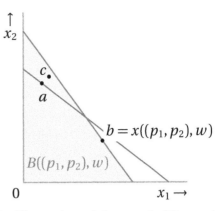

(a) The bundle a is revealed to be better than b.

(b) An illustration of the proof of Proposition 5.3.

Figure 5.6

the budget set $B((p_1, p_2), w)$ contains both a and b, $p_1 b_1 + p_2 b_2 < w$, and $x((p_1, p_2), w) = a$.

We now define a property that is satisfied by every demand function rationalized by a monotone preference relation.

Definition 5.7: Weak axiom of revealed preference (WARP)

A demand function satisfies the *weak axiom of revealed preference* (WARP) if for no bundles a and b, both a is revealed to be at least as good as b and b is revealed to be better than a.

Proposition 5.3: Demand function of rational consumer satisfies WARP

A demand function that is rationalized by a monotone preference relation satisfies the weak axiom of revealed preference.

Proof

Let x be a demand function that is rationalized by the monotone preference relation $\succsim$. Assume, contrary to the result, that (*i*) a is revealed to be at least as good as b and (*ii*) b is revealed to be better than a. Given (*i*), we have $a \succsim b$. By (*ii*) there are prices p_1 and p_2 and wealth w such that $b = x((p_1, p_2), w)$ and $p_1 a_1 + p_2 a_2 < w$. Let c be a bundle in $B((p_1, p_2), w)$ with $c_1 > a_1$ and $c_2 > a_2$. (Refer to Figure 5.6b.) By the monotonicity of the preference relation we have $c \succ a$, and since b is chosen from $B((p_1, p_2), w)$

we have $b \succcurlyeq c$. It follows from the transitivity of the preference relation that $b \succ a$, contradicting $a \succcurlyeq b$.

Propositions 2.1 and 2.2 show that for a general choice problem, a choice function is rationalizable if and only if it satisfies property α. Notice that by contrast, Proposition 5.3 provides only a necessary condition for a demand function to be rationalized by a monotone preference relation, not a sufficient condition. We do not discuss a sufficient condition, called the strong axiom of revealed preference.

5.6   Properties of demand functions

A demand function describes the bundle chosen by a consumer as a function of the prices and the consumer's wealth. If we fix the price of good 2 and the consumer's wealth, the demand function describes how the bundle chosen by the consumer varies with the price of good 1. This relation between the price of good 1 and its demand is called the consumer's regular, or Marshallian, demand function for good 1 (given the price of good 2 and wealth). The relation between the price of good 2 and the demand for good 1 (given a price of good 1 and the level of wealth), is called the consumer's cross-demand function for good 2. And the relation between the consumer's wealth and his demand for good i (given the prices) is called the consumer's Engel function for good i.

Definition 5.8: Regular, cross-demand, and Engel functions

Let x be the demand function of a consumer.

- For any given price p_2^0 of good 2 and wealth w^0, the function x_1^* defined by $x_1^*(p_1) = x_1((p_1, p_2^0), w^0)$ is the consumer's *regular (or Marshallian) demand function for good 1 given* (p_2^0, w^0), and the function $\hat{x}_2$ defined by $\hat{x}_2(p_1) = x_2((p_1, p_2^0), w^0)$ is the consumer's *cross-demand function for good 2 given* (p_2^0, w^0).

- For any given prices (p_1^0, p_2^0), the function $\overline{x}_k$ defined by $\overline{x}_k(w) = x_k((p_1^0, p_2^0), w)$ is the consumer's *Engel function for good k given* (p_1^0, p_2^0).

Consider, for example, a consumer who spends the fraction α of his budget on good 1 and the rest on good 2, so that $x((p_1, p_2), w) = (\alpha w / p_1, (1 - \alpha) w / p_2)$. The consumer's regular demand function for good 1 given p_2^0 and w^0 is given by $x_1^*(p_1) = \alpha w^0 / p_1$ (and in particular does not depend on p_2^0), his cross-demand function for good 2 given p_2^0 and w^0 is the constant function $\hat{x}_2(p_1) =$

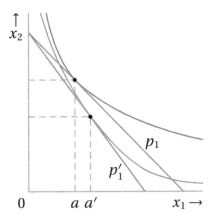

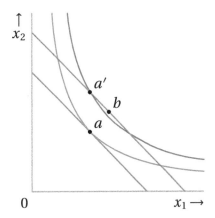

(a) An example in which the demand for good 1 increases when the price of good 1 increases.

(b) An illustration of the proof of Proposition 5.4.

Figure 5.7

$(1-\alpha)w^0/p_2^0$, and his Engel function for good 1 given the prices (p_1^0, p_2^0) is the linear function $\overline{x}_1(w) = \alpha w/p_1^0$.

We now introduce some terminology for various properties of the demand function.

Definition 5.9: Normal, regular, and Giffen goods

A good is *normal* for a given consumer if, for any given prices, the consumer's Engel function for the good is increasing. A good is *regular* for the consumer if for any price of the other good and any wealth, the consumer's regular demand function for the good is decreasing, and *Giffen* if his regular demand function for the good is increasing.

This terminology can also be applied locally: we say, for example, that good 1 is a Giffen good at $((p_1^0, p_2^0), w^0)$ if the demand function is increasing around p_1^0 given p_2^0 and w^0 (but is not necessarily increasing at all values of p_1).

It is common to assume that every good is regular: as the price of the good increases, given the price of the other good and the consumer's wealth, the consumer's demand for the good decreases. The demand function of a rational consumer whose preference relation satisfies the standard assumptions of monotonicity, continuity, convexity and differentiability does not necessarily have this property. We do not give an explicit example but Figure 5.7a is suggestive: as the price of good 1 increases from p_1 to p_1', given the price of good 2 and the consumer's wealth, the consumer's demand for good 1 increases from a to a'.

The following result gives a condition on the preference relation that guarantees that a good is normal.

Proposition 5.4: MRS and normal good

The demand function of a rational consumer whose marginal rate of substitution $MRS(x_1, x_2)$ is increasing in x_2 for every value of x_1 has the property that good 1 is normal (the consumer's Engel function for the good is increasing).

Proof

Fix p_1^0 and p_2^0 and let $w' > w$. Let a be a solution of the consumer's problem for the budget set $B((p_1^0, p_2^0), w)$ and let a' be a bundle on the frontier of $B((p_1^0, p_2^0), w')$ with $a_1' = a_1$. (Refer to Figure 5.7b.) By the assumption on the marginal rate of substitution, $MRS(a') > MRS(a)$, and hence the solution, b, of the consumer's problem for the budget set $B((p_1^0, p_2^0), w')$ has $b_1 > a_1' = a_1$.

The analysis in this section compares the choices of a consumer for two sets of parameters. Such analyses are called comparative statics. The word statics refers to the fact that the comparison does not involve an analysis of the path taken by the outcome through time as the parameters change; we simply compare one outcome with the other. For example, the properties of the regular demand function can be viewed as answering the comparative statics question of how a consumer's behavior differs for two sets of parameters (prices and wealth) that differ only in the price of one of the goods. Phenomena related to the fact that people's behavior when they confront one budget set depends also on their behavior in a budget set they faced previously are not captured by this exercise.

The following comparative static result involves a consumer whose demand function satisfies the weak axiom of revealed preference and who chooses a bundle on the budget line. The result considers the effect of a change in the price of a good when the consumer's wealth is adjusted so that he has exactly enough wealth to purchase the bundle he chose before the change. The result asserts that if the consumer's wealth is adjusted in this way when the price of good 1 increases, then the consumer purchases less of good 1.

Proposition 5.5: Slutsky property

Assume that the demand function x of a rational consumer is single-valued, satisfies the weak axiom of revealed preference, and satisfies $p_1 x_1((p_1, p_2), w) + p_2 x_2((p_1, p_2), w) = w$ for all $((p_1, p_2), w)$. Let $p_1' > p_1$ and let w' be the cost of the bundle $x((p_1, p_2), w)$ for the pair of prices

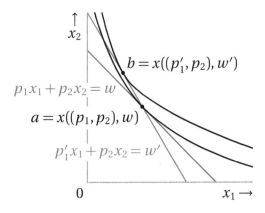

Figure 5.8 An illustration of the proof of Proposition 5.5.

$(p_1', p_2): w' = p_1' x_1((p_1, p_2), w) + p_2 x_2((p_1, p_2), w)$. Then $x_1((p_1', p_2), w') \leq x_1((p_1, p_2), w)$.

Proof

Let $a = x((p_1, p_2), w)$ and $b = x((p_1', p_2), w')$ (see Figure 5.8). By construction a is in the budget set $B((p_1', p_2), w')$ and therefore b is revealed to be at least as good as a. The slope of the budget line for the price p_1' is larger than the slope for the price p_1. Therefore if $b_1 > a_1$ then b is in the interior of $B((p_1, p_2), w)$. As a is chosen from $B((p_1, p_2), w)$ and b is interior, a is revealed to be better than b. This conclusion contradicts the assumption that the demand function satisfies the weak axiom of revealed preference.

Problems

1. *Lexicographic preferences.* Find the demand function of a rational consumer with lexicographic preferences (with first priority on good 1).

2. *Cobb-Douglas preferences.* A consumer's preference relation is represented by the utility function $x_1^\alpha x_2^{1-\alpha}$ where $0 < \alpha < 1$. These preferences are convex and differentiable. Show that for all prices and wealth levels the consumer spends the fraction α of his budget on good 1.

3. *Rationalizing a demand function I.* Consider the demand function for which the consumer spends his entire wealth on the two goods and the ratio of the amount spent on good 1 to the amount spent on good 2 is p_2/p_1. Show that the preference relation represented by the utility function $\sqrt{x_1} + \sqrt{x_2}$ rationalizes this demand function.

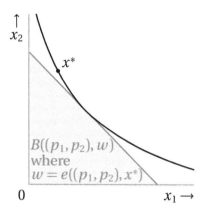

Figure 5.9 The budget set $B((p_1, p_2), e((p_1, p_2), x^*))$ (see Problem 5).

4. *Rationalizing a demand function II.* A consumer chooses the bundle at the intersection of the budget line and a ray from the origin orthogonal to the frontier. Can this demand function be rationalized by a monotone preference relation?

5. *Expenditure function.* A consumer's preference relation is monotone, continuous, and convex. Let $x^* = (x_1^*, x_2^*)$ be a bundle. For any pair (p_1, p_2) of prices, let $e((p_1, p_2), x^*)$ be the smallest wealth that allows the consumer to purchase a bundle that is at least as good for him as x^*:

$$e((p_1, p_2), x^*) = \min_{(x_1, x_2)} \{p_1 x_1 + p_2 x_2 : (x_1, x_2) \succsim (x_1^*, x_2^*)\}.$$

(See Figure 5.9.)

a. Show that the function e is increasing in p_1 (and p_2).

b. Show that for all $\lambda > 0$ and every pair (p_1, p_2) of prices we have $e((\lambda p_1, \lambda p_2), x^*) = \lambda e((p_1, p_2), x^*)$.

6. *Rationalizing a demand function.* If the cost of buying 10 units of good 1 is less than $\frac{1}{2}w$, a consumer buys 10 units of good 1 and spends his remaining wealth on good 2. Otherwise he spends half of his wealth on each good. Show that this behavior is rationalized by a preference relation represented by the utility function

$$u(x_1, x_2) = \begin{cases} x_1 x_2 & \text{if } x_1 \leq 10 \\ 10 x_2 & \text{if } x_1 > 10. \end{cases}$$

7. *Consumer with additive utility function.* Suppose that the two goods are food (z) and money (m). A consumer's preference relation is represented by the

utility function $m + v(z)$, where v is increasing and concave and has a continuous derivative. The price of a unit of food in terms of money is α. The consumer initially has M units of money and no food.

a. Characterize the solution of the consumer's problem.

b. Compare the consumption of food of a consumer who faces two budget sets that differ only in the price of food. Show that when the price of food is β the amount of food consumed is not more than the amount consumed when the price of food is $\alpha < \beta$.

8. *Time preferences I.* Consider a consumer who chooses how much to consume at each of two dates and can transfer consumption from one date to the other by borrowing and lending. We can model his behavior by treating consumption at date 1 and consumption at date 2 as the two different goods in the model studied in this chapter.

Assume that the consumer is endowed with y units of money at each date and faces an interest rate $r > 0$ for both borrowing and lending, so that he can exchange 1 unit at date 1 for $1 + r$ units at date 2. The consumer's budget set is then
$$\{(x_1, x_2) \in X : (1 + r)x_1 + x_2 \leq (1 + r)y + y\}.$$

Denote the consumer's demand function by $x(r, y)$. Assume that (*i*) x satisfies the weak axiom of revealed preference, (*ii*) for every pair (r, y) the consumer chooses a bundle on the budget line $\{(x_1, x_2) \in X : (1 + r)x_1 + x_2 = (1 + r)y + y\}$, and (*iii*) consumption at each date is a normal good.

a. Show that if the consumer borrows when the interest rate is r_1 then he borrows less (and may even save) when the interest rate is $r_2 > r_1$.

b. Show that if the consumer chooses to lend when the interest rate is r_1 then he does not borrow when the interest rate is $r_2 > r_1$.

9. *Time preferences II.* For the same model as in the previous question, assume that the consumer has a preference relation $\succcurlyeq$ that is monotone, continuous, convex, and differentiable.

a. Say that the preference relation is *time neutral* if for all s and t we have $(s, t) \sim (t, s)$. (That is, for any amounts s and t of consumption, the consumer is indifferent between consuming s units at date 1 and t units at date 2 and consuming t units at date 1 and s at date 2.) Show that for all values of t we have $MRS(t, t) = 1$.

b. We say that the preference relation has *present bias* if whenever $t > s$ we
have $(t,s) \succ (s,t)$. Show that for all values of t we have $MRS(t,t) \geq 1$.

c. Show, using only the assumption that the preferences are present biased,
that if $r \leq 0$ then any solution of the consumer's problem has at least as
much consumption at date 1 as it does at date 2.

Notes

Giffen goods were named after Robert Giffen by Marshall (1895, 208). Engel functions are named after Ernst Engel. The Slutsky property is due to Slutsky (1915).
The theory of revealed preference is due to Samuelson (1938). The exposition of
the chapter draws upon Rubinstein (2006a, Lecture 5).

6 Producer behavior

We suggest that you begin by responding to the following question, to which we return at the end of the chapter.

> Assume that you are a vice president of a package delivery company. The company employs 196 workers in addition to its management team. It was founded five years ago and is owned by three families.
>
> The work is unskilled; each worker needs one week of training. All the company's employees have been with the company for three to five years. The company pays its workers more than the minimum wage and provides the benefits required by law. Until recently, it was making a large profit. As a result of a recession, profit has fallen significantly, but is still positive.
>
> You attend a meeting of management to decide whether to lay off some workers. The company's Finance Department has prepared the following forecast of annual profit.
>
> | Number of workers who will continue to be employed | Expected annual profit in millions of dollars |
> |---|---|
> | 0 (all workers will be laid off) | Loss of 8 |
> | 50 (146 workers will be laid off) | Profit of 1 |
> | 65 (131 workers will be laid off) | Profit of 1.5 |
> | 100 (96 workers will be laid off) | Profit of 2 |
> | 144 (52 workers will be laid off) | Profit of 1.6 |
> | 170 (26 workers will be laid off) | Profit of 1 |
> | 196 (no layoffs) | Profit of 0.4 |
>
> How many workers would you continue to employ?

6.1 The producer

Producers, like consumers, play a central role in economic models. A consumer can trade goods, changing the distribution of goods among the agents in the economy. A producer can change the availability of goods, transforming inputs, which may be physical goods, like raw materials, or mental resources, like information and attention, into outputs.

Chapter of *Models in Microeconomic Theory* by Martin J. Osborne and Ariel Rubinstein. Version 2023.5.30 (h).
© 2023 Martin J. Osborne and Ariel Rubinstein CC BY-NC-ND 4.0. https://doi.org/10.11647/OBP.0362.06

In the model we study, a producer is specified by (*i*) a technology, which describes his ability to transform inputs into outputs, and (*ii*) the motives that guide his decision regarding the amounts of inputs and outputs. Many producers are not individuals, but organizations, like collectives, families, or firms. Such organizations typically have hierarchical structures and mechanisms to make collective decisions. The model we study does not consider how these mechanisms affect the production decision.

We study a simple model in which the producer can transform a single good, input, into another good, output. The technology available to him is modeled by a function f, where $f(a) = y$ means that the quantity a of input yields y units of output. We assume that a positive output requires a positive input ($f(0) = 0$) and more input produces at least as much output (f is nondecreasing). We further assume that the impact on output of an extra unit of input is no larger for large amounts of the input than it is for small amounts of the input (f is concave) and this impact goes to zero as the amount of input increases without bound (the producer's effectiveness is spread more thinly as output increases).

Definition 6.1: Production function

A *production function* is a function $f : \mathbb{R}_+ \to \mathbb{R}_+$, giving the quantity of output for any quantity of the input, that is continuous, nondecreasing, and concave, satisfies $f(0) = 0$, and has the property that for any $\varepsilon > 0$ there is a quantity y such that $f(y+1) - f(y) < \varepsilon$.

We assume that the producer operates in an environment in which he has to pay for the input and is paid for the output according to given prices. In this chapter we assume that the producer believes his actions do not affect these prices. That is, the producer, like the consumer in the previous chapters, is a price-taker. This assumption fits situations in which the amount of input used by the producer and the amount of his output are both small compared with the total amounts of these goods in the economy, so that the producer's actions have little effect on the aggregates and thus do not significantly affect the prices of the goods. The assumption is not appropriate for a producer whose use of an input or production of an output dominates the markets for those goods, so that his actions do affect the market prices. We consider such a producer in the next chapter.

Denote the price of output by p and the price of input by w. A producer who uses a units of input to produce y units of output obtains the revenue py and profit $\pi = py - wa$. We assume that the producer has preferences over the triples (a, y, π). That is, he potentially cares about the amount of input he uses, the amount of output he produces, and the amount of profit he obtains. Here are some possible forms for his preferences.

Output maximization

The producer prefers (a, y, π) to (a', y', π') if (i) $y > y'$ and $\pi \geq 0$, or (ii) $\pi \geq 0$ and $\pi' < 0$. Such a producer chooses (a, y) to maximize output subject to profit being nonnegative. The producer's preference for profit to be nonnegative may be due to the difficulty of surviving when he makes a loss.

Profit maximization

The producer prefers (a, y, π) to (a', y', π') if and only if $\pi > \pi'$. Such a producer chooses (a, y) to maximize profit.

Profit maximization with lower bar on output

For some given output $\overline{y}$, the producer prefers (a, y, π) to (a', y', π') if (i) $\pi > \pi'$ and $y \geq \overline{y}$, or (ii) $y \geq \overline{y}$ and $y' < \overline{y}$. Such a producer chooses (a, y) to maximize profit subject to producing at least $\overline{y}$. If $\overline{y}$ is small, the constraint does not bind. But if it is large, it constrains the amount of the input to at least the number $\overline{a}$ for which $f(\overline{a}) = \overline{y}$.

A cooperative

Assume that the producer is an organization that decides the number of its members and divides its profit equally among them. It employs only its own members. Each member contributes one unit of labor, so that the amount a of the input is the number of members of the cooperative. The cooperative aims to maximize the profit per member, π/a.

In this chapter we explore the implications of only the first two forms of preferences: output maximization and profit maximization.

6.2   Output maximization

We start by considering a producer who aims to maximize the amount of output subject to not making a loss.

Definition 6.2: Output-maximizing producer

Given the prices p for output and w for input, an *output-maximizing producer with production function f* chooses the amount a of input to solve the problem

$$\max_a f(a) \text{ subject to } pf(a) - wa \geq 0.$$

Figure 6.1a illustrates such a producer's decision problem. The producer's profit is given by the difference between the red curve labelled $pf(a)$ and the line labelled wa. If, in addition to the assumptions we have made about the production function f, it is strictly concave, then either profit is negative for all

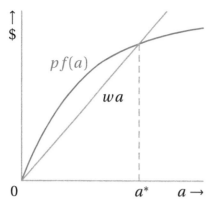 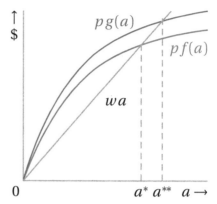

(a) A case in which an output-maximizing producer chooses a positive amount, a^*, of the input.

(b) The effect of a technological improvement for an output-maximizing producer.

Figure 6.1 An output-maximizing producer

positive values of a or there is a unique positive number a^* such that $pf(a^*) - wa^* = 0$. (Figure 6.1a illustrates the second case.)

Proposition 6.1: Optimal input for output-maximizing producer

If the production function f is strictly concave then the amount of input chosen by an output-maximizing producer with production function f facing the price w of input and the price p of output is

$$\begin{cases} 0 & \text{if } pf(a) - wa < 0 \text{ for all } a > 0 \\ a^* & \text{otherwise} \end{cases}$$

where a^* is the unique positive number for which $pf(a^*) - wa^* = 0$.

The implications for the producer's optimal action of changes in the prices of the input and output and in the technology follow immediately from Figure 6.1a (for prices) and from Figure 6.1b (for technology).

Proposition 6.2: Comparative statics for output-maximizing producer

If the production function f is strictly concave then a decrease in the price of the input, an increase in the price of output, and a technological improvement that changes the production function from f to g with $g(a) \geq f(a)$ for all a, all cause the amount of input (and output) chosen by an output-maximizing producer with production function f to increase or stay the same.

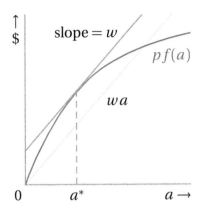

(a) The amount a^* of input chosen by a profit-maximizing producer.

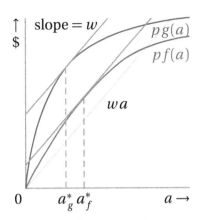

(b) A possible effect of an improvement in technology for a profit-maximizing producer.

Figure 6.2 A profit-maximizing producer

6.3 Profit maximization

Producers are more commonly assumed to be profit-maximizers than output-maximizers.

Definition 6.3: Profit-maximizing producer

Given the prices p for output and w for input, a *profit-maximizing producer with production function f* chooses the amount of input to solve the problem

$$\max_a pf(a) - wa.$$

Figure 6.2a illustrates such a producer's decision problem. If the production function is differentiable and strictly concave then a solution of the producer's problem is characterized as follows.

Proposition 6.3: Optimal input for profit-maximizing producer

If the production function f is differentiable and strictly concave then the amount of input chosen by a profit-maximizing producer with production function f facing the price w of input and the price p of output is

$$\begin{cases} 0 & \text{if } pf(a) - wa < 0 \text{ for all } a > 0 \\ a^* & \text{otherwise} \end{cases}$$

where a^* is the unique positive number for which $pf'(a^*) - w = 0$.

Proof

The producer's profit when he chooses the amount a of input is $pf(a) - wa$. Given that f is strictly concave, this function is strictly concave in a. The result follows from the standard conditions for a maximizer of a differentiable function.

A change in the price of input or the price of output changes the amount of input chosen by a profit-maximizing producer in the same direction as it does for an output-maximizing producer.

Proposition 6.4: Comparative statics for profit-maximizing producer

An increase in the price of input or a decrease in the price of output causes the amount of input chosen by a profit-maximizing producer to decrease or remain the same.

Proof

Denote by $\alpha(w)$ the amount of input chosen by the producer when the input price is w. By definition,

$$pf(\alpha(w)) - w\alpha(w) \geq pf(a) - wa \text{ for all } a,$$

or

$$p[f(\alpha(w)) - f(a)] \geq w[\alpha(w) - a] \text{ for all } a.$$

In particular, for the prices w^1 and w^2 of the input,

$$p[f(\alpha(w^1)) - f(\alpha(w^2))] \geq w^1[\alpha(w^1) - \alpha(w^2)]$$

and

$$p[f(\alpha(w^2)) - f(\alpha(w^1))] \geq w^2[\alpha(w^2) - \alpha(w^1)].$$

Adding these inequalities yields

$$0 \geq (w^1 - w^2)(\alpha(w^1) - \alpha(w^2)).$$

Thus if $w^1 < w^2$ then $\alpha(w^1) \geq \alpha(w^2)$. A similar argument applies to changes in the price p of output.

Note that this proof does not use any property of the production function, so that the result in particular does not depend on the concavity of this function.

If the production function is differentiable, we can alternatively prove the result as follows, given Proposition 6.3. If $pf'(0) < w$ then increasing w preserves the inequality and the optimal production remains 0. If $pf'(0) \geq w$ then increasing w does not increase the solution of the equation $pf'(a) = w$, given that f is concave.

Unlike an output-maximizer, a profit-maximizer may decrease output when the technology improves; Figure 6.2b gives an example. However, as you can verify, if the production function is differentiable and the technological improvement from f to g is such that $g'(a) \geq f'(a)$ for all a, then a profit-maximizing producer does increase the amounts of input and output.

6.4   Cost function

Given a production function, we can find the cost of producing any amount of output. Specifically, for the production function f, the cost of producing y units of output is $wf^{-1}(y)$. Sometimes it is convenient to take the cost function as the primitive of the model, rather than deriving it from the production function. That is, we start with a function C that specifies the cost $C(y)$ of producing any amount y of output. This approach is appropriate if we are interested only in the market for output.

A natural assumption is $C(0) = 0$. We assume also that the average cost $C(y)/y$ of producing y units eventually exceeds any given bound. Some cost functions C have the form $C(y) = k + c(y)$ for $y > 0$, where $k > 0$ and c is an increasing function with $c(0) = 0$. In such cases, we refer to k as the fixed cost of production and to $c(y)$ as the variable cost.

Definition 6.4: Cost function

A *cost function* is an increasing function $C : \mathbb{R}_+ \to \mathbb{R}_+$ with $C(0) = 0$ such that for all $L > 0$ there exists (a large) number y such that $C(y)/y > L$. If this function takes the form

$$C(y) = \begin{cases} 0 & \text{if } y = 0 \\ k + c(y) & \text{if } y > 0 \end{cases}$$

for some increasing function $c : \mathbb{R}_+ \to \mathbb{R}_+$ with $c(0) = 0$ and some $k > 0$, then C is called a *cost function with a fixed cost k and variable cost function c*.

The function $\text{AC}(y) = C(y)/y$ for $y > 0$ is the *average cost function for C*, and if C is differentiable at y then $\text{MC}(y) = C'(y)$ is the *marginal cost for C at y*.

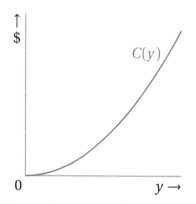

(a) A cost function with no fixed cost.

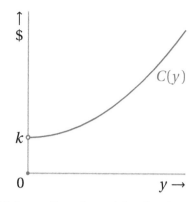

(b) A cost function with a fixed cost k.

Figure 6.3

Cost functions with and without a fixed cost are shown in Figures 6.3a and 6.3b. Average and marginal cost functions are shown in Figures 6.4a and 6.4b.

Note that if output is produced by a single input, as we assumed before, and the production function is f, then $C(y) = wf^{-1}(y)$, a cost function with no fixed cost (C is increasing since f is increasing). Given that f is concave, C is convex in this case.

The following properties of the average and marginal cost functions are sometimes useful.

Proposition 6.5: Properties of the average and marginal cost functions

Let C be a cost function (without any fixed cost).

a. If C is convex then AC is nondecreasing.

b. If C is differentiable then $\lim_{y \to 0} AC(y) = MC(0)$.

c. If C is differentiable then AC is increasing at y if $AC(y) < MC(y)$ and decreasing at y if $MC(y) < AC(y)$.

Proof

a. Let $a > b$ and $\lambda = b/a$. Then $\lambda a + (1 - \lambda)0 = b$, so that by the convexity of C we have $C(b) \leq \lambda C(a) + (1 - \lambda)C(0) = \lambda C(a)$ and thus $AC(b) = C(b)/b \leq C(a)/a = AC(a)$.

b. We have

$$\lim_{y \to 0} AC(y) = \lim_{y \to 0} \frac{C(y)}{y} = \lim_{y \to 0} \frac{C(y) - C(0)}{y - 0} = C'(0).$$

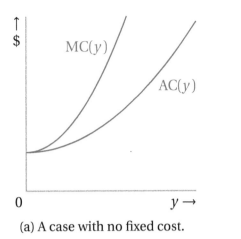
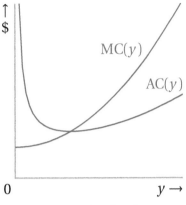

(a) A case with no fixed cost.   (b) A case with a fixed cost.

Figure 6.4 Average and marginal cost functions.

c. Differentiating AC we get

$$AC'(y) = C'(y)/y - C(y)/y^2 = (MC(y) - AC(y))/y,$$

from which the result follows.

An intuition for part c of the result is that $C(y)$ is the sum of the marginal costs up to y, so that $AC(y)$ is the average of $MC(z)$ for $0 \le z \le y$. Thus if $MC(y) > AC(y)$ and y increases then we add a cost greater than $AC(y)$, so that the average increases.

The profit of a producer with cost function C who faces the price p for output and produces y units of output is

$$py - C(y).$$

The following result, for an output-maximizing producer, is immediate. An example in which the producer's optimal output is positive is given in Figure 6.5a.

Proposition 6.6: Output chosen by output-maximizing producer

An output-maximizing producer with cost function C who faces the price p for output chooses the largest positive output y^* for which $C(y^*)/y^* = AC(y^*) = p$ if such an output exists, and otherwise chooses output 0.

The output chosen by a profit-maximizing producer with a convex differentiable cost function is also easy to characterize. An example in which the producer's optimal output is positive is shown in Figure 6.5b.

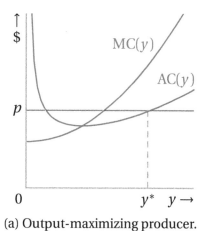

(a) Output-maximizing producer.

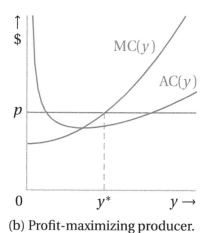

(b) Profit-maximizing producer.

Figure 6.5 The output chosen by a producer facing the price p.

Proposition 6.7: Output chosen by profit-maximizing producer

A profit-maximizing producer with a convex differentiable cost function C who faces the output price p chooses an output y^* for which $C'(y^*) = \mathrm{MC}(y^*) = p$ if $p \geq \mathrm{AC}(y^*)$ and otherwise chooses output 0.

Proof

Given the convexity of C, the function $py - C(y)$ is concave in y, so that the result follows from the standard conditions for a maximizer of a differentiable function.

6.5   Producers' preferences

We have discussed two possible preferences for producers, output maximization and profit maximization. Many other textbooks restrict attention to profit maximization. By contrast, the preferences of individuals in consumer theory are usually taken to be subject only to mild assumptions (discussed in Chapter 4).

    Why is profit maximization usually assumed? Some people think of it as a normative assumption: producers should maximize profit. Others consider it descriptive: the main goal of producers is to maximize profit. Some researchers think that the assumption of profit-maximization is made only because it allows economists to draw analytically interesting and nontrivial results. Yet others think that the assumption is so that students believe that profit-maximization is the only legitimate goal of producers.

We refrain from expressing our opinion on the issue. We suggest only that you consider it taking into account how students of economics and other disciplines have responded to the question at the beginning of the chapter.

Did you decide to maximize profit and lay off 96 workers? Or did you decide to give up all profit and not lay off any worker? Or did you compromise and choose to lay off only 26 or 52 workers? Surely you did not lay off more than 96 workers, since doing so is worse than laying off 96 in terms of both the number of layoffs and profit.

When the question is posed to students in various disciplines, students of economics tend to lay off more workers than students in philosophy, law, mathematics, and business. It is not clear whether this effect is due to selection bias (students who choose to study economics are different from students in the other disciplines) or to indoctrination (studying material in which profit-maximization is assumed has an effect). In any case, even among students of economics, only about half choose the profit-maximizing option. So maybe profit-maximization is not the only goal of producers that we should investigate?

Problems

1. *Comparative statics.* Propositions 6.2 and 6.4 give comparative static results for a producer with a concave production function. Consider analogous results for a producer with a convex cost function.

   For an output maximizer and a profit maximizer, analyze diagrammatically the effect of (a) an increase in the price of output and (b) a technological change such that all marginal costs decrease.

2. *Two factories.* A producer can use two factories to produce output. The production functions for the factories are $f(a_1) = \sqrt{a_1}$ and $g(a_2) = \sqrt{a_2}$, where a_i is the amount of input used in factory i. The cost of a unit of input is 1 and the cost of activating a factory is $k > 0$. Calculate the producer's cost function.

3. *A producer with a cost of firing workers.* A producer uses one input, workers, to produce output according to a production function f. He has already hired a_0 workers. He can fire some or all of them, or hire more workers. The wage of a worker is w and the price of output is p. Compare the producer's behavior if he maximizes profit to his behavior if he also takes into account that firing workers causes him to feel as if he bears the cost $l > 0$ per fired worker.

4. *Robinson Crusoe.* Robinson Crusoe is both a producer and a consumer. He has one unit of time, which he can divide between leisure and work. If he devotes the amount of time x to work then his output is $f(x)$, where f is increasing and strictly concave. He has a monotone convex preference relation over the set of leisure–consumption pairs (l,c) that is represented by a differentiable utility function u.

   a. Formally state the problem that Crusoe's optimal choice of (l,c) solves.

   b. Calculate the solution of Crusoe's problem for $f(x)=\sqrt{x}$ and $u(l,c)=lc$.

   c. Explain why the marginal rate of substitution between leisure and consumption at the pair (l^*,c^*) chosen by Crusoe is equal to $f'(1-l^*)$ (the marginal product at $1-l^*$).

(More difficult) Now assume that Crusoe has two independent decision-making units. One unit decides the amount to produce and the other decides how much to consume. The units make their decisions simultaneously. Each unit takes the value of a unit of time devoted to work to be some number w. The consumption unit chooses a leisure-consumption pair (l,c) that maximizes $u(l,c)$ given the budget constraint $c = w(1-l)+\pi$, where π is the profit of the production unit. The production unit maximizes its profit given that it has to pay w for a unit of time devoted to work.

The units are in harmony in the sense that given the price w, the decision of how much to consume is consistent with the decision of how much to produce.

   d. Give the formal conditions required for harmony between the consumption and production units to prevail.

   e. Find the value of w^*, and the associated pair (l^*,c^*), that satisfies the conditions in the previous part when $f(x)=\sqrt{x}$ and $u(l,c)=lc$.

   f. Demonstrate graphically why Crusoe behaves in the same way if he makes his decision as in the first part of the problem as he does if he makes his decision using two separate units, as in the second part of the problem.

   g. Suppose that Crusoe's production unit acts as an output maximizer rather than a profit maximizer. Show diagrammatically that the pair (l^*,c^*) that is in harmony differs from the pair that maximizes $u(l,c)$ subject to $c = f(1-l)$.

Notes

See Rubinstein (2006b) for the issue discussed in Section 6.5. The exposition of the chapter draws upon Rubinstein (2006a, Lecture 6b).

7 Monopoly

7.1 Basic model

In the previous chapter we consider a producer who acts as if his behavior has no effect on the prices of the input or output. We argue that this assumption may be appropriate if the producer's quantities of inputs and output are small relative to the total volume of trade in the markets.

In this chapter we study several variants of a model that fits a very different situation, in which the producer of a single good is the only one serving a market. The variants differ in the type of options the producer can offer potential buyers. In the basic case, the producer can post a price per unit, and each buyer can purchase any amount of the good at that price. In other cases, the producer has other instruments like offering all consumers a set of price-quantity pairs. In each case, every potential buyer chooses the option he most prefers. The producer predicts correctly the buyers' responses and acts to advance his target (like maximizing profit or increasing production).

We allow for the possibility that the market has a number of segments, with distinct demand functions. Thus a specification of the market consists of two elements, (*i*) a demand function for each segment and (*ii*) a description of a producer, which includes his cost function and preferences.

Definition 7.1: Monopolistic market

A *monopolistic market* $\langle (q_i)_{i=1}^k, C, \succsim \rangle$ for a single good has the following components.

Demand
  A collection $(q_i)_{i=1}^k$ of decreasing functions, where $q_i : \mathbb{R}_+ \to \mathbb{R}_+$. The function q_i, the *demand function in segment i*, associates with every price p_i for segment i the total amount $q_i(p_i)$ of the good demanded in that segment.

Producer
  A single producer, called a *monopolist*, characterized by a cost function C that is continuous and convex and satisfies $C(0) = 0$, and a preference

---

Chapter of *Models in Microeconomic Theory* by Martin J. Osborne and Ariel Rubinstein. Version 2023.5.30 (h).
© 2023 Martin J. Osborne and Ariel Rubinstein CC BY-NC-ND 4.0.   https://doi.org/10.11647/OBP.0362.07

relation $\succcurlyeq$ over pairs $((y_1, \ldots, y_k), \pi)$, where y_i is the quantity sold in segment i for $i = 1, \ldots, k$ and π is the producer's profit.

7.2 Uniform-price monopolistic market

We first consider a monopolist who sets a single price, the same for all segments of the market. The monopolist might act in this way because he is prohibited by law from setting different prices for different segments of the market. (For example, charging men and women different prices may be outlawed.) Also, a producer's ability to enforce different prices in different segments of the market is limited if individuals can buy the good in one segment at a low price and sell it in another segment at a high price. (Such arbitrage is easier for some goods, like books, than it is for others, like haircuts.)

Definition 7.2: Uniform-price monopolistic market

A *uniform-price monopolistic market* is a monopolistic market in which the producer chooses a single price, the same in all segments.

7.2.1 Profit-maximizing monopolist

Let $\langle (q_i)_{i=1}^k, C, \succcurlyeq \rangle$ be a uniform-price monopolistic market. Define the total demand function Q by $Q(p) = \sum_{i=1}^k q_i(p)$ for all p. The profit of a producer who sets the price p in a uniform-price monopolistic market is $\pi(p) = pQ(p) - C(Q(p))$. Given that each function q_i is decreasing, the function Q is decreasing, and hence has an inverse, say P. Thus the producer's setting a price p and obtaining the profit $\pi(p)$ is equivalent to his choosing the output $y = Q(p)$ and obtaining the profit $\Pi(y) = P(y)y - C(y)$.

   A useful concept in the analysis of a uniform-price monopolistic market is marginal revenue.

Definition 7.3: Marginal revenue

The *marginal revenue* at the output y for the differentiable (demand) function Q is
$$\mathrm{MR}(y) = [P(y)y]' = P(y) + P'(y)y,$$
where P is the inverse of Q.

   The number $\mathrm{MR}(y)$ is the rate of change in revenue as output increases. If the function P is decreasing, we have $\mathrm{MR}(y) \leq P(y)$ for all y. The intuitive reason for this inequality is that selling an additional unit of the good increases revenue by approximately $P(y)$ but also causes a reduction in the price of all y units sold.

Usually the function MR is assumed to be decreasing, but this property does not follow from the assumptions we have made. The derivative of MR at y is $2P'(y) + P''(y)y$, so that if $P''(y)$ is positive and large enough, the derivative is positive even if P is decreasing. The following example illustrates this point in an environment in which the good is indivisible.

Example 7.1: Monopoly with marginal revenue that is not decreasing

Consider a market for an indivisible good and three consumers, each of whom buys either one unit of the good or no units. One consumer buys one unit of the good if and only if the price is at most 10; the cutoff prices for the two other consumers to buy a unit are 6 and 5. In this context, $P(y)$ is the highest price at which the producer can sell y units of the good. Thus $P(1) = 10$, $P(2) = 6$, and $P(3) = 5$. Given the indivisibility of the good, we define the marginal revenue at the output y as $\text{MR}(y) = P(y)y - P(y-1)(y-1)$, yielding the following numbers, where $\text{MR}(3) > \text{MR}(2)$.

y	Revenue(y)	MR(y)
1	10	10
2	12	2
3	15	3

The next result gives a necessary condition for an output to maximize the profit of a producer in a uniform-price monopolistic market.

Proposition 7.1: Uniform-price profit-maximizing monopolist

Consider a uniform-price monopolistic market $\langle (q_i)_{i=1}^k, C, \succcurlyeq \rangle$ in which C and each function q_i is differentiable. For any price p, let $Q(p) = \sum_{i=1}^k q_i(p)$, let MR be the marginal revenue function for Q, and let MC be the marginal cost function for C. If the monopolist's preferences $\succcurlyeq$ are profit-maximizing and his optimal output y^* is positive, then $\text{MR}(y^*) = \text{MC}(y^*)$.

Proof

The monopolist chooses p to maximize $pQ(p) - C(Q(p))$, or equivalently y to maximize $P(y)y - C(y)$, where P is the inverse of Q. The result follows from the standard necessary condition for an interior maximizer of a differentiable function.

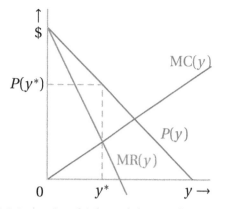

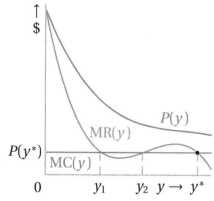

(a) A case in which MR(y) = MC(y) for only one value of y.

(b) A case in which MR(y) = MC(y) for multiple values of y.

Figure 7.1 The output y^* chosen by a profit-maximizing producer in a uniform-price monopolistic market, and the resulting price $P(y^*)$.

Note that the condition in the result is only necessary, not sufficient. In the left panel of Figure 7.1, a single output satisfies the condition, and this output maximizes profit. In the right panel, three outputs satisfy the condition. The output labeled y^* is the profit-maximizer, because the difference between the area under the MR curve (the total revenue) and the area under the MC curve (the total cost) up to y^* is larger than the difference between these areas for y_1 and y_2.

Inefficiency   Since MR(y) < $P(y)$ for all y, an implication of Proposition 7.1 is that the price charged by a profit-maximizing producer in a uniform-price monopolistic market is greater than the marginal cost at this output. As a consequence, an inefficiency of sorts exists in such a market: the cost of production of another unit of the good is less than the price that some buyers are willing to pay for the good. The monopolist does not produce the extra unit because he takes into account that the price reduction necessary to sell the extra unit will affect all the other units, too, causing his profit to fall.

Sometimes the area under the inverse demand function,

$$W(y) = \int_0^y P(x)\,dx, \tag{7.1}$$

is used as a measure of the consumers' welfare when y units of the good are sold. The logic behind this definition is clear when the good is indivisible, each consumer either buying one unit or none. The number $P(1)$ is then the highest price that any consumer in the market is willing to pay for the good, $P(2)$ is the

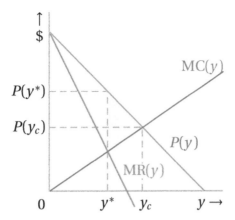

Figure 7.2 The reduction in $W(y)$ caused by the reduction in output from y_c to y^*.

highest price any remaining consumer is willing to pay, and so forth. The integral is analogous to the sum $P(1) + P(2) + \cdots + P(y)$, the maximum amount of money for which y units can be sold.

The area under the marginal cost function between 0 and y is the total cost of producing y. Thus it is common to interpret the integral between 0 and y of the difference between the demand function and the marginal cost function as a measure of the welfare added to the world by the production of y units of the good. This measure of welfare is maximized at the quantity y_c for which $P(y_c) = \mathrm{MC}(y_c)$. Thus the loss of welfare due to the operation of the producer as a monopolist is the yellow triangle in Figure 7.2. This triangle is called the *deadweight loss* due to the monopoly.

Two policies to control a monopolist's behavior involve setting a maximum price and providing the monopolist with a subsidy.

Maximum price   If the maximum price the monopolist is allowed to charge is $p_{\max}$, then for outputs y with $P(y) < p_{\max}$ the value of MR remains the same as before, while for outputs such that $p(y) > p_{\max}$ we have $\mathrm{MR}(y) = p_{\max}$. That is, the function MR is not continuous and has two segments, as shown in Figure 7.3a.

If $p_{\max}$ is set equal to the price $P(y_c)$, where y_c is the output for which $P(y_c) = \mathrm{MC}(y_c)$, then the producer chooses y_c, reducing his profit and eliminating the deadweight loss.

Subsidy   Suppose that the producer gets a subsidy of t units of money for each unit he sells, in addition to the amount the consumers pay. Such a subsidy raises the MR curve by t, so that the intersection of the new MR and MC is at a higher quantity. For an appropriate value of the subsidy the monopolist optimally produces the quantity y_c (see Figure 7.3b). However, if the consumers pay the subsidy then this policy may not improve their welfare.

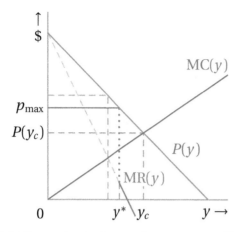
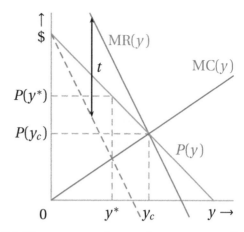

(a) The output chosen by a monopolist who can set a price of at most p_{max}.

(b) The output chosen by a monopolist who receives a subsidy of t per unit sold.

Figure 7.3 The effect of policies to change the output of a producer in a uniform-price monopolistic market.

7.2.2   Output-maximizing monopolist

As we discussed in the previous chapter, profit maximization is not the only possible target for a producer. Consider a monopolist who maximizes output subject to obtaining nonnegative profit. Such a monopolist produces the quantity y^* for which $\mathrm{AC}(y^*) = P(y^*)$ (see Figure 7.4). This output is larger than the output y_c that maximizes the consumers' welfare $W(y)$.

7.3   Discriminatory monopoly

We now consider a monopolistic market in which the producer can set different prices in different segments.

> **Definition 7.4: Discriminatory monopolistic market**
>
> A *discriminatory monopolistic market* is a monopolistic market in which the producer chooses a collection of prices, one for each segment of the market.

Note that the model assumes that the demand in each segment depends only on the price in that segment. In particular, this demand does not depend on the prices in other segments, so that we are assuming implicitly that consumers' demands are not affected by any feeling they may have that charging different prices to different groups is unfair.

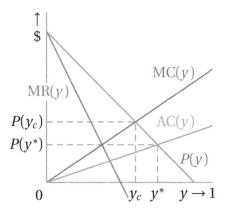

Figure 7.4 The output y^* chosen by an output-maximizing producer in a uniform-price monopolistic market, and the resulting price $P(y^*)$.

Let $\langle (q_i)_{i=1}^k, C, \succcurlyeq \rangle$ be a discriminatory monopolistic market in which the producer's preferences are profit-maximizing, so that his problem is

$$\max_{y_1,\ldots,y_k} \left[\sum_{i=1}^k P_i(y_i)y_i - C\left(\sum_{i=1}^k y_i \right) \right], \tag{7.2}$$

where P_i is the inverse of q_i. Note that this problem cannot be decomposed into k independent problems because the cost is a function of the total output.

The next result generalizes the necessary condition for an output to maximize the producer's profit in a uniform-price monopolistic market (Proposition 7.1).

Proposition 7.2: Discriminatory profit-maximizing monopolist

Consider a discriminatory monopolistic market $\langle (q_i)_{i=1}^k, C, \succcurlyeq \rangle$ in which C and each function q_i is differentiable. For each segment i, let MR_i be the marginal revenue function for q_i, and let MC be the marginal cost function for C. If the monopolist's preferences are profit-maximizing and his optimal output y_i^* in segment i is positive, then

$$MR_i(y_i^*) = MC\left(\sum_{j=1}^k y_j^* \right).$$

Proof

The result follows from the standard necessary condition for a maximizer of a differentiable function, applied to (7.2).

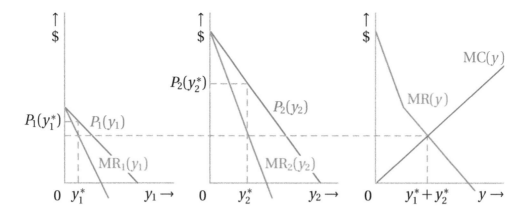

Figure 7.5 The outputs chosen by a profit-maximizing producer in each segment of a discriminatory monopolistic market. In segment i the output is y_i^* and the price is $P_i(y_i^*)$.

Two intuitions lie behind this result. First, the marginal revenues for all segments in which output is positive must be the same since otherwise the producer could increase his profit by moving some production from a segment with a low marginal revenue to one with a high marginal revenue. Second, if the marginal cost is higher than the common marginal revenue then the producer can increase his profit by reducing production, and if the marginal cost is smaller than the common marginal revenue he can increase his profit by increasing production.

The result is illustrated in Figure 7.5. The curve $\mathrm{MR}(y)$ is the horizontal sum of the MR_i curves. For any output y, $\mathrm{MR}(y)$ is the marginal revenue of the monopolist given that he allocates the output y optimally between the segments.

7.4 Implicit discrimination

In this section we assume that the monopolist is aware that the consumers have different demand functions, but cannot discriminate between them explicitly, either because he is prohibited from doing so or because he does not know who is who. We consider the possibility that he can offer an arbitrary set of pairs (q, m), where q is an amount of the good and m is the (total) price of purchasing q. He offers the same set to all consumers, each of whom is limited to choosing one member of the set or not buying the good at all.

Specifically, we consider a market for a good that can be consumed in any quantity between 0 and 1. Each consumer i is willing to pay up to $V^i(q)$ for the quantity q, where the function V^i is increasing and continuous, and $V^i(0) = 0$. A single producer (a monopolist) produces the good at no cost.

The monopolist offers a finite set of pairs (q, m), referred to as a menu. If consumer i chooses (q, m), then his utility is $V^i(q) - m$. Each consumer chooses

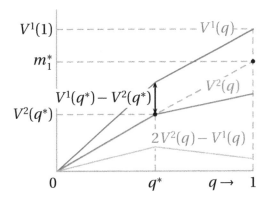

Figure 7.6 An example of a monopolistic market with a menu in which the profit-maximizing menu for the monopolist contains two options, $(q^*, V^2(q^*))$ and $(1, m_1^*)$, where $m_1^* = V^1(1) - (V^1(q^*) - V^2(q^*))$.

an option in the menu for which his utility is highest, if this maximal utility is nonnegative; otherwise, he buys nothing. The monopolist assumes that the consumers behave optimally and chooses a menu for which his profit, the total amount paid by the consumers, is maximal.

Definition 7.5: Monopolistic market with a menu

A *monopolistic market with a menu* has the following components.

Demand

A collection $(V^i)_{i=1}^n$ of increasing continuous functions, where $V^i : [0, 1] \to \mathbb{R}_+$ and $V^i(0) = 0$. The function V^i is the *value function for consumer i*, giving the maximum amount $V^i(q)$ consumer i is willing to pay for q units of the good.

Producer

A single producer, called a *monopolist*, with no costs, who chooses a set M of pairs, called a *menu*, where a pair (q, m) represents the option to buy q units of the good at the (total) price m.

If $V^i(q) - m \geq 0$ for some $(q, m) \in M$, consumer i chooses an option $(q, m) \in M$ for which $V^i(q) - m$ is maximal; otherwise he buys nothing. The producer chooses M so that the consumers' choices maximize his profit.

We now analyze a monopolistic market with a menu in which there are two consumers, one of whom values each additional unit of the good more than the other. One implication of the following result is that for some such markets, offering a menu that consists of more than one pair is optimal for the monopolist.

Proposition 7.3: Monopolistic market with a menu

Consider a two-consumer monopolistic market with a menu (V^1, V^2) in which $V^1(q^1) - V^1(q^2) > V^2(q^1) - V^2(q^2)$ whenever $q^1 > q^2 \geq 0$. Let q^* be a maximizer of $2V^2(q) - V^1(q)$. The monopolist's maximal profit is

$$\max\{V^1(1), 2V^2(1), V^1(1) + 2V^2(q^*) - V^1(q^*)\}.$$

- If $V^1(1)$ is the largest term, then $\{(1, V^1(1))\}$ is an optimal menu and consumer 1 alone purchases the single option.

- If $2V^2(1)$ is the largest term, then $\{(1, V^2(1))\}$ is an optimal menu and both consumers purchase the single option.

- If $V^1(1) + 2V^2(q^*) - V^1(q^*)$ is the largest term, then $M^* = \{(q^*, V^2(q^*)), (1, V^1(1) - (V^1(q^*) - V^2(q^*)))\}$ is an optimal menu; consumer 2 purchases the first option and consumer 1 purchases the second option.

Proof

First note that the monopolist cannot gain by offering options not chosen by any consumer. Thus an optimal menu consisting of one or two options exists.

Consider menus that consist of a single option, (q, m). (*i*) If $V^1(q) < m$, then neither consumer chooses the option and the monopolist's profit is 0. (*ii*) If $V^2(q) < m \leq V^1(q)$, then consumer 1 alone chooses the option. Out of these menus, the best one for the monopolist is $\{(1, V^1(1)\}$, which yields the profit $V^1(1)$. (*iii*) If $m \leq V^2(q)$, then both consumers choose the option. Out of these menus, the best one for the monopolist is $\{(1, V^2(1))\}$, which yields the profit $2V^2(1)$.

Now consider the set $\mathcal{M}_2$ of menus that consist of two options, one chosen by each consumer. The menu M^* specified in the proposition belongs to $\mathcal{M}_2$. (Consumer 1 is indifferent between the two options. Consumer 2 is indifferent between $(q^*, V^2(q^*))$ and not buying anything, and his utility from $(1, V^1(1) - (V^1(q^*) - V^2(q^*)))$ is nonpositive by the assumption about the relation between the two value functions.)

We argue that if the menu $\{(q^1, m^1), (q^2, m^2)\}$ is optimal in $\mathcal{M}_2$ and consumer i chooses (q^i, m^i), then the menu is M^*.

Step 1 $V^2(q^2) = m^2$.

Proof. Given that both consumers purchase an option, we have $V^i(q^i) \geq$

m^i for $i = 1, 2$. We now argue that $V^i(q^i) = m^i$ for some i. If $V^i(q^i) > m^i$ for both consumers, then there exists $\varepsilon > 0$ (small enough) such that increasing m^i by ε increases the monopolist's profit by 2ε. We need $V^2(q^2) = m^2$ since if $V^1(q^1) = m^1$ then, given that $V^1(q) > V^2(q)$ for all q, we have $0 = V^1(q^1) - m^1 \geq V^1(q^2) - m^2 > V^2(q^2) - m^2$, contradicting $V^2(q^2) \geq m^2$. ◁

Step 2 $(q^1, m^1) = (1, V^1(1) - (V^1(q^2) - V^2(q^2)))$.

Proof. For consumer 1 to choose (q^1, m^1) we need $V^1(q^1) - m^1 \geq V^1(q^2) - m^2 = V^1(q^2) - V^2(q^2)$ (using Step 1), or $m^1 \leq V^1(q^1) - (V^1(q^2) - V^2(q^2))$. Given (q^2, m^2), the best (q^1, m^1) satisfying this condition is $(1, V^1(1) - (V^1(q^2) - V^2(q^2)))$. ◁

By Steps 1 and 2, the optimal menu in $\mathcal{M}_2$ has the form $\{(q^2, V^2(q^2)), (1, V^1(1) - (V^1(q^2) - V^2(q^2)))\}$. This menu yields the profit $V^2(q^2) + V^1(1) - (V^1(q^2) - V^2(q^2)) = 2V^2(q^2) + V^1(1) - V^1(q^2)$, which is maximized by $q^2 = q^*$. Thus M^* is optimal in $\mathcal{M}_2$.

Figure 7.6 shows an example of a monopolistic market with a menu in which a menu with two options is optimal.

Problems

1. *Double margins.* A profit-maximizing producer in a uniform-price monopolistic market has no production cost.

   a. Suppose that the good in the market is indivisible. There are two consumers, each of whom wants to purchase either one or zero units of the good. One consumer is willing to pay \$10 for the good and the other is willing to pay \$8. What price does the monopolist set?

   Assume now that the monopolist does not sell the good directly to the consumers, but sells it to an intermediary, who sells it to the consumers at a uniform price.

   b. Under the assumptions of the previous part, find the demand function of the intermediary and analyze the behavior of the producer.

   c. Repeat the previous parts when the good is divisible, the monopolist's cost function is $c(y) = y^2$, and the consumer's inverse demand function is $P(y) = 1 - y$.

d. Prove that if the monopolist's cost function is convex and the consumers' inverse demand function is $P(y) = A - By$ then in the presence of an intermediary the output of the monopolist is at most his output when he sells directly to consumers.

2. *Imposing a tax.*

   a. Imposing a sales tax can cause a profit-maximizing monopolist in a uniform-price monopolistic market to increase the price he charges by more than the tax. To verify this claim, consider a monopolist selling a single good who has no costs and faces two consumers, 1 and 2. Consumer i purchases one unit if the price he pays does not exceed v^i. Assume $v^1 = 1 > v^2 = v > 0$. Show that for some values of v and t, the imposition of a tax of t causes the price charged by the monopolist to rise by more than t.

   b. Show that if the monopolist faces a linear inverse demand function $P(q) = A - Bq$ and constant marginal cost of c, then the price increase due to a tax of t is less than t.

3. *Monopolist interested in fairness.* Consider a monopolist who faces a market with two segments, with demand functions q_1 and q_2, and has no production cost. Suppose that he maximizes profit subject to the constraint that the outcome is fair in the sense that $W_1(q_1(p_1)) - p_1q_1(p_1) = W_2(q_2(p_2)) - p_2q_2(p_2)$, where p_i is the price in segment i and $W_i(q)$ is the area under the inverse demand function P_i between 0 and q, as in (7.1). (Recall that $W_i(q)$ is a rough measure of the welfare of consumers in segment i from purchasing q units of the good.)

   Formulate the optimization problem of this monopolist and solve the problem when $q_i(p_i) = a_i - p_i$ for $i = 1, 2$, with $a_1 \geq a_2$. Compare the outcome with the one generated by a profit-maximizing monopolist.

4. *Nonlinear prices.* Consider a market for a single indivisible good; each individual can consume either one or two units of the good. A monopolist has no cost of production and faces two consumers. Consumer i (= 1, 2) is willing to pay up to $V^i(q)$ for q units of the good, where $V^i(2) > V^i(1) > V^i(0) = 0$. The monopolist cannot discriminate between the consumers, but can offer nonlinear prices: the price of the first unit a consumer buys does not have to be the same as the price of the second unit.

   Give an example in which a profit-maximizing monopolist optimally chooses a price schedule for which the price of the second unit is less than the price of the first unit, and also an example in which the reverse is true.

5. *Bundling.* A profit-maximizing monopolist produces two indivisible goods, A and B, at zero cost. He confronts a population in which individual i is willing to pay up to v_a^i for good A, v_b^i for good B, and $v_a^i + v_b^i$ for both goods. The monopolist can sell either each good separately or a bundle of both goods; he is restricted to charge the same price for all individuals. Construct two examples, one in which the monopolist's optimal policy is to offer the two goods in a bundle, and one in which the optimal policy is to sell the two goods separately.

6. *Two-part tariff.* Assume that a profit-maximizing monopolist with a differentiable cost function C confronts a single consumer, who has a continuous decreasing inverse demand function P. Let $W(q) = \int_0^q P(x)\,dx$, the maximum amount the consumer is willing to pay for q units of the good. The monopolist makes an offer (A, p), where A is the cost of the option to purchase from the monopolist and p is a price per unit, so that a consumer who purchases any amount $x > 0$ pays $A + px$. Formulate the monopolist's problem and prove that an output $q > 0$ that maximizes the monopolist's profit satisfies $P(q) = MC(q)$.

7. *Implicit discrimination.* Consider a market with two consumers and a good that is available in discrete amounts. The maximum amount $V^i(q)$ that each consumer i is willing to pay for q units of the good, for $q = 1$ or 2, is given in the following table, which shows also each consumer's marginal valuation $MV^i(q) = V^i(q) - V^i(q-1)$, the maximum amount i is willing to pay for an additional unit when she has $q - 1$ units.

q	$V^1(q)$	$MV^1(q)$	$V^2(q)$	$MV^2(q)$
0	0		0	
1	12	12	10	10
2	19	7	13	3

Consider a profit-maximizing monopolist whose cost of production is zero.

a. Find the price charged by the monopolist if he can offer only a uniform price to all consumers.

b. Suppose the monopolist can offer only a single option (q, m), where q is an amount of the good and m is an amount of money. Each consumer can either pay m and get q units of the good, or buy nothing. Find the option chosen by the monopolist.

c. Now suppose that the monopolist can offer the consumers a menu consisting of two such options (q, m). Each consumer either chooses one of the options or buys nothing. Show that the menu $\{(1,10),(2,17)\}$ is profit-maximizing and yields the profit 27 (consumer 1 chooses $(2,17)$ and consumer 2 chooses $(1,10)$).

8. *Coupons.* Some stores issue coupons, giving a discount to a customer who has one. To understand the logic of this phenomenon, consider a profit-maximizing monopolist with no production cost who faces two equal-sized groups of consumers. Each member of group 1 is willing to pay 7 for the monopolist's good and incurs a cost of 4 to search for a coupon, and each member of group 2 is willing to pay up to 5 for the good and incurs a cost of 1 to search for a coupon. What price and discount does the monopolist offer?

9. *Two workers and one employer.* An employer has two workers, a and b. Each worker can produce any quantity in $[0,1]$. The payoff of worker i $(= a, b)$ if he produces y_i and is paid m_i is $m_i - e_i(y_i)$, where the (effort cost) function e_i is increasing, differentiable, and convex, and satisfies $e_i(0) = 0$, $e_i'(0) < 1$, and $e_i'(1) > 1$. Assume that $e_a'(y) < e_b'(y)$ for all $y > 0$. The employer's profit is $y_a + y_b - m_a - m_b$.

   The employer offers a menu of contracts, each of which is a pair (y, m) with the interpretation that the employer will pay m to a worker who produces y. Each worker chooses the contract he prefers or rejects all contracts.

   Show that if it is optimal for a profit-maximizing employer to offer a menu consisting of two distinct contracts, (y_a, m_a), chosen by a, and (y_b, m_b), chosen by b, then $e_b'(y_b) = 1$, $1 - e_a'(y_a) = e_a'(y_a) - e_b'(y_a)$, $m_a = e_a(y_a)$, and $m_b = e_b(y_b) + m_a - e_b(y_a)$.

Notes

The material in this chapter is standard. Problem 1 is based on Tirole (1988, 174).

Equilibrium

8 A jungle

In this chapter and the next we study a society consisting of a set of individuals and a set of houses. Each house can accommodate only one person and each person can occupy only one house. Different people may have different preferences over the houses, but everyone prefers to occupy any house than to be homeless.

In this chapter we analyze a model in which the assignment of houses is determined by the individuals' strengths; the concepts of property and ownership do not exist. A person who wants to occupy a house currently occupied by a weaker person can do so simply by presenting himself to the current occupant. The process is orderly: everyone knows everyone else's strength, and on seeing that a stronger person wants to occupy his house, a person vacates it without a fight, which he knows he would lose.

We study the existence and character of a stable assignment of houses to individuals. Will the people forever be evicting each other, or does an assignment of people to houses exist in which no one wants the house of anyone who is weaker than him? What are the properties of such an assignment?

8.1 Model

Society

A society is defined by a set of individuals, a set of houses, and the individuals' preferences over the houses. To simplify the analysis, we assume that the number of houses is equal to the number of individuals and that no individual is indifferent between any two houses.

> **Definition 8.1: Society**
>
> A *society* $\langle N, H, (\succsim^i)_{i \in N} \rangle$ consists of
>
> **individuals**
>   a finite set N

Chapter of *Models in Microeconomic Theory* by Martin J. Osborne and Ariel Rubinstein. Version 2023.5.30 (h).

houses

a finite set H with the same number of members as N

preferences

for each individual $i \in N$, a strict preference relation $\succ^i$ over H.

We interpret $h \succ^i h'$ to mean that individual i prefers to occupy house h than house h'. Notice that we assume that each individual cares only about the house he occupies, not about the house anyone else occupies. We discuss this assumption in Section 8.6.

An outcome of the model is an assignment of houses to individuals. Formally, an assignment is a function from the set N of individuals to the set H of houses. We typically denote an assignment by a, with $a(i)$ being the house assigned to individual i. Since we assume that a house can be occupied by at most one individual, an assignment is feasible only if it assigns different individuals to different houses (that is, only if it is a one-to-one function). We call such an assignment an allocation.

Definition 8.2: Assignment and allocation

An *assignment* for a society $\langle N, H, (\succ^i)_{i \in N} \rangle$ is a function from the set N of individuals to the set H of houses, associating a house with every individual. An *allocation* is an assignment in which each house is assigned to exactly one individual.

Example 8.1

The following table gives an example of a society with four individuals, 1, 2, 3, and 4, and four houses, A, B, C, and D. Each column indicates the preference ordering of an individual, with the individual's favorite house at the top. For example, individual 1's preference ordering is $B \succ^1 C \succ^1 D \succ^1 A$.

Individuals

1	2	3	4
B	B	A	B
C	D	B	C
D	A	C	A
A	C	D	D

One allocation, in which individuals 1, 2, 3, and 4 occupy houses D, A, C, and B respectively, is highlighted.

Power

What determines the allocation of houses? Presumably the individuals' preferences play a role. In this chapter, we focus on an additional factor: the individuals' relative power. We assume that between any two individuals there is a stable power relation: either i is stronger than j, or j is stronger than i. No two individuals are equally powerful. Precisely, we take as given a binary relation $\rhd$ on the set of individuals, where $i \rhd j$ means that i is more powerful than j, in which case i can take over the house occupied by j.

> **Definition 8.3: Jungle**
>
> A *jungle* $\langle N, H, (\succsim^i)_{i \in N}, \rhd \rangle$ consists of a society $\langle N, H, (\succsim^i)_{i \in N} \rangle$ and a *power relation* $\rhd$, a complete, transitive, antisymmetric binary relation on the set N of individuals.

Comments

1. *Power is not only physical.* One individual may be more powerful than another because he is physically stronger. But alternatively, his social status, ability to persuade, or seniority may be sufficient to allow him to force another individual to relinquish the house that individual occupies.

2. *No property rights.* The model makes no reference to property rights. An individual can occupy a house, but does not *own* it. No legal system by which an individual can defend his occupation of a house exists. In many societies, property rights interfere, to some extent, with the exercise of power. Many models in economics consider the extreme case in which property rights are perfectly enforced. In this chapter, we consider the other extreme, where power alone determines the outcome.

3. *Outcome of a struggle is deterministic.* The notion of power is deterministic: if $i \rhd j$, then in a contest between i and j, i wins for sure; there is no chance that j wins.

4. *No cost of fighting.* Vacating a house involves no cost. Whenever the occupant of a house is confronted by a stronger individual, the occupant recognizes his inferiority and costlessly vacates his house.

5. *No coalitions.* The model specifies the actions possible for each individual; it does not include any separate specification of the actions possible for groups of individuals. This formulation reflects an implicit assumption that each individual acts on his own; no group can achieve any outcome that its members cannot achieve by themselves.

8.2 Equilibrium

An equilibrium in a model is generally an outcome that is stable given the forces assumed to be active. In a jungle, a stable outcome is an allocation in which no individual prefers any house that he can obtain to the one he occupies. Thus an allocation is *not* an equilibrium if some individual prefers the house occupied by a weaker individual to the house he currently occupies.

More precisely, an equilibrium of a jungle is an allocation a for which no individual i prefers the house $a(j)$ occupied by any individual j who is weaker than i to the house $a(i)$ that he occupies.

Definition 8.4: Equilibrium

An *equilibrium* of the jungle $\langle N, H, (\succcurlyeq^i)_{i \in N}, \rhd \rangle$ is an allocation a^* such that for no individuals $i, j \in N$ is it the case that $i \rhd j$ and $a^*(j) \succ^i a^*(i)$.

Example 8.2

For the jungle consisting of the society in Example 8.1 together with the power relation $\rhd$ for which $1 \rhd 2 \rhd 3 \rhd 4$, the allocation (B, D, A, C), highlighted in the following table, is an equilibrium.

Individuals

1	2	3	4
B	B	A	B
C	D	B	C
D	A	C	A
A	C	D	D

Individuals 1 and 3 occupy their favorite houses. Individuals 2 and 4 do not occupy their favorite house, which is occupied by a stronger individual. Individual 2 prefers D to the houses occupied by the individuals weaker than him, namely 3 and 4; no individual is weaker than 4.

Every jungle has an equilibrium. That is, for every set of individuals, set of houses, profile of preference relations, and power relation, an allocation—at least one, possibly more than one—is stable against the exercise of power.

We prove this result by showing that an allocation generated by a procedure called *serial dictatorship* is an equilibrium. This procedure is defined for an arbitrary ordering of the individuals. It assigns to the first individual in the ordering his favorite house, say h_1, and to the second individual in the ordering his favorite house among all those that remain after removing h_1. It continues in the same way according to the ordering of the individuals, assigning to each individual his favorite house among all houses that remain after removing the ones assigned to the individuals who precede him in the ordering.

Procedure: Serial dictatorship

For the society $\langle N, H, (\succeq^i)_{i \in N} \rangle$ and ordering i_1, i_2, ..., i_n of the members of N, the *serial dictatorship procedure* generates the allocation defined inductively as follows.

Initialization

The house h_1 allocated to individual i_1 is the best house in H according to i_1's preference relation, $\succeq^{i_1}$.

Inductive step

For every $k \geq 2$, the house h_k allocated to individual i_k is the best house in $H \setminus \{h_1, \ldots, h_{k-1}\}$ according to i_k's preference relation, $\succeq^{i_k}$.

If we apply this procedure to the society in Example 8.1 and the ordering 1, 2, 3, 4 then we get the allocation (B, D, A, C), which Example 8.2 shows is an equilibrium of the jungle with the power relation $\rhd$ for which $1 \rhd 2 \rhd 3 \rhd 4$. We now show that this result is general.

Proposition 8.1: Every jungle has an equilibrium

For any jungle $\langle N, H, (\succeq^i)_{i \in N}, \rhd \rangle$, the allocation generated by the serial dictatorship procedure for the society $\langle N, H, (\succeq^i)_{i \in N} \rangle$ and the ordering $\rhd$ is an equilibrium.

Proof

Let a be the assignment generated by the serial dictatorship procedure for the society $\langle N, H, (\succeq^i)_{i \in N} \rangle$ and the ordering $\rhd$. The number of houses is the same as the number of individuals, so the procedure assigns to every individual a house. Every house is assigned only once, so the assignment a is feasible, and hence an allocation. The allocation is an equilibrium because the house assigned to each individual is the best house, according to the individual's preferences, among all the houses not assigned to stronger individuals.

Note that the serial dictatorship procedure is not the equilibrium concept; it is only a means by which to prove that an equilibrium exists. Proposition 8.1 leaves open the possibility that other equilibria, constructed differently, exist, but we now show that in fact no other equilibria exist.

Proposition 8.2: Every jungle has a unique equilibrium

Every jungle has a unique equilibrium.

Proof

Consider the jungle $\langle N, H, (\succeq^i)_{i \in N}, \rhd \rangle$. Without loss of generality assume that $N = \{1, \ldots, n\}$ and $1 \rhd 2 \rhd \cdots \rhd n$. Assume, contrary to the claim, that a and b are two equilibria of the jungle. Denote by i^* the strongest individual i for whom $a(i) \neq b(i)$. That is, $a(i) = b(i)$ for all $i < i^*$ and $a(i^*) \neq b(i^*)$, as illustrated in the following diagram.

The set of houses allocated to individuals 1 through $i^* - 1$ is the same in a and b, so the set of houses allocated to i^* through n is also the same in the two allocations. Thus the house $a(i^*)$ (orange in the diagram) is allocated by b to some individual j less powerful than i^*: $a(i^*) = b(j)$. Also the house $b(i^*)$ (blue) is allocated by a to some individual k less powerful than i^*: $b(i^*) = a(k)$. (Individual j could be more or less powerful than k; in the diagram he is more powerful.) The fact that a is an equilibrium implies that $a(i^*) \succ_{i^*} a(k) = b(i^*)$ and the fact that b is an equilibrium implies that $b(i^*) \succ_{i^*} b(j) = a(i^*)$, a contradiction.

Comments

1. *Equilibrium is static.* The concept of equilibrium in a jungle, like the other equilibrium concepts in this part of the book, is static. Problem 5 describes a dynamic process that starts from an arbitrary initial allocation and asks you to show that this process converges to an equilibrium.

2. *Strict preferences.* The assumption that the individuals' preferences are strict (that is, no individual is indifferent between any two houses), is essential for this result. Problem 1 asks you to show that if one or more individuals are indifferent between two houses then a jungle may have more than one equilibrium.

8.3   Pareto stability

Now suppose that the allocation of houses to people is determined not by the balance of power, but by mutual agreement. One allocation is replaced by another only if everyone agrees: no one objects and at least one person prefers the new allocation. Thus an allocation is immune to replacement if no allocation is better for some people and no worse for anyone.

Formally, an allocation b Pareto dominates an allocation a if for every individual the house assigned by b is at least as good as the house assigned by a, and at least one individual prefers the house assigned by b to the one assigned by a. An allocation is Pareto stable if no allocation Pareto dominates it.

> **Definition 8.5: Pareto stability**
>
> The allocation b in the society $\langle N, H, (\succeq^i)_{i \in N} \rangle$ *Pareto dominates* the allocation a if $b(i) \succeq^i a(i)$ for all $i \in N$ and $b(i) \succ^i a(i)$ for some $i \in N$. An allocation is *Pareto stable* if no allocation Pareto dominates it.

Consider the allocation in Example 8.1; denote it by a. Let b be the allocation in which $b(1) = C$, $b(2) = D$, $b(3) = A$, and $b(4) = B$. Individuals 1, 2, and 3 prefer the house assigned to them by b to the one assigned to them by a, and individual 4 occupies the same house in both allocations. Thus b Pareto dominates a and hence a is not Pareto stable.

Note that under the assumption that no individual is indifferent between any two houses, an allocation a is Pareto stable if for no allocation b does every individual who is allocated different houses by a and b prefer the house he is allocated by b to the one he is allocated by a.

Comments

1. *Terminology.* You may have previously encountered the term "Pareto optimal" or "Pareto efficient". These terms are different names for "Pareto stable". We use this terminology for two reasons. First, we want to emphasize that Pareto stability is an equilibrium concept. The force that can upset an allocation is an agreement between all individuals to replace the allocation with another one. Second, we want to use a name that has no normative flavor. A Pareto stable allocation might be good or bad, fair or unfair. Making such assessments requires information not present in the model.

2. *The notion of Pareto stability does not involve power.* Whether an allocation is Pareto stable depends only on the characteristics of the society, not on the power relation.

3. *Another potential source of instability.* Behind the definition of Pareto stability lies the assumption that whenever one allocation is Pareto dominated by another, the latter will replace the former. This assumption is strong. If the allocations b and c both Pareto dominate a, and b is better than c for some

individuals whereas c is better than b for others, then the individuals might disagree about the allocation that should replace a. The concept of Pareto stability implicitly assumes that this disagreement is not an obstacle to the replacement of a.

We now show that for any society and *any* ordering of the individuals, the allocation generated by the serial dictatorship procedure is Pareto stable.

Proposition 8.3: Serial dictatorship allocation is Pareto stable

For any society and any ordering of the individuals, the allocation generated by the serial dictatorship procedure is Pareto stable.

Proof

Let $\langle N, H, (\succeq^i)_{i \in N} \rangle$ be a society and $i_1, i_2, \ldots, i_n$ an ordering of the individuals in N. Denote by a the allocation generated by the serial dictatorship procedure for the society with this ordering. That is, $a(i_1)$ is i_1's most preferred house, $a(i_2)$ is i_2's most preferred house in $H \setminus \{a(i_1)\}$, and so on.

Suppose, contrary to the claim that a is Pareto stable, that b is an allocation with $b(i) \succeq^i a(i)$ for every individual $i \in N$ and $b(i) \succ^i a(i)$ for at least one individual $i \in N$. Let i_r be the first individual in the ordering $i_1, i_2, \ldots, i_n$ for whom $b(i_r) \succ^{i_r} a(i_r)$. Then $b(i_q) = a(i_q)$ for every $q < r$ (because no individual is indifferent between any two houses), as illustrated in the following diagram.

$$
\begin{array}{ccccccccc}
i: & i_1 & i_2 & \ldots & i_{r-1} & i_r & \ldots & i_s & \ldots & i_n \\
a(i): & \blacksquare & \blacksquare & \ldots & \blacksquare & \blacksquare & \ldots & \blacksquare & \ldots & \blacksquare \\
b(i): & \blacksquare & \blacksquare & \ldots & \blacksquare & \blacksquare & \ldots & \blacksquare & \ldots & \blacksquare
\end{array}
$$

Therefore $b(i_r) = a(i_s)$ for some individual i_s with $s > r$, and hence $a(i_s) \succ^{i_r} a(i_r)$, contradicting the fact that $a(i_r)$ is i_r's favorite house among the houses that remain after removing those allocated to individuals who precede him in the ordering.

8.4 Equilibrium and Pareto stability in a jungle

We now connect the notion of equilibrium, which requires that an outcome be immune to the use of power, to the concept of Pareto stability, which requires that the outcome be immune to a reallocation to which everyone agrees.

> ### Proposition 8.4: Equilibrium of every jungle is Pareto stable
>
> The equilibrium of every jungle is Pareto stable.

> **Proof**
>
> By Proposition 8.2 every jungle has a unique equilibrium, and by Proposition 8.1 this equilibrium is obtained by applying the serial dictatorship procedure for the power relation. Thus by Proposition 8.3 the equilibrium is Pareto stable.

In Section 8.6 we show that this result depends on the assumption that each individual cares only about the house he occupies: equilibria of some jungles in which individuals care about the houses occupied by other individuals are not Pareto stable.

8.5 Which allocations can be obtained by a social planner who controls the power relation?

Now consider a social planner who can determine the power relation in the society but cannot dictate the allocation of houses. We assume that the planner believes that whatever power relation he dictates, the outcome will be an equilibrium of the jungle for that power relation. Which allocations can the planner induce? More precisely, for which allocations a is there a power relation such that a is an equilibrium of the jungle with that power relation? By Proposition 8.4 all equilibria are Pareto stable, so a necessary condition for an allocation to be achievable as an equilibrium for some power relation is that it be Pareto stable. We now show that this condition is in fact also sufficient. That is, a planner can, by choosing the power relation appropriately, induce any Pareto stable allocation. To prove this result we use the following lemma.

> ### Lemma 8.1: Pareto stable allocation and favorite houses
>
> In every Pareto stable allocation of any society, at least one individual is allocated his favorite house.

> **Proof**
>
> Let a be an allocation in the society $\langle N, H, (\succsim^i)_{i \in N} \rangle$ for which $a(i) \neq h^*(i)$ for every $i \in N$, where $h^*(i)$ is i's favorite house. We show that a is not Pareto stable.

Choose, arbitrarily, individual i_1. By our assumption, $a(i_1) \neq h^*(i_1)$: i_1 does not occupy his favorite house. So that house, $h^*(i_1)$, is occupied by some other individual, say i_2: $a(i_2) = h^*(i_1)$.

Similarly, i_2's favorite house, $h^*(i_2)$, is occupied by an individual other than i_2, say i_3: $a(i_3) = h^*(i_2)$. This individual could be i_1 or some other individual.

If $i_3 = i_1$, define the allocation b by $b(i_1) = a(i_2) = h^*(i_1)$, $b(i_2) = a(i_1) = h^*(i_2)$, and $b(j) = a(j)$ for every other individual. That is, switch the houses of i_1 and i_2 and keep everyone else's house the same. Then both i_1 and i_2 prefer the house allocated to them in b to the house allocated to them in a, and everyone else occupies the same house in both allocations. Thus a is not Pareto stable.

If $i_3 \neq i_1$, continue in the same way to construct a sequence of individuals such that for each k, i_k's favorite house, $h^*(i_k)$, is $a(i_{k+1})$, the one allocated by a to i_{k+1}. Because the set of houses is finite, for some $k \leq n$ we have $i_k = i_m$ for some $m < k$.

The following diagram illustrates the construction. An arrow from i to j means that i's favorite house is the one allocated by a to j.

$$i_1 \rightarrow i_2 \rightarrow \cdots \rightarrow i_m \rightarrow i_{m+1} \rightarrow \cdots \rightarrow i_k$$

Now define the allocation b by $b(i_j) = a(i_{j+1})$ for all $j = m, \ldots, k-1$, $b(i_k) = a(i_m)$, and $b(i) = a(i)$ for every other i. Every individual i_j for $j = m, \ldots, k$ prefers the house allocated to him in b to the one allocated to him in a and every other individual occupies the same house in both allocations. Thus a is not Pareto stable.

We now show that by choosing the power relation appropriately, a social planner can achieve any Pareto stable allocation as the unique equilibrium.

Proposition 8.5: Pareto stable allocation is equilibrium for some power relation

Let a be a Pareto stable allocation of a society $\langle N, H, (\succcurlyeq^i)_{i \in N} \rangle$. There exists a power relation $\rhd$ such that a is the only equilibrium of the jungle $\langle N, H, (\succcurlyeq^i)_{i \in N}, \rhd \rangle$.

Proof

We construct the power relation $\rhd$ as follows.

By Lemma 8.1, at least one individual is allocated his favorite house by *a*. Let i_1 be such an individual, and start constructing $\triangleright$ by making i_1 the most powerful individual.

Now remove i_1 from the set of individuals and $a(i_1)$ from the set of houses. That is, consider the society in which the set of individuals is $N \setminus \{i_1\}$ and the set of houses is $H \setminus \{a(i_1)\}$. The allocation a restricted to the individuals in this smaller society—that is, the allocation a' defined by $a'(i) = a(i)$ for all $i \in N \setminus \{i_1\}$—is Pareto stable in the smaller society. The reason is that if it were not, there would be an allocation b' in the smaller society for which some individual in the smaller society is better off than he is in a', and no individual is worse off than he is in a'. But then in the allocation b in the original society defined by $b(i_1) = a(i_1)$ and $b(i) = b'(i)$ for all $i \in N \setminus \{i_1\}$ Pareto dominates a, contradicting the Pareto stability of a in the original society.

Given the Pareto stability of a' in the smaller society, again by Lemma 8.1 there exists an individual, say i_2, who is allocated his favorite house in $H \setminus \{a(i_1)\}$ by a'. We continue the construction of $\triangleright$ by making him the second most powerful individual.

Continue in the same way. At stage $k + 1$, identify an individual i_{k+1} for whom $a(i_{k+1})$ is the favorite house among $H \setminus \{a(i_1), \ldots, a(i_k)\}$ and make him the $(k + 1)$th most powerful individual.

By construction, for any individual i the house $a(i)$ allocated to him is better according to his preferences than every house allocated to an individual who is weaker according to $\triangleright$. Thus a is an equilibrium, and hence by Proposition 8.2 the only equilibrium, of the jungle $\langle N, H, (\succeq^i)_{i \in N}, \triangleright \rangle$.

Comment

Assume that you observe a group of individuals occupying a set of houses. You know the preferences of each individual (so that you know the society) but you do not know the power relation in the group. You want to determine whether the allocation you observe is consistent with an equilibrium of a jungle. To do so, you need to check whether there is a power relation such that the allocation you observe is the equilibrium of the jungle consisting of the society accompanied by that power relation.

By Proposition 8.4 an allocation that is not Pareto stable is not an equilibrium, so that its appearance is inconsistent with equilibrium. On the other hand, by Proposition 8.5 every Pareto stable allocation *is* an equilibrium of some jungle. So the observation of an allocation over which individuals do not quarrel is consistent with the allocation's being the outcome of the power struggle captured by a jungle.

8.6   Externalities

So far we have assumed that each individual cares only about the house he occupies. In fact, people may care not only about the houses they occupy but also about the allocation of houses to other people. For example, people generally care about their neighbors. They may care also about the appropriateness of other people's houses relative to their needs. They may consider, in addition, the fairness of the allocation. For example, a person may prefer an allocation in which everyone gets his second best house to an allocation in which he gets his favorite house but others get houses they rank near the bottom of their preferences.

The influence of one person's action on another person is called an externality by economists. We now extend the model of a jungle to allow for externalities. The following definition of a society differs from our previous definition in two respects. First, the preferences of each individual are defined over the set of allocations rather than the set of houses. Second, these preferences are not required to be strict. We allow non-strict preferences to include cases in which some individuals care only about the houses occupied by a specific group of individuals, possibly only himself. An individual who has such preferences is indifferent between allocations that differ only in the houses assigned to individuals outside the group.

Definition 8.6: Society with externalities

A *society with externalities* $\langle N, H, (\succeq^i)_{i \in N} \rangle$ consists of

individuals
  a finite set N

houses
  a finite set H with the same number of members as N

preferences
  for each individual $i \in N$, a preference relation $\succeq^i$ over the set of allocations.

The definition of a jungle with externalities differs from our previous definition only in that the society is replaced by a society with externalities.

Definition 8.7: Jungle with externalities

A *jungle with externalities* $\langle N, H, (\succeq^i)_{i \in N}, \rhd \rangle$ consists of a society with externalities $\langle N, H, (\succeq^i)_{i \in N} \rangle$ and a power relation $\rhd$, a complete, transitive, antisymmetric binary relation on the set N of individuals.

Despite the similarity of this definition with our original definition of a jungle, the meanings of the power relation $\triangleright$ in the definitions differ. In a jungle, $i \triangleright j$ means simply that i can take over the house occupied by j. In a jungle with externalities, $i \triangleright j$ means that individual i can take over the house occupied by j *and* force j to occupy the house currently occupied by i. When considering whether to force such an exchange, individual i compares the current allocation with the one in which he and individual j exchange houses.

Definition 8.8: Equilibrium of jungle with externalities

An *equilibrium* of the jungle with externalities $\langle N, H, (\succeq^i)_{i \in N}, \triangleright \rangle$ is an allocation a^* such that for no individuals $i, j \in N$ is it the case that $i \triangleright j$ and $b \succ^i a^*$, where b is the allocation that differs from a^* only in that $b(i) = a^*(j)$ and $b(j) = a^*(i)$.

The following examples show that the two basic results about the equilibrium of a jungle without externalities, its existence (Proposition 8.1) and its Pareto stability (Proposition 8.4), do not hold in a jungle with externalities.

Example 8.3: Nonexistence of equilibrium in jungle with externalities

Suppose $N = \{1, 2, 3\}$ and $H = \{\text{⌂}, \text{⌂}, \text{⌂}\}$, and think of the houses as being located on a circle, as in the following figure.

Assume that $1 \triangleright 2 \triangleright 3$ and suppose that individual 1 most prefers any of the three allocations in which he is individual 2's clockwise neighbor, and individual 2 most prefers any of the three allocations in which he is individual 1's clockwise neighbor.

In an equilibrium, 1 must be the clockwise neighbor of 2, because if 3 is the clockwise neighbor of 2, individual 1 can become the clockwise neighbor of 2 by forcing 3, who is less powerful than his, to exchange houses with his. Similarly, in an equilibrium, 2 must also be the clockwise neighbor of 1. But in no allocation is 1 the clockwise neighbor of 2 and 2 the clockwise neighbor of 1. Thus no equilibrium exists.

Example 8.4: Equilibria not Pareto stable in jungle with externalities

Consider a jungle that differs from the one in the previous example only in the individuals' preferences. Individual 1 most prefers to be individual 2's clockwise neighbor, individual 2 most prefers to be 3's clockwise neighbor, and individual 3 most prefers to be 1's clockwise neighbor. Each individual prefers every allocation in which his clockwise neighbor is the individual he most prefers in that position to any other allocation. In addition, among the three allocations a, b, and c in which each individual has his favorite clockwise neighbor, shown in the following figures, each individual prefers a to b to c.

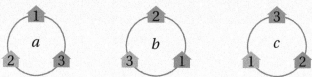

These three allocations are all equilibria, but b and c are not Pareto stable: all three individuals prefer a to both b and c. (For another example of an equilibrium in a jungle with externalities that is not Pareto stable, see Problem 6.)

Problems

1. *Jungle with preferences with indifference.* In a variant of a jungle in which the individuals' preferences are not necessarily strict, show the following results.

   a. An equilibrium exists, but may not be unique.

   b. An equilibrium may not be Pareto stable.

2. *Comparative statics.* Two jungles have the same set of individuals, the same set of houses, and the same preference profile (that is, the same society), but different power relations. The power relations differ only in that two individuals exchange positions. Compare the equilibria of the two jungles. Which individuals are necessarily assigned the same houses in both jungles? How are the individuals who exchange positions affected? How are the other individuals affected?

3. *Manipulability.* To prevent unnecessary clashes, the individuals in the jungle decide that a computer will calculate the equilibrium and they will abide by its recommendation. The computer is informed of the power relation, and each individual reports to the computer his preference relation. Then the computer calculates the equilibrium (given the reported preference relations), and the individuals abide by the allocation. Show that no individual can do better than reporting his true preference relation, regardless of the other individuals' reports.

4. *The jungle with insufficient housing.* Extend the model of the jungle to the case in which the number of houses is smaller than the number of individuals. In this case, an allocation is a function from the set of individuals to the set $H \cup \{homeless\}$ with the property that no two individuals are assigned to the same house. Each individual has a preference ordering over $H \cup \{homeless\}$. Assume, as before, that this ordering is strict; assume also that every individual prefers to be allocated any house than to be homeless. Define an equilibrium for this extended model and show that it exists.

5. *A dynamic process.* Consider the following dynamic process for the jungle $\langle N, H, (\succsim^i)_{i \in N}, \rhd \rangle$. At each stage, each member of a subset of the individuals occupies a distinct house.

   At stage 0, no individual occupies any house.

   For any $t \geq 0$, at stage $t + 1$ every individual goes to the house that is best for him among the houses that, at the end of stage t, are either vacant or are occupied by him or by individuals weaker than him. For each house h, the individual who occupies h at the end of stage $t + 1$ is defined as follows. If exactly one individual goes to h, then he occupies h. If more than one individual goes to h, then the strongest among these individuals occupies h (and the other individuals at h do not occupy any house). If no individual goes to h, then it is unoccupied.

   Show that this process converges (at the latest at stage $|N|$) to an equilibrium of $\langle N, H, (\succsim^i)_{i \in N}, \rhd \rangle$.

6. *The cream guard.* An organization consists of n workers and n jobs, with $n \geq 3$. A manager, who is not one of the workers, assigns the workers to the jobs. The workers differ in their influence on the manager. If i has a larger influence than j, then i can persuade the manager to exchange i's and j's jobs. The nickname of one worker is "the cat"; he is at the bottom of the influence ladder. The jobs in the organization have an agreed ranking in terms of prestige, $h_1, h_2, \ldots, h_n$, and every individual wants a job that is as prestigious as possible.

   However, there is a small complication. The most prestigious job h_1 is the "cream guard". Every worker benefits from the situation in which the cat, rather than anyone else, guards the cream. Everyone is willing to sacrifice one place in the prestige ranking (but not more) to have the cat guard the cream.

   a. Find the equilibrium of this jungle with externalities.

   b. Explain why the equilibrium you found is not Pareto stable.

7. *Pareto instability and pairwise exchange.* Construct a society with an allocation that is not Pareto stable but for which no pair of individuals want to exchange their houses.

8. *Unique Pareto stable allocation.* Characterize the societies that have a unique Pareto stable allocation.

9. *Change requires majority approval.* Consider a variant of Pareto stability in which an allocation a is dominated by another allocation b if and only if $b(i) \succ^i a(i)$ for a strict majority of individuals. Construct a society in which no allocation is stable in this sense.

10. *Preference for strong neighbors.* Suppose $N = \{1, 2, \ldots, 2k\}$ where $1 \vartriangleright 2 \vartriangleright \cdots \vartriangleright 2k$ and $H = \{1a, 1b, 2a, 2b, \ldots, ka, kb\}$. Every individual can force an individual who is weaker than him to exchange apartments. Every pair of apartments ma and mb for $m = 1, \ldots, k$ are adjacent. Every individual has a preference relation over the pairs (h, j), where h is the apartment he occupies and j is the occupant of the adjacent apartment.

   Characterize the equilibrium of the jungle with externalities that models this situation under the assumption that every individual prefers (h, j) to (h', j') if and only if j is stronger than j'. That is, he cares only about the strength of his neighbor, not about the apartment he occupies. Is an equilibrium of this jungle Pareto stable?

Notes

This chapter is based on Piccione and Rubinstein (2007) and Rubinstein (2012, Chapter 3).

9 A market

As in the previous chapter, a society consists of a set of individuals and a set of houses; each house can accommodate only one person and each person can occupy only one house. Different individuals may have different preferences over the houses, but everyone prefers to occupy any house than to be homeless.

In this chapter, unlike in the previous one, we assume that the ownership of a house is recognized and protected. Each house is initially owned by some individual. Houses can be exchanged only with the mutual consent of both owners; no individual can force another individual to give up his house.

The model allows us to introduce the central economic idea of prices as a means of guiding the individuals to a reallocation of the houses in which no group of individuals want to voluntarily exchange their houses.

9.1 Model

A society is defined as in the previous chapter. In particular, we assume that each individual cares only about the house that he occupies, not about the houses occupied by other individuals. Also, we continue to assume, for simplicity, that preferences are strict: no individual is indifferent between any two houses.

We study a model called a market, which differs from a jungle in that ownership replaces power and an initial pattern of ownership replaces the power relation. A market consists of a society and an allocation e, where $e(i)$ is the house initially owned by individual i.

> ### Definition 9.1: Market
>
> A *market* $\langle N, H, (\succeq^i)_{i \in N}, e \rangle$ consists of a society $\langle N, H, (\succeq^i)_{i \in N} \rangle$ and an allocation e for the society, called the *initial allocation*, which represents the initial ownership of the houses.

> ### Example 9.1
>
> Consider the market $\langle N, H, (\succeq^i)_{i \in N}, e \rangle$ in which $N = \{1, 2, 3, 4\}$, $H = \{A, B, C, D\}$, and the individuals' preferences and the initial allocation are given in the following table. Each column indicates the preference ordering of

Chapter of *Models in Microeconomic Theory* by Martin J. Osborne and Ariel Rubinstein. Version 2023.5.30 (h).
ⓒ 2023 Martin J. Osborne and Ariel Rubinstein CC BY-NC-ND 4.0.   https://doi.org/10.11647/OBP.0362.09

an individual, with the individual's favorite house at the top; the initial allocation is highlighted.

Individuals

1	2	3	4
B	A	A	A
C	B	C	D
D	C	D	B
A	D	B	C

Individual 1 initially owns house A, which is the one he least prefers and everyone else most prefers. Thus every other individual wants to exchange houses with individual 1. Individual 2 can offer him the most attractive exchange, because he initially owns house B, which is individual 1's favorite. Thus we might expect that the outcome includes an exchange between individuals 1 and 2.

Example 9.2

Consider the market in the following table.

Individuals

1	2	3	4
D	A	A	B
C	D	C	C
A	C	D	D
B	B	B	A

Individuals 1 and 3 are interested in exchanging their houses, and so are individuals 2 and 4. These two exchanges lead to the allocation indicated in red in the left-hand table below. After the exchanges, no further reallocation within any group is mutually desirable.

Individuals   Individuals

1	2	3	4		1	2	3	4
D	A	A	B		D	A	A	B
C	D	C	C		C	D	C	C
A	C	D	D		A	C	D	D
B	B	B	A		B	B	B	A

Another possible outcome of exchange is indicated in the right-hand table. This allocation may be achieved by an agreement between individuals 1, 2, and 4. Alternatively, it may be achieved by individual 1 first exchanging his house, A, with individual 2, which leads individual 1 to hold B, and then exchanging B with individual 4. After the first exchange, individual 1 holds a house, B, that he does not like; but he knows that he can subsequently exchange it with individual 4 for D, his favorite house.

Equilibrium of market

The central concept in this chapter is that of an equilibrium of a market. In an equilibrium, a number is attached to each house. We may interpret the number as the value or price of the house. Each individual can exchange the house he owns initially only for houses with lower or equal prices. An equilibrium satisfies two conditions. First, each individual chooses the house that is best for him among the houses with prices at most equal to the price of the house he initially owns. Second, the outcome is harmonious in the sense that the individuals' independent choices generate an allocation, in which each house is chosen by precisely one individual.

Definition 9.2: Equilibrium of market

An *equilibrium* of the market $\langle N, H, (\succeq^i)_{i \in N}, e \rangle$ is a pair (p, a) where

- p, a *price system*, is a function that attaches a number $p(h)$ (a *price*) to each house $h \in H$

- a is an assignment

such that

optimality of choices
  for every individual $i \in N$, the house $a(i)$ maximizes i's preference relation $\succeq^i$ over his *budget set* $\{h \in H : p(h) \leq p(e(i))\}$:

$$a(i) \succeq^i h \text{ for all } h \in H \text{ with } p(h) \leq p(e(i))$$

feasibility
  a is an allocation.

Notice the structure of the definition, which is common to many definitions of equilibrium. First we specify the nature of a candidate for equilibrium, which in this case is a pair consisting of a price system and an assignment. Then we specify the conditions for such a candidate to be an equilibrium.

Example 9.3

Consider Example 9.2. The allocation that results from the first pair of exchanges, $a = (C, D, A, B)$, is not an outcome of any market equilibrium, by the following argument. If there is a price system p such that (p, a) is an equilibrium then we need $p(A) = p(C)$: since C must be in the budget set of individual 1, we need $p(C) \leq p(A)$, and since A must be in the budget set of individual 3, we need $p(A) \leq p(C)$. Similarly, $p(B) = p(D)$. But if $p(A) \geq p(D)$ then individual 1 chooses house D, which is his favorite, not C, and if $p(A) < p(D) = p(B)$ then individual 2 chooses house A, not D. Thus for no price system p is (p, a) a market equilibrium.

The allocation that results from the second group of exchanges, $b = (D, A, C, B)$, is the outcome of a market equilibrium with a price system p satisfying $p(A) = p(B) = p(D) > p(C)$. (In fact, Proposition 9.5 implies that b is the only equilibrium allocation of this market.)

Example 9.4: Market with common preferences

Consider a market $\langle N, H, (\succsim^i)_{i \in N}, e \rangle$ in which all individuals have the same preference relation: $\succsim^i \, = \, \succsim$ for all $i \in N$. Let p be a price system that reflects $\succsim$ in the sense that for any houses h and h', $p(h) > p(h')$ if and only if $h \succ h'$. (In the terminology of Chapter 1, p is a utility function that represents $\succsim$.) Then the pair (p, e) is an equilibrium: the assignment e is an allocation; the budget set of each individual i consists of the house $e(i)$ and all houses that are inferior according to the common preferences $\succsim$, and thus his most preferred house in this set is $e(i)$. Notice that any equilibrium allocation a satisfies $a(i) \succsim e(i)$ for all i and thus $a = e$.

If every individual has a different favorite house, then there is an equilibrium that assigns the same price to every house.

Example 9.5: Market in which individuals have different favorite houses

Consider a market $\langle N, H, (\succsim^i)_{i \in N}, e \rangle$ in which each individual has a different favorite house. Then (p, a) is an equilibrium if p assigns the same price to all houses and for every individual i, $a(i)$ is i's favorite house. For this price system all budget sets are equal to H, so that each individual optimally chooses his favorite house; since no two individuals have the same favorite house, a is an allocation. In fact, in any equilibrium allocation a each individual gets his favorite house. Otherwise, let h^* be a most expensive house in $\{h \in H :$

h is not the favorite house of the individual i for whom $a(i)=h$}. Let i^* be the individual for whom $a(i^*) = h^*$. Then i^*'s favorite house is not more expensive than h^* and thus given that he can afford $a(i^*)$ he can afford his favorite house, so that $a(i^*)$ is not optimal for i^* in his budget set, a contradiction.

Comments

1. Note that the notion of equilibrium does not require an individual to be aware of the preferences of the other individuals. Each individual has to know only the price system to make his choice.

2. The notion of equilibrium is static. If a society is at an equilibrium, there is no reason for it to move away. But we do not specify a process by which a society that is not at an equilibrium might move to an equilibrium.

Any allocation can be transformed into any other allocation by implementing a set of trading cycles, each of which is a rotation of houses within a set of individuals.

For example, the move from (A, B, C, D) to (C, D, A, B) can be achieved by individual 1 exchanging his house with individual 3 and individual 2 exchanging his house with individual 4. In this case, each trading cycle consists of a single bilateral exchange; we denote these cycles by $(1, 3)$ and $(2, 4)$.

As another example, the move from (A, B, C, D) to (D, A, C, B) can be achieved by individuals 1, 2, and 4 agreeing on a rotation of the houses they initially own so that individual 1 get 4's house, 4 gets 2's house, and 2 gets 1's house, while individual 3 keeps his house. We denote these trading cycles by $(1, 4, 2)$ and (3). Note that the trading cycle $(1, 4, 2)$ can be achieved also by individual 1 first exchanging his house with individual 4, to yield the allocation (D, B, C, A), and then individual 4 exchanging his house (which is now A) with individual 2.

In general, a trading cycle is a sequence $(i_1, \ldots, i_k)$ of individuals, with the interpretation that (either by simultaneous rotations of houses or by a sequence of bilateral exchanges) individual i_j gets the house originally owned by i_{j+1} for $j = 1, \ldots, k-1$ and i_k gets the house owned initially by i_1. A trading cycle consisting of a single individual, for example (i_1), means that the individual keeps the house he owns.

Definition 9.3: Trading cycle and trading partition

A *trading cycle* in a market $\langle N, H, (\succsim^i)_{i \in N}, e \rangle$ is a finite sequence of distinct individuals (members of N). A *trading partition* is a set of trading cycles such that every individual belongs to exactly one of the cycles. A trading partition $\{(i^1_1,\dots,i^1_{k_1}),\dots,(i^m_1,\dots,i^m_{k_m})\}$ *transforms the allocation a to the allocation b for which for each* $j = 1,\dots,m$ *we have* $b(i^j_l) = a(i^j_{l+1})$ *for* $l = 1,\dots,k_j-1$ *and* $b(i^j_{k_j}) = a(i^j_1)$.

We now show that for any pair of allocations, a unique trading partition transforms one allocation to the other.

Lemma 9.1: Uniqueness of transforming trading partition

For any allocations a and b in a market, a unique trading partition transforms a to b.

Proof

We construct the trading partition T inductively. Start with an arbitrary individual i_1. If $b(i_1) = a(i_1)$, add the (degenerate) trading cycle (i_1) to T. Otherwise, let i_2 be the individual for whom $a(i_2) = b(i_1)$. If $b(i_2) = a(i_1)$, add the trading cycle (i_1, i_2) to T. Otherwise let i_3 be the individual for whom $a(i_3) = b(i_2)$, and continue in same way until an individual i_k is reached for whom $b(i_k) = a(i_1)$; the number of individuals is finite, so such an individual exists. At this point, add the trading cycle $(i_1, i_2, \dots, i_k)$ to T.

If any individuals remain, select one of them arbitrarily and repeat the construction. Continue until every individual is a member of a trading cycle in T. By construction, T transforms a to b and is a trading partition because no individual appears in more than one of the trading cycles it contains. Given that for any individual i, the individual j for whom $b(j) = a(i)$ is unique, T is the only trading partition that transforms a to b.

We now show that for any equilibrium allocation a the prices of all houses initially owned by the members of each trading cycle in the trading partition that transforms e to a are the same.

Proposition 9.1: Transforming initial allocation to equilibrium by trade

Let (p, a) be an equilibrium of the market $\langle N, H, (\succsim^i)_{i \in N}, e\rangle$. The prices of all houses initially owned by the members of each trading cycle in the trading partition that transforms e to a are the same.

Proof

Let $(i_1, \dots, i_k)$ be a trading cycle in the trading partition that transforms e to a (described in the proof of Lemma 9.1). Then $a(i_l) = e(i_{l+1})$ for

$l = 1, \ldots, k-1$ and $a(i_k) = e(i_1)$. Thus for $l = 1, \ldots, k-1$ we need $e(i_{l+1})$ to be in i_l's budget set, so that $p(e(i_l)) \geq p(e(i_{l+1}))$, and we need $e(i_1)$ to be in i_k's budget set, so that $p(e(i_k)) \geq p(e(i_1))$. Hence $p(e(i_1)) \geq p(e(i_2)) \geq \cdots \geq p(e(i_k)) \geq p(e(i_1))$, so that all these prices are equal.

9.2 Existence and construction of a market equilibrium

We now show that every market has an equilibrium. In fact, we show how to construct an equilibrium. The construction involves a sequence of trading cycles. We start by identifying a trading cycle that gives every individual in the cycle his favorite house. We call such a cycle a top trading cycle.

Definition 9.4: Top trading cycle

The trading cycle $(i_1, \ldots, i_k)$ in the market $\langle N, H, (\succsim^i)_{i \in N}, e \rangle$ is a *top trading cycle* if for $l = 1, \ldots, k$ individual i_l's favorite house is initially owned by individual i_{l+1}, where $i_{k+1} = i_1$. That is, $e(i_{l+1}) \succsim^{i_l} h$ for $l = 1, \ldots, k$ and all $h \in H$.

To find a top trading cycle, first choose an arbitrary individual, say i_1. If he initially owns his favorite house, then (i_1) is a (degenerate) top trading cycle. Otherwise, let i_2 be the initial owner of i_1's favorite house. If i_2 initially owns his favorite house, then (i_2) is a top trading cycle; if i_1 initially owns this house then (i_1, i_2) is a top trading cycle; otherwise let i_3 be the owner. Continue in the same way, at each step k checking whether the owner of k's favorite house is a member of the sequence $(i_1, \ldots, i_k)$, say i_l, in which case $(i_l, \ldots, i_k)$ is a top trading cycle, and otherwise adding the owner to the list as i_{k+1}. The number of individuals is finite, so eventually the procedure identifies a top trading cycle. The procedure is illustrated in the following diagram, in which an arrow from i to j means that j is the owner of i's favorite house, and then defined more formally.

$$i_1 \to i_2 \to \cdots \to i_l \to i_{l+1} \to \cdots \to i_k$$

Procedure 9.1: Procedure for generating a top trading cycle

For a market $\langle N, H, (\succsim^i)_{i \in N}, e \rangle$, the following inductive procedure generates a top trading cycle.

Initialization

Choose an arbitrary individual $i_1 \in N$, and define the sequence (i_1).

Inductive step

Let $(i_1, \ldots, i_k)$ be the sequence of individuals in N that is obtained in step k, so that $e(i_{l+1})$ is i_l's favorite house for $l = 1, \ldots, k-1$.

- If the owner of i_k's favorite house is a member of the sequence, say i_l, stop; the sequence $(i_l, \ldots, i_k)$ is a top trading cycle.

- Otherwise, add the owner of i_k's favorite house to the sequence as i_{k+1}, to generate the sequence $(i_1, \ldots, i_k, i_{k+1})$, so that $e(i_{l+1})$ is i_l's favorite house for $l = 1, \ldots, k$, and continue.

Notice that the procedure is initialized with an arbitrary individual. The individual chosen may affect the top trading cycle that is generated. Consider, for example, a market in which individual i initially owns his favorite house, individual j owns the favorite house of individual k, and individual k owns the favorite house of individual j. Then the procedure generates the (degenerate) cycle (i) if we initially select individual i and the cycle (j, k) if we initially select individual j.

We now specify an iterative procedure that generates an equilibrium of a market. The procedure first finds a top trading cycle in the market, assigns the same arbitrary price, say p_1, to all the houses initially owned by individuals in the cycle, and assigns to each individual in the cycle his favorite house (that is, the house owned by the next individual in the cycle). It then removes all these individuals (and the houses they initially own) from the market, and finds a top trading cycle in the smaller market. It assigns an arbitrary price p_2 with $p_2 < p_1$ to the houses initially owned by the individuals in this cycle and assigns to each individual in the cycle his favorite house among those available in the smaller market. It then removes the individuals in the cycle from the smaller market, to produce an even smaller market. The procedure continues in the same way until no individuals remain.

Procedure 9.2: Top trading procedure

For a market $\langle N, H, (\succeq^i)_{i \in N}, e \rangle$, the *top trading procedure* is defined as follows. First, for any set $N' \subseteq N$, define $M(N')$ be the market in which the set of individuals is N', the set H' consists of the houses owned initially by members of N', the preference relation of each member of N' is his original preference relation restricted to H', and the initial allocation assigns to each member of N' the house he owns in the original market.

Initialization

Start with the set of individuals $N_1 = N$, and any number $p_0 > 0$.

Inductive step

For a given set of individuals $N_s \subseteq N$, find a top trading cycle in the market $M(N_s)$; denote by I_s the set of individuals in the cycle.

Assign a price p_s with $0 < p_s < p_{s-1}$ to all the houses initially owned by the individuals in I_s, and assign to each member of I_s his favorite house in $M(N_s)$ (the house initially owned by the individual who follows him in the top trading cycle).

Let $N_{s+1} = N_s \setminus I_s$. If $N_{s+1} = \emptyset$, stop; otherwise continue with N_{s+1}.

This procedure generates a price system and an assignment.

As we mentioned previously, a market may contain more than one top trading cycle, so different operations of the procedure may lead to different outcomes. We now show that every outcome of the procedure is an equilibrium of the market.

Proposition 9.2: Existence of a market equilibrium

Every market has an equilibrium; any pair consisting of a price system and an assignment generated by the top trading procedure is an equilibrium.

Proof

The assignment and price system generated by the top trading procedure is an equilibrium because (1) every house is assigned only once, so that the assignment is an allocation, and (2) every individual is assigned his favorite house among all houses that are not more expensive than the house he owns initially.

Example 9.6

For the market in Example 9.1, the top trading procedure operates as follows. The only top trading cycle in the entire market is $(1,2)$. We assign a price p_1 to the houses initially owned by individuals 1 and 2, A and B, allocate to each of these individuals his favorite house ($a(1) = B$ and $a(2) = A$), and remove these individuals from the market.

The smaller market has two top trading cycles, (3) and (4). If we choose (3), then we assign a price $p_2 < p_1$ to the house individual 3 initially owns, C, allocate this house to him, and remove him from the market.

Now only individual 4 remains, and in this market the only top trading cycle is (4). So we assign a price $p_3 < p_2$ to the house individual 4 initially owns, D, and assign this house to him.

Thus the pair consisting of the allocation (B, A, C, D) and price system p with $p(D) < p(C) < p(A) = p(B)$ is an equilibrium of the market.

If, at the second stage, we select individual 4 instead of individual 3, we generate the same allocation (B, A, C, D), but a price system p with $p(C) < p(D) < p(A) = p(B)$, so such a pair is also an equilibrium of the market.

Example 9.7

For the market in Example 9.2, the top trading procedure operates as follows. The only top trading cycle of the market is $(1, 4, 2)$. We assign some price p_1 to the houses initially owned by individuals 1, 2, and 4, allocate to each of these individuals his favorite house ($a(1) = D$, $a(2) = A$, and $a(4) = B$), and remove the individuals from the market.

The only individual remaining in the market is 3, and thus the only top trading cycle in the smaller market is (3). We assign a price $p_2 < p_1$ to the house individual 3 initially owns, C, and assign this house to him.

Thus the pair consisting of the allocation (D, A, B, C) and price system p with $p(C) < p(A) = p(B) = p(D)$ is an equilibrium of the market, as we saw in Example 9.2.

Proposition 9.2 does not assert that the equilibrium is unique, and indeed the ranking of prices may differ between equilibria, as Example 9.6 shows. However, in both examples the procedure finds only one equilibrium *allocation*, and this property is general: every market has a unique equilibrium allocation. We defer this result, Proposition 9.5, to a later section because its proof is somewhat more complex than the other proofs in this chapter.

Say that i is richer than j if $p(e(i)) > p(e(j))$, so that i can afford any house that j can afford and also at least one house that j cannot afford. What makes an individual in a market richer than other individuals? One factor that seems intuitively important in making i rich is the number of individuals whose favorite house is the house initially owned by i. The more individuals who like i's house, the more likely i is to be a member of a top trading cycle that appears early in the procedure in the proof of Proposition 9.2, so that a high price is attached to his house. But the ranking of an individual's house by the other individuals is not the only factor in determining his wealth. The house owned initially by i may be the favorite house of many individuals, but those individuals may initially own houses that no one likes. In this case, although many individuals desire i's house,

i will not necessarily be relatively rich. Another contributor to a high market price for i's house is the attractiveness of the houses owned by the individuals who like i's house. Overall, it is the coordination of desires that makes a person rich in this model. For example, if for two individuals i and j, i's favorite house is the one initially owned by j, and vice versa, and these houses are at the bottom of the rankings of all other individuals, the equilibrium price of the two houses could be higher than the equilibrium price of any other house.

9.3   Equilibrium and Pareto stability

Proposition 8.4, in the previous chapter, shows the Pareto stability of any equilibrium of a jungle without externalities (in which each individual cares only about the house he occupies and not about the house anyone else occupies). We now show an analogous result for a market. That is, if each individual cares only about the house he occupies, then for any equilibrium allocation in a market, no other allocation is at least as good for every individual and preferred by at least one individual.

Proposition 9.3: Pareto stability of equilibrium allocation

For any market, every equilibrium allocation is Pareto stable.

Proof

Let (p, a) be an equilibrium of the market $\langle N, H, (\succeq^i)_{i \in N}, e \rangle$. If a is not Pareto stable then for some allocation b we have $b(i) \succeq^i a(i)$ for every $i \in N$ and $b(i) \succ^i a(i)$ for some $i \in N$. For any i for which $b(i) \succ^i a(i)$ we have $p(b(i)) > p(a(i))$, since otherwise $p(b(i)) \leq p(a(i)) = p(e(i))$ and thus $a(i)$ is not optimal for i in the set $\{h \in H : p(h) \leq p(e(i))\}$. For any other i, $b(i) = a(i)$ (because each preference relation is strict) and thus $p(b(i)) = p(a(i))$. Hence $\sum_{i \in N} p(b(i)) > \sum_{i \in N} p(a(i))$. But a and b are both allocations, so each side of this inequality is equal to $\sum_{i \in N} p(e(i))$. This contradiction implies that no such allocation b exists, and hence a is Pareto stable.

The name conventionally given to this result and similar results for other models of economies is the "first fundamental theorem of welfare economics". However, the result establishes only that an equilibrium is Pareto stable, a concept unrelated to welfare. The concept of a market specifies only the individuals' ordinal preferences, not any measure of their welfare in the everyday sense of the word. The result says that for any equilibrium allocation, no other allocation exists for which some individual is better off and no individual is worse off.

But allocations may exist in which the vast majority of individuals, and even all individuals but one, are better off. For these reasons, we refrain from using the conventional label for the result.

An implication of Proposition 9.3 is that if the initial allocation is not Pareto stable, every equilibrium involves trade: at least two individuals trade their houses. We now show conversely that if the initial allocation is Pareto stable then no trade occurs in equilibrium.

Proposition 9.4: No trade from a Pareto stable allocation

Let $\langle N, H, (\succeq^i)_{i \in N}, e \rangle$ be a market. If e is Pareto stable then for every equilibrium (p, a) of the market we have $a = e$.

Proof

Let (p, a) be an equilibrium of the market. Since $e(i)$ is in the budget set of individual i given the price system p, $a(i) \succeq^i e(i)$ for all $i \in N$. If $a \neq e$ then $a(i) \succ^i e(i)$ for some individual i, which means that e is not Pareto stable.

A conclusion from Propositions 9.3 and 9.4 is that if a market starts operating at date 1 and results in an equilibrium allocation, and then is opened again at date 2 with initial endowments equal to the equilibrium allocation at the end of date 1, then no trade occurs in the equilibrium of the market at date 2.

Proposition 9.4 has an interpretation parallel to the one we give to Proposition 8.5 for a jungle. We interpret that result to mean that an authority in the society that controls the power relation and is aware of the individuals' preferences can obtain any Pareto stable allocation as an equilibrium by choosing the power relation appropriately. Proposition 9.4 may be given a similar interpretation. Suppose that an authority in the society can allocate initial property rights but cannot prevent individuals from trading. If trade is conducted according to the equilibrium concept we have defined, the authority can induce any Pareto stable allocation by assigning the initial rights appropriately. In this way, ownership in a market plays a role parallel to power in a jungle.

Proposition 9.4 is often called the "second fundamental theorem of welfare economics". We refrain from using this name because as for Proposition 9.3, we regard the word "welfare" as inappropriate in the context of the result.

9.4   Uniqueness of market equilibrium

The uniqueness of equilibrium in an economic model is appealing because it means that the model narrows down the outcome as much as possible. It also simplifies an analysis of the effect of a change in a parameter of the model.

The ranking of the prices in an equilibrium of a market is not necessarily unique, as Example 9.6 shows. But we now show that every market has a unique equilibrium *allocation*. This result depends on our assumption that no individual is indifferent between any two houses (see Problem 7).

Proposition 9.5: Uniqueness of equilibrium

Every market has a unique equilibrium allocation.

Proof

Assume, contrary to the claim, that the market $\langle N, H, (\succsim^i)_{i \in N}, e \rangle$ has equilibria (p, a) and (q, b) with $a \neq b$. Let i_1 be an individual whose initial house $e(i_1)$ has the highest price according to p. Let $(i_1, i_2, \ldots, i_{k^*})$ be a trading cycle in the trading partition that transforms e into a. By Proposition 9.1, $p(e(i))$ is the same for all $i \in I = \{i_1, i_2, \ldots, i_{k^*}\}$, so that every house is in the budget set of every $i \in I$, and hence $a(i)$ is i's favorite house in H for every $i \in I$.

Now consider the equilibrium (q, b). Without loss of generality, $e(i_1)$ is the most expensive house according to q among the houses in $\{e(i) : i \in I\}$. That is, $q(e(i_1)) \geq q(e(i))$ for all $i \in I$. Since $e(i_2) = a(i_1)$ is i_1's favorite house in H, in the equilibrium (q, b) individual i_1 chooses $e(i_2)$. That is, $b(i_1) = e(i_2)$. Therefore, by Proposition 9.1, $q(e(i_2)) = q(e(i_1))$, so that i_2 also owns a most expensive house according to q among the houses in $\{e(i) : i \in I\}$. Continue in this way to conclude that $(i_1, i_2, \ldots, i_k)$ is also a trading cycle in the trading partition that transforms e to b.

Now delete from the set of individuals and the set of houses the members of this trading cycle and their initial houses. We are left with a smaller market and two equilibria of this market. The reason is that if, before the deletion, every individual chose the best house that he could afford given the equilibrium prices, the deletion of the houses that he did not choose does not affect the optimality of his choice. Therefore we can continue with the restricted market and choose again a trading cycle with the highest price according to p.

Continuing in this way, we conclude that the trading partition that transforms e into a is the same as the one that transforms e into b, so that $a = b$.

More formally, we can prove the result by induction on the number of individuals. A market with one individual of course has a unique equilibrium allocation. If every market with not more than $n - 1$ individuals has a unique equilibrium allocation, then the argument we have made shows that a market with n individuals also has a unique equilibrium allocation.

Problems

1. *Trade for an allocation that is not Pareto stable.* Show that if an allocation is not Pareto stable then some (nonempty) group of individuals can exchange the houses they own among themselves in such a way that all members of the group are better off.

2. *Examples of markets.*

   a. Consider a market in which some individual initially owns his favorite house. Show that in any equilibrium this individual is allocated this house.

   b. What can you say about the equilibrium allocation in a market equilibrium in which every house has a different price?

   c. Show that in an equilibrium of any market consistent with the following table, individual 4 is allocated his favorite house.

Individual	1	2	3	4
Initial allocation	D	C	B	A
Favorite house	A	A	D	?

3. *Effect of removing an individual.* Give an example of a market for which removing one of the individuals, together with the house he initially owns, makes one of the remaining individuals better off and another of the remaining individuals worse off.

4. *Effect of changes in one individual's preferences.*

   a. Let M_1 be a market and let (p, a) be an equilibrium of M_1. Assume that M_2 differs from M_1 only in that $a(1)$ moves up in individual 1's preferences. What can you say about the equilibrium allocations in the two markets?

   b. (More difficult.) In the market M_1, individual 1 initially owns house A. The market M_2 differs from M_1 only in that in M_2 the ranking of A in individual 2's preferences is higher than it is in M_1. Show that individual 1 is not worse off, and may be better off, in the equilibrium of M_2 than in the equilibrium of M_1.

5. *Manipulation.* Explain why no individual in a market is better off behaving as if his preferences are different from his actual preferences. That is, if the markets M and M' differ only in the preferences of individual i, then the equilibrium allocation in M' is no better according to i's preferences in M than the equilibrium allocation in M.

6. *The core.* Like Pareto stability, the core is a notion of stability. An allocation a is in the core of a market if no set of individuals can leave the market with their initial houses and reallocate them among themselves (in any way, not necessarily consistent with equilibrium) so that all of them are better off than in a. Show that the equilibrium of any market is in the core.

7. *Market with indifferences.* Some of the results in this chapter rely on the assumption that the individuals' preference relations do not have indifferences. Construct a market in which individuals have preferences with indifferences, some equilibrium is not Pareto stable, and there is more than one equilibrium allocation.

Notes

The model presented in this chapter is due to Shapley and Scarf (1974), who attribute the proof for the existence of a market equilibrium to David Gale. The presentation here draws upon Rubinstein (2012, Chapter 3).

10 An exchange economy

In this chapter we study a market in which the goods, unlike the houses in the previous two chapters, can be consumed in any quantity: they are divisible. As in the previous chapter, the ownership of goods is recognized and protected. Each individual initially owns a bundle of goods. We look for a distribution of the goods among the individuals and a price system with the property that for each good the total amount the individuals want to purchase is equal to the total amount other individuals want to sell: demand and supply are equal.

10.1 Model

In a market there are two goods, called 1 and 2. Each good can be consumed in any (nonnegative) quantity. As in Chapter 4, a bundle is a pair (x_1, x_2), where x_k, the quantity of good k for $k = 1, 2$, is a nonnegative number, so that the set of all possible bundles is $\mathbb{R}_+^2$. The set of individuals in the market is denoted N. Each individual $i \in N$ initially owns the bundle $e(i) = (e_1(i), e_2(i))$. We take these initial bundles as given; we do not ask where they come from. We assume that the total amount of each good initially owned by all individuals is positive (not zero).

Each individual cares about the bundle he owns after trading. Sometimes we say he "consumes" this bundle. As in the previous two chapters, we assume that each individual has no interest, selfish or altruistic, in the bundles chosen by other individuals. Thus the desires of each individual i are captured by a preference relation over the set $\mathbb{R}_+^2$ of possible bundles, which we assume is monotone and continuous.

Collecting these elements, we define an exchange economy as follows.

Definition 10.1: Exchange economy

An *exchange economy* $\langle N, (\succeq^i)_{i \in N}, e \rangle$ consists of

individuals
  a finite set N

preferences
  for each individual $i \in N$, a monotone and continuous preference relation $\succeq^i$ over $\mathbb{R}_+^2$

Chapter of *Models in Microeconomic Theory* by Martin J. Osborne and Ariel Rubinstein. Version 2023.5.30 (h).
© 2023 Martin J. Osborne and Ariel Rubinstein CC BY-NC-ND 4.0.   https://doi.org/10.11647/OBP.0362.10

---

initial allocation

a function e that assigns to each individual $i \in N$ a bundle $e(i) \in \mathbb{R}^2_+$, the bundle that i initially owns, with $\sum_{i \in N} e_k(i) > 0$ for $k = 1, 2$.

Comments

1. The model of an exchange economy is closely related to that of a market discussed in the previous chapter. In the model of a market, each house is an indivisible good that can be consumed by only a single individual. In the model of an exchange economy, each good is divisible, and the total amount of it can be divided arbitrarily among the individuals. The analogue of the set H in the previous chapter is the set $\mathbb{R}^2_+$ here.

2. Many goods are in fact not divisible. For example, you can own four or six chairs, but not 5.3. We assume divisibility because it simplifies the analysis without, apparently, significantly affecting the conclusions.

3. Like the houses in the previous chapters, any given amount of each good in our model can be consumed by only one individual: the total amount of the good available has to be divided up among the individuals. This formulation excludes from consideration goods like information that can be simultaneously consumed by many individuals.

10.1.1 Prices and budget sets

A price system is a pair of nonnegative numbers $p = (p_1, p_2)$ different from $(0,0)$. Given a price system p, the value of the bundle $x = (x_1, x_2)$ is $p_1 x_1 + p_2 x_2$, which we write also as px (the inner product of the vectors p and x). By exchanging some or all of his initial bundle $e(i)$ with other individuals, i can obtain any bundle x whose value px does not exceed $pe(i)$, the value of $e(i)$; that is, he can obtain any bundle x for which $px \leq pe(i)$. As before we refer to the set of such bundles as the budget set of individual i and denote it $B(p, e(i))$. Given our assumption that each individual's preference relation is monotone, a bundle is optimal in i's budget set if and only if it is optimal on the budget line $\{x \in \mathbb{R}^2_+ : px = pe(i)\}$.

Definition 10.2: Price system and budget set

A *price system* is a pair of nonnegative numbers different from $(0,0)$. The *value of the bundle $x = (x_1, x_2)$ according to the price system $p = (p_1, p_2)$ is*

$px = p_1x_1 + p_2x_2$, and for the exchange economy $\langle N, (\succsim^i)_{i \in N}, e \rangle$, the *budget set of individual* $i \in N$ given the price system p is

$$B(p, e(i)) = \{x \in \mathbb{R}_+^2 : px \leq pe(i)\}.$$

We have in mind two interpretations of a price system. The first and most literal is that the prices are quoted in a monetary unit. Each individual can sell any amounts of the goods in his initial bundle and use the monetary proceeds to buy amounts of other goods. If, for example, he sells y_1 units of good 1 then he obtains the amount of money p_1y_1, which he can use to buy the amount z_2 of good 2 for which $p_1y_1 = p_2z_2$. The second interpretation is that the prices represent the ratio at which the goods may be exchanged. Specifically, the price system (p_1, p_2) means that one unit of good 1 may be exchanged for p_1/p_2 units of good 2.

Note that in both interpretations a price system p is equivalent to any price system of the form $\lambda p = (\lambda p_1, \lambda p_2)$ for $\lambda > 0$ (that is, a price system in which all prices are multiplied by a positive number), because $B(\lambda p, e(i)) = B(p, e(i))$ for all values of p and $e(i)$.

10.1.2 Allocations

The total amount of each good k available in the economy is $\sum_{i \in N} e_k(i)$. An *allocation* is a distribution of these total amounts among the individuals.

Definition 10.3: Assignment and allocation

An *assignment* in an exchange economy $\langle N, (\succsim^i)_{i \in N}, e \rangle$ is a function from the set N of individuals to the set $\mathbb{R}_+^2$ of possible bundles of goods. An *allocation* is an assignment a for which the sum of the assigned bundles is the sum of the initial bundles:

$$\sum_{i \in N} a(i) = \sum_{i \in N} e(i).$$

10.2 Competitive equilibrium

The central concept in this chapter is competitive equilibrium. A competitive equilibrium consists of a price system and an assignment such that each individual's bundle in the assignment is optimal for him given the price system and his initial endowment, and the assignment is an allocation. If this condition is not satisfied then either at least one individual does not choose his optimal bundle or, for at least one of the goods, the total amount that the individuals want to purchase is different from the total amount available.

Definition 10.4: Competitive equilibrium of exchange economy

A *competitive equilibrium* of the exchange economy $\langle N, (\succsim^i)_{i \in N}, e \rangle$ is a pair (p, a) in which

- $p = (p_1, p_2)$ is a price system

- a is an assignment

such that

optimality of choices
  for every individual $i \in N$ the bundle $a(i)$ is optimal according to $\succsim^i$ in the budget set $B(p, e(i))$ (that is, $B(p, e(i))$ contains no bundle b for which $b \succ^i a(i)$)

feasibility
  a is an allocation.

  An allocation a is a *competitive equilibrium allocation* of the exchange economy $\langle N, (\succsim^i)_{i \in N}, e \rangle$ if for some price system p, (p, a) is a competitive equilibrium of $\langle N, (\succsim^i)_{i \in N}, e \rangle$.

Note that if (p, a) is a competitive equilibrium of $\langle N, (\succsim^i)_{i \in N}, e \rangle$ then so is $(\lambda p, a)$ for any $\lambda > 0$, because $B(\lambda p, e(i)) = B(p, e(i))$ for all $i \in N$.

In a competitive equilibrium all individuals face the same price system and each individual chooses an optimal bundle from a budget set defined by this price system, which is not affected by the individual's choice. This assumption seems reasonable when the market contains a large number of individuals, none of whom initially owns a large fraction of the total amount of any good. It is less reasonable when the number of individuals is small, in which case some individuals' actions may significantly affect the prices. Note, however, that the concept of competitive equilibrium is well-defined regardless of the number of individuals and the distribution of their initial bundles. In particular, it is well-defined even for an economy with only one individual; only the reasonableness of the concept is questionable in this case.

Figure 10.1 illustrates a competitive equilibrium for an exchange economy with two individuals. In this figure, the orange vectors are equal in length and opposite in direction, so that the sum of the individuals' optimal bundles is equal to the sum of their initial bundles.

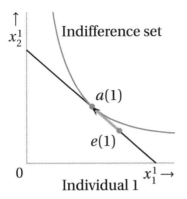
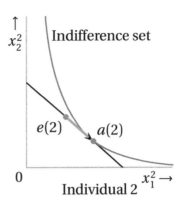

Figure 10.1 A competitive equilibrium in an exchange economy with two individuals. The ratio p_1/p_2 of the prices is the (common) slope of the (black) budget frontiers, and $a(1)$ and $a(2)$ are the bundles the individuals optimally choose. The prices are consistent with a competitive equilibrium because the orange vectors exactly cancel each other out: $e(1) - a(1) = -(e(2) - a(2))$, so that $a(1) + a(2) = e(1) + e(2)$.

Example 10.1: Competitive equilibrium with substitutable goods

Consider an exchange economy $\langle N, (\succeq^i)_{i \in N}, e \rangle$ for which $N = \{1, 2\}$, $e(1) = (\alpha, 0)$, and $e(2) = (0, \beta)$ (with $\alpha > 0$ and $\beta > 0$), so that each good is initially owned exclusively by one individual, and each individual's preference relation $\succeq^i$ is represented by the utility function $x_1 + x_2$ (Example 4.1 with $v_1/v_2 = 1$).

In this economy, (p, a) with $p = (1, 1)$ and $a = e$ is a competitive equilibrium. In this equilibrium, the budget lines of individuals 1 and 2 are $\{(x_1, x_2) \in \mathbb{R}_+^2 : x_1 + x_2 = \alpha\}$ and $\{(x_1, x_2) \in \mathbb{R}_+^2 : x_1 + x_2 = \beta\}$, so that each individual i is indifferent between all bundles on his budget line and the bundle $e(i)$, in particular, is optimal for him (see Example 5.6). Note that the concept of competitive equilibrium requires only that the bundle assigned to each individual is optimal for the individual, not that it is the *only* bundle optimal for him.

More generally, every pair (p, a) where $p = (1, 1)$, $a(1) = (\alpha - \varepsilon, \varepsilon)$, and $a(2) = (\varepsilon, \beta - \varepsilon)$, with $0 \le \varepsilon \le \min\{\alpha, \beta\}$, is a competitive equilibrium. In such an equilibrium each individual exchanges ε units of the good he initially owns for ε units of the other good. Neither individual can do better because given the price system, for every bundle an individual can achieve by exchange, the sum of the amounts of the two goods is the same.

This economy has no equilibrium in which the prices of the goods are not equal. For any such price system, each individual's unique optimal bundle contains none of the more expensive good and thus is not consistent with a competitive equilibrium.

Example 10.2: Competitive equilibrium with complementary goods

Consider an exchange economy $\langle N, (\succsim^i)_{i \in N}, e \rangle$ for which $N = \{1, 2\}$, $e(1) = (\alpha, 0)$, and $e(2) = (0, \beta)$, as in the previous example, but each individual's preference relation is represented by the utility function $\min\{x_1, x_2\}$ (Example 4.4).

For any price system p in which $p_1 > 0$ and $p_2 > 0$, the bundles optimally chosen by the individuals are

$$x^1(p) = \left(\frac{\alpha p_1}{p_1 + p_2}, \frac{\alpha p_1}{p_1 + p_2} \right) \quad \text{and} \quad x^2(p) = \left(\frac{\beta p_2}{p_1 + p_2}, \frac{\beta p_2}{p_1 + p_2} \right)$$

(see Example 5.5). For this pair of bundles to be an allocation we need

$$\frac{\alpha p_1}{p_1 + p_2} + \frac{\beta p_2}{p_1 + p_2} = \alpha \quad \text{and} \quad \frac{\alpha p_1}{p_1 + p_2} + \frac{\beta p_2}{p_1 + p_2} = \beta.$$

The left-hand sides of these equations are the same, so that if $\alpha = \beta$ then for every price system p with $p_1 > 0$ and $p_2 > 0$ the economy has a competitive equilibrium (p, a) with $a(1) = x^1(p)$ and $a(2) = x^2(p)$.

If $\alpha \neq \beta$ then no equilibrium in which both prices are positive exists, but the economy has an equilibrium in which one of the prices is zero. Suppose that $\alpha > \beta$. Then the economy has an equilibrium in which the price system is $(0, 1)$ (good 1, of which there is a surplus, has no value). Given that the price of good 1 is zero, individual 2 can consume any quantity of good 1, so that any bundle (x_1^2, β) with $x_1^2 \geq \beta$ is optimal for him. Individual 1, who has only good 1, is indifferent between all bundles $(x_1^1, 0)$ on his budget line. For a competitive equilibrium we need $x_1^1 + x_1^2 = \alpha$, so $((0, 1), a)$ is a competitive equilibrium if and only if $a(1) = (x_1^1, 0)$ and $a(2) = (\alpha - x_1^1, \beta)$, with $x_1^1 \leq \alpha - \beta$. In particular, $((0, 1), a)$ with $a(1) = (\alpha - \beta, 0)$ and $a(2) = (\beta, \beta)$ is a competitive equilibrium.

This example shows, incidentally, that an individual who destroys some of his initial bundle may *improve* the bundle he consumes in a competitive equilibrium. If $\alpha > \beta$, then the bundle individual 1 consumes in a competitive equilibrium is $(x_1^1, 0)$ where $x_1^1 \leq \alpha - \beta$. If he destroys some of his initial holding of good 1, reducing the amount to γ with $0 < \gamma < \beta$, then the competitive equilibrium price system changes from $(0, 1)$ to $(1, 0)$ and the equilibrium allocations a have $a(1) = (\gamma, \beta - x_2^2)$ and $a(2) = (0, x_2^2)$ for $0 \leq x_2^2 \leq \beta - \gamma$. Individual 1 prefers all of these allocations to the ones in the original equilibrium. The fact that an individual may benefit from destroying some of the goods he initially owns does not depend on an equilibrium price being zero; other examples show that the phenomenon may occur when both equilibrium prices are positive.

The definition of a competitive equilibrium requires that the sum of the bundles optimal for the individuals, given the prices, is equal to the sum of the initial bundles (demand is equal to supply for all goods). The next result says that given any price system and any assignment that consists of optimal bundles (given the price system), if for one good the sum of the assigned quantities is equal to the sum of the individuals' initial holdings, then the same is true also for the other good. This result is useful when calculating competitive equilibria, because it means that if we find a price system for which demand and supply are equal for one good then we know that they are equal for the other good, so that the price system is consistent with competitive equilibrium.

Proposition 10.1: Property of assignment of bundles on budget lines

Consider an exchange economy $\langle N, (\succsim^i)_{i \in N}, e \rangle$. Let p be a price system with $p_1 > 0$ and $p_2 > 0$. Consider an assignment a with $pa(i) = pe(i)$ for all $i \in N$. (That is, $a(i)$ is on i's budget line for each i.) If the sum of the quantities of one good in the bundles in the assignment a is equal to the sum of the quantities of the good in the initial bundles then this equality holds also for the other good. That is,

$$\sum_{i \in N} a_1(i) = \sum_{i \in N} e_1(i) \quad \Leftrightarrow \quad \sum_{i \in N} a_2(i) = \sum_{i \in N} e_2(i).$$

Proof

The fact that $pa(i) = pe(i)$ for each $i \in N$ means that $p_1 a_1(i) + p_2 a_2(i) = p_1 e_1(i) + p_2 e_2(i)$ for each $i \in N$, and hence

$$\sum_{i \in N} [p_1 a_1(i) + p_2 a_2(i)] = \sum_{i \in N} [p_1 e_1(i) + p_2 e_2(i)].$$

Thus

$$p_1 \left(\sum_{i \in N} a_1(i) - \sum_{i \in N} e_1(i) \right) = p_2 \left(\sum_{i \in N} e_2(i) - \sum_{i \in N} a_2(i) \right),$$

so that given $p_1 > 0$ and $p_2 > 0$,

$$\sum_{i \in N} a_2(i) - \sum_{i \in N} e_2(i) = 0 \quad \Leftrightarrow \quad \sum_{i \in N} e_1(i) - \sum_{i \in N} a_1(i) = 0.$$

Example 10.3

Consider an exchange economy $\langle N,(\succsim^i)_{i\in N}, e\rangle$ in which, as in the previous two examples, $N = \{1,2\}$, $e(1) = (\alpha, 0)$, and $e(2) = (0, \beta)$. Assume now that each individual's preference relation is represented by the utility function $x_1 x_2$. Recall that the optimal bundle for such an individual has the property that the amount the individual spends on each good is the same (see Example 5.7). Now, if $((p_1, 1), a)$ is a competitive equilibrium with $p_1 > 0$, then individual 1 spends $p_1\alpha/2$ on each good and thus $a(1) = (\alpha/2, p_1\alpha/2)$. Similarly $a(2) = (\beta/(2p_1), \beta/2)$. By Proposition 10.1, $((p_1, 1), a)$ is a competitive equilibrium if and only if $\alpha/2 + \beta/(2p_1) = \alpha$. The economy has no equilibrium in which a price is zero, so (p, a) with $p = (\beta/\alpha, 1)$ and $a(1) = a(2) = (\alpha/2, \beta/2)$ is the only equilibrium.

10.3   Existence of a competitive equilibrium

A result that gives precise conditions under which an exchange economy has a competitive equilibrium requires mathematical tools beyond the level of this book. However, we can establish the following result, for the case in which each individual has a continuous demand function. When each individual is rational and has strictly convex and continuous preferences, his optimal choice as a function of the price system results in such a demand function. The result states that if every individual wants to obtain more of a good than he initially owns when its price is low enough and sell some of his initial holding when its price is high enough, then a competitive equilibrium exists.

Proposition 10.2: Existence of competitive equilibrium

Let $\langle N,(\succsim^i)_{i\in N}, e\rangle$ be an exchange economy. For each $i \in N$ and every price system p with $p_1 > 0$ and $p_2 > 0$, let $x^i(p)$ be a bundle that maximizes $\succsim^i$ in the budget set $B(p, e(i))$. Let $d^i(p_1) = x_1^i(B((p_1, 1), e(i)))$, individual i's demand for good 1 given the price system $(p_1, 1)$. Assume that

- each function d^i is continuous

- for some price p_1 low enough we have $d^i(p_1) > e_1(i)$ for all $i \in N$ (every individual wants to consume more of good 1 than he initially owns)

- for some price p_1 high enough we have $d^i(p_1) < e_1(i)$ for all $i \in N$ (every individual wants to sell some of the amount of good 1 that he initially owns).

Then the exchange economy has a competitive equilibrium.

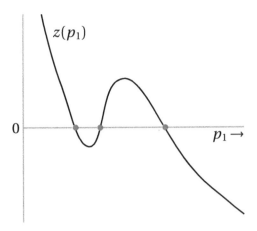

Figure 10.2 An example of an excess demand function z for good 1 satisfying the conditions of Proposition 10.2. The three red disks indicate competitive equilibrium prices for good 1.

Proof

For any price p_1, let $z(p_1) = \sum_{i\in N}[d^i(p_1) - e_1(i)]$, the difference between the total demand for good 1 when the price system is $(p_1, 1)$ and the total amount of good 1 available. By the assumption that each function d^i is continuous, the function z is continuous. By the assumptions about the values of the demand functions for low and high values of p_1, $z(p_1)$ is positive for p_1 small enough and negative for p_1 high enough. (A function z satisfying these conditions is shown in Figure 10.2.) By the Intermediate Value Theorem the value of this function z is thus zero for at least one price p_1^*. (It may be zero for more than one price.)

We claim that $((p_1^*, 1), (x^i(p_1^*, 1))_{i\in N})$ is a competitive equilibrium. The optimality condition is satisfied by the definition of the demand functions. The feasibility condition follows from Proposition 10.1, which states that if the excess demand for one good is zero, so is the excess demand for the second good.

An exchange economy in which some individuals' preferences are not convex may not have a competitive equilibrium; Problem 5 asks you to study an example. Example 10.2 shows that an exchange economy may have multiple equilibria, differing both in the price system and the equilibrium allocation.

10.4 Reopening trade

Consider an exchange economy $\langle N, (\succsim^i)_{i\in N}, e\rangle$ in which each individual i initially holds the bundle $e(i)$. Suppose that the individuals trade according to a competitive equilibrium (p,a). After trade, each individual i holds the bundle $a(i)$. Now suppose that the possibility of trade reopens; the exchange economy $\langle N,(\succcurlyeq^i)_{i\in N},a\rangle$, in which the initial bundle of each individual i is $a(i)$, models the situation. Does (p,a) remain a competitive equilibrium in this economy? The next result states that it does.

Proposition 10.3: No trade from competitive equilibrium

A competitive equilibrium (p,a) of the exchange economy $\langle N,(\succcurlyeq^i)_{i\in N},e\rangle$ is a competitive equilibrium of the exchange economy $\langle N,(\succcurlyeq^i)_{i\in N},a\rangle$.

Proof

The feasibility condition for competitive equilibrium is satisfied because a by definition is an allocation. The optimality condition is satisfied also: since $pa(i)=pe(i)$, the budget sets $B(p,e(i))$ and $B(p,a(i))$ are the same, so that the bundle $a(i)$, which is optimal in the budget set $B(p,e(i))$, is optimal for individual i also in $B(p,a(i))$.

10.5   Equilibrium and Pareto stability

We now show that a competitive equilibrium allocation is Pareto stable.

Proposition 10.4: Pareto stability of competitive equilibrium allocation

Every competitive equilibrium allocation of an exchange economy is Pareto stable.

Proof

Let (p,a) be a competitive equilibrium of the exchange economy $\langle N,(\succcurlyeq^i)_{i\in N},e\rangle$. Assume that a is not Pareto stable. That is, assume that there is an allocation y such that $y(i)\succcurlyeq^i a(i)$ for every individual i and $y(j)\succ^j a(j)$ for some individual j.

The optimality of $a(i)$ according to $\succcurlyeq^i$ in i's budget set implies that $py(i)\geq pe(i)$: if $py(i)<pe(i)$ then the budget set contains a bundle that i prefers to $y(i)$ and hence to $a(i)$. Furthermore, the optimality of $a(j)$ in j's budget set implies that $py(j)>pe(j)$. Thus $p\sum_{i\in N}y(i)>p\sum_{i\in N}e(i)$, contradicting the feasibility of y, which requires $\sum_{i\in N}y(i)=\sum_{i\in N}e(i)$. Hence a is Pareto stable.

Comments

1. The conclusion of this result depends critically on the assumption that each individual cares only about the bundle he consumes. Consider a variant of an exchange economy in which individuals care also about the bundles consumed by other individuals. Suppose specifically that the economy contains two individuals, with initial bundles $(1,0)$ and $(0,1)$. Individual 1 is negatively affected by individual 2's consumption of good 2; his utility from any allocation a is $a_1(1) + a_2(1) - 2a_2(2)$. Individual 2 cares only about his own consumption; his utility from a is $2a_1(2) + 3a_2(2)$. Assuming that each individual takes the consumption of the other individual as given, the only price systems $(p_1, 1)$ for which the demands for each good is equal to 1 satisfy $\frac{2}{3} \le p_1 \le 1$ and no trade occurs (the induced allocation is the initial allocation). This outcome is not Pareto stable: the allocation b for which $b(1) = (0, 0.5)$ and $b(2) = (1, 0.5)$ is preferred by both individuals.

2. An allocation is Pareto stable if no other allocation is at least as good for all individuals and better for at least one. We suggest that you verify that under either of the following conditions, an allocation is Pareto stable if and only if no other allocation is better for every individual.

   a. The individuals' preference relations are convex and every bundle in the allocation contains a positive quantity of each good.

   b. The individuals' preference relations are strongly monotone.

3. An implication of Proposition 10.4 is an analogue of Proposition 9.4. If the exchange economy $\langle N, (\succsim^i)_{i \in N}, e \rangle$ has a competitive equilibrium (p, a), then $a(i) \succsim^i e(i)$ for every individual $i \in N$. Thus if the initial allocation e is Pareto stable, then every individual i is indifferent between $a(i)$ and $e(i)$, so that (p, e) is also a competitive equilibrium of the economy. Suppose an authority that is able to redistribute goods between individuals wants the allocation in the economy to be some Pareto stable allocation a. The result says that if the authority redistributes goods to generate a, subsequently opening up trade will not undo the redistribution, in the sense that the outcome will be an allocation b for which $b(i) \sim^i a(i)$ for every individual i.

4. Proposition 10.4 is an analogue of Proposition 9.3. Like that result, it is conventionally referred to as the "first fundamental theorem of welfare economics". The result in the previous comment is an analogue of Proposition 9.4 and is conventionally referred to as the "second fundamental theorem of welfare economics". For the reasons we give in the discussion following Proposition 9.3, we regard these names as inappropriate.

10.6   The core

Proposition 10.4 says that no allocation is unanimously preferred to a competitive equilibrium allocation. In fact, a stronger result holds: for any competitive equilibrium allocation a, no group of individuals can benefit from seceding from the economy and reallocating their initial bundles among themselves (without exchanging goods with any individuals outside the group), in such a way that they are all better off than they are in a. To state the result, we use a stability concept called the core.

> **Definition 10.5: Core**
>
> Consider the exchange economy $\langle N, (\succ^i)_{i \in N}, e \rangle$. A nonempty set $S \subseteq N$ of individuals can *improve upon* an allocation a if for some collection $(b(i))_{i \in S}$ of bundles with $\sum_{i \in S} b(i) = \sum_{i \in S} e(i)$ we have $b(i) \succ^i a(i)$ for all $i \in S$. An allocation a is in the *core* if no set of individuals can improve upon it.

Note that whether an allocation is in the core, unlike its Pareto stability, depends on the allocation of the initial bundles.

The following example shows that an allocation can be Pareto stable and preferred by every individual to his initial bundle and yet not be in the core.

> **Example 10.4: Pareto stable allocation not in core**
>
> Consider an exchange economy with two individuals of type 1 and two of type 2. Each individual of type 1 has the initial bundle $(1,0)$ and a preference relation represented by the utility function $\min\{x_1, x_2\}$. Each individual of type 2 has the initial bundle $(0,1)$ and a preference relation represented by the utility function $x_1 + x_2$.
>
> Consider the allocation a in which each individual of type 1 is assigned the bundle $(0.1, 0.1)$ and each individual of type 2 is assigned the bundle $(0.9, 0.9)$. Each individual prefers his assigned bundle in this allocation to his initial bundle. The allocation is Pareto stable (for every bundle preferred by any individual, the sum of the amounts of the goods exceeds the sum of the amounts he is allocated). However, all members of a set S consisting of two individuals of type 1 and one of type 2, can improve upon the allocation: if each individual of type 1 is assigned the bundle $(0.2, 0.2)$ and the individual of type 2 is assigned the bundle $(1.6, 0.6)$, then all three individuals are better off than they are in the original allocation a.

> ### Proposition 10.5: Competitive equilibrium is in core
>
> Every competitive equilibrium allocation of an exchange economy is in the core of the economy.

> ### Proof
>
> Let (p, a) be a competitive equilibrium of the exchange economy $\langle N, (\succsim^i)_{i \in N}, e \rangle$. Suppose that a is not in the core of the economy. Then there is a nonempty set $S \subseteq N$ and a collection $(b(i))_{i \in S}$ of bundles with $\sum_{i \in S} b(i) = \sum_{i \in S} e(i)$ such that $b(i) \succ^i a(i)$ for all $i \in S$. Now, the fact that (p, a) is a competitive equilibrium means that for each individual i, the bundle $a(i)$ is optimal according to $\succsim^i$ in i's budget set. Thus $b(i) \succ^i a(i)$ implies that $pb(i) > pe(i)$, so that $p \sum_{i \in S} b(i) > p \sum_{i \in S} e(i)$. This inequality contradicts the condition $\sum_{i \in S} b(i) = \sum_{i \in S} e(i)$. Thus a is in fact in the core.

10.7 Competitive equilibrium based on demand functions

The individuals in an exchange economy are characterized by their preference relations and initial bundles. In a competitive equilibrium, each individual chooses his favorite bundle, according to his preferences, from his budget set. In a variant of the model, individuals are characterized instead by their demand functions and initial bundles, with the demand function of each individual specifying the bundle he consumes for each price system, given his initial bundle. These demand functions may not be rationalized by preference relations. (See Section 5.5 for examples of such demand functions.)

A competitive equilibrium of this variant of an exchange economy is a pair (p, a) consisting of a price system p and an assignment a such that (1) for each individual i the bundle $a(i)$ is the one specified by his demand function given the price system p and his initial bundle $e(i)$ and (2) a is an allocation.

> ### Example 10.5: Competitive equilibrium based on demand functions
>
> Consider an economy with two individuals in which individual 1 consumes only the good with the higher price; if the prices of the goods are the same, he consumes only good 1. No monotone preference relation rationalizes this demand function (see Example 5.11). Assume that individual 2 demands a bundle that maximizes the function $x_1 + x_2$ over his

budget set, so that if the prices of the goods differ, he demands only the good with the lower price.

Suppose that $e(1) = (\alpha, 0)$ and $e(2) = (0, \beta)$. Then every pair (p, a) in which p is a price system with $p_1 \geq p_2 = 1$ and a is the allocation with $a(1) = (\alpha, 0)$ and $a(2) = (0, \beta)$ is a competitive equilibrium since individual 1 demands only the first (and more expensive) good and individual 2 demands only the second (and cheaper) good.

For (p, a) with $p_1 < p_2 = 1$ to be an equilibrium we need $a(1) = (0, \alpha p_1)$ and $a(2) = (\beta / p_1, 0)$. These two bundles sum to the total bundle (α, β) if and only if $p_1 = \beta / \alpha$. Thus for such an equilibrium to exist we need $\beta < \alpha$. Indeed, if $\beta < \alpha$ then in addition to the equilibria in the previous paragraph, the pair (p, a) in which $p = (\beta / \alpha, 1)$, $a(1) = (0, \beta)$, and $a(2) = (\alpha, 0)$ is a competitive equilibrium.

10.8 Manipulability

Can an individual bias a competitive equilibrium in his favor by acting as if his preferences differ from his true preferences? The next example shows that the answer to this question is affirmative. (By contrast, Problem 5 in Chapter 9 shows that such manipulation is not possible in the markets studied in that chapter.)

Example 10.6: Manipulability of competitive equilibrium

Consider an exchange economy with two individuals in which the preference relation of individual 1 is represented by the function $x_1 + x_2$, the preference relation of individual 2 is represented by the function $\min\{x_1, x_2\}$, and the initial bundles are $e(1) = (1, 0)$ and $e(2) = (0, 1)$. This economy has a unique competitive equilibrium (p, a), with $p = (1, 1)$ and $a(1) = a(2) = (\frac{1}{2}, \frac{1}{2})$.

If individual 1 acts as if his preferences are represented by the function $3x_1 + x_2$ (which means that he acts as if good 1 is more desirable to him than it really is) then the competitive equilibrium prices are $(3, 1)$ and the equilibrium allocation gives him the bundle $(\frac{3}{4}, \frac{3}{4})$, which is better for him than the bundle $(\frac{1}{2}, \frac{1}{2})$ he receives in the equilibrium when he acts according to his true preferences.

10.9 Edgeworth box

The Edgeworth box is a graphical tool for analyzing an exchange economy with two individuals and two goods. We take a diagram like the one in Figure 10.1

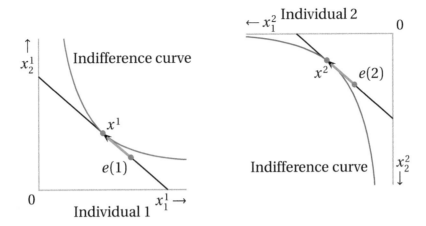

Figure 10.3 The competitive equilibrium in Figure 10.1, with the diagram for individual 2 rotated 180 degrees.

and rotate the right-hand panel, which represents individual 2's optimization problem, 180 degrees, to get Figure 10.3. Then we move the panels together, so that the initial bundles (represented by small green disks) coincide, to get Figure 10.4a. In this diagram, a point in the rectangle bounded by the two sets of axes represents an allocation, with the bundle assigned to individual 1 plotted relative to the axes with origin at the bottom left, and the bundle assigned to individual 2 plotted relative to the axes with origin at the top right.

The green disk in the figure represents the individuals' initial bundles; the segment of the black line between the blue disks (viewed relative to individual 1's axes) represents individual 1's budget set, and the segment between the violet disks (viewed relative to individual 2's axes) represents individual 2's budget set. The line corresponds to a competitive equilibrium if the disk representing the optimal bundle x^1 of individual 1 coincides with the disk representing the optimal bundle x^2 for individual 2, as it does in Figure 10.4a, because in this case the assignment in which each individual gets his optimal bundle given the price system is an allocation. Figure 10.4b shows a price system that does not correspond to a competitive equilibrium: the total amount of good 1 demanded is less than the total amount available and the total amount of good 2 demanded exceeds the total amount available.

The set of Pareto stable allocations and the core are shown in Figure 10.5. Every allocation on the line colored black and red connecting individual 1's origin to individual 2's origin is Pareto stable. The reason is that every allocation on or above the indifference curve of one individual through the allocation is below (relative to other individual's origin) the indifference curve of the other individual through the allocation. Similarly, any allocation not on the black and red line is not Pareto stable, because there is another allocation in which both individuals are better off.

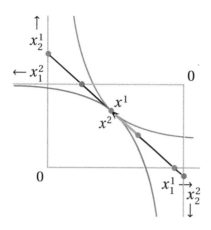
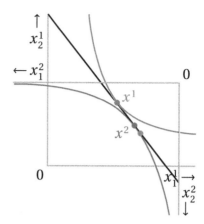

(a) The competitive equilibrium in Figure 10.1, with the diagram for individual 2 rotated 180 degrees and moved so that the points representing the individuals' initial bundles coincide.

(b) A price system that is not consistent with a competitive equilibrium.

Figure 10.4 Edgeworth boxes.

An allocation is in the core of this two-individual economy if and only if it is Pareto stable and each individual likes the allocation at least as much as his initial bundle. Thus the core is the set of allocations on the red line in Figure 10.5.

Problems

1. *Examples.* Consider the following exchange economies, in which n^A individuals have preferences represented by the utility function u^A and initial bundle e^A and n^B individuals have preferences represented by the utility function u^B and initial bundle e^B.

economy	n^A	n^B	u^A	u^B	e^A	e^B
E_1	1	1	$x_1 + x_2$	$\min\{x_1, x_2\}$	$(\alpha, 0)$	$(0, \beta)$
E_2	1	2	$x_1 + x_2$	$\min\{x_1, x_2\}$	$(1, 0)$	$(0, 1)$
E_3	n^A	n^B	x_2	x_1	$(\alpha, 0)$	$(0, \beta)$
E_4	1	1	$x_1 x_2$	$x_1^2 x_2$	$(2, 3)$	$(5, 4)$

   a. Characterize the competitive equilibria of E_1 for $\alpha \le \beta \le 2\alpha$. Draw the Edgeworth box of E_1 and indicate the set of Pareto stable allocations and the core.

   b. Characterize the competitive equilibria of E_2.

   c. Characterize the competitive equilibria of E_3.

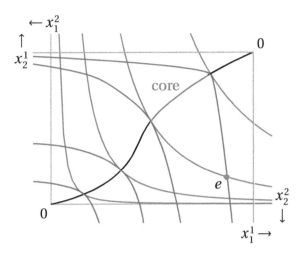

Figure 10.5 The core (red line) and set of Pareto stable allocations (core plus black lines).

    d. Find the competitive equilibria of E_4. (Ariel does not like problems like this one, but suggests you do the problem, so that you appreciate what you would be missing.) You should conclude that the competitive price system is $(\frac{25}{16}, 1)$.

2. *A market with perfectly complementary goods.* All individuals in an exchange economy have preferences represented by the function $\min\{x_1, x_2\}$; n_1 of them have the initial bundle $(1, 0)$ and the remaining n_2 have the initial bundle $(0, 1)$, where $n_1 \geq n_2$.

    a. Show that the allocation in which each individual holds the bundle $(n_1/(n_1 + n_2), n_2/(n_1 + n_2))$ is Pareto stable.

    b. Show that this allocation is in the core if and only if $n_1 = n_2$.

    c. What are the competitive equilibria of the economy when $n_1 > n_2$?

3. *Replicating a market.* Let $M_1 = \langle N, (\succsim^i)_{i \in N}, e \rangle$ be an exchange economy in which $N = \{A, B\}$. Let M_n be the exchange economy containing n individuals identical to A (type A) and n individuals identical to B (type B).

    a. Suppose that (p, a) is a competitive equilibrium of M_1 and that the assignment b in M_n gives each of the n individuals of type A the bundle $a(A)$ and each of the n individuals of type B the bundle $a(B)$. Show that (p, b) is a competitive equilibrium of M_n.

    b. Show that if all individuals have strictly convex preferences and (p, b) is a competitive equilibrium of M_n, then all individuals of type A consume the same bundle, say x_A, and all individuals of type B consume the same bundle, say x_B, and (p,a) with $a(A) = x_A$ and $a(B) = x_B$ is a competitive equilibrium of M_1.

4. *Robinson Crusoe economy.* Consider an exchange economy with a single individual, R, who has the initial bundle e. A competitive equilibrium of this economy is a pair (p, x^*) where p is a price system and x^* is a bundle, with x^* optimal for R in $\{x \in \mathbb{R}_+^2 : px = pe\}$ and $x^* = e$. Assume that R's preference relation is monotone, continuous, and convex. Explain graphically why this economy has a competitive equilibrium.

5. *Economy with nonconvex preferences.* We remark before Proposition 10.2 that one of the sufficient conditions for the existence of a competitive equilibrium in an exchange economy is that the individuals' preferences are convex. In this question you will see that competitive equilibrium may exist if the individuals' preferences are not convex. Consider an exchange economy with two individuals whose preferences are represented by the utility function $(x_1)^2 + (x_2)^2$, and thus are not convex (see Problem 1a in Chapter 4). Assume that $e_k(1) + e_k(2) > 0$ for $k = 1, 2$.

   a. Show that the economy with $e(1) = (\alpha, 0)$ and $e(2) = (0, \beta)$ has a competitive equilibrium.

   b. Show that if the economy has a competitive equilibrium then the equilibrium prices are equal.

   c. Show that if $e(1) = e(2) = (2, 1)$ then the economy has no competitive equilibrium.

   d. Characterize all initial allocations for which the economy has a competitive equilibrium.

6. *Integration of exchange market and housing market.* In the exchange economy $\langle N, (\succsim^i)_{i \in N}, e \rangle$ the initial bundle of each individual differs from the initial bundle of every other individual ($e(i) \neq e(j)$ for all $i \neq j$ in N). Each individual has a monotone, continuous, and convex preference relation. Rather than assuming that each individual can choose any bundle in $\mathbb{R}_+^2$, assume that each individual can choose only one of the bundles held initially by one of the individuals.

   a. Assume that in equilibrium a price is attached to each bundle (not each good). Explain how the housing model of Chapter 9 can be applied to define an equilibrium of the market.

   b. Construct an example of such an economy with four individuals where $e(1) = (2,0)$, $e(2) = (0,2)$, $e(3) = (1,0)$, and $e(4) = (0,1)$ such that any

competitive equilibrium price function p is not linear in the sense that
for no (p_1, p_2) is it the case that $p(e(i)) = p_1 e_1(i) + p_2 e_2(i)$ for all i.

7. *Economy with differentiable preferences.* Characterize in an Edgeworth box
(Section 10.9) all the Pareto stable allocations in an exchange economy with
two individuals in which the sum of the individuals' initial bundles is $(1, 1)$,
the individuals' preference relations are strictly monotone, convex, and differentiable, and, for each individual, the marginal rate of substitution is less
than 1 at each bundle (x_1, x_2) for which $x_1 + x_2 > 1$, greater than 1 at each bundle for which $x_1 + x_2 < 1$, and equal to 1 at each bundle for which $x_1 + x_2 = 1$.

8. *Exchange economy with one indivisible good.* Consider an exchange econ-
omy $\langle N, (\succsim^i)_{i \in N}, e \rangle$ in which $N = \{1, \ldots, n\}$, where n is odd. Good 1 can be
consumed only in the amounts 0, 1, or 2 whereas good 2 can be consumed in
any amount. Assume that each individual i has a preference relation represented by the function $t^i x_1 + x_2$, where $t^1 > t^2 > \cdots > t^n > 0$, and initially has
the bundle $(1, M^i)$, where $M^i > t^1$. Characterize the competitive equilibria of
this economy.

9. *One individual determines the prices.* Consider an exchange economy with
two individuals in which individual 2 chooses the price ratio and commits to
comply with any exchange that individual 1 chooses given that ratio. Individual 2 foresees 1's response and chooses the exchange rate so that individual
1's response is best for him (individual 2). Use an Edgeworth box to show
graphically the following two results.

   a. The outcome of the procedure might (and typically does) differ from a
   competitive equilibrium, and when it differs it is better for individual 2.

   b. Proposition 10.3 does not hold for the procedure: if the outcome of the
   procedure is the allocation b and the individuals are assigned the bundles $b(1)$ and $b(2)$ then individual 2 can achieve a bundle better than $b(2)$
   by announcing a price for a trade away from b.

Notes

The modern theory of competitive equilibrium, which has its origins in the work
of Walras (1874), was developed by Kenneth J. Arrow, Gerard Debreu, and Lionel
McKenzie (see for example Arrow and Debreu 1954, Debreu 1959, and McKenzie
1954, 1959). The Edgeworth box (Section 10.9) was introduced by Edgeworth
(1881, 28, 114).

11 Variants of an exchange economy

In this chapter we study two variants of the model of an exchange economy that demonstrate the richness of the model. In the first variant we insert into the framework the basic model of supply and demand for a single indivisible good (with which you may be familiar from an introductory course in economics). In the second variant we use the framework to capture a situation in which individuals face uncertainty about the future resources. This variant is used to analyze markets for insurance and bets.

11.1 Market with indivisible good and money

A single indivisible good is traded in a market for money. Each person can consume either one unit of the good, or none of it. Consuming more than one unit, or a fraction of a unit, is impossible. A ticket for a performance and membership in a club are examples of such goods. Some people initially own one unit of the good and some do not. Every person is characterized by the monetary value he assigns to having one unit of the good. There is room for trade if the value assigned by some person who initially has the good is lower than the value assigned by some person who does not initially have the good. In that case, many transactions may be mutually beneficial for the pair of people. We are interested in who buys the good, who sells it, and the prices at which the transactions take place.

11.1.1 Model

The model is a variant of an exchange economy with two goods. Good 1 is money, which can be held in any nonnegative amount, and good 2 is an indivisible good, which can be held (1) or not held (0). Thus a bundle is a pair (x_1, x_2), where x_1 is a nonnegative number and x_2 is either 0 or 1. Formally, the set of possible bundles of goods (which is $\mathbb{R}_+^2$ in the previous chapter) is

$$X = \{(x_1, x_2) : x_1 \in \mathbb{R}_+ \text{ and } x_2 \in \{0, 1\}\} = \mathbb{R}_+ \times \{0, 1\}.$$

We assume that the preferences over X of each individual i are represented by the function $x_1 + v^i x_2$ where $v^i \geq 0$. Thus individual i prefers the bundle $(s, 1)$ to

Chapter of *Models in Microeconomic Theory* by Martin J. Osborne and Ariel Rubinstein. Version 2023.5.30 (h).

the bundle $(t,0)$ if and only if $s+v^i > t$. That is, he prefers holding the indivisible good to not owning it if and only if he has to give up less than v^i units of money to obtain it. We refer to v^i as i's *valuation* of the good.

We assume that every individual who does not own the indivisible good initially has enough money to pay his valuation to obtain the good: no individual is cash constrained. That is, for every individual i whose initial bundle $e(i)$ has $e_2(i)=0$ we assume that $e_1(i) \geq v^i$.

Definition 11.1: Exchange economy with indivisible good and money

An *exchange economy with an indivisible good and money* $\langle N, (v^i)_{i \in N}, e \rangle$ has the following components.

Individuals

  A finite set N.

Valuations

  For each individual $i \in N$, a nonnegative number v^i (i's *valuation* of the good); the preference relation of each individual i over $X = \mathbb{R}_+ \times \{0,1\}$ is represented by the function u^i defined by $u^i(x_1, x_2) = x_1 + v^i x_2$.

Initial allocation

  A function e that assigns to each individual i a bundle $e(i) \in X$, the bundle that i initially owns, with $e_1(i) \geq v^i$ if $e_2(i)=0$.

  Individual i is a (potential) *buyer* if $e_2(i) = 0$ and a (potential) *seller* if $e_2(i)=1$. To avoid degenerate cases, we assume that the economy contains at least one buyer and one seller.

As for an exchange economy studied in the previous chapter, we assume that a single price for the indivisible good prevails. No individual has the power to influence the price and every individual believes that he can trade the good at this price, and only at this price.

The assumption that all transactions take place at the same price is not obviously reasonable. Consider, for example, the economy that consists of two buyers, B_4 and B_{10}, with valuations 4 and 10, and two sellers, S_0 and S_6, with valuations 0 and 6. If first B_{10} meets S_6 they may trade at a price between 6 and 10. If, subsequently, B_4 meets S_0 they may trade at a price between 0 and 4. Whether such a sequence of transactions occurs might depend on the information available to the individuals about other individuals' valuations and the pattern in which they meet. For example, if B_{10} realizes that S_0 is about to sell the good at a price of at most 4, he might approach S_0 and offer him a price between 4 and 6. The concept of competitive equilibrium that we study in this chapter does not model the formation of prices; it simply assumes that somehow a price emerges and becomes known to all individuals.

As the equilibrium notion we adapt the concept of competitive equilibrium for an exchange economy. We set the price of money to be 1. Thus a price system is a pair $(1, p)$, where p is the amount of money transferred from a buyer to a seller in exchange for the indivisible good. The budget set of each seller i contains two bundles, $(e_1(i), 1)$ (he retains the good) and $(e_1(i) + p, 0)$ (he sells the good). He optimally sells the good if $p > v^i$, and is indifferent between selling and not if $p = v^i$. Similarly, the budget set of each buyer i contains two bundles, $(e_1(i) - p, 1)$ (he buys the good) and $(e_1(i), 0)$ (he does not). He optimally buys the good if $p < v^i$, and is indifferent between buying and not if $p = v^i$. A price p is an equilibrium price if the number of units buyers wish to purchase is equal to the number of units sellers wish to sell.

Definition 11.2: Competitive equilibrium of exchange economy with indivisible good and money

A *competitive equilibrium* of the exchange economy with an indivisible good and money $\langle N, (v^i)_{i \in N}, e \rangle$ is a pair (p, a) where

- p is a nonnegative number (the price of the indivisible good)
- $a = (a(i))_{i \in N}$ is a profile of bundles

such that

optimality of choices
  for each individual i, (*i*) $a_2(i) = 1$ if $p < v^i$, (*ii*) $a_2(i) = 0$ if $p > v^i$, and (*iii*) $a_1(i) = e_1(i) + p(e_2(i) - a_2(i))$.

feasibility
  $\sum_{i \in N} a(i) = \sum_{i \in N} e(i)$.

Notice the analogue of Proposition 10.1 for this model: if the total amount of the indivisible good demanded by all individuals is equal to the total amount available, that is, $\sum_{i \in N} a_2(i) = \sum_{i \in N} e_2(i)$, then the total amount of money demanded by all individuals, $\sum_{i \in N} (e_1(i) + p(e_2(i) - a_2(i)))$, is equal to $\sum_{i \in N} e_1(i)$, the total amount of money available.

Consider the economy with four individuals we specified earlier. Every price p with $4 \leq p \leq 6$ is part of an equilibrium, in which B_{10} buys the good, S_0 sells the good, and the other two individuals refrain from trade. A price greater than 6 is not part of an equilibrium since for such a price at most one individual, B_{10}, wants to have the indivisible good but two units of it are available. By a similar argument, a price less than 4 is not part of an equilibrium.

Example 11.1

An exchange economy with an indivisible good and money contains 14 sellers with valuation 0 and 17 buyers with valuation 100.

This economy has no equilibrium with a price less than 100, because at such a price all 17 buyers optimally choose to have the good, but only 14 units of the good are available. Also the economy has no equilibrium with a price greater than 100, because at such a price no individual wants to have the good. Thus the only possible equilibrium price is 100. At this price, all 14 sellers optimally wish to sell the good and every buyer is indifferent between buying and not buying the good. Therefore the price 100 together with a profile of choices in which every seller sells his unit, 14 of the 17 buyers choose to buy a unit, and the remaining 3 buyers choose not to do so, is a competitive equilibrium.

Note that a competitive equilibrium may involve no trade. If the valuation of every seller exceeds the valuation of every buyer, in no competitive equilibrium does any trade take place; an equilibrium price is any number between the lowest valuation among the sellers and the highest valuation among the buyers.

The following result proves that competitive equilibrium exists and characterizes all equilibria.

Proposition 11.1: Characterization of competitive equilibrium

Let $\langle N,(v^i)_{i\in N},e \rangle$ be an exchange economy with an indivisible good and money. Denote the number of individuals by n and name them so that $v^1 \geq v^2 \geq \cdots \geq v^n$. Denote by s the number of sellers (equal to the number of units of the indivisible good available). A number p is a competitive equilibrium price for the economy if and only if $v^{s+1} \leq p \leq v^s$.

Proof

Let $p \in [v^{s+1}, v^s]$ and define the allocation a as follows.

individuals	$a(i)$
buyers $i \in \{1,\ldots,s\}$	$(e_1(i)-p,1)$
sellers $i \in \{1,\ldots,s\}$	$(e_1(i),1)$
buyers $i \in \{s+1,\ldots,n\}$	$(e_1(i),0)$
sellers $i \in \{s+1,\ldots,n\}$	$(e_1(i)+p,0)$

The optimality condition is satisfied since any individual whose valuation is greater than p is in $\{1,\ldots,s\}$ and any individual whose valuation is less

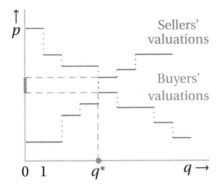 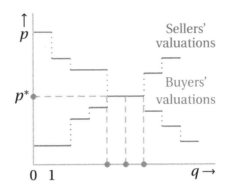

Figure 11.1 Equilibria of exchange economies with an indivisible good and money. The red lines represent the sellers' valuations and the blue lines represent the buyers' valuations. The green line segment and disk on the vertical axis represent the equilibrium prices and the green disks on the horizontal axis represent the number of units traded in an equilibrium.

than p is in $\{s+1,\ldots,n\}$. The allocation is feasible because $\sum_{i \in N} a_2(i) = s = \sum_{i \in N} e_2(i)$. Thus (p, a) is a competitive equilibrium.

A price greater than v^s is not an equilibrium price because for such a price the number of individuals who optimally hold the good is less than s. Similarly, a price less than v^{s+1} is not an equilibrium price.

Comments

1. This result is illustrated in Figure 11.1. The blue lines show the buyers' valuations, plotted in descending order. The length of each solid line segment is the number of buyers whose valuations are equal to the height of the segment. The red lines similarly show the sellers' valuations, plotted in ascending order. In the left panel economy, there is a range of competitive equilibrium prices, indicated in green; in every equilibrium the total amount of the good traded is q^*. In the right panel economy, there is a unique competitive equilibrium price p^* and a range of possible equilibrium quantities.

2. The result implies that an economy has a unique equilibrium price if and only if $v^s = v^{s+1}$. In this case, as in the right-hand panel of Figure 11.1, the number of equilibrium transactions is not unique. For example, if s is a seller and $s+1$ is a buyer, then there is an equilibrium in which these two trade, and also an equilibrium in which they do not.

We now characterize the Pareto stable allocations and prove that, as in the model of the previous chapter, every competitive equilibrium allocation is Pareto stable.

Proposition 11.2: Pareto stable allocations

Let $\langle N,(v^i)_{i\in N},e\rangle$ be an exchange economy with an indivisible good and money. (*a*) An allocation a is Pareto stable if and only if $v^i \geq \min\{v^j,a_1(j)\}$ for any pair (i,j) of individuals in which i holds the good $(a_2(i)=1)$ and j does not $(a_2(j)=0)$. (*b*) Every competitive equilibrium allocation is Pareto stable.

Proof

(*a*) Consider an allocation a which in which $a_2(i)=1$, $a_2(j)=0$, and $v^i < \min\{v^j,a_1(j)\}$. Let b be the allocation identical to a except that $b(i) = (a_1(i)+\delta,0)$ and $b(j)=(a_1(j)-\delta,1)$ where $v^i < \delta < \min\{v^j,a_1(j)\}$. Then b is feasible and Pareto dominates a, so that a is not Pareto stable.

Now let a be an allocation such that for any pair of individuals i and j for which $a_2(i)=1$ and $a_2(j)=0$, we have $v^i \geq \min\{v^j,a_1(j)\}$. We argue that a is Pareto stable.

Suppose the allocation b Pareto dominates a. By the feasibility of a and b, the number k of individuals who hold the good in a but not in b is equal to the number of individuals who hold the good in b but not in a (refer to Figure 11.2). Denote by v the lowest valuation of an individual who holds the good in a.

If $b_2(i)=a_2(i)$ then $b_1(i)\geq a_1(i)$. For each of the k individuals for whom $a_2(i)=1$ and $b_2(i)=0$, we have $b_1(i)\geq a_1(i)+v^i \geq a_1(i)+v$. For each of the k individuals for whom $a_2(i)=0$ and $b_2(i)=1$ we have $b_1(i)+v^i \geq a_1(i)$ and $b_1(i)\geq 0$. Thus $b_1(i)\geq a_1(i)-\min\{v^i,a_1(i)\}$. By the assumption on a, $v^j \geq \min\{v^i,a_1(i)\}$ for all j who hold the good in a so $v \geq \min\{v^i,a_1(i)\}$ and thus $b_1(i)\geq a_1(i)-v$. For at least one individual the inequality is strict, so that $\sum_{i\in N} b_1(i) > \sum_{i\in N} a_1(i)$, contradicting the feasibility of b. Thus no allocation Pareto dominates a.

(*b*) Let (p^*,a) be a competitive equilibrium. Then for every individual i who holds the good $v^i \geq p^*$, and for every individual j who does not hold the good $v^i \leq p^*$. Then (*a*) implies that a is Pareto stable.

Recall that an allocation is in the core of an exchange economy if no subset of individuals can secede from the economy and allocate their initial bundles (in this case, units of the good and money) between themselves so that they are all better off. Proposition 10.5, showing that a competitive equilibrium allocation is in the core of an exchange economy, holds also for an exchange economy with an indivisible good and money (as you can verify). Further, for such an economy,

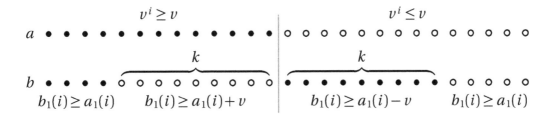

Figure 11.2 An illustration of the argument in the second part of the proof of part (a) of Proposition 11.2. Each disk represents an individual who holds the indivisible good, and each circle represents an individual who does not hold the good.

a stronger result is true: every core allocation is a competitive equilibrium allocation, so that the core is exactly the set of competitive allocations.

Proposition 11.3: Core and competitive equilibrium

For every allocation a in the core of an exchange economy with an indivisible good and money there is a number p such that (p, a) is a competitive equilibrium of the economy.

Proof

Denote the economy $\langle N, (v^i)_{i \in N}, e \rangle$. We have $a_1(i) + v^i a_2(i) \geq e_1(i) + v^i e_2(i)$ for every individual i since otherwise i can improve upon a by himself. Also, if $a_2(i) = e_2(i)$ then $a_1(i) = e_1(i)$ because if $a_1(i) > e_1(i)$ then the set $N \setminus \{i\}$ of individuals can improve upon a (it has the same amount of the indivisible good in a and e but has less money in a).

If $a = e$ then the valuation of every individual who holds the good in a is at least as high as the valuation of any individual who does not hold the good, since otherwise such a pair can improve upon a (given the assumption that each buyer i has at least v^i units of money). In this case (p, a) is an equilibrium for any p with $\max_{i \in N}\{v^i : a_2(i) = 0\} \leq p \leq \min_{i \in N}\{v^i : a_2(i) = 1\}$.

Now suppose $a \neq e$. Let $B = \{i \in N : e_2(i) = 0 \text{ and } a_2(i) = 1\}$ and $S = \{i \in N : e_2(i) = 1 \text{ and } a_2(i) = 0\}$. Since $a \neq e$ both B and S are nonempty and by the feasibility of a they have the same size. For every other individual i we have $a(i) = e(i)$.

If $a_1(j) - e_1(j) < e_1(i) - a_1(i)$ for some $j \in S$ and $i \in B$ (seller j receives less than buyer i pays) then for any number p with $a_1(j) - e_1(j) < p < e_1(i) - a_1(i)$ the set $\{i, j\}$ can improve upon a with the bundles $(e_1(i) - p, 1)$ for i and $(e_1(j) + p, 0)$ for j.

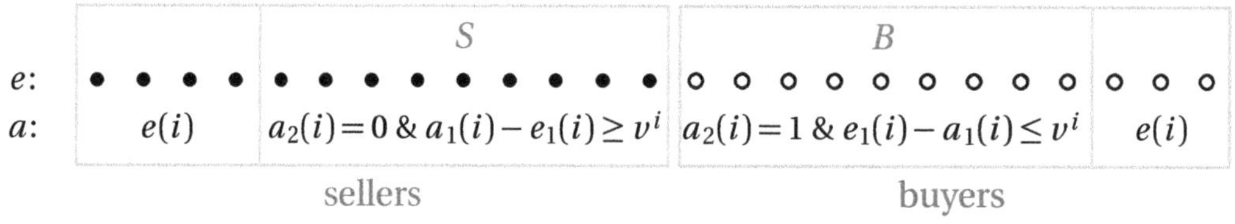

	S		B	
e:	• • • • • • • • • • • •		○ ○ ○ ○ ○ ○ ○ ○ ○	○ ○ ○
a:	$e(i)$	$a_2(i)=0$ & $a_1(i)-e_1(i)\geq v^i$	$a_2(i)=1$ & $e_1(i)-a_1(i)\leq v^i$	$e(i)$
		sellers		buyers

Figure 11.3 An illustration of the sets S and B in the proof of Proposition 11.3.

Thus for all $i \in B$ and $j \in S$ we have $e_1(i)-a_1(i) \leq a_1(j)-e_1(j)$. By the feasibility of a, $\sum_{i\in B}(e_1(i)-a_1(i))=\sum_{j\in S}(a_1(j)-e_1(j))$ (given that $a_1(k)=e_1(k)$ for all $k \notin B\cup S$). Thus $e_1(i)-a_1(i)$ is the same for all $i \in B$, $a_1(j)-e_1(j)$ is the same for all $j \in S$, and these amounts are equal. Denote their common value by p.

It remains to show that (p,a) is an equilibrium. Consider an individual i with $e_2(i)=0$. If $v^i < p$ then $i \notin B$ because if $i \in B$ then $a_1(i)=e_1(i)-p$ and hence $e_1(i)>a_1(i)+v^i$ (buyer i pays more than v^i for the good) so that $e(i)$ is better for i than $a(i)$. If $v^i > p$ then $i \in B$ since otherwise $a(i)=e(i)$ and i can join with any $j \in S$ to improve upon a (i is willing to pay more than the amount j receives). Similarly for an individual i with $e_2(i)=1$.

11.2   Exchange economy with uncertainty

People are uncertain about the future, and often believe that their wealth depends on it. To mitigate the impact of uncertainty, they engage in contracts involving payments that depend on the form the future may take. By using such contracts, they may insure each other. For example, if in future A person 1 has a high wealth and in future B he has a low wealth, and the reverse is true for person 2, then they may both be better off with a contract that transfers money from person 1 to person 2 in future A in exchange for a transfer from person 2 to person 1 in future B. We study the terms of such contracts in an equilibrium of a model like the one in Chapter 10.

11.2.1   Model

We call each possible future a state of the world, or simply a state, and assume for simplicity that only two states, called 1 and 2, are possible. Every individual believes that the probability of state k is π_k, with $\pi_k > 0$. All individuals agree on these probabilities. The individuals buy and sell contracts that specify payments depending on the state that occurs. We model these contracts by stretching the notion of a good: good k is a payment of 1 unit of money if state k occurs

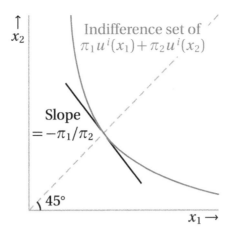

Figure 11.4 An indifference set of an individual whose preference relation is represented by a utility function $\pi_1 u^i(x_1) + \pi_2 u^i(x_2)$, where u^i is a Bernoulli utility function.

and nothing otherwise. Thus the owner of the bundle (x_1, x_2) obtains x_1 units of money if the state is 1 and x_2 units of money if the state is 2. Each individual i starts with the initial bundle $e(i)$.

We assume that each individual's enjoyment of the money he gets is independent of the state. Thus a bundle (x_1, x_2) is viewed by each individual as a lottery that gives x_1 units of money with probability π_1 and x_2 with probability π_2. In particular, if $x_1 = x_2$ then the bundle gives the same amount in each state, and thus corresponds to a sure outcome.

The preferences over lotteries of each individual i are assumed to be represented by the expected value of a Bernoulli utility function u^i, so that his preference relation over the set of bundles (x_1, x_2) is represented by the utility function $U^i(x_1, x_2) = \pi_1 u^i(x_1) + \pi_2 u^i(x_2)$. We assume that each individual is risk-averse, so that u^i is concave, and for convenience assume also that u^i is differentiable. The marginal rate of substitution for individual i at (x_1, x_2) is thus $\pi_1 u_i'(x_1)/\pi_2 u_i'(x_2)$. Thus it is π_1/π_2 if $x_1 = x_2$, greater than π_1/π_2 if $x_1 < x_2$, and less than π_1/π_2 if $x_1 < x_2$ as illustrated in Figure 11.4.

To summarize, we study the following model.

Definition 11.3: Exchange economy with uncertainty

An *exchange economy with uncertainty* $\langle N, (u^i)_{i \in N}, (\pi_1, \pi_2), e \rangle$ consists of

individuals
     a finite set N

utility functions
     for each individual $i \in N$, a differentiable concave function $u^i : \mathbb{R} \to \mathbb{R}$
     (i's Bernoulli utility function)

> **probabilities of states**
> probabilities π_1 and π_2 with $\pi_1 + \pi_2 = 1$ (π_k is the probability that each individual assigns to state k)
>
> **initial allocation**
> a function e that assigns to each individual i a bundle $e(i) \in \mathbb{R}^2$, the bundle that i initially owns.

The notion of equilibrium we use is an adaptation of the notion of competitive equilibrium for an exchange economy.

> **Definition 11.4: Competitive equilibrium of economy with uncertainty**
>
> A *competitive equilibrium* of the exchange economy with uncertainty $\langle N, (u^i)_{i \in N}, (\pi_1, \pi_2), e \rangle$ is a competitive equilibrium of the exchange economy $\langle N, (\succsim^i)_{i \in N}, e \rangle$ where $\succsim^i$ is a preference relation represented by the utility function $\pi_1 u^i(x_1) + \pi_2 u^i(x_2)$.

11.2.2 Uncertainty about distribution of wealth

We start by considering an economy in which the total amount of money available to all individuals is independent of the state of the world, but the distribution of the money among the individuals may depend on the state. We show that if each individual is strictly risk-averse (his Bernoulli utility function is strictly concave) then in a competitive equilibrium the individuals perfectly insure each other, consuming the same bundle in each state.

> **Proposition 11.4: Competitive equilibrium of economy with uncertainty**
>
> Let $\langle N, (u^i)_{i \in N}, (\pi_1, \pi_2), e \rangle$ be an exchange economy with uncertainty in which each function u^i is strictly concave. Assume that $\sum_{i \in N} e(i) = (c, c)$ for some $c > 0$. This economy has a unique competitive equilibrium (p, a) in which $p_1/p_2 = \pi_1/\pi_2$ and $a(i) = (\pi_1 e_1(i) + \pi_2 e_2(i), \pi_1 e_1(i) + \pi_2 e_2(i))$ for each individual i. That is, each individual consumes with certainty the expected amount of money he owns initially.

> **Proof**
>
> We first argue that (p, a) is a competitive equilibrium. We have $p_1/p_2 = \pi_1/\pi_2$, so that a bundle (x_1, x_2) is on individual i's budget line if $\pi_1 x_1 + \pi_2 x_2 = \pi_1 e_1(i) + \pi_2 e_2(i)$. That is, all bundles on the budget line represent

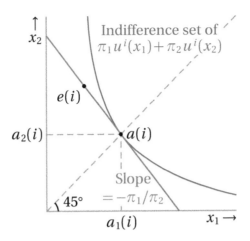

Figure 11.5 If $p_1/p_2 = \pi_1/\pi_2$ then an individual i for whom u^i is strictly concave optimally consumes the bundle $a(i)$ on his budget line for which $a_1(i) = a_2(i)$.

lotteries with the same expectation. Therefore, by i's strict risk aversion the only optimal bundle for him is $a(i)$, which gives the amount $\pi_1 e_1(i) + \pi_2 e_2(i)$ with certainty. (See Figure 11.5.) The allocation a is feasible because for each good k

$$\sum_{i \in N} a_k(i) = \sum_{i \in N}(\pi_1 e_1(i) + \pi_2 e_2(i)) = \pi_1 \sum_{i \in N} e_1(i) + \pi_2 \sum_{i \in N} e_2(i) = \pi_1 c + \pi_2 c = c.$$

The economy has no competitive equilibrium (q, b) with $q_1/q_2 \neq \pi_1/\pi_2$. If $q_1/q_2 < \pi_1/\pi_2$ then the bundle $b(i)$ optimal for each individual i satisfies $b_1(i) > b_2(i)$, so that $\sum_{i \in N} b_1(i) > \sum_{i \in N} b_2(i)$, contradicting the feasibility condition that the total amount in each state is the same, equal to c. Similarly the economy has no equilibrium in which $q_1/q_2 > \pi_1/\pi_2$.

11.2.3 Collective uncertainty

Now suppose that state 1 is a disaster that reduces the total wealth. Then the equilibrium price ratio is greater than π_1/π_2 and every individual consumes less in state 1 than in state 2.

Proposition 11.5: Competitive equilibrium of economy with uncertainty

Let $\langle N, (u^i)_{i \in N}, (\pi_1, \pi_2), e \rangle$ be an exchange economy with uncertainty in which each function u^i is strictly concave and $\sum_{i \in N} e_1(i) < \sum_{i \in N} e_2(i)$. In a competitive equilibrium (p, a), (i) $p_1/p_2 > \pi_1/\pi_2$ and (ii) $a_1(i) < a_2(i)$ for every individual i.

Proof

(*i*) If $p_1/p_2 \leq \pi_1/\pi_2$ then the bundle $x(i)$ optimal for individual i satisfies $x_1(i) \geq x_2(i)$ and thus $\sum_{i \in N} e_1(i) = \sum_{i \in N} x_1(i) \geq \sum_{i \in N} x_2(i) = \sum_{i \in N} e_2(i)$, which contradicts our assumption that the total wealth is less in state 1 than in state 2. (*ii*) Since the marginal rate of substitution at (x_1, x_2) with $x_1 \geq x_2$ is at most π_1/π_2, (*i*) implies $a_1(i) < a_2(i)$.

11.2.4   An economy with a risk-neutral insurer

Now suppose that each individual owns one unit of wealth, which will be wiped out if state 1 occurs. The market is served by an insurer who is involved also in many other markets. The risks in each market are independent of the risks in every other market, so that the insurer faces little risk in aggregate. Thus it seems reasonable to model the insurer as acting in any given market to maximize his expected wealth $(\pi_1 x_1 + \pi_2 x_2)$. That is, we model the insurer as being risk-neutral. The next result shows that in a competitive equilibrium in such an economy the risk-averse individuals may be fully insured or only partially insured, depending on the size of the insurer's initial resources.

Proposition 11.6: Competitive equilibrium in market with insurer

Let $\langle N, (u^i)_{i \in N}, (\pi_1, \pi_2), e \rangle$ be an exchange economy with uncertainty in which $N = \{I\} \cup M$, where I is risk-neutral and all m members of M are strictly risk-averse, with the same strictly concave utility function u. Assume that $e(I) = (\alpha, \alpha)$ and $e(i) = (0, 1)$ for every $i \in M$.

  a. If $\alpha \geq m\pi_2$ then the economy has a unique competitive equilibrium (p, a), in which $p_1/p_2 = \pi_1/\pi_2$, $a(I) = (\alpha - m\pi_2, \alpha + m\pi_1)$, and $a(i) = (\pi_2, \pi_2)$ for all $i \in M$.

  b. If $\alpha < m\pi_2$ then the economy has a competitive equilibrium. In any equilibrium $p_1/p_2 > \pi_1/\pi_2$, $a(I) = (0, \alpha(1 + p_1/p_2))$, and $a(i) = (\alpha/m, 1 - \alpha p_1/(m p_2))$ for all $i \in M$.

Proof

First note that in both cases the economy has no equilibrium with $p_1/p_2 < \pi_1/\pi_2$, since for such a price ratio we have $a_1(I) > \alpha$, so that the insurer's demand for good 1 exceeds the amount available in the economy.

a. We first show that (p, a) is the unique equilibrium with $p_1/p_2 = \pi_1/\pi_2$. For such a price system the only optimal bundle of each individual $i \in M$ is $a(i) = (\pi_2, \pi_2)$. Given $\alpha \geq m\pi_2$, in any such equilibrium feasibility requires that the insurer chooses the bundle $a(I) = (\alpha - m\pi_2, \alpha + m\pi_1)$. This bundle is on the insurer's budget line and hence is optimal for him since all bundles on his budget line yield the same expected utility. Thus the pair (p, a) is the unique equilibrium.

The economy has no equilibrium (q, b) in which $q_1/q_2 > \pi_1/\pi_2$. For such a price ratio, I's optimal bundle is $(0, \alpha(q_1 + q_2)/q_2)$ (see the left panel in Figure 11.6) and $b_1(i) < q_2/(q_1 + q_2)$ for each $i \in M$ (see the right panel in Figure 11.6). Hence

$$b_1(I) + \sum_{i \in M} b_1(i) < m \frac{q_2}{q_1 + q_2} = m \frac{1}{1 + q_1/q_2} < m \frac{1}{1 + \pi_1/\pi_2} = m\pi_2 \leq \alpha$$

contradicting the equilibrium condition that the total demand for good 1 is equal to α.

b. The economy has no equilibrium with price ratio π_1/π_2 since then each individual $i \in M$ optimally chooses the bundle (π_2, π_2), contradicting the feasibility requirement, given $\alpha < m\pi_2$.

Thus in any equilibrium (q, b) we have $q_1/q_2 > \pi_1/\pi_2$ and hence the insurer chooses $b(I) = (0, \alpha(q_1 + q_2)/q_2)$ (as in the left panel of Figure 11.6). The feasibility constraint then requires that $b_1(i) = \alpha/m$ for all $i \in M$. Thus the price system q is part of an equilibrium if and only if q_1/q_2 is equal to the marginal rate of substitution for each member of M at $(\alpha/m, 1 - \alpha q_1/(mq_2))$. Our assumptions ensure that at least one such price system exists. Although this result is intuitively plausible, the proof is beyond the scope of this book. The main idea of the proof is that the amount of good 1 demanded by an individual is π_2 if $q_1/q_2 = \pi_1/\pi_2$ and is close to 0 if q_1/q_2 is large enough, so that for some intermediate value of q_1/q_2 his demand is α/m.

Comment

One purpose in building and analyzing formal models is to test our intuitions about the world. The analysis may sharpen our intuition or, alternatively, suggest that our assumptions are not reasonable. Proposition 11.6 leads us to a conclusion of the latter type. In a competitive equilibrium, the insurer's profit is zero, whereas the individuals prefer the bundles they are allocated to their initial

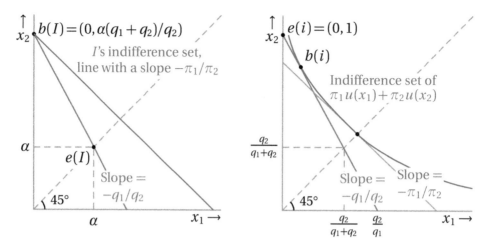

Figure 11.6 If $q_1/q_2 > \pi_1/\pi_2$ then the insurer's optimal bundle is $(0, \alpha(q_1 + q_2)/q_2)$ (left panel) and individual i's optimal bundle $b(i)$ satisfies $b_1(i) < q_2/(q_1 + q_2)$ (right panel).

bundles. This result conflicts with our intuition that a large insurer will achieve a large profit at the expense of the risk-averse individuals. The result appears to depend on the assumption that the single large insurer takes prices as given, an assumption that does not seem reasonable. Our intuition suggests that a large monopolistic insurer will be able to exercise market power, committing to prices that generate a positive profit.

11.2.5 Heterogeneous beliefs

We have assumed so far that the probability assigned to any given state is the same for all individuals. The next example considers an economy in which the individuals' beliefs about the states differ.

Example 11.2: Exchange economy with uncertainty and heterogeneous beliefs

Consider a variant of an exchange economy with uncertainty in which the probabilities the individuals assign to the states differ. The set of individuals is $N = \{1, 2\}$ and each individual i's Bernoulli utility function is $u^i(x) = x$, his initial bundle is $e(i) = (1, 1)$, and he assigns probability $\pi_1(i)$ to state 1 and $\pi_2(i)$ to state 2. We suggest you verify that the following table describes the unique competitive equilibrium for various configurations of the individuals' beliefs.

	p	$a(1)$	$a(2)$
$\frac{1}{2} < \pi_1(2) < \pi_1(1)$	$(\pi_1(2), \pi_2(2))$	$(1/\pi_1(2), 0)$	$(2 - 1/\pi_1(2), 2)$
$\pi_1(2) < \frac{1}{2} < \pi_1(1)$	$(\frac{1}{2}, \frac{1}{2})$	$(2, 0)$	$(0, 2)$
$\pi_1(2) < \pi_1(1) < \frac{1}{2}$	$(\pi_1(1), \pi_2(1))$	$(2, 2 - 1/\pi_2(1)))$	$(0, 1/\pi_2(1)))$

Thus when both individuals believe that state 1 is more likely than state 2 and individual 1 assigns higher probability than individual 2 to state 1 then the only equilibrium prices coincide with the probabilities that individual 2 assigns to the states, and individual 1 bets only on state 1. When the individuals disagree about the more likely state then in the unique equilibrium each of them bets on the state he believes to be more likely.

Problems

Section 11.1

1. *In equilibrium the sum of utilities is maximized.* Show that in any competitive equilibrium of an exchange economy with an indivisible good and money the sum of the individuals' utilities is maximized.

2. *Equilibrium with cash constraints.* In an exchange economy with an indivisible good and money, each buyer is assumed to have at least as much money as her valuation. Consider the following example of a variant of such an economy with five individuals in which some buyers have less money than their valuations. Characterize the competitive equilibrium of this economy under the assumption that no individual can spend more money than he originally holds.

i	1	2	3	4	5
v^i	2	10	8	4	6
$e_1(i)$	13	6	5	2	10
$e_2(i)$	0	0	0	1	1

3. *Comparative statics.* Consider an exchange economy with an indivisible good and money in which the unique competitive equilibrium price is p^*.

   a. Show that if the valuation of one of the individuals (either a buyer or a seller) increases then any equilibrium price in the new economy is at least as high as p^*.

   b. Show that the addition of a buyer cannot decrease the equilibrium price of the good and the addition of a seller cannot increase this price.

4. *Manipulability.* Consider an exchange economy with an indivisible good and money with a unique competitive equilibrium price. Give an example in which an individual can benefit (according to his original preferences) from acting as if he has a different valuation.

5. *Transaction costs.* Consider a variant of an exchange economy with an indivisible good and money in which every individual has to decide to go to the market or stay home. Going to the market involves a monetary loss of $c > 0$. A candidate for an equilibrium is now a price of the good and a profile of decisions for the individuals, where each individual has three alternatives: (*i*) stay home with his initial bundle; (*ii*) go to the market and trade at the equilibrium price; (*iii*) go to the market and do not trade.

   Define equilibrium to be a price and a decision profile such that (*a*) the action of every individual is optimal, given the price and (*b*) the number of individuals who go to the market and buy the good is equal to the number of individuals who go to the market and sell the good.

   Show that any equilibrium price is an equilibrium price in the market without transaction costs in which each seller with original valuation v has valuation $v + c$ and each buyer with original valuation v has valuation $v - c$.

6. *Payments not to participate in the market.* Construct an example of an exchange economy with an indivisible good and money where it is worthwhile for one of the individuals to offer other individuals the following deal: "don't participate in the market and I will compensate you with a sum of money that will make you better off than if you refuse my offer and participate in the market".

Section 11.2

7. *Heterogeneous beliefs.* Two individuals in an exchange economy with uncertainty have the same Bernoulli utility function, u, which is increasing, strictly concave, and differentiable. Individual 1 believes that the probability that the yellow basketball team will win the next game is t and individual 2 believes that this probability is s, where $0 < s \leq t < 1$. The two goods in the economy are tickets that pay \$1 if the yellow team wins and \$1 if the yellow team loses. Each individual initially has 100 tickets of each type.

   a. Analyze the competitive equilibrium of this market when $t = s$.

   b. Assume that $t > s$. Show, graphically, that in a competitive equilibrium individual 1 holds more tickets that pay \$1 if the yellow team wins than tickets that pay \$1 if the team loses.

8. *Exchange economy with uncertainty and indivisible goods.* A show will take place only if the weather permits. To watch the show, a person needs a ticket, which will not be refunded if the show is cancelled. Each individual has a

Bernoulli utility function that takes the value $10+m$ if the individual watches the show and m if he does not, where m is the amount of money he holds. Of the $n = n_1 + n_0$ individuals, n_1 each initially holds a single ticket and n_0 each has initially an amount of money greater than 10 but no ticket. Each individual i believes that the show will take place with probability t^i where $0 < t^n < t^{n-1} < \cdots < t^2 < t^1 < 1$. Define and characterize the competitive equilibria of the variant of an exchange economy with an indivisible good and money that models this situation.

9. *Betting market.* Two candidates, A and B run for office. An even number n of individuals gamble on the outcome of the election. All gamblers are risk-neutral. Gambler i assigns probability α_i to A's winning and probability $1 - \alpha_i$ to B's winning. Each gambler chooses whether to bet on A or B. An individual who bets on A pays a price p and gets \$1 if A wins, and an individual who bets on B pays $1 - p$ and gets \$1 if B wins.

   a. Define an equilibrium price as the price for which the number of individuals who bet on A is equal to the number of individuals who bet on B. What is a rationale for this definition?

   b. Find the equilibrium prices if there are eight gamblers and $(\alpha_1,\ldots,\alpha_8) = (0.95, 0.9, 0.8, 0.7, 0.6, 0.4, 0.1, 0)$.

10. *Time preferences.* Consider an economy with two types of individuals; each individual lives for two periods. There are n individuals of generation 1, each of whom holds \$1 in period 1, and n individuals of generation 2, each of whom holds \$1 in period 2. A bundle is a pair (x_1, x_2) with the interpretation that its holder consumes x_t units at time $t = 1, 2$. The preferences of each individual are represented by the utility function $U(x_1, x_2) = u(x_1) + \delta u(x_2)$, where $0 < \delta < 1$ and u is increasing and strictly concave.

   a. Characterize the competitive equilibria of this economy. Are the individuals of generation 1 better off than those of generation 2, or vice versa?

   b. (If you wish) Calculate the equilibria for the case that $u(x) = \sqrt{x}$.

Notes

The adaptation of the model of an exchange economy to an environment with uncertainty in Section 11.2 was suggested by Arrow (1964) (originally published in French in 1953).

Problem 9 is inspired by the Iowa election markets (see `http://tippie.uiowa.edu/iem/markets/`).

12 A market with consumers and producers

This chapter describes two models that extend the model of an exchange economy to economies in which goods are produced. We do not analyze the models in detail, but only prove, for each model, one result regarding the Pareto stability of the equilibrium outcome.

12.1 Production economy

12.1.1 Introduction

Every day has a morning and an afternoon. All decision-makers face the same price system, which remains the same during the day. Each production unit is controlled by a manager and is owned by consumers. In the morning, each manager chooses a feasible production plan. Here we assume that the manager's objective is to maximize the profit of the production unit, on the assumption that all of the output will be sold at the given prices. After lunch the profit of each production unit is divided among the owners of the unit. Every individual observes the sum of the profits he has received from the production units in which he has an ownership share. In the afternoon he chooses a consumption bundle that is optimal for him in the budget set determined by his income and the price system.

If every consumer is able to purchase a bundle that is optimal for him and no surplus of any good remains, then the producers' and consumers' decisions are in harmony and the prices are consistent with equilibrium. If a surplus or shortage of some good exists (goods remain on the shelves or the shelves are empty and some consumers cannot purchase as much as they desire), then the economy is not in equilibrium, and we expect prices to change.

12.1.2 Model

The economy has two goods, 1 and 2, a set I of consumers, and a set J of producers. Each consumer i is characterized by an increasing, continuous, and convex preference relation $\succsim^i$ on the set of bundles $\mathbb{R}^2_+$. Each producer j is characterized by a technology, a set $T(j) \subseteq \mathbb{R}^2_+$ of all the bundles he can produce.

Chapter of *Models in Microeconomic Theory* by Martin J. Osborne and Ariel Rubinstein. Version 2023.5.30 (h).
© 2023 Martin J. Osborne and Ariel Rubinstein CC BY-NC-ND 4.0.   https://doi.org/10.11647/OBP.0362.12

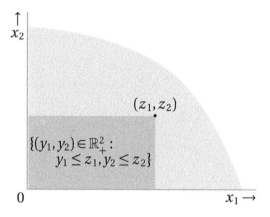

Figure 12.1 An example of a technology: a closed, bounded, convex subset of $\mathbb{R}^2_+$ that includes $(0,0)$ and has the property that for every point (z_1, z_2) in the set, every point $(y_1, y_2) \in \mathbb{R}^2_+$ with $y_1 \leq z_1$ and $y_2 \leq z_2$ is in the set.

Each producer j chooses a member of $T(j)$. Notice that this formalization of the producer's decision is simplistic: he is endowed with production abilities and needs merely to choose a combination of goods to produce. (He incurs no cost.) We assume that each $T(j)$ is a technology, defined as follows and illustrated in Figure 12.1.

Definition 12.1: Technology

A *technology* T is a set $T \subseteq \mathbb{R}^2_+$ that is closed, bounded, and convex, and has the property that if $(x_1, x_2) \in T(j)$, $y_1 \leq x_1$, and $y_2 \leq x_2$ then $(y_1, y_2) \in T(j)$ (that is, goods can be *freely disposed*).

Each producer j, when choosing the output of his production unit (an element in $T(j)$) takes as given the price system (p_1, p_2) prevailing in the market and maximizes the value of this output (the unit's profit). That is, producer j chooses a solution of the problem

$$\max_{x \in T(j)} px$$

where $px = p_1 x_1 + p_2 x_2$.

The last element of the model provides a link between the production units' profits and the consumers' budgets. We assume that the profit of each unit is divided among the consumers. Denote by $\alpha(i, j)$ the fraction of the profit of producer j that belongs to consumer i. All the profit of each production unit is distributed to consumers, so $\sum_{i \in I} \alpha(i, j) = 1$ for every j. Each consumer chooses a bundle to maximize his preferences given his wealth, which is the total profit he receives. Note that the model takes the ownership shares as given; it does not include the process by which ownership is determined.

Definition 12.2: Production economy

A *production economy* $\langle I, J, (\succsim^i)_{i \in I}, (T(j))_{j \in J}, \alpha \rangle$ consists of

consumers
a finite set I

producers
a finite set J

consumers' preferences
for each consumer $i \in I$, a preference relation $\succsim^i$ over $\mathbb{R}_+^2$ that is monotone, continuous, and convex

technologies
for each producer $j \in J$, a technology $T(j) \subseteq \mathbb{R}_+^2$, the set of bundles that j can produce

ownership shares
for every consumer $i \in I$ and producer $j \in J$, a number $\alpha(i, j) \in [0, 1]$ with $\sum_{i \in I} \alpha(i, j) = 1$ for every $j \in J$; $\alpha(i, j)$ is the fraction of producer j's profit owned by consumer i.

A feasible outcome in the economy specifies the bundle chosen by each producer and by each consumer such that the total amount of each good produced is equal to the total amount of each good consumed.

Definition 12.3: Consumption-production plan

A *consumption-production plan* in the production economy $\langle I, J, (\succsim^i)_{i \in I}, (T(j))_{j \in J}, \alpha \rangle$ is a pair (x, y) where $x = (x(i))_{i \in I}$ is an assignment of bundles to consumers and $y = (y(j))_{j \in J}$ is an assignment of bundles to producers such that $y(j) \in T(j)$ for every producer $j \in J$ and $\sum_{i \in I} x(i) = \sum_{j \in J} y(j)$.

A candidate for a competitive equilibrium of a production economy consists of a price system $p^* = (p_1^*, p_2^*)$, a consumption decision $x^*(i)$ for every consumer $i \in I$, and a production decision $y^*(j)$ for every producer $j \in J$. A candidate is a competitive equilibrium if the following conditions are satisfied.

- For every consumer i, the bundle $x^*(i)$ is optimal given p^* and the income i gets from his shares of the producers' profits.

- For every producer j, the bundle $y^*(j)$ maximizes j's profit given p^* and his technology $T(j)$.

- The combination of consumption and production decisions is feasible: it is a consumption-production plan.

Definition 12.4: Competitive equilibrium of production economy

A *competitive equilibrium* of the production economy $\langle I, J, (\succcurlyeq^i)_{i \in I}, (T(j))_{j \in J}, \alpha \rangle$ is a pair $(p, (x, y))$ consisting of

- a price system $p = (p_1, p_2)$ and

- an assignment of bundles to consumers $x = (x(i))_{i \in I}$ and an assignment of bundles to producers $y = (y(j))_{j \in J}$

such that

optimality of consumers' choices
    for every consumer $i \in I$, the bundle $x(i)$ is maximal according to $\succcurlyeq^i$ in the set $\{x \in \mathbb{R}_+^2 : px = \sum_{j \in J} \alpha(i, j)\pi(j)\}$, where $\pi(j) = py(j)$ for each $j \in J$ (the profit of producer j)

optimality of producers' choices
    for every producer $j \in J$, the bundle $y(j)$ maximizes pz subject to $z \in T(j)$

feasibility
    (x, y) is a consumption-production plan.

The notion of Pareto stability can be applied to a production economy: a consumption-production plan is Pareto stable if no consumption-production plan is at least as good for all consumers and better for at least one of them.

Definition 12.5: Pareto stable consumption-production plan

The consumption-production plan (x', y') in the production economy $\langle I, J, (\succcurlyeq^i)_{i \in I}, (T(j))_{j \in J}, \alpha \rangle$ *Pareto dominates* the consumption-production plan (x, y) if $x'(i) \succcurlyeq^i x(i)$ for all $i \in I$ and $x'(i) \succ^i x(i)$ for some $i \in I$. The consumption-production plan (x, y) is *Pareto stable* if no plan (x', y') Pareto dominates it.

12.1.3 Competitive equilibrium

We now show that the consumption-production plan generated by a competitive equilibrium of a production economy is Pareto stable (a counterpart of Proposition 10.4 for an exchange economy).

> ### Proposition 12.1: Pareto stability of competitive equilibrium
>
> The consumption-production plan **generated by any** competitive equilibrium of a production economy **is** Pareto stable.

> ### Proof
>
> Let $(p,(x,y))$ be a competitive equilibrium of the production economy $\langle I, J, (\succsim^i)_{i \in I}, (T(j))_{j \in J}, \alpha \rangle$. Assume that the consumption-production plan (x', y') Pareto dominates (x, y). The optimality of the producers' choices in the competitive equilibrium implies that $py(j) \geq py'(j)$ for every $j \in J$, so that
>
> $$p \sum_{j \in J} y(j) \geq p \sum_{j \in J} y'(j).$$
>
> Also, $px'(i) \geq px(i)$ for every consumer $i \in I$ (if $px'(i) < px(i)$ then given that $x'(i) \succsim^i x(i)$ and that $\succsim^i$ is monotone, there is a bundle z with $pz < px(i)$ and $z \succ^i x(i)$, contradicting the optimality of $x(i)$). For the consumer i for whom $x'(i) \succ^i x(i)$, we have $px'(i) > px(i)$ (otherwise $x(i)$ is not optimal for i given the price system p). Thus
>
> $$p \sum_{i \in I} x'(i) > p \sum_{i \in I} x(i).$$
>
> But the feasibility requirement of the equilibrium, $\sum_{i \in I} x(i) = \sum_{j \in J} y(j)$, so
>
> $$p \sum_{i \in I} x'(i) > p \sum_{i \in I} x(i) = p \sum_{j \in J} y(j) \geq p \sum_{j \in J} y'(j),$$
>
> contradicting $\sum_{i \in I} x'(i) = \sum_{j \in J} y'(j)$.

Note that the proof of this result does not use the convexity of the preferences or of the technology. However, without these assumptions a competitive equilibrium may not exist. Consider a production economy with one producer and one consumer, who owns the producer's profit. The consumer's preference relation is convex, and is represented by the function $\min\{x_1, x_2\}$. The technology is the set T as depicted in Figure 12.2. For any price system, the production bundle that maximizes profit is either a or b (or both). But for any budget set the consumer's optimal bundle involves equal amounts of the goods. So for no price system does the consumer's optimal bundle coincide with the producer's optimal bundle, as competitive equilibrium requires in this economy.

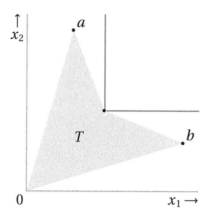

Figure 12.2 An economy with production with a single consumer and single production unit in which the technology is not convex.

12.2   An economy with capital and labor

12.2.1   Introduction

A capitalist uses the labor of a worker to produce a good. Given the wage rate, the capitalist decides how much labor time to buy, and the production process he owns yields a quantity of the good; he uses some of the output to pay the worker and consumes the remainder. The worker decides how long to work, is paid, and consumes his income and any remaining leisure time. In an equilibrium, wages are such that the amount of time the worker wants to work is equal to the quantity of labor the capitalist wants to buy.

12.2.2   Model

There are two goods, a consumption good and leisure, and two individuals, a capitalist and a worker. The production process transforms an amount of time into an amount of the consumption good. The production function f describes this process: the output produced by a units of time is $f(a)$. We assume that f is increasing and concave, and satisfies $f(0)=0$. (Figure 12.3 shows an example.)

   The worker has one unit of time and decides how to divide it between leisure and work. He is characterized by a preference relation on $\{(l,x):0\le l\le 1,x\ge 0\}$, where l is an amount of leisure and x is an amount of the consumption good. We assume that this preference relation is monotone, continuous, and convex.

> **Definition 12.6: Capitalist-worker economy**
>
> A *capitalist-worker economy* $\langle f, \succcurlyeq \rangle$ consists of

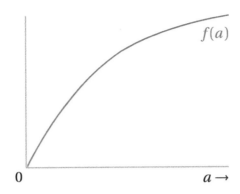

Figure 12.3 A production function.

capitalist's technology

   an increasing concave function $f : \mathbb{R}_+ \to \mathbb{R}_+$ with $f(0) = 0$, the *production function* available to the capitalist, which associates with every nonnegative number a (an amount of labor) a nonnegative number $f(a)$ (the amount of a consumption good produced).

worker's preferences

   a monotone, continuous, and convex preference relation $\succeq$ over $\mathbb{R}_+^2$ (the worker's preferences over pairs (l,x) consisting of an amount l of leisure and an amount x of the consumption good).

We assume one individual of each type only for simplicity. The model can easily be extended to include multiple capitalists and workers.

Given a wage rate, the producer chooses the amount of labor time to buy. We assume here that he aims to maximize profit. That is, given the wage rate w (measured in units of the consumption good per unit of time) the producer chooses a to maximize $f(a) - wa$. The worker decides the amount of time l to keep for leisure; he chooses the value of l that generates the pair $(l, w(1-l))$ that is best according to his preferences.

Definition 12.7: Consumption-production plan

A *consumption-production plan* in the capitalist-worker economy $\langle f, \succeq \rangle$ is a pair $((l,x),(a,z))$ consisting of an amount l of leisure for the worker, an amount x of the consumption good assigned to the worker, an employment level a, and an amount z of the consumption good assigned to the capitalist, with $a = 1 - l$ and $f(a) = x + z$.

The following definition of Pareto stability is appropriate for the model.

> ### Definition 12.8: Pareto stability
>
> A consumption-production plan $((l,x),(a,z))$ in the capitalist-worker economy $\langle f, \succcurlyeq \rangle$ is *Pareto stable* if there is no consumption-production plan $((l',x'),(a',z'))$ for which $z' \geq z$ and $(l',x') \succcurlyeq (l,x)$, with at least one strict inequality.

A competitive equilibrium consists of a wage rate w^*, an employment level a^*, and a consumption bundle (l^*,x^*) for the worker such that

- the bundle (l^*,x^*) is optimal for the consumer and the employment level a^* maximizes the capitalist's profit, given the wage rate

- the amount of time the worker wants to devote to production is equal to the amount of labor time the capitalist wants to use (the employment level).

> ### Definition 12.9: Competitive equilibrium of capitalist-worker economy
>
> A *competitive equilibrium* of a capitalist-worker economy $\langle f, \succcurlyeq \rangle$ is a pair $(w^*,((l^*,x^*),(a^*,z^*)))$ consisting of a positive number w^* (the wage rate) and a pair of choices, one for the worker, (l^*,x^*), and one for the capitalist, (a^*,z^*), such that
>
> **optimality of worker's choice**
> (l^*,x^*) is maximal with respect to $\succcurlyeq$ in the budget set $\{(l,x) : 0 \leq l \leq 1, x = w^*(1-l)\}$ (the worker chooses amounts of leisure and consumption that he likes best given the wage rate)
>
> **optimality of capitalist's choice**
> a^* maximizes $f(a) - w^*a$ (the employment level maximizes the capitalist's profit, given the wage rate) and $z^* = f(a^*) - w^*a^*$
>
> **feasibility**
> $((l^*,x^*),(a^*,z^*))$ is a consumption-production plan.

A competitive equilibrium is illustrated in Figure 12.4. Given the wage rate w^*, the capitalist optimally chooses the employment level a^*, resulting in the output $x^* + z^*$. The worker optimally supplies a^* units of labor time, earning w^*a^* and thus facing the budget set indicated. In this set, the optimal bundle for the consumer is (l^*,x^*).

> ### Proposition 12.2: Pareto stability of competitive equilibrium
>
> The consumption-production plan in any competitive equilibrium of a capitalist-worker economy is Pareto stable.

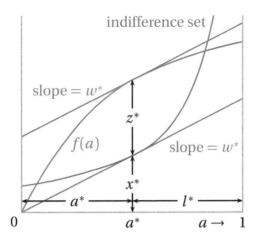

Figure 12.4 An illustration of a competitive equilibrium in a capitalist-worker economy.

> **Proof**
>
> Consider a competitive equilibrium $(w^*, ((l^*, x^*), (a^*, z^*)))$. Let $((l', x'), (a', z'))$ be a consumption-production plan that Pareto dominates $((l^*, x^*), (a^*, z^*))$. Thus $z' \geq z^*$ and $(l', x') \succcurlyeq (l, x)$ with at least one strict inequality. By the optimality of (l^*, x^*) in the set $\{(l, x) : 0 \leq l \leq 1, x = w^*(1 - l)\}$ we have $x' \geq w^*(1 - l')$. Therefore one of the inequalities $z' \geq z^*$ and $x' \geq w^*(1 - l')$ must be strict. By the feasibility of the plan, $x' + z' = f(a')$ and $a' = (1 - l')$. Thus $f(a') - w^* a' = f(a') - w^*(1 - l') \geq f(a') - x' = z' \geq z^* = f(a^*) - w^* a^*$ with one of the inequalities strict. Thus $f(a') - w^* a' > f(a^*) - w^* a^*$, contradicting the optimality of a^* for the capitalist.

We close the chapter by emphasizing again that Pareto stability is not a normative notion. The fact that a consumption-production plan is Pareto stable means only that any plan that one of the individuals (the capitalist and the worker) prefers is worse for the other individual. A competitive equilibrium may be just or unjust; a regulation like a minimum wage may lead to a consumption-production plan that is not Pareto stable but is fairer.

Problems

1. *Comparative advantage and specialization.* Consider an economy with two goods and a set $N = \{1, \ldots, n\}$ of individuals. Each individual is both a consumer and a producer. Individual i chooses a bundle from the set $T(i) = \{(y_1, y_2) : t^i y_1 + y_2 \leq c^i\}$, where c^i and t^i are positive constants, with $t^1 < t^2 < \cdots < t^n$. Each individual can trade the bundle he produces for another bundle at the market prices.

a. Given a price system p, define a p-production-consumption plan for individual i to be a pair $(x(i), y(i))$ such that $y(i) \in T(i)$ and $px(i) = py(i)$. Define an appropriate concept of competitive equilibrium.

b. Show that given the price system (p_1, p_2), every individual for whom $t^i < p_1/p_2$ produces only good 1, every individual for whom $t^i > p_1/p_2$ produces only good 2, and every individual for whom $t^i = p_1/p_2$ are indifferent between all p-production-consumption plans.

c. Show that if all individuals have the same preference relation, represented by the utility function $tx_1 + x_2$, then the economy has a competitive equilibrium in which each individual consumes the bundle that he produces.

d. Assume that $n = 2$ and each individual has preferences represented by the utility function $\min\{x_1, x_2\}$. Give an example of an economy in which $t^1 < t^2$ (individual 1 has a *comparative advantage* in producing good 1) with a competitive equilibrium in which individual 1 produces both goods.

2. *Capitalist-worker economy with output-maximizing capitalist.* Assume that in a capitalist-worker economy the capitalist maximizes output subject to the constraint that profit is nonnegative (see Section 6.2). Illustrate in a diagram like Figure 12.4 a competitive equilibrium of the economy. Is an equilibrium outcome necessarily Pareto stable?

3. *Technological improvement in capitalist-worker economy.* Show by examples that a technological improvement in a capitalist-worker economy (in which the capitalist maximizes profit) may change the competitive equilibrium so that the capitalist is worse off or the worker is worse off.

4. *Production chain.* Consider an economy with two producers. Producer 1 makes the good X using his own labor time; t units of time generate the output $f(t)$. Producer 2 makes good Y using X as an input; his production function is g. Both f and g are strictly concave, increasing, and differentiable. Producer 1 has a differentiable, monotone, and convex preference relation over pairs consisting of amounts of Y and leisure. Producer 2 chooses the amount of X to maximize his profit. Each producer is the sole owner of his technology.

    A candidate for a competitive equilibrium consists of (i) a price p^* of X in terms of Y, (ii) the amount of time t^* that producer 1 devotes to making X, and (iii) the quantity x^* of X that producer 2 uses. A candidate (p^*, t^*, x^*) is a competitive equilibrium if (i) producer 1's decision maximizes his preference relation given p^*, (*ii*) producer 2's decision maximizes his profit, and (*iii*) the supply of X by producer 1 is equal to the demand for X by producer 2.

Show that the outcome of a competitive equilibrium is Pareto stable.

5. *Pollution.* In an economy in which one individual's action has a direct effect on another individual, a competitive equilibrium may not be Pareto stable. To demonstrate this point, consider an economy with two goods, N producers, and N consumers. Each producer has the production technology $T = \{(y_1, y_2) : 2y_1 + y_2 = 2\}$ (and incurs no cost), and maximizes his profit. The producers' profits are divided equally among all consumers. Consumption of good 2 produces pollution. The pollution index is 1.5 times the average consumption of good 2. Each consumer has the utility function $x_1 + x_2 - z$, where z is the pollution index. When choosing a bundle a consumer takes the pollution index as given. (This assumption seems reasonable when N is large.) Define an appropriate notion of symmetric competitive equilibrium in which all consumers choose the same bundle and all producers choose the same member of T. Show that any symmetric equilibrium outcome is not Pareto stable.

13 Equilibrium with prices and expectations

In the models of markets we have discussed so far, equilibrium prices make the individuals' decisions compatible. Each individual takes the prices as given when deciding on his action, and at the equilibrium prices the demand and supply of every good are equal.

In this chapter, an individual's behavior is affected not only by the prices but also by his expectations regarding other parameters. Each individual takes these expectations, like the prices, as given. In equilibrium, each individual behaves optimally, the supply and demand for each good are equal, and the expectations of individuals are correct.

We present three models. In the first model, each individual chooses one of two bank branches. His decision is affected only by his belief about the expected service time in each branch. In the second model, potential buyers of a used car, who cannot observe the quality of the cars for sale, take into account their expectation of the average quality of these cars as well as the price. In the third model, the unit cost of catching fish depends on the total amount of fish caught. Each fisher makes his decision taking as given both the price of fish and his expectation about the unit cost he will incur.

13.1 Distributing customers among bank branches

13.1.1 Introduction

Individuals live on the long main street of a town. At each end of the street there is a branch of a bank. Each individual cares only about the amount of time he spends dealing with the bank, which is the sum of his travel time and waiting time. The waiting time in each branch depends on the number of individuals who patronize the branch; each individual forms expectations about these waiting times. We are interested in the distribution of the individuals between the branches in an equilibrium in which each individual's expectations are correct.

13.1.2 Model

We model the street along which the individuals live as the interval $[0, 1]$; the bank branches are located at the points 0 and 1. The set of individuals is the

Chapter of *Models in Microeconomic Theory* by Martin J. Osborne and Ariel Rubinstein. Version 2023.5.30 (h).
© 2023 Martin J. Osborne and Ariel Rubinstein CC BY-NC-ND 4.0.   https://doi.org/10.11647/OBP.0362.13

interval $[0,1]$, with the interpretation that individual z resides at point z. Thus for each $z \in [0,1]$, the fraction z of individuals reside to the left of z and the fraction $1-z$ reside to the right of z. The assumption that the set of individuals is infinite aims to capture formally a situation in which the number of individuals is very large and each individual's behavior has a negligible effect on the waiting times in the branches, even though these waiting times are determined by the aggregate behavior in the population.

The waiting time in each branch depends on the number of individuals who use that branch. Specifically, if the fraction of individuals who use branch j (i.e. the branch located at j, which is 0 or 1) is n_j, then the waiting time in that branch is $f_j(n_j)$. We assume that each function f_j is increasing and continuous, with $f_j(0) = 0$ (i.e. if there are no customers in a branch, the waiting time in that branch is zero).

We assume, for simplicity, that an individual's travel time from x to branch z is the distance $d(z,x) = |z - x|$ between x and z. Every individual prefers the branch for which the sum of the travel time and the waiting time is smallest.

Definition 13.1: Service economy

A *service economy* $\langle B, I, (f_j)_{j \in B}, d \rangle$ consists of

branches
   a set $B = \{0, 1\}$

individuals
   a set $I = [0, 1]$

waiting time technology
   continuous increasing functions $f_j : [0,1] \to \mathbb{R}$ with $f_j(0) = 0$ for $j = 0, 1$, where $f_j(n_j)$ is the waiting time at branch j when the fraction of individuals who choose branch j is n_j

preferences
   each individual $i \in I$ prefers a smaller loss to a larger one, where the loss from choosing branch j when t_j is the waiting time in that branch is $d(i,j) + t_j$, where $d(i,j) = |i - j|$.

Note that the bank branches are not decision-makers in this model: their locations and service technologies are fixed. The only decision-makers are the individuals.

13.1.3 Equilibrium

We define an equilibrium in the spirit of competitive equilibrium. Each individual has beliefs about the waiting times and assumes that his action does not affect these waiting times. This assumption is analogous to our earlier assumption when defining competitive equilibrium that consumers and producers take prices as given, ignoring the effect of their own actions on the prices. Each individual chooses the branch that minimizes the time he spends dealing with the branch, given his beliefs about the waiting times. In equilibrium the individuals' beliefs are correct. Behind this definition is the assumption that agents' holding incorrect beliefs is a source of instability in the interaction; for stability, we need not only the individuals' actions to be optimal but also their beliefs to be correct.

A candidate for equilibrium consists of two numbers, t_0 and t_1, the individuals' (common) beliefs about the waiting times in the branches, and a function $l : [0,1] \to \{0,1\}$, assigning to every individual at point x the branch $l(x)$ (either 0 or 1) that he chooses.

To be an equilibrium, a candidate has to satisfy two conditions.

- The decision of each individual is optimal given his beliefs about the waiting times in the branches.

- The individuals' decisions and beliefs are consistent in the sense that the belief about the waiting time in each branch is correct, given the service technology and the fraction of individuals who select that branch.

Definition 13.2: Equilibrium of service economy

An *equilibrium* of the service economy $\langle B, I, (f_j)_{j \in B}, d \rangle$ is a pair $((t_0, t_1), l)$, consisting of a pair of numbers (t_0, t_1) (the waiting times in the branches) and a function $l : I \to B$ (an assignment of each $x \in I$ to a branch), such that

optimality of individuals' choices

$$l(x) = 0 \quad \Rightarrow \quad x + t_0 \leq (1-x) + t_1$$
$$l(x) = 1 \quad \Rightarrow \quad (1-x) + t_1 \leq x + t_0$$

(each individual is assigned to a branch for which the travel time plus waiting time for that branch is at most the travel time plus waiting time for the other branch)

consistency

$$t_j = f_j(\alpha(l, j)) \text{ for each } j \in B$$

where $\alpha(l, j)$ is the fraction of individuals assigned to branch j by the function l.

13.1.4 Analysis

We now prove the existence of an equilibrium in this model, characterize it, and show that it is Pareto stable. We start by showing that there is a unique point z^* such that if all individuals to the left of z^* use branch 0 and all individuals to the right of z^* use branch 1 then individual z^* is indifferent between the two branches.

Lemma 13.1

There is a unique number z^* such that $z^* + f_0(z^*) = 1 - z^* + f_1(1 - z^*)$.

Proof

The function $z + f_0(z)$ is continuous and increasing in z and takes the value 0 at the point 0 and the value $1 + f_0(1)$ at the point 1. The function $1 - z + f_1(1 - z)$ is continuous and decreasing in z and takes the value $1 + f_1(1)$ at 0 and the value 0 at 1. So the graphs of the functions have a unique intersection.

Next we show that for any expected waiting times, if for an individual at x branch 0 is at least as good as branch 1, then all individuals to the left of x prefer branch 0 to branch 1 (and analogously for an individual for whom branch 1 is at least as good as branch 0).

Lemma 13.2

For any pair of expected waiting times, if branch 0 is at least as good as branch 1 for an individual at x then branch 0 is better than branch 1 for every individual y with $y < x$, and if branch 1 is at least as good as branch 0 for an individual at x then branch 1 is better than branch 0 for every individual y with $y > x$.

Proof

Denote by t_0 and t_1 the expected waiting times in the branches. For branch 0 to be at least as good as branch 1 for an individual at x we need

$$t_0 + d(x, 0) \leq t_1 + d(x, 1).$$

If $y < x$ then $d(y, 0) < d(x, 0)$ and $d(y, 1) > d(x, 1)$, so that $t_0 + d(y, 0) < t_1 + d(y, 1)$. A similar argument applies to the other case.

We can now prove the existence and uniqueness of an equilibrium in a service economy.

> ## Proposition 13.1: Equilibrium of service economy
>
> Every service economy has a unique equilibrium (up to the specification of the choice at one point).

> ## Proof
>
> We first show that every service economy has an equilibrium. Let z^* be the number given in Lemma 13.1. Let $(t_0^*, t_1^*) = (f_0(z^*), f_1(1 - z^*))$ and let l^* be the function that assigns 0 to all individuals in $[0, z^*]$ and 1 to all individuals in $(z^*, 1]$. We now argue that $((t_0^*, t_1^*), l^*)$ is an equilibrium.
>
> **Optimality of individuals' choices**
>
>   Individual z^* is indifferent between the two branches since $z^* + t_0^* = z^* + f_0(z^*) = 1 - z^* + f_1(1 - z^*) = 1 - z^* + t_1^*$ (using the definition of z^*). By Lemma 13.2, all individuals on the left of z^* prefer 0 to 1 and all on the right of z^* prefer branch 1 to 0.
>
> **Consistency**
>
>   The proportion $\alpha(l^*, 0)$ of individuals who choose branch 0 is z^*. Therefore $t_0^* = f_0(z^*) = f_0(\alpha(l^*, 0))$. Similarly, the proportion $\alpha(l^*, 1)$ of individuals who choose branch 1 is $1 - z^*$, so that $t_1^* = f_1(1 - z^*) = f_1(\alpha(l^*, 1))$.
>
>   We now show that the equilibrium is unique. First note that a service economy has no equilibrium in which one branch is not used since if there were such an equilibrium, the waiting time at the unused branch would be 0 while the waiting time at the other branch would be positive, and hence individuals who are located close to the unused branch would prefer that branch to the other one.
>
>   Let $((t_0, t_1), l)$ be an equilibrium. By Lemma 13.2, there is a point z such that all individuals to the left of z choose 0 and all individuals to the right of z choose 1. Thus an individual at z is indifferent between the branches, so that $z + t_0 = 1 - z + t_1$, and hence $z = z^*$ by Lemma 13.1. Therefore l is identical to l^* up to the assignment at z^*. By the consistency condition for equilibrium, $t_0 = f_0(z^*)$ and $t_1 = f_1(1 - z^*)$.

We now define the notion of Pareto stability for a service economy and show that the equilibrium of such an economy is Pareto stable.

Definition 13.3: Pareto stability

Consider a service economy $\langle B, I, (f_j)_{j \in B}, d \rangle$. For any assignment l and individual $x \in I$ define $L_x(0, l) = x + f_0(\alpha(l, 0))$, the loss of x from choosing 0 given that all other individuals behave according to l. Similarly define $L_x(1, l) = 1 - x + f_1(\alpha(l, 1))$.

An assignment l is *Pareto stable* if there is no assignment l' that *Pareto dominates* l in the sense that $L_x(l'(x), l') \leq L_x(l(x), l)$ for all $x \in I$, with strict inequality for some $x \in I$.

Proposition 13.2: Pareto stability of equilibrium of service economy

Every equilibrium of a service economy is Pareto stable.

Proof

Let $((t_0^*, t_1^*), l^*)$ be an equilibrium of the service economy $\langle B, I, (f_j)_{j \in B}, d \rangle$. Let l' be an assignment. If the proportions of individuals at each branch are the same in l^* and l', then the waiting times induced by the two assignments are the same. Since all individuals make the optimal choices in l^*, the assignment l' does not Pareto dominate l^*.

If more individuals are assigned to branch 0 (say) by l' than l^*, then some individuals who are assigned to branch 1 by l^* are assigned to branch 0 by l'. In the equilibrium such individuals like branch 1 at least as much as branch 0. Under l', branch 0 is less attractive for each of them since the waiting time at that branch is greater than it is under l^*. Hence l' does not Pareto dominate l^*.

13.2 Asymmetric information and adverse selection

13.2.1 Introduction

Second-hand cars of a particular model may differ substantially in quality. Each owner knows the quality of his car, but no buyer knows the quality of any given car. Because cars are indistinguishable to buyers, the price of every car is the same. Each owner decides whether to offer his car for sale, given this price. The decision of each potential buyer depends on his expectation of the quality of the cars offered for sale. A buyer may believe that the quality of the cars offered for sale is low, because owners of high-quality cars are not likely to want to sell, given the uniform price. The fact that the cars selected for sale by the owners have low quality is often called *adverse selection*.

13.2.2 Model

The set of individuals in the market consists of a finite set S of owners and a larger finite set B of potential buyers. Each $i \in S$ owns a car of quality $Q(i) \in (0, 1]$, which he knows. The utility of an owner of a car of quality q is q if he keeps it and p if he sells it at the price p. Each potential buyer obtains the utility $\alpha q - p$, where $\alpha > 1$, if he purchases a car of quality q at the price p, and the utility 0 if he does not purchase a car. The assumption that $\alpha > 1$ implies that mutually beneficial trade is possible: every car is valued more highly by every potential buyer than by its owner.

A potential buyer does not know and cannot determine the quality of any specific car before purchasing it, and no owner can credibly communicate the quality of his car to a potential buyer. Thus for a potential buyer, purchasing a car is a lottery with prizes equal to the possible qualities of the car. We assume that a buyer maximizes his expected utility, so his decision depends on his expectation $\hat{q}$ of the quality of the cars for sale; he wishes to purchase a car if the amount he pays for it is less than $\alpha \hat{q}$.

Definition 13.4: Second-hand car market

A *second-hand car market* $\langle S, B, Q, \alpha \rangle$ consists of

owners
>   a finite set S, each member of which owns one car

buyers
>   a finite set B with $|B| > |S|$, each member of which buys at most one car

qualities
>   a function $Q : S \to (0, 1]$, where $Q(i)$ is the quality of the car owned by i

preferences
>   the owner of a car of quality q prefers to sell it if in exchange he gets an amount of money $p > q$ and prefers not to sell it if he gets an amount of money $p < q$
>
>   a potential buyer prefers to buy a car than not to do so if $\alpha \hat{q} > p$, prefers not to buy it if $\alpha \hat{q} < p$, and is indifferent between the two options if $\alpha \hat{q} = p$, where $\alpha > 1$ and p is the amount he pays and $\hat{q}$ is his belief about the expected quality of the cars for sale.

13.2.3 Equilibrium

Two parameters determine the behavior of the buyers and owners: the price of a car and the belief of the potential buyers about the expected quality of the cars

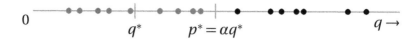

Figure 13.1 Equilibrium of a second-hand car market. Each small disk represents a car; the red ones are offered for sale.

for sale. An equilibrium consists of a price p^*, a (common) belief q^* of the potential buyers about the expected quality of cars for sale, a specification of the owners who offer their cars for sale, and a specification of the potential buyers who purchase cars, such that

- the decision of every owner and potential buyer is optimal, given p^* and q^*

- the number of cars offered for sale is equal to the number of buyers who wish to purchase a car

- if at least one car is traded, the buyers' belief about the expected quality of the cars offered for sale is correct (if there is no trade the belief is not restricted).

Definition 13.5: Equilibrium of second-hand car market

An *equilibrium* (p^*, q^*, S^*, B^*) of a second-hand car market (S, B, Q, α) consists of a number $p^* \geq 0$ (the price of a car), a number $q^* \geq 0$ (the potential buyers' common belief about the expected quality of the cars offered for sale), a set $S^* \subseteq S$ (the set of owners who offer their cars for sale), and a set $B^* \subseteq B$ (the set of potential buyers who purchase a car) such that

optimality of choices

for potential buyers: if $B^* \neq \varnothing$ then $p^* \leq \alpha q^*$ and if $B \setminus B^* \neq \varnothing$ then $p^* \geq \alpha q^*$

for owners: if $i \in S^*$ then $p^* \geq Q(i)$ and if $i \in S \setminus S^*$ then $p^* \leq Q(i)$

consistency

$|S^*| = |B^*|$ (the number of owners who sell their cars is equal to the number of potential buyers who buy a car)

if $S^* \neq \varnothing$ then $q^* = \sum_{i \in S^*} Q(i)/|S^*|$, the average quality of the cars owned by the members of S^* (the potential buyers' belief about the expected quality of the cars offered for sale is correct).

An equilibrium in which $\varnothing \subset B^* \subset B$, so that $p^* = \alpha q^*$, is illustrated in Figure 13.1.

13.2.4 Analysis

We now show that every second-hand car market has an equilibrium in which trade occurs (the set of owners who sell their cars is nonempty).

Proposition 13.3: Equilibrium of second-hand car market

Let $\langle S, B, Q, \alpha \rangle$ be a second-hand car market. Name the owners so that $S = \{s_1, \ldots, s_{|S|}\}$ with $Q(s_1) \leq Q(s_2) \leq \cdots \leq Q(s_{|S|})$. The market has an equilibrium (p^*, q^*, S^*, B^*) with $S^* \neq \varnothing$. In any equilibrium the quality of every car that is sold is no greater than the quality of every other car.

Proof

For $m = 1, \ldots, |S|$, let $A(m)$ be the average quality of the m lowest quality cars: $A(m) = \sum_{i=1}^{m} Q(s_i)/m$. Given $\alpha > 1$, we have $\alpha A(1) > Q(s_1)$. Let m^* be the maximal m for which $\alpha A(m) \geq Q(s_m)$. Let $p^* = \alpha A(m^*)$, $q^* = A(m^*)$, and $S^* = \{s_1, \ldots, s_{m^*}\}$; let B^* be a subset of B with m^* members. Then (p^*, q^*, S^*, B^*) is an equilibrium. To verify the optimality of the individuals' choices, note that $p^* = \alpha q^* = \alpha A(m^*) \geq Q(s_{m^*}) \geq Q(s_m)$ for every $m \leq m^*$, so that each owner $s_1, \ldots, s_{m^*}$ optimally sells his car. Also $p^* = \alpha A(m^*) \leq \alpha A(m^* + 1) < Q(s_{m^*+1}) \leq Q(s_m)$ for all $m \geq m^*+1$, so that each owner $s_{m^*+1}, \ldots, s_{|S|}$ optimally does not sell his car. Each potential buyer is indifferent between buying and not buying a car since $\alpha q^* = p^*$.

The last claim in the proposition follows from the optimality of the owners' equilibrium choices. The quality of the cars of owners who sell is at most p^* and the quality of the other owners' cars is at least p^*.

Every second-hand car market has also an equilibrium in which no car is traded. Let p^* be a positive number less than $Q(s_1)$, the lowest quality, and let q^* be such that $\alpha q^* < p^*$. Then $(p^*, q^*, \varnothing, \varnothing)$ is an equilibrium: no potential buyer is willing to pay p^* for a car, given his belief that the average quality of the cars for sale is q^*, and no owner has a car whose quality is low enough to justify his selling it for p^*. In this equilibrium, the potential buyers expect that the average quality of cars for sale is less than the lowest quality of all owners' cars. Note that the definition of equilibrium does not restrict the belief of the potential buyers when no owner offers a car for sale. We might regard the belief q^* that we have assumed to be unreasonable. For example, if potential buyers know the range of qualities of the owners' cars, then their expectation should reasonably lie within this range, in which case an equilibrium in which no trade occurs does not exist.

Note that the equilibrium constructed in the proof of Proposition 13.3 is not Pareto stable unless $S^* = S$. If $S^* \subset S$, suppose that the owner of a car of quality q who has not sold the car transfers it to a potential buyer who has not purchased a car, in exchange for an amount of money between q and αq. Then both the owner and the buyer are better off.

For some second-hand car markets, in all equilibria with trade only the lowest quality car is traded. Suppose for example that the set of car qualities is $\{1,2,\ldots,|S|\}$ and $\alpha < \frac{4}{3}$. In an equilibrium there is a number m^* such that S^* consists of the owners of cars with qualities $1,2,\ldots,m^*$ and $m^* \leq \alpha q^*$, where q^* is the average quality of the cars for sale, which is $\frac{1}{2}(1+m^*)$. That is, $m^* \leq \frac{1}{2}\alpha(1+m^*) < \frac{2}{3}(1+m^*)$, which is satisfied only by $m^* = 1$.

13.3   A fishing economy

13.3.1   Introduction

A community of fishers and consumers lives near a lake. Each fisher decides how many fish to catch and each consumer decides how many fish to buy, given the price of fish. The cost of catching fish increases with the number of fish caught. In an equilibrium, the total amount of fish the fishers decide to catch is equal to the total amount the consumers decide to buy. Will the fishers catch too much in the sense that if they reduced their catch the price would adjust in such a way that everybody would be better off?

13.3.2   Model

The set of individuals in the economy consists of a set I of consumers and a set J of fishers. Each fisher decides how many fish to catch, up to a limit of L. If the total amount of fish caught by all fishers is T then the cost for a fisher to catch x fish is $c(T)x$, where c is a continuous, increasing function with $c(0)=0$. That is, the larger is the total catch the more costly it is to fish. Each consumer decides how much fish to consume, up to a limit of one unit. Each consumer's preferences are represented by the function $vx + m$, with $v > 0$, where m is the amount of money he has and x is the amount of fish he consumes.

To make the main point of this section we analyze the model under the additional assumptions that (i) $c(|J|L) > v$ (if all fishers operate at full capacity then their unit cost exceeds the value of a unit to consumers), (ii) $c(0) < v$ (if all fishers are idle then their unit cost is less than the value of a unit to the consumers), and (iii) $|J|L \leq |I|$ (if all fishers operate at full capacity, their total output is less than the maximum possible total amount the consumers can consume).

Definition 13.6: Fishing economy

A *fishing economy* $\langle I, J, v, L, c \rangle$ consists of

consumers
    a finite set I

fishers
 a finite set J

consumers' preferences
 a number $v > 0$, the consumers' monetary equivalent of a unit of fish, so that each consumer's preferences are represented by the utility function $vx + m$, where m is the amount of money the consumer has and $x \in [0, 1]$ is the amount of fish he consumes

fishers' technology
 a number L with $0 < L \leq |I|/|J|$ and an increasing and continuous function $c : [0, |J|L] \to \mathbb{R}$ with $c(0) < v$ and $c(|J|L) > v$ (a fisher can catch up to L units of fish and one who catches y units incurs the cost $c(T)y$ when the total amount of fish caught by all fishers is T).

13.3.3 Equilibrium

A candidate for an equilibrium of a fishing economy consists of a price for a unit of fish, the fishers' common expectation about the unit cost of fishing, the amount of fish that each fisher decides to catch, and the amount of fish chosen by each consumer, such that

- every fisher chooses the amount of fish he catches to maximize his profit given the price and his expectation of the cost of fishing

- every consumer chooses his consumption optimally given the price

- the expectations of the fishers about the cost of fishing are correct

- the total amount of fish caught is equal to the total amount the consumers choose to consume.

Definition 13.7: Competitive equilibrium of fishing economy

A *competitive equilibrium* (p^*, c^*, y^*, x^*) of the fishing economy $\langle I, J, v, L, c \rangle$ consists of a positive number p^* (the price of a unit of fish), a non-negative number c^* (the fishers' belief about the unit cost of fishing), a non-negative number y^* (the amount of fish caught by each fisher), and a non-negative number x^* (the amount of fish chosen by each consumer) such that

optimality of choices
 for consumers: x^* maximizes the utility $vx - p^*x$ over $[0, 1]$

 for fishers: y^* maximizes the profit $p^*y - c^*y$ over $[0, L]$

feasibility

$|I|x^* = |J|y^*$ (the total amount of fish consumed is equal to the total amount of fish caught)

consistency

$c^* = c(|J|y^*)$ (the fishers' expectation about the unit fishing cost is correct).

13.3.4 Analysis

Proposition 13.4: Competitive equilibrium of fishing economy

A fishing economy $\langle I, J, v, L, c \rangle$ has a unique competitive equilibrium (p^*, c^*, y^*, x^*), in which $p^* = v = c^* = c(|J|y^*)$ and $|I|x^* = |J|y^*$.

Proof

First, given $c(0) < v$, $c(|J|L) > v$, and the continuity of c there exists a number y^* such that $c(|J|y^*) = v$. Now, given that $c(|J|y^*) = v$, our assumptions that $c(|J|L) > v$ and c is increasing imply that $y^* < L$ and our assumption that $L \leq |I|/|J|$ implies that $x^* < 1$. The tuple (p^*, c^*, y^*, x^*) is a competitive equilibrium because all consumers and fishers are indifferent between all their possible actions, total production is equal to total consumption, and the fishers' expectation about the unit cost is correct.

To prove that the economy has no other equilibrium, suppose that (p', c', y', x') is an equilibrium.

If $p' > v$ then the optimal choice of every consumer is 0, so that $x' = y' = 0$. But then $c' = c(0) < v$, so that the optimal choice of every fisher is L, violating feasibility.

If $p' < v$ then the optimal choice of every consumer is 1, so that $x' = 1$ and by the feasibility condition $y' = |I|/|J|$. By the consistency condition $c' = c(|I|)$ and by our assumption that $|J|L \leq |I|$ we have $c(|I|) \geq c(|J|L) > v$, so that catching a positive amount of fish is not optimal for any fisher.

Therefore $p' = v$. It now suffices to show that $c' = p'$, since then by consistency we have $v = c(|J|y')$ and by feasibility $|J|y' = |I|x'$. If $c' > p'$ then the optimality of the fishers' choices implies that $y' = 0$; hence $x' = 0$, so that the optimality of the consumers' choices requires $p' \geq v$. But now by consistency $c' = c(0) < v$, a contradiction. A similar argument shows that $c' < p'$ is not possible.

A competitive equilibrium outcome is not Pareto stable, by the following argument. Let (p^*, c^*, y^*, x^*) be a competitive equilibrium. The utility of each consumer is $vx^* - p^*x^* = 0$ and the profit of each fisher is $p^*y^* - c(|J|y^*)y^* = 0$. Now consider $\hat{y}$ and $\hat{k}$ with $0 < \hat{y} < y^*$ and $c(|J|\hat{y}) < \hat{k} < v$. The production-consumption plan in which each fisher catches $\hat{y}$ fish and receives $\hat{k}\hat{y}$ units of money and each consumer receives $\hat{y}|J|/|I|$ fish and pays $\hat{k}\hat{y}|J|/|I|$ generates positive utility to all consumers and positive profits to all fishers.

This model is used by many economists (including MJO, but not AR) to argue that a tax-redistribution scheme can make all agents (consumers and fishers) better off. Assume that each fisher has to pay a tax $t = v - c(|J|\hat{y})$ per unit of fish caught (where $0 < \hat{y} < y^*$), so that in equilibrium the unit cost for a fisher is $c^* + v - c(|J|\hat{y})$. This tax changes the unit cost of fishing when the total amount of fish caught is T from $c(T)$ to $d(T) = c(T) + v - c(|J|\hat{y})$, so that $d(|J|\hat{y}) = v$. Thus Proposition 13.4 implies that the economy with the tax has a unique equilibrium, in which each fisher catches $\hat{y}$ fish, the price paid by consumers is v, and each consumer purchases $\hat{y}|J|/|I|$ fish. In this equilibrium the utility of every consumer and the profit of every fisher is zero. The taxes collected can be distributed among the consumers and producers to make every consumer's utility and every fisher's profit positive.

Problems

1. *Service economy.*

   a. Compare the equilibrium of the service economy $\langle B, I, (f_j)_{j \in B}, d \rangle$ with the equilibrium of the service economy that differs only in that f_0 is replaced by $\hat{f}_0$ with $\hat{f}_0(x) < f_0(x)$ for all $x > 0$ (branch 0 becomes more efficient). Show that more individuals use branch 0 in an equilibrium of the modified economy than in an equilibrium of the original economy.

   b. Show that if branch 0 is more efficient than branch 1 in the sense that $f_0(x) < f_1(x)$ for every $x > 0$, then in equilibrium the waiting time in branch 1 is larger than it is in branch 0.

   c. Some evidence suggests that some people exaggerate their estimate of the time they spend in activities like going to a bank. (See for example Jones and Hwang 2005.) Assume that an individual who spends the total amount of time t acts as if this total time is λt, with $\lambda > 1$. How does the equilibrium change?

   d. How does the equilibrium change if individuals exaggerate only the waiting time in a branch, not the transportation time?

2. *Total loss in equilibrium of service economy.* Consider a service economy. Suppose that all individuals to the left of z use branch 0 and the remainder use branch 1. Then the total time spent by the individuals is

$$\int_0^z [x + f_0(z)]\, dx + \int_z^1 [(1-x) + f_1(z)]\, dx.$$

Explain why the equilibrium may not (and typically does not) minimize the total time spent by all individuals even though we know from Proposition 13.2 that the equilibrium is Pareto stable. (If you wish, just calculate the equilibrium for the service economy with $f_0(x) = x$ and $f_1(x) = 2x$ and show that the assignment of individuals to branches that minimize the total loss differs from the equilibrium allocation.)

3. *Fund-raising party.* Each of the 1,200 participants at a fund-raising event can choose a raffle ticket marked L or H. One ticket marked L is randomly chosen and its holder is given the prize L, and one ticket marked H is randomly chosen and its holder is given the prize H, where $0 < L < H$. The preferences of each individual i over the set of lotteries are represented by the expected value of a Bernoulli utility function u^i with $u^i(0) = 0$, $u^i(H) = 1$, and $u^i(L) = v$, where $0 < v < 1$.

   a. Formulate an equilibrium concept in the spirit of this chapter.

   b. What is the equilibrium if $v = \frac{1}{3}$?

4. *Matching.* Individuals are divided into a members of type A and b members of type B, where $a \ge b$. Each individual wishes to be matched with an individual of the other type. An individual can be matched with only one other individual. Matches can occur in two possible venues, 1 and 2. Each individual chooses one of these venues. Given that α individuals of type A and β individuals of type B choose a venue, the probability of a type A individual being matched at that venue is $\min\{\alpha, \beta\}/\alpha$ and the probability of a type B individual being matched is $\min\{\alpha, \beta\}/\beta$. Each individual chooses a venue to maximize the probability he is matched.

   A profile is a list (a_1, b_1, a_2, b_2) of nonnegative real numbers for which $a_1 + a_2 = a$ and $b_1 + b_2 = b$, with the interpretation that a_i and b_i are the numbers of type A and type B individuals who choose venue i. For simplicity, we do not require these numbers to be integers. A candidate for equilibrium is a profile (a_1, b_1, a_2, b_2) and a vector of nonnegative numbers (p_1, p_2, q_1, q_2) with $p_1 + p_2 = 1$ and $q_1 + q_2 = 1$, where p_i is the probability a type A individual assigns to being matched in venue i and q_i is the probability that a type B individual assigns to being matched in venue i. A candidate is an equilibrium if the following two conditions are satisfied.

Optimality

If some type A individual is assigned to venue i ($a_i > 0$) then $p_i \geq p_j$, where $j \neq i$, and if some type B individual is assigned to venue i ($b_i > 0$) then $q_i \geq q_j$.

Consistency

We have $p_i = \min\{1, b_i/a_i\}$ and $q_i = \min\{1, a_i/b_i\}$ for $i = 1, 2$. (Define $\min\{1, 0/0\} = 0$ and for every $x \neq 0$ define $\min\{1, x/0\} = 1$.)

a. Show that any profile (a_1, b_1, a_2, b_2) satisfying $b_1/a_1 = b_2/a_2 = b/a$ together with the vector (p_1, p_2, q_1, q_2) with $p_i = b/a$ and $q_i = 1$ for $i = 1, 2$ is an equilibrium.

b. Characterize all the equilibria for which individuals of each type choose each venue.

c. Find an equilibrium in which every individual chooses venue 1.

5. *Health services.* Consider a market for health services in which there is a large number n of individuals, each with a large amount of money m. Each individual can purchase a quantity of health services. If individual i buys $y(i)$ units of health services, the probability that he survives is $\alpha(y(i), y^*)$, where y^* is the average level of health services obtained by all individuals. Individuals take y^* as given although it is influenced by their behavior. The function α is increasing and concave. Each individual aims to maximize the product of the amount of money he is left with and the probability of survival. That is, he chooses $y(i)$ to maximize $(m - p^* y(i)) \alpha(y(i), y^*)$.

a. Define an equilibrium. Write the equations that characterize an equilibrium in which all agents purchase a positive quality of health services. Assume that the function α is differentiable.

b. Explain why an equilibrium is not Pareto stable.

Notes

The model in Section 13.2 is due to Akerlof (1970).

14 A market with asymmetric information

In this chapter we study an equilibrium concept that differs from the notions of competitive equilibrium discussed in Chapters 9–12. The models in the earlier chapters specify the precise set of economic agents who operate in the market, and an equilibrium specifies the terms of trade (prices) for which the aggregate demand and supply of these agents are equal. The model we study in this chapter does not explicitly specify the set of agents. As a consequence, the equilibrium notion is more abstract. A set of contracts is an equilibrium if no agent who offers a contract wants to withdraw it, and no agent can profit by adding a contract.

We illustrate the concept by applying it to a model central to the economics of information. The problems at the end of the chapter demonstrate the use of the concept to study other economic interactions.

14.1 Introductory model

To explain the logic of the solution concept, we start with a model of a simple labor market without asymmetric information. The market contains employers and workers. Employers post wage offers. Workers are identical, with productivity, if employed, equal to $v > 0$. Each worker either selects a posted offer that is best for him or, if no posted offer is better for him than being unemployed, does not select any offer. A worker who selects an offer is matched with the employer posting the offer; he produces v and receives the posted wage. The profit of an employer who pays a wage w to a worker is $v - w$.

We say that a wage offer (a nonnegative number) is optimal for a worker given the set W of offers if it is the highest wage in W. (We assume that not accepting any offer is equivalent to receiving a wage of 0.) An equilibrium is a finite set W of wage offers for which

I. every offer in W is optimal for a worker

II. no offer in W generates a loss to an employer who posts it

III. no offer $w \notin W$ is optimal for a worker, given the offers in $W \cup \{w\}$, and would yield an employer who posts it a positive profit.

Chapter of *Models in Microeconomic Theory* by Martin J. Osborne and Ariel Rubinstein. Version 2023.5.30 (h).
© 2023 Martin J. Osborne and Ariel Rubinstein CC BY-NC-ND 4.0.   https://doi.org/10.11647/OBP.0362.14

Condition I captures the idea that offers that are not accepted by any worker do not survive. Condition II requires that no offer that is accepted yields a loss to the employer who posts it. Condition III requires that no employer can post a new offer that is optimal for a worker and yields the employer a positive profit.

The notion of equilibrium differs from the ones we analyze in earlier chapters in that it does not specify the choices made by specific participants. An equilibrium is a set of acceptable contracts in the market. The equilibrium is silent about who makes which offer.

We claim that the set $\{v\}$, consisting of the single wage offer v, is an equilibrium. Workers optimally choose it, as it is better than not accepting an offer; it yields zero profit to an employer; and any new offer is either not accepted (if it is less than v) or is accepted (if it is greater than v) but yields negative profit to the employer who posts it.

In fact, $\{v\}$ is the only equilibrium. Let W^* be an equilibrium. If $W^* = \varnothing$ then any offer w with $0 < w < v$ is optimal given $W^* \cup \{w\} = \{w\}$ and yields an employer who posts it a positive profit, violating III. By I, if $W^* \neq \varnothing$ then W^* consists of a single offer, say w^*. By II, $w^* \leq v$. If $w^* < v$, then an offer w with $w^* < w < v$ is optimal for a worker given $W^* \cup \{w\}$ and yields a positive profit, violating III.

14.2   Labor market with education

Imagine a labor market in which employers do not know, before hiring workers, how productive they will be, but do know their educational backgrounds. If education enhances productivity, we might expect employers to be willing to pay higher wages to more educated workers. We study a model in which education does *not* affect productivity, but productivity is negatively related to the cost of acquiring education: the more productive a worker, the less costly it is for him to acquire education. Under this assumption, we might expect employers to be willing to pay a high wage to a worker with a high level of education because they believe that acquiring such an education is worthwhile only for high productivity workers. The model we study investigates whether such a relation between wages and education exists in equilibrium.

In the model there are two types of worker, H and L. When employed, a type H worker creates output worth v_H and a type L worker creates output worth v_L, where $0 < v_L < v_H$. The proportion of workers of type L in the population is α_L and the proportion of workers of type H is α_H, with $\alpha_H + \alpha_L = 1$. No employer knows the type of any given worker before hiring him.

If an employer offers a wage w and a worker who accepts the offer is of type H with probability γ_H and type L with probability γ_L then the employer obtains an expected profit of $\gamma_H v_H + \gamma_L v_L - w$. If a contract is simply a wage offer, then by the argument in the previous section the only equilibrium is $\{\bar{v}\}$, where $\bar{v} = \alpha_H v_H + \alpha_L v_L$, the expected productivity of a worker.

We now add education to the model. Each worker chooses a level of education, which does *not* affect his productivity. The cost of obtaining education is linear in the level of education and is higher for type L workers (who have lower productivity) than it is for type H workers. Specifically, the income of a type X worker with t years of education who is paid the wage w is $w - \beta_X t$, with $0 < \beta_H < \beta_L$.

An employer can observe a worker's education but not his productivity. A contract now specifies a wage and a minimal acceptable number of years of education.

Facing a set of contracts, an individual who is planning his career chooses his education level bearing in mind the maximal wage that this level allows him to obtain. Thus his decision is to choose one of the available contracts (or to choose not to be employed). We assume that each worker's preferences over contracts are lexicographic: his first priority is high income (taking into account the cost of the required level of education), and among contracts that yield him the same income, he prefers one with a lower educational requirement. Thus no worker is indifferent between any two contracts.

Definition 14.1: Labor market with asymmetric information

A *labor market with asymmetric information* is a list of numbers $(v_L, v_H, \alpha_L, \alpha_H, \beta_L, \beta_H)$, where $0 < v_L < v_H$, $\alpha_L \geq 0$, $\alpha_H \geq 0$, $\alpha_L + \alpha_H = 1$, and $0 < \beta_H < \beta_L$. The market consists of *employers* and *workers*. The workers are of two types.

Type L (fraction α_L)
    Productivity v_L and cost β_L for each unit of education

Type H (fraction α_H)
    Productivity v_H and cost β_H for each unit of education.

   A *contract* is a pair (t, w) of nonnegative numbers; t is the number of units of education required for the job and w is the wage.

We now specify a worker's preferences over contracts.

Definition 14.2: Worker's preferences

In a labor market with asymmetric information $(v_L, v_H, \alpha_L, \alpha_H, \beta_L, \beta_H)$, the *income* of a worker of type X $(= H, L)$ who accepts the contract (t, w) is

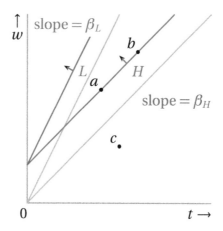

Figure 14.1 Iso-income lines for workers. Along each blue line the income of a worker of type L is constant, and along each red line the income of a worker of type H is constant. Income is higher along the darker lines. A type H worker prefers a to b because a requires less education and both contracts yield him the same income. If only c is offered, each type of worker prefers not to accept any offer, because c yields negative income.

$w - \beta_X t$. The preference relation $\succsim^X$ of a worker of type X over the set of contracts is lexicographic, giving first priority to larger income $w - \beta_X t$ and second priority to smaller values of the education requirement t.

For any set C of contracts the alternative that is *optimal given C for a worker of type X $(= H, L)$* is

$$\begin{cases} (t, w) \in C & \text{if } w - \beta_X t \geq 0 \text{ and } (t, w) \succsim^X (t', w') \text{ for all } (t', w') \in C \\ \phi & \text{if } w' - \beta_X t' < 0 \text{ for every } (t', w') \in C, \end{cases}$$

where ϕ means that the worker does not accept any contract.

Figure 14.1 shows iso-income lines for each type of worker. The blue lines belong to a type L worker; their slope is β_L. Each additional unit of education has to be compensated by an increase β_L in the wage to keep the income of such a worker the same. The red iso-income lines belong to a type H worker; their slope is β_H. Incomes for each type increase in a northwesterly direction: every worker prefers contracts with lower educational requirements and higher wages.

Given that the set of contracts offered is C, an employer who offers a contract $c = (t, w)$ expects a payoff that depends on the types of workers for whom c is optimal given C. If c is not optimal given C for any worker, the employer's payoff is zero; if c is optimal given C only for type X workers, his payoff is $v_X - w$, the profit from hiring a type X worker; and if c is optimal for all workers, his payoff is $\alpha_L v_L + \alpha_H v_H - w$.

> ### Definition 14.3: Employer's payoff
>
> In a labor market with asymmetric information $(v_L, v_H, \alpha_L, \alpha_H, \beta_L, \beta_H)$, for any set C of contracts and any $c = (t, w) \in C$, the *payoff* $\pi(c, C)$ of an employer who offers the contract c when C is the set of posted contracts is
>
> $$\begin{cases} 0 & \text{if } c \text{ is not optimal given } C \text{ for either type of worker} \\ v_X - w & \text{if } c \text{ is optimal given } C \text{ only for type } X \text{ workers} \\ \alpha_L v_L + \alpha_H v_H - w & \text{if } c \text{ is optimal given } C \text{ for both types of worker.} \end{cases}$$
>
> The payoff of an employer who does not offer a contract is 0.

Equilibrium An equilibrium is a finite set C^* of contracts for which (I) every contract in C^* is optimal for at least one type of worker given C^*, (II) no contract in C^* yields a negative payoff to an employer, and (III) no contract $c \notin C^*$ that is optimal for at least one type of worker given $C^* \cup \{c\}$ yields a positive payoff for an employer.

Note that this notion of equilibrium reflects an assumption that an employer who considers offering a new contract correctly anticipates the types of workers for whom the contract is optimal given the other contracts offered.

> ### Definition 14.4: Equilibrium of labor market
>
> An *equilibrium* of a labor market with asymmetric information $(v_L, v_H, \alpha_L, \alpha_H, \beta_L, \beta_H)$ is a finite set C^* of contracts such that
>
> I. each $c \in C^*$ is optimal given C^* for at least one type of worker
>
> II. if $c \in C^*$, then $\pi(c, C^*) \geq 0$ (no employer wants to withdraw a contract)
>
> III. if $c \notin C^*$ and c is optimal given $C^* \cup \{c\}$ for some type of workers, then $\pi(c, C^* \cup \{c\}) \leq 0$ (no employer wants to add a contract).
>
> An equilibrium C^* for which the same alternative is optimal given C^* for both types of worker is a *pooling equilibrium*. An equilibrium for which a different alternative is optimal given C^* for each type is a *separating equilibrium*.

We first argue that the set consisting solely of the contract $b = (0, \overline{v}) = (0, \alpha_H v_H + \alpha_L v_L)$ is not an equilibrium. The reason is that the contract a in Figure 14.2a, like any contract in the area shaded green, is optimal given the set

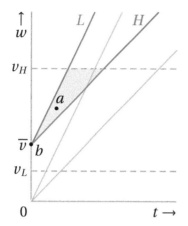

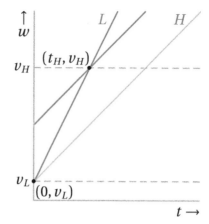

(a) Illustration of the argument that $\{(0,\overline{v})\}$ is not an equilibrium.

(b) The contracts offered in an equilibrium (Proposition 14.1), if one exists.

Figure 14.2

$\{a,b\}$ for a type H worker but not for a type L worker. Thus, given that the wage in a is less than v_H, an employer who offers a when the only other contract is b obtains a positive payoff, violating condition III in Definition 14.4.

The next result shows more generally that a labor market with asymmetric information has no pooling equilibrium and that an equilibrium, if one exists, is separating, containing two contracts, one of which is optimal for each type of worker. These contracts are illustrated in Figure 14.2b. The contract optimal for a type L worker entails a wage equal to his productivity, v_L, and no education ($t = 0$). The contract optimal for a type H worker also pays a wage equal to his productivity, v_H, but requires enough education that a type L worker is not better off choosing it.

Proposition 14.1: Characterization of equilibrium of labor market

If a labor market with asymmetric information $(v_L, v_H, \alpha_L, \alpha_H, \beta_L, \beta_H)$ has an equilibrium C^*, then $C^* = \{c_L^*, c_H^*\}$ where $c_L^* = (0, v_L)$, $c_H^* = (t_H, v_H)$, and t_H satisfies $v_H - \beta_L t_H = v_L$. Given C^*, the contract c_L^* is optimal for a type L worker and c_H^* is optimal for a type H worker.

Proof

Consider an equilibrium C^*.

Step 1 *The action ϕ (not accepting any offer) is not optimal for either type of worker given C^* and thus in particular C^* is not empty.*

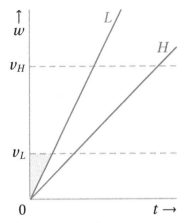

(a) Step 1 of the proof of Proposition 14.1.

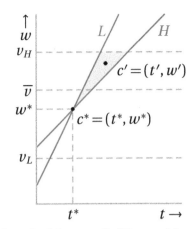

(b) Step 2 of the proof of Proposition 14.1.

Figure 14.3

Proof. Suppose that ϕ is optimal for some type X worker given C^*. Then no contract in the region shaded green in Figure 14.3a is in C^* (because if it were it would be better than ϕ for type X given C^*). Thus any such contract c is optimal for type X given $C^* \cup \{c\}$. Whether X is L or H, the contract c yields a positive payoff for an employer (the wage is less than v_L), and thus violates condition III.   ◁

Step 2 C^* *is not a pooling equilibrium.*

Proof. Assume C^* is a pooling equilibrium. By Step 1, C^* is nonempty, so some contract, say $c^* = (t^*, w^*)$, is optimal given C^* for both types, and by condition I, C^* contains no other contract.

Suppose that $w^* > \bar{v} = \alpha_H v_H + \alpha_L v_L$. Then $\pi(c^*, C^*) = \bar{v} - w^* < 0$, violating condition II.

Now suppose that $w^* \leq \bar{v}$. Consider a contract $c' = (t', w')$ in the green triangle in Figure 14.3b. That is, $w^* + \beta_H(t' - t^*) < w' < \min\{w^* + \beta_L(t' - t^*), v_H\}$. The contract c' is optimal given $\{c^*, c'\}$ for type H, and is not optimal given $\{c^*, c'\}$ for type L (who prefer c^*). Thus $\pi(c', \{c^*, c'\}) = v_H - w' > 0$, violating condition III.   ◁

Given Step 1, Step 2, condition I, and the fact that no worker is indifferent between any two contracts, C^* contains exactly two contracts, say $C^* = \{c_L, c_H\}$, where $c_L = (t_L, w_L)$ is optimal given C^* for type L workers and $c_H = (t_H, w_H)$ is optimal given C^* for type H workers. We now characterize these two contracts.

Step 3 $w_X \leq v_X$ *for* $X = H, L$.

Proof. For an employer who offers the contract c_X, $\pi(c_X, C^*) = v_X - w_X$, so that $w_X \leq v_X$ condition II.   ◁

Step 4 $c_L = c_L^* = (0, v_L)$.

Proof. By Step 3, $w_L \leq v_L$. If $w_L < v_L$ then the contract $c = (t_L, \frac{1}{2}(v_L + w_L))$ is optimal given $C^* \cup \{c\}$ for (at least) type L workers, so that $\pi(c, C^* \cup \{c\}) \geq v_L - \frac{1}{2}(v_L + w_L) = \frac{1}{2}(v_L - w_L) > 0$, violating condition III. Thus $w_L = v_L$.

If $t_L > 0$, let $c' = (t_L', w_L')$ with $t_L' < t_L$, $w_L' < w_L$, and $w_L' - \beta_L t_L' > w_L - \beta_L t_L$. That is, c' reduces the education requirement and the wage in such a way that the income of a type L worker increases. Then c' is optimal given $C^* \cup \{c'\}$ for at least type L workers, so that $\pi(c', C^* \cup \{c'\}) \geq v_L - w_L' > 0$, violating condition III. Thus $t_L = 0$.   ◁

Step 5 $w_H = v_H$ *and* c_L *and* c_H *yield the same income for a type L worker, so that* $v_H - \beta_L t_H = v_L$.

Proof. By Step 3, $w_H \leq v_H$. Given that c_H is optimal given C^* only for a type H worker and c_L is optimal only for a type L worker, c_H lies in the green region in Figure 14.4. If c_H is not c_H^* (the point at the intersection of the horizontal line $w = v_H$ and the line $w - \beta_L t = v_L$) then any contract c_H' in the interior of the dark green region is better for type H workers than c_H but worse for type L workers than c_L. Thus c_H' is optimal given $\{c_L, c_H, c_H'\}$ only for type H workers, so that $\pi(c_H', \{c_L, c_H, c_H'\}) > 0$, violating condition III. Hence $w_H = v_H$ and $v_H - \beta_L t_H = v_L$, so that $c_H = c_H^*$.   ◁

Whether the set of contracts specified in this result is in fact an equilibrium depends on the proportions of the types of workers in the population. Let $m = v_H - \beta_H t_H$ so that the contract $(0, m)$ yields type H workers the same income as does c_H^*.

If the proportion of type L workers is high enough that the average productivity in the entire population, $\bar{v}$, is less than m (as in Figure 14.5a), then C^* is an equilibrium, by the following argument.

- Each c_X^* is optimal for workers of type X.

- Each contract c_X^* yields a payoff of zero to an employer.

- Any contract $c = (t, w)$ that is optimal given $\{c_L^*, c_H^*, c\}$ only for type H workers is in the area shaded green in Figure 14.5a, so that $w > v_H$ and thus the contract does not yield a positive profit.

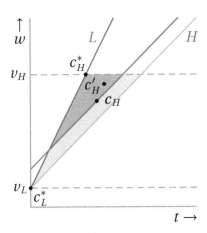

Figure 14.4 Step 5 of the proof of Proposition 14.1.

- Any contract $c = (t, w)$ that is optimal given $\{c_L^*, c_H^*, c\}$ for type L workers has $w > v_L$, so that if c is optimal only for type L workers it yields a negative profit.

- Any contract $c = (t, w)$ that is optimal given $\{c_L^*, c_H^*, c\}$ for both types of worker lies above the iso-income curve of a type H worker through c_H^* (the dark red line in Figure 14.5a), so that $w > m$; since $m > \overline{v}$ we have $w > \overline{v}$, so that c is not profitable.

If, on the other hand, the proportion of workers of type H is large enough that the average productivity in the population exceeds m, then an employer who adds the contract $(0, m)$ (or any other contract in the green triangle in Figure 14.5b) attracts workers of both types and obtains a positive profit. Thus in this case the set C^* of contracts is not an equilibrium.

Comment

The model is related to the "handicap principle" in biology. This principle provides an explanation for phenomena like the long horns of male deer. The male deer signals his unobserved fitness (biological value) by wasting resources on useless horns. The usefulness of the signal depends on the fact that spending resources on useless horns is less costly for fitter animals. In the economic story, a worker signals his unobserved quality by obtaining education, which has no effect on his productivity but is less costly for workers with high productivity.

Problems

1. *Quality certificate.* A market contains producers, each of whom can produce one unit of a good. The quality of the good produced by half of the producers

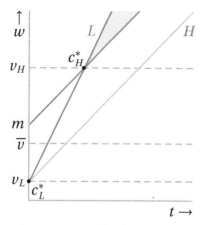 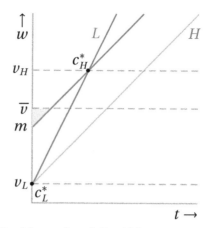

(a) In this market, $\{c_H^*, c_L^*\}$ is a separating equilibrium.

(b) In this market, $\{c_H^*, c_L^*\}$ is not a separating equilibrium.

Figure 14.5 Existence or nonexistence of equilibria in labor markets with asymmetric information.

(type L) is low, and the quality of the good produced by the remaining half (type H) is high. Each producer knows the quality of his output and has no production cost.

The market contains also traders, each of whom can buy a unit of the good from a producer. If a trader buys a unit, he can sell it for the price 20 if it is high quality and for the price 10 if it is low quality. No trader can verify the quality of a good prior to purchasing it.

A producer can obtain a certificate that says that his output has high quality. The cost of such a certificate is 4 for type H and 12 for type L. (A type L producer has to bribe the agency who gives the certificate.)

Traders make offers. An offer has either the form $(+, p)$, a promise to pay p for a good with a certificate, or the form $(-, p)$, a promise to pay p for a good without a certificate. Traders maximize profits.

Each producer has to decide whether to accept one of the offers or to reject all offers (in which case his profit is 0). Producers maximize profits. A producer who is indifferent between two offers chooses the one without the certificate.

A candidate for equilibrium is a set of offers. Define a notion of equilibrium in the spirit of this chapter and characterize all equilibria.

2. *Sorting students.* Consider a world in which entrepreneurs offer education services to the students in a city. All students must choose a school (if one exists). Every student appreciates the closeness of a school to the city. There

are two styles of schools, A and B. A school is a pair (x, d), where x is the style and d is the distance from the city. (The notion of school is analogous to that of a contract in the body of the chapter.) For any value of d, every student prefers (A, d) to (B, d).

The students are of two types.

- A student of type 1 is willing to travel an extra 10 kilometers to get to an A-school. That is, $(A, d) \succeq^1 (B, d')$ if and only if $d \leq d' + 10$. A student of this type fits better at an A-school.

- A student of type 2 is willing to travel only an extra 5 kilometers to study in an A-school. That is, $(A, d) \succeq^2 (B, d')$ if and only if $d \leq d' + 5$. A student of this type fits better at a B-school.

If $(A, d) \sim^i (B, d')$, so that $d > d'$, then a student of type i chooses school B.

Assume that a new school is established only if it is expected that all the students who find it optimal fit its style. An existing school closes if no student attends it or if all students who find it optimal fit the other style of school. Note the following asymmetry: an existing school remains open if it attracts a mixed population whereas to be established, a new school has to expect to attract only students that fit its style.

Define a notion of equilibrium and characterize it.

Notes

The economic example in this chapter is based on Spence (1973) but the analysis follows Rothschild and Stiglitz (1976). The handicap principle is due to Zahavi (1975).

||| Game theory

15 Strategic games

The model of a strategic game is central to game theory. In a strategic game, each individual chooses an action from a given set and is affected not only by this action but also by the other individuals' actions. We study mainly the notion of Nash equilibrium, according to which a profile of actions is stable if no individual wants to deviate from his action given the other individuals' actions.

15.1 Strategic games and Nash equilibrium

A strategic game consists of a set of players, each of whom is characterized by the set of actions available to him and a preference relation over action profiles (lists of actions, one for each player). Each player chooses one of his available actions, so that an outcome of the game is an action profile. We often work with utility functions that represent the players' preference relations, rather than explicitly with preferences, and refer to the utility functions as payoff functions.

Definition 15.1: Strategic game

A *strategic game* $\langle N, (A^i)_{i \in N}, (\succsim^i)_{i \in N} \rangle$ consists of

players
 a set $N = \{1, \dots, n\}$

actions
 for each player $i \in N$, a set A^i of actions

preferences
 for each player $i \in N$, a preference relation $\succsim^i$ over the set $A = \times_{i \in N} A^i$ of *action profiles*.

A function $u^i : A \to \mathbb{R}$ that represents $\succsim^i$ is a *payoff function* for player i.

This model differs from the models discussed in Part II in two main ways. First, in a strategic game the set of alternatives of each player is fixed, whereas in the market models the set of alternatives available to an individual is determined by the equilibrium. Second, in the market models an individual's preferences are defined over his own choices, whereas in a strategic game a player's preferences

Chapter of *Models in Microeconomic Theory* by Martin J. Osborne and Ariel Rubinstein. Version 2023.5.30 (h).
© 2023 Martin J. Osborne and Ariel Rubinstein CC BY-NC-ND 4.0.   https://doi.org/10.11647/OBP.0362.15

are defined over the set of action profiles, so that they take into account the effect of other players' actions on the player.

The main solution concept we study is Nash equilibrium. A Nash equilibrium is an action profile with the property that no deviation by any player leads to an action profile that the player prefers. That is, every player's action in a Nash equilibrium is best for him given the other players' actions.

Definition 15.2: Nash equilibrium of strategic game

In a strategic game $\langle N, (A^i)_{i \in N}, (\succsim^i)_{i \in N} \rangle$, an action profile $a = (a^i) \in A$ is a *Nash equilibrium* if for every player $i \in N$ we have

$$(a^i, a^{-i}) \succsim^i (x^i, a^{-i}) \text{ for all } x^i \in A^i$$

where (x^i, a^{-i}) denotes the action profile that differs from a only in that the action of individual i is x^i rather than a^i.

Like the other equilibrium concepts we discuss, Nash equilibrium is static: we do not consider either a dynamic process or a reasoning process that might lead each player to choose his Nash equilibrium action. Note also that the notion of Nash equilibrium does not consider the instability that might arise if groups of players act together. It simply identifies outcomes that are stable against deviations by individuals, without specifying how these outcomes are attained.

We can express the condition for a Nash equilibrium differently using the notion of a best response.

Definition 15.3: Best response

In a strategic game $\langle N, (A^i)_{i \in N}, (\succsim^i)_{i \in N} \rangle$, the action $a^i \in A^i$ of player i is a *best response* to the list a^{-i} of the other players' actions if

$$(a^i, a^{-i}) \succsim^i (x^i, a^{-i}) \text{ for all } x^i \in A^i.$$

Denote by $BR(a^{-i})$ the set of player i's best responses to a^{-i}. Then an action profile a is a Nash equilibrium if and only if $a^i \in BR(a^{-i})$ for each player i.

15.2   Basic examples

Example 15.1: Traveler's dilemma

Each of two people chooses a number of dollars between \$180 and \$300. Each person receives the lower of the two amounts chosen. In addition, if the amounts chosen differ, $5 is transferred from the person who chose the larger amount to the person who chose the smaller one. (If the amounts chosen are the same, no transfer is made.)

The name traveler's dilemma comes from a story used to add color (a part of the charm of game theory). Each of two travelers takes a suitcase containing an identical object on a flight. The value of the object is known to be between $180 and $300. The suitcases are lost and the airline has to compensate the travelers. The airline asks each traveler to name an integer between 180 and 300. Each traveler gets (in dollars) the smaller of the numbers chosen, and, if the numbers differ, in addition $5 is transferred from the traveler who names the larger number to the one who names the smaller number.

A strategic game that models this situation has $N = \{1,2\}$, $A^i = \{180, 181, \ldots, 300\}$ for $i = 1, 2$, and

$$u^i(a^1, a^2) = \begin{cases} a^i + 5 & \text{if } a^i < a^j \\ a^i & \text{if } a^i = a^j \\ a^j - 5 & \text{if } a^i > a^j, \end{cases}$$

where j is the player other than i.

Claim *The only Nash equilibrium of the traveler's dilemma is* $(180, 180)$.

Proof. First note that $(180, 180)$ is indeed a Nash equilibrium. If a player increases the number he names, his payoff falls by 5.

No other pair (a^1, a^2) is an equilibrium. Without loss of generality, assume $a^1 \geq a^2$. If $a^1 > a^2$, then a deviation of player 1 to a^2 increases his payoff from $a^2 - 5$ to a^2. If $a^1 = a^2 \neq 180$, then a deviation of player i to $a^i - 1$ increases his payoff from a^i to $a^i + 4$.   ◁

When people are asked to play the game (without the suitcase interpretation), most say they would choose a number different from 180. For example, among 21,000 students of courses in game theory around the world who have responded at `https://arielrubinstein.org/gt`, only 22% have chosen 180. The most popular choice is 300 (43%). About 8% chose 299 and 7% chose a number in the range 295–298. The action 298 is the best action given the distribution of the participants' choices.

One possible explanation for the difference between these results and Nash equilibrium is that the participants' preferences are not those specified in the game. Most people care not only about the dollar amount they receive. Some perceive 300 to be the socially desirable action especially if they anticipate that most other people would choose 300. Many people dislike gaining a few dollars at the expense of another person, especially if they believe the other person is not trying to game the system. Thus, for example, player 1 may prefer the outcome $(300, 300)$ to $(299, 300)$, even though the latter involves a higher monetary reward. In this case, the experimental results conflict less with Nash equilibrium as $(300, 300)$ is an equilibrium in the game with these modified preferences.

The next few examples are two-player games with a small number of alternatives for each player. Such a game may conveniently be presented in a table with one row for each action of player 1, one column for each action of player 2, and two numbers in each cell, that are payoffs representing the players' preferences. For example, the following table represents a game in which player 1's actions are T and B, and player 2's are L and R. Each cell corresponds to an action profile. For example, the top left cell corresponds to (T, L). The preferences of player 1 over the set of action profiles are represented by the numbers at the left of each cell and those of player 2 are represented by the numbers at the right of each cell. Thus, for example, the worst action profile for player 1 is (B, R) and the best action profile for player 2 is (B, L).

	L	R
T	5,0	−1,1
B	3,7	−2,0

Example 15.2: Prisoner's dilemma

The Prisoner's dilemma is the most well-known strategic game. The story behind it involves two suspects in a robbery who are caught conducting a lesser crime. The police have evidence regarding only the lesser crime. If both suspects admit to the robbery, each is sentenced to six years in jail. If one of them admits to the robbery and implicates the other, who does not admit to it, then the former is set free and the latter is sentenced to seven years in jail. If neither admits to the robbery then each is sentenced to one year in jail. Each person aims to maximize the number of free years within the next seven years.

The structure of the incentives in this story is shared by many other situations. The essential elements are that each of two individuals has to choose between two courses of action, C (like not admitting) and D

(like admitting), each individual prefers D to C regardless of the other individual's action, and both individuals prefer (C,C) to (D,D).

We can model the situation as a strategic game in which $N = \{1,2\}$, $A^i = \{C,D\}$ for $i = 1, 2$, and the players' preferences are represented by the payoffs in the following table.

	C	D
C	6,6	0,7
D	7,0	1,1

Each player's optimal action is D, independent of the other player's action. Thus (D,D) is the only Nash equilibrium of the game.

The action profile (D,D) is not Pareto stable: both players prefer (C,C). This fact sometimes leads people to use the game to argue that rational behavior by all players may lead to an outcome that is socially undesirable.

Note that in the situation the game is intended to model, some people, at least, would probably not have the preferences we have assumed: the guilt from choosing D when the other person chooses C would lead them to prefer (C,C) to the action profile in which they choose D and the other person chooses C. In the game in which each player has such modified preferences, (C,C) is a Nash equilibrium.

The previous two strategic games, the traveler's dilemma and the prisoner's dilemma, are symmetric: the set of actions of each player is the same and the payoff of player 1 for any action pair (a^1, a^2) is the same as the payoff of player 2 for the action pair (a^2, a^1).

Definition 15.4: Symmetric two-player game

A two-player strategic game $\langle\{1,2\}, (A^i)_{i\in\{1,2\}}, (\succsim^i)_{i\in\{1,2\}}\rangle$ is *symmetric* if $A^1 = A^2$ and $(a^1, a^2) \succsim^1 (b^1, b^2)$ if and only if $(a^2, a^1) \succsim^2 (b^2, b^1)$.

In other words, if u^1 represents $\succsim^1$ then the function u^2 defined by $u^2(a^1, a^2) = u^1(a^2, a^1)$ represents $\succsim^2$. In a symmetric game, a player's preferences can be described by using only the terms "the player" and "the other player", without referring to the player's name.

Example 15.3: Where to meet? (Bach or Stravinsky)

Two people can meet at one of two locations, B (perhaps a concert of music by Bach) or S (perhaps a concert of music by Stravinsky). One person prefers to meet at B and the other prefers to meet at S. Each person prefers to meet somewhere than not to meet at all and is indifferent between the outcomes in which he alone shows up at one of the locations.

This situation is modeled by the following game.

	B	S
B	2,1	0,0
S	0,0	1,2

The game has two Nash equilibria, (B,B) and (S,S). The first equilibrium can be thought of as representing the convention that player 2 yields to player 1, while the second equilibrium represents the convention that player 1 yields to player 2. These interpretations are particularly attractive if the people who engage in the game differ systematically. For example, if player 1 is older than player 2, then the first equilibrium can be interpreted as a norm that the younger player yields to the older one.

Note that the situation can be modeled alternatively as a symmetric game where each player has the two actions F (favorite) and N, as follows.

	F	N
F	0,0	2,1
N	1,2	0,0

Although this game is symmetric, its two Nash equilibria, (N,F) and (F,N), are not symmetric.

Example 15.4: Odds or evens (matching pennies)

In a two-person game played by children, each player presents between 1 and 5 fingers. One player, say player 1, wins if the sum is odd and the other player, 2, wins if the sum is even. Each player prefers to win than to lose.

In one strategic game that models this situation, each player has five actions.

	1	2	3	4	5
1	0,1	1,0	0,1	1,0	0,1
2	1,0	0,1	1,0	0,1	1,0
3	0,1	1,0	0,1	1,0	0,1
4	1,0	0,1	1,0	0,1	1,0
5	0,1	1,0	0,1	1,0	0,1

Obviously, what matters is only whether a player chooses an odd or even number of fingers. So in another strategic game that models the situation, each player's actions are *odd* and *even*.

	odd	*even*
odd	0,1	1,0
even	1,0	0,1

Unlike the previous two examples, these games are *strictly competitive*: an outcome is better for player 1 if and only if it is worse for player 2. Neither game has a Nash equilibrium. That makes sense: no deterministic stable mode of behavior is to be expected given that the game is used to make random choices. We return to the game in Section 15.7, when discussing a notion of equilibrium that involves randomization.

Note that if each of two players has to choose a side of a coin, *Head* and *Tail*, and player 1 prefers to mismatch player 2's choice whereas player 2 prefers to match 1's choice, we get the same payoffs. For this reason, such an interaction is known also as *matching pennies*.

Example 15.5: Coordination game

Two people can meet at one of three stadium gates, Yellow, Blue, or Green. They want to meet and do not care where. This situation is modeled by the following strategic game.

	Y	B	G
Y	1,1	0,0	0,0
B	0,0	1,1	0,0
G	0,0	0,0	1,1

Each of the three action pairs in which both players choose the same action is a Nash equilibrium. An equilibrium, for example (Yellow, Yellow), makes sense if the Yellow gate is a salient meeting place.

15.3   Economic examples

We start with two examples of auctions. In a *sealed-bid auction*, n players bid for an indivisible object. Player i's monetary valuation of the object is $v^i > 0$, $i = 1, \dots, n$. Assume for simplicity that no two players have the same valuation, so that without loss of generality $v^1 > v^2 > \cdots > v^n$. Each player's bid is a nonnegative number, and the object is given to the player whose bid is highest; in case of a tie, the object is given to the player with the lowest index among those who submit the highest bid. That is, the winner $W(b^1, \dots, b^n)$ is the smallest i such that

$b^i \geq b^j$ for $j = 1, \ldots, n$. We assume that each player cares only about whether he wins the object and how much he pays and, for example, does not regret that he did not bid slightly more if doing so would have caused him to win. The auctions we study differ in the rule determining the amount the players pay. If player i wins and pays p then his payoff is $v^i - p$ and if he does not win and pays p then his payoff is $-p$.

Example 15.6: First-price auction

A first-price auction is a sealed-bid auction in which the player who wins the object (the one with the lowest index among the players whose bids are highest) pays his bid and the others pay nothing, so that player i's payoff function is

$$u^i(b^1, \ldots, b^n) = \begin{cases} v^i - b^i & \text{if } W(b^1, \ldots, b^n) = i \\ 0 & \text{otherwise.} \end{cases}$$

This game has many Nash equilibria. Here are some of them.

- $b^1 = v^2$ and $b^i = v^i$ for all other i. Player 1's payoff is $v^1 - v^2$. He cannot increase his payoff: if he lowers his bid then he is no longer the winner, so that his payoff falls to 0. Any other player can obtain the object only if he bids more than v^2, which causes his payoff to be negative.

- $b^1 = b^2 = v^2$ and $b^i = 0$ for all other i.

- $b^i = p$ for all i, where $v^2 \leq p \leq v^1$.

Claim *In all Nash equilibria of a first-price auction, player 1 gets the object and pays a price in $[v^2, v^1]$.*

Proof. Let $(b^1, \ldots, b^n)$ be a Nash equilibrium. Suppose the winner is $i \neq 1$. We need $b^i \leq v^i$ (otherwise player i's payoff is negative, and he can increase it to 0 by bidding 0). Thus player 1 can deviate to a bid between v^2 and v^1, thereby winning the object and getting a positive payoff.

Now suppose that the winner is 1. We have $b^1 \leq v^1$ (as before). If $b^1 < v^2$ then player 2 can raise his bid to a number between b^1 and v^2 and get a positive payoff. Thus $b^1 \in [v^2, v^1]$.   ◁

In fact, $(b^1, \ldots, b^n)$ is a Nash equilibrium of the game if and only if $b^1 \in [v^2, v^1]$, $b^i \leq b^1$ for all $i \neq 1$, and $\max_{i \neq 1} b^i = b^1$.

Example 15.7: Second-price auction

A second-price auction is a sealed-bid auction in which the player who wins the object pays the highest of the *other* bids and the other players pay nothing, so that player i's payoff function is

$$u^i(b^1,\ldots,b^n)=\begin{cases} v^i-\max_{j\neq i}\{b^j\} & \text{if } W(b^1,\ldots,b^n)=i \\ 0 & \text{otherwise.} \end{cases}$$

To get some intuition about the Nash equilibria of this game, suppose first that $n=2$, $v^1=10$, and $v^2=5$. In this case the Nash equilibria of the game include $(7,7)$, $(8,2)$, $(3,12)$, and $(10,5)$.

We now show that the auction has a wide range of Nash equilibria.

Claim *For every player i and every price $p\leq v^i$ a second-price auction has a Nash equilibrium in which i obtains the object and pays p.*

Proof. Consider the action profile in which player i bids $b^i > v^1$, some other player j bids p, and every other player bids 0. Player i wins and his payoff is v^i-p. If he changes his bid, his payoff either remains the same or becomes 0. The payoff of every other player is 0, and remains 0 unless he increases his bid and becomes the winner, in which case his bid must be at least $b^i > v^1$, so that his payoff is negative.   ◁

The result shows, in particular, that the auction has an equilibrium in which each player bids his valuation. This equilibrium is attractive because it has the special property that regardless of the other players' bids, i's action, to bid his valuation v^i, is at least as good for him as any other action: $u^i(v^i,b^{-i})\geq u^i(b^i,b^{-i})$ for all b^{-i} and b^i. We return to this property in Chapter 17 (see Problem 2). Although the equilibrium is attractive, in experiments a majority of subjects do not bid their valuations (see for example Kagel and Levin 1993).

Example 15.8: Location game

The inhabitants of a town are distributed uniformly along the main street, modeled as the interval $[0,1]$. Two sellers choose locations in the interval. Each inhabitant buys a unit of a good from the seller whose location is closer to his own location. Thus if the sellers' locations are a^1 and a^2 with $a^1 < a^2$ then all inhabitants with locations less than $\frac{1}{2}(a^1+a^2)$ patronize seller 1 and all inhabitants with locations greater than $\frac{1}{2}(a^1+a^2)$ patronize seller 2; the fraction of inhabitants with location exactly $\frac{1}{2}(a^1+a^2)$ is zero, so we can ignore it. Each seller wants to sell to the largest proportion of inhabitants possible.

We can model this situation as a strategic game in which $N = \{1,2\}$ and, for $i = 1, 2$, $A^i = [0,1]$ and

$$u^i(a^1,a^2) = \begin{cases} \frac{1}{2}(a^1+a^2) & \text{if } a^i < a^j \\ \frac{1}{2} & \text{if } a^i = a^j \\ 1 - \frac{1}{2}(a^1+a^2) & \text{if } a^i > a^j. \end{cases}$$

Note that the game is strictly competitive.

Claim *The only Nash equilibrium of the location game is $(\frac{1}{2},\frac{1}{2})$.*

Proof. The action pair $(\frac{1}{2},\frac{1}{2})$ is a Nash equilibrium: any deviation from $\frac{1}{2}$ by a seller reduces the fraction of inhabitants who patronize the seller.

The game has no other equilibria. If the sellers choose different locations then for each of them a deviation towards the other improves his market share. If the sellers choose the same location, different from $\frac{1}{2}$, then a deviation by a seller to $\frac{1}{2}$ increases the proportion of inhabitants who patronize him.   ◁

Notice that a player who chooses the location $\frac{1}{2}$ guarantees that his payoff is at least $\frac{1}{2}$, and a player cannot guarantee to himself more than $\frac{1}{2}$. Such an action, which guarantees a certain payoff and has the property that no other action guarantees a higher payoff, is called a *maxmin action*.

Comment   The variant of the game with three players has no Nash equilibrium, by the following argument.

For an action profile in which all players' locations are the same, either a move slightly to the right or a move slightly to the left, or possibly both, increase a player's payoff to more than $\frac{1}{3}$.

For any other action profile, there is a player who is the only one choosing his location and the locations of both other players are either to the left or to the right of his location. Such a player can increase his payoff by moving closer to the other players' locations.

Example 15.9: Effort game

Two players are involved in a joint project. Each player chooses an effort level in $A^i = [0,\infty)$. A player who chooses the level e bears the quadratic

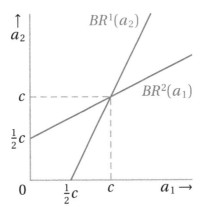

Figure 15.1 The players' best response functions for the effort game in Example 15.9. The game has a unique Nash equilibrium, (c, c).

cost e^2. The project yields player i the amount $a^i(c + a^j)$, where j is the other player and c is a positive constant. Player i's payoff function is given by $u^i(a^i, a^j) = a^i(c + a^j) - (a^i)^2$.

A simple calculation shows that each player i's unique best response to a^j is $\frac{1}{2}(c + a^j)$; the best response functions are shown in Figure 15.1. The equations $a^1 = BR^1(a^2) = \frac{1}{2}(c + a^2)$ and $a^2 = BR^2(a^1) = \frac{1}{2}(c + a^1)$ have a unique solution, $(a^1, a^2) = (c, c)$ (the intersection of the lines in the figure), which is thus the unique Nash equilibrium of the game.

Example 15.10: Quantity-setting oligopoly (Cournot)

Two producers of a good compete in a market. Each of them chooses the quantity of the good to produce. When the total amount they produce is Q, the price in the market is $1 - Q$ if $Q \leq 1$ and 0 otherwise. Each producer incurs the cost cq when he produces q units, where $c \in (0, 1)$, and aims to maximize his profit.

This situation is modeled by a strategic game in which $N = \{1, 2\}$ and for $i = 1, 2$, $A^i = [0, 1]$ and

$$u^i(q^i, q^j) = \begin{cases} (1 - q^i - q^j - c)q^i & \text{if } q^i + q^j \leq 1 \\ -cq^i & \text{if } q^i + q^j > 1 \end{cases}$$

(where j is the other player).

To find the Nash equilibria of the game, we find the best response function of each player i. If $q^j > 1 - c$ then for every output of player i the price is less than c, so that i's profit is negative; in this case his optimal output is 0. Otherwise his optimal output is $(1 - q^j - c)/2$.

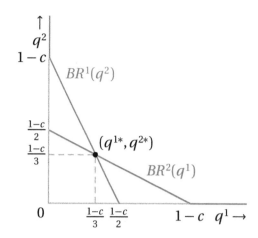

Figure 15.2 The best response functions in a quantity-setting duopoly game in which the inverse demand function is $P = 1 - Q$ and the cost function of each firm is cq. The unique Nash equilibrium is $(q^{1*}, q^{2*}) = (\frac{1}{3}(1-c), \frac{1}{3}(1-c))$.

The best response functions are shown in Figure 15.2. They intersect at $(q^1, q^2) = (\frac{1}{3}(1-c), \frac{1}{3}(1-c))$, which is thus the only Nash equilibrium of the game.

More generally, with n producers the payoff function of player i is

$$u^i(q^1,\ldots,q^n) = \begin{cases} (1 - q^i - \sum_{j\neq i} q^j - c)q^i & \text{if } \sum_{j=1}^n q^j \leq 1 \\ -cq^i & \text{if } \sum_{j=1}^n q^j > 1. \end{cases}$$

Thus player i's best response function is

$$BR^i(q^{-i}) = \max\{0, \tfrac{1}{2}(1 - c - \sum_{j\neq i} q^j)\}.$$

In equilibrium, $2q^i = 1-c-\sum_{j\neq i} q^j$ for each i, so that $q^i = 1-c-\sum_{i=1}^n q^j$ for each i. Therefore q^i is the same for all i, and is thus equal to $(1-c)/(n+1)$. The price in this equilibrium is $1 - (1-c)n/(n+1)$. As $n \to \infty$ this price converges to c and each producer's profit converges to 0.

Example 15.11: Price-setting duopoly (Bertrand)

As in the previous example, two profit-maximizing producers of a good compete in a market with a mass of consumers of size 1. But now we assume that each of them chooses a price (rather than a quantity). Each consumer buys one unit of the good from the producer whose price is lower if this price is at most 1 and nothing otherwise; if the prices are the same, the consumers are split equally between the producers. Each firm produces the amount demanded from it and in doing so incurs the cost $c \in [0,1)$ per unit. Thus, if producer i's price p^i is lower than producer j's price p^j, producer i's payoff is $p^i - c$ if $p^i \leq 1$ and 0 if $p^i > 1$, and producer j's payoff is 0; if the prices are the same, equal to p, each producer's payoff is $\frac{1}{2}(p - c)$ if $p \leq 1$ and 0 if $p > 1$.

In the strategic game that models this situation, for some actions of one producer the other producer has no best response: if one producer's price is between c and 1, the other producer has no optimal action. (A price slightly lower than the other producer's price is a good response in this case, but given that price is modeled as a continuous variable, no price is optimal.) Nevertheless, the game has a unique Nash equilibrium.

Claim *The only Nash equilibrium of a price-setting duopoly is (c,c).*

Proof. The action pair (c,c) is a Nash equilibrium: if a producer increases his price his profit remains 0, and if he reduces his price his profit becomes negative.

We now argue that (c,c) is the only Nash equilibrium. Suppose that (p^1, p^2) is a Nash equilibrium.

We have $\min\{p^1, p^2\} \geq c$, since otherwise a producer who charges $\min\{p^1, p^2\}$ makes a loss, which he can avoid by raising his price to c. Also $\min\{p^1, p^2\} \leq 1$, since otherwise each producer's payoff is 0 and either producer can increase his payoff by reducing his price to 1.

Also, $p^1 = p^2$, because if $c \leq p^i < p^j$ (and $p^i \leq 1$) then i can increase his payoff by raising his price to any value less than $\min\{1, p^j\}$.

Finally, if $c < p^1 = p^2 \leq 1$ then each player's payoff is positive and either player can reduce his price slightly and almost double his payoff.   ◁

15.4 Existence of Nash equilibrium

As we have seen (Example 15.4) some strategic games do not have a Nash equilibrium. We now present two results on the existence of Nash equilibrium in certain families of games. More general results use mathematical tools above the level of this book.

15.4.1 Symmetric games

Our first result is for a family of two-player symmetric games in which each player's set of actions is a closed and bounded interval and his best response function is continuous.

Proposition 15.1: Existence of Nash equilibrium in symmetric game

Let $G = \langle \{1,2\}, (A^i)_{i \in \{1,2\}}, (\succsim^i)_{i \in \{1,2\}} \rangle$ be a two-player symmetric game in which $A^1 = A^2 = I \subset \mathbb{R}$ is a closed and bounded interval for $i = 1, 2$, and each player has a unique best response to every action of the other player, which is a continuous function of the other player's action. Then there exists $x \in I$ such that (x, x) is a Nash equilibrium of G.

Proof

Let $I = [l, r]$. Under the assumptions of the result, the function $g(x) = BR^1(x) - x$, where BR^1 is player 1's best response function, is a continuous function from $[l, r]$ to $\mathbb{R}$ with $g(l) \geq 0$ and $g(r) \leq 0$. Thus by the intermediate value theorem there is a number x^* such that $g(x^*) = 0$, or $BR^1(x^*) = x^*$. Given that the game is symmetric, also $BR^2(x^*) = x^*$, so that (x^*, x^*) is a Nash equilibrium.

An example in which each player's best response is increasing in the other player's action is shown in Figure 15.3a. In this example the game has more than one equilibrium. Such a game does not have any asymmetric equilibria: if (x, y) with $x > y$ were an equilibrium then we would have $BR^1(x) = y$ and $BR^2(y) = x$ and thus also $BR^1(y) = x$, contradicting the assumption that the function BR^1 is increasing.

If each player's best response is decreasing in the other player's action then in addition to symmetric equilibria, the game may have asymmetric equilibria, as in the following example.

Example 15.12

Consider the two-player symmetric game where $N = \{1, 2\}$, $A^i = [0, 1]$, and $u^i(a^1, a^2) = -|1 - a^1 - a^2|$ for $i = 1, 2$. The best response function of player i is given by $BR^i(a^j) = 1 - a^j$, which is continuous. Every action pair $(x, 1-x)$ for $x \in [0, 1]$ is an equilibrium; only $(\frac{1}{2}, \frac{1}{2})$ is symmetric. The best response functions, which coincide, are shown in Figure 15.3b.

15.4.2 Supermodular finite games

The next result concerns games in which the players' best response functions are nondecreasing; such games are called *supermodular*.

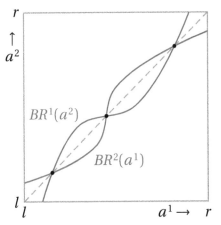
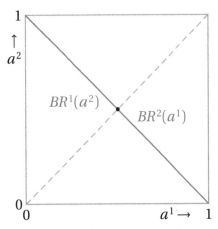

(a) The players' best response functions in a symmetric two-player game. The three small black disks indicate the Nash equilibria.

(b) The players' best response functions in the game in Example 15.12. Every pair $(x, 1-x)$ is a Nash equilibrium. The small black disk indicates the symmetric equilibrium.

Figure 15.3

Proposition 15.2: Existence of equilibrium in finite supermodular two-player game

Consider a two-player strategic game $\langle\{1,2\},(A^i)_{i\in\{1,2\}},(\succsim^i)_{i\in\{1,2\}}\rangle$ in which $A^1 = \{1,\ldots,K\}$, $A^2 = \{1,\ldots,L\}$, and all payoffs of each player are distinct, so that each player has a unique best response to each action of the other player. If each best response function is nondecreasing then the game has a Nash equilibrium.

The result assumes that all payoffs of each player are distinct only for simplicity; it remains true without this assumption.

Figure 15.4a shows an example of best response functions satisfying the conditions in the result, with $K = 8$ and $L = 7$. The function BR^1 is indicated by the blue disks and the function BR^2 is indicated by the red disks. The action pair $(6,5)$, colored both blue and red, is a Nash equilibrium.

Proof

Partition the set A^1 into intervals $I_1,\ldots,I_M$ such that for all actions in any given interval I_m the best response of player 2 is the same, equal to b_m $(BR^2(x) \equiv b_m$ for all $x \in I_m)$ and $b_m < b_{m'}$ for $m < m'$. (See Figure 15.4b for an illustration.) For each $m = 1,\ldots,M$, let $BR^1(b_m) = a_m$. If for some value of m we have $a_m \in I_m$ then (a_m, b_m) is a Nash equilibrium. Otherwise,

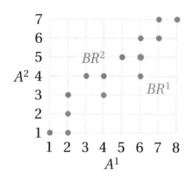
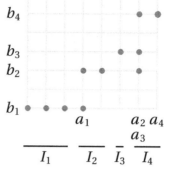

(a) Best response functions in a game satisfying the conditions of Proposition 15.2. The action pair $(6,5)$ is a Nash equilibrium of the game.

(b) An illustration of the proof of Proposition 15.2.

Figure 15.4

denote by $I_{m(i)}$ the interval to which a_i belongs. The fact that BR^2 is non-decreasing implies that $m(i+1) \geq m(i)$ for all i. Now, $m(1) > 1$ (otherwise $(1,1)$ is an equilibrium) and thus $m(2) \geq m(1) \geq 2$, which implies $m(2) > 2$ (otherwise $(2,2)$ is an equilibrium). Continuing the argument we get $m(M) > M$, contradicting $m(M) \leq M$.

15.5 Strictly competitive games

A strategic game is strictly competitive if it has two players and the interests of the players are completely opposed.

Definition 15.5: Strictly competitive game

A two-player strategic game $\langle \{1,2\}, (A^i)_{i \in \{1,2\}}, (\succsim^i)_{i \in \{1,2\}} \rangle$ is *strictly competitive* if for any action pairs a and b,

$$a \succsim^1 b \text{ if and only if } b \succsim^2 a.$$

Strictly competitive games are often called zero-sum games. The reason is that if the function u^1 represents $\succsim^1$ then $\succsim^2$ can be represented by the function u^2 defined by $u^2(a) = -u^1(a)$ for each action pair a, in which case the sum of the players' payoffs is zero for every action pair.

Most economic situations have elements of both conflicting and common interests, and thus cannot be modeled as strictly competitive games. The family of strictly competitive games fits situations for which the central ingredient of the interaction is conflictual. For example, the game of chess is strictly competitive (assuming that each player prefers to win than to tie than to lose). The competition between two politicians for votes may also be modeled as a strictly competitive game.

Consider the following (pessimistic) reasoning by a player: "Whatever action I take, the outcome will be the worst among all outcomes that might occur, given my action. Therefore, I will choose an action for which that worst outcome is best for me." In a two-player game, this reasoning leads player 1 to choose a solution to the problem

$$\max_{a^1 \in A^1}[\min_{a^2 \in A^2} u^1(a^1, a^2)]$$

and player 2 to choose a solution to the problem

$$\max_{a^2 \in A^2}[\min_{a^1 \in A^1} u^2(a^1, a^2)].$$

The maximum in each case is the highest payoff that each player can guarantee for himself.

Consider, for example, the following variant of Bach or Stravinsky.

	B	S
B	2, 1	0.5, 0.5
S	0, 0	1, 2

The game has two Nash equilibria, (B, B) and (S, S). Suppose that each player chooses an action using the pessimistic reasoning we have described. If player 1 chooses B, then the worst outcome for him is (B, S), and if he chooses S, the worse outcome is (S, B). The former is better than the latter for him, so he chooses B. Similarly, player 2 chooses S. Thus, if the two players reason in this way, the outcome is (B, S) (and the players do not meet).

Consider now the location game of Example 15.8. This game, as we noted, is strictly competitive: whenever the market share of one player increases, the market share of the other player decreases. The game has a unique Nash equilibrium, in which both players choose the middle point, $\frac{1}{2}$. A player who chooses this location guarantees that his market share is at least $\frac{1}{2}$. If he chooses any other location, then if the other player chooses a point between the middle point and his point, he gets less than half the market. For example, if a player chooses 0.6 then he gets less than half the market if the other player chooses 0.55. Thus for this game, unlike the variant of Bach or Stravinsky, which is not strictly competitive, Nash equilibrium and the pessimistic reasoning we have described lead to the same conclusion. We now show that the same is true for any strictly competitive game, and hence if a strictly competitive game has more than one equilibrium then each player's payoff in every equilibrium is the same.

Proposition 15.3: Maxminimization and Nash equilibrium

Let $G = \langle \{1,2\}, (A^i)_{i \in \{1,2\}}, (\succcurlyeq^i)_{i \in \{1,2\}} \rangle$ be a strictly competitive game. (i) If (a^1, a^2) is a Nash equilibrium of G, then for each player i, a^i is a solution of $\max_{x^i \in A^i}[\min_{x^j \in A^j} u^i(x^1, x^2)]$, where u^i represents $\succcurlyeq^i$ and j is the other player. (ii) If G has a Nash equilibrium, then each player's payoff is the same in all equilibria.

Proof

(i) Assume that (a^1, a^2) is a Nash equilibrium of G. If player 2 chooses an action different from a^2, his payoff is not higher than $u^2(a^1, a^2)$, so that player 1's payoff is not lower than $u^1(a^1, a^2)$. Thus the lowest payoff player 1 obtains if he chooses a^1 is $u^1(a^1, a^2)$:

$$u^1(a^1, a^2) = \min_{x^2 \in A^2} u^1(a^1, x^2).$$

Hence, by the definition of a maximizer,

$$u^1(a^1, a^2) \le \max_{x^1 \in A^1} \min_{x^2 \in A^2} u^1(x^1, x^2).$$

Now, given that (a^1, a^2) is a Nash equilibrium of G, $u^1(a^1, a^2) \ge u^1(x^1, a^2)$ for all $x^1 \in A^1$. Thus $u^1(a^1, a^2) \ge \min_{x^2 \in A^2} u^1(x^1, x^2)$ for all $x^1 \in A^1$, and hence

$$u^1(a^1, a^2) \ge \max_{x^1 \in A^1} \min_{x^2 \in A^2} u^1(x^1, x^2).$$

We conclude that

$$u^1(a^1, a^2) = \max_{x^1 \in A^1} \min_{x^2 \in A^2} u^1(x^1, x^2).$$

(ii) That player 1's payoff is the same in all equilibria follows from (i).

Note that the result does not claim that a Nash equilibrium exists. Indeed, we have seen that the game odds or evens, which is strictly competitive, has no Nash equilibrium.

By Proposition 15.3, a player's payoff in a Nash equilibrium of a strictly competitive game is the maximum payoff the player can guarantee. We show now that it is also the lowest payoff the other player can inflict on him. As we noted earlier, we can take player 2's payoff function to be the negative of player 1's, $(u^2(x^1, x^2) = -u^1(x^1, x^2)$ for all $(x^1, x^2))$ and thus by Proposition 15.3, if (a^1, a^2) is a Nash equilibrium of the game then

$$-u^1(a^1,a^2) = u^2(a^1,a^2) = \max_{x^2 \in A^2} \min_{x^1 \in A^1} (-u^1(x^1,x^2))$$
$$= \max_{x^2 \in A^2} (-\max_{x^1 \in A^1} (u^1(x^1,x^2))) = -\min_{x^2 \in A^2} \max_{x^1 \in A^1} u^1(x^1,x^2),$$

so that

$$u^1(a^1,a^2) = \max_{x^1 \in A^1} \min_{x^2 \in A^2} u^1(x^1,x^2) = \min_{x^2 \in A^2} \max_{x^1 \in A^1} u^1(x^1,x^2).$$

That is, if the game has a Nash equilibrium then the maximum payoff a player can guarantee is the same as the lowest payoff the other player can inflict on him. For a game that is not strictly competitive, this equality does not generally hold, but the maximum payoff that a player can guarantee is never higher than the minimum that the other player can inflict on his (see Problem 12).

15.6   Kantian equilibrium

Nash equilibrium is the most commonly used solution concept for strategic games, but it is not the only possible solution concept. We now briefly discuss one alternative concept, Kantian equilibrium.

At a Nash equilibrium, no player wants to deviate under the assumption that the other players will not change their actions. At a Kantian equilibrium, no player wants to deviate under the assumption that if he does so, the other players will change their actions in the same way as he has. To complete the definition we need to specify the meaning of "the same way".

We illustrate the concept with a simple example. Consider a two-player game in which each player i's set of actions is $(0,1]$ and his preferences are represented by u^i. Assume that a player who considers deviating from an action pair, increasing or decreasing his action by a certain percentage, imagines that the other player will change his action in the same direction, by the same percentage. In equilibrium no player wishes to change his action under this assumption about the resulting change in the other player's action. Formally, (a^1,a^2) is a *Kantian equilibrium* if $u^i(a^1,a^2) \geq u^i(\lambda a^1, \lambda a^2)$ for $i = 1, 2$ and for all $\lambda > 0$.

We calculate the Kantian equilibrium for the quantity-setting duopoly in Example 15.10 with $c = 0$. For (a^1,a^2) to be a Kantian equilibrium of this game we need

$$u^1(a^1,a^2) = a^1(1-a^1-a^2) \geq \max_{\lambda > 0} \lambda a^1(1-\lambda a^1 - \lambda a^2)$$

and similarly for player 2. The solution of the maximization problem is $\lambda^* = 1/(2(a^1+a^2))$. For equilibrium we need $\lambda^* = 1$, so that $a^1 + a^2 = \frac{1}{2}$. The condition for player 2 is identical, so any pair (a^1, a^2) for which $a^1 + a^2 = \frac{1}{2}$ is a Kantian equilibrium.

By contrast, the game has a unique Nash equilibrium, $(\frac{1}{3}, \frac{1}{3})$. So the total output produced in a Kantian equilibrium is less than the total output produced in a Nash equilibrium. The reason that $(\frac{1}{4}, \frac{1}{4})$ is not a Nash equilibrium is that an increase in output by a single player, assuming the other player does not change his output, is profitable. It is a Kantian equilibrium because an increase in output by a single player from $\frac{1}{4}$ is not profitable if it is accompanied by the same increase in the other player's output.

15.7   Mixed strategies

Consider the game matching pennies, specified as follows.

	H	T
H	0,1	1,0
T	1,0	0,1

As we have seen, this game has no Nash equilibrium.

Imagine that two large populations of individuals play the game, members of population 1 playing the role of player 1 and members of population 2 playing the role of player 2. From time to time, an individual is drawn randomly from each population and these two individuals play the game. Each individual in each population chooses the same action whenever he plays the game, but the individuals within each population may choose different actions. When two individuals are matched to play the game, neither of them knows the identity of the other player. We are interested in steady states in which each individual's belief about the distribution of actions in the other population is correct (perhaps because of his long experience playing the game) and each individual chooses his best action given these beliefs.

An implication of the game's not having a Nash equilibrium is that no configuration of choices in which all members of each population choose the same action is stable. For example, the configuration in which every individual in population 1 chooses T and every individual in population 2 chooses H is not consistent with a stable steady state because every individual in population 2, believing that he certainly faces an opponent who will choose T, is better off choosing T.

Now consider the possibility that some individuals in each population choose H and some choose T. Denote by p^H the fraction of individuals in population 1 who choose H. Then an individual in population 2 gets a payoff of 1 with probability p^H if he chooses H and with probability $1 - p^H$ if he chooses T. Thus if $p^H > \frac{1}{2}$ then every individual in population 2 prefers H to T, in which case the individuals in population 1 who choose H are not acting optimally. Hence the game has no steady state with $p^H > \frac{1}{2}$. Similarly, it has no steady state with $p^H < \frac{1}{2}$.

What if $p^H = \frac{1}{2}$? Then every individual in population 2 is indifferent between H and T: both actions yield the payoff 1 with probability $\frac{1}{2}$. Thus any distribution of actions among the individuals in population 2 is consistent with each of these individuals acting optimally. In particular, a distribution in which half the individuals choose each action is consistent. And given that distribution, by the same argument every individual in population 1 is indifferent between H and T, so that in particular half of them choosing H and half choosing T is consistent with each individual in population 1 choosing his action optimally, given the distribution of actions in population 2. In summary, every individual's action is optimal given the distribution of actions in the other population if and only if each action is chosen by half of each population.

In the remainder of the chapter we identify population i with player i and refer to a distribution of actions in a population as a mixed strategy. (The terminology "mixed strategy" relates to another interpretation of equilibrium, in which a player chooses a probability distribution over his actions. We do not discuss this interpretation.)

> **Definition 15.6: Mixed strategy**
>
> Given a strategic game $\langle N, (A^i)_{i \in N}, (\succsim^i)_{i \in N} \rangle$, a *mixed strategy* for player i is a probability distribution over A^i. A mixed strategy α^i that is concentrated on one action (i.e. $\alpha^i(a^i) = 1$ for some $a^i \in A^i$) is a *pure strategy*.

If A^i consists of a finite (or countable) number of actions, a mixed strategy α^i of player i assigns a nonnegative number $\alpha^i(a^i)$ to each $a^i \in A^i$, and the sum of these numbers is 1. We interpret $\alpha^i(a^i)$ as the proportion of population i that chooses the action a^i.

If some players' mixed strategies are not pure, players face uncertainty. To analyze their choices, we therefore need to know their preferences over lotteries over action profiles, not only over the action profiles themselves. Following convention we adopt the expected utility approach (see Section 3.3) and assume that the preferences of each player i over lotteries over action profiles are represented by the expected value of some function u^i that assigns a number to each action profile. *Thus in the remainder of this section, in Section 15.9, and in the exercises for these sections, we specify the preferences of each player i in a strategic game by giving a Bernoulli function u^i whose expected value represents the player's preferences over lotteries over action profiles* (rather than a preference relation over action profiles).

We now define a concept of equilibrium in the spirit of Nash equilibrium in which the behavior of each player is described by a mixed strategy rather than an action. We give a definition only for games in which the number of actions of each player is finite or countably infinite. A definition for games with more general action sets is mathematically more subtle.

Definition 15.7: Mixed strategy equilibrium of strategic game

Let $G = \langle N, (A^i)_{i \in N}, (u^i)_{i \in N} \rangle$ be a strategic game for which the set A^i of actions of each player i is finite or countably infinite. A profile $(\alpha^i)_{i \in N}$ of mixed strategies is a *mixed strategy equilibrium* of G if for every player $i \in N$ and every action $a^i \in A^i$ for which $\alpha^i(a^i) > 0$, i's expected payoff (according to u^i) from a^i given α^{-i} is at least as high as his expected payoff from x^i given α^{-i} for any $x^i \in A^i$.

The notion of mixed strategy equilibrium extends the notion of Nash equilibrium in the sense that (*i*) any Nash equilibrium is a mixed strategy equilibrium in which each player's mixed strategy is a pure strategy and (*ii*) if α is a mixed strategy equilibrium in which each player's mixed strategy is pure, with $\alpha^i(a^i) = 1$ for every player i, then $(a^i)_{i \in N}$ is a Nash equilibrium.

Although not every strategic game has a Nash equilibrium, every game in which each player's set of actions is finite has a mixed strategy equilibrium. A proof of this result is beyond the scope of this book.

Example 15.13: Mixed strategy equilibrium in matching pennies

	H	T
H	0,1	1,0
T	1,0	0,1

Let (α^1, α^2) be a pair of mixed strategies. Let $p^1 = \alpha^1(H)$ and $p^2 = \alpha^2(H)$. The pair is not a mixed strategy equilibrium if $\alpha^i(a^i) = 1$ for some action a^i, for either player i. If $p^1 = 1$, for example, then the only optimal action of player 2 is H but if $p^2 = 1$ then player 1's action H is not optimal.

For (α^1, α^2) to be an equilibrium with $p^1 \in (0, 1)$, both actions of player 1 must yield the same expected payoff, so that $1 - p^2 = p^2$, and hence $p^2 = \frac{1}{2}$. The same consideration for player 2 implies that $p^1 = \frac{1}{2}$. Thus the only mixed strategy equilibrium of the game is the mixed strategy pair in which half of each population chooses each action.

The next example shows that a game that has a Nash equilibrium may have also mixed strategy equilibria that are not pure.

Example 15.14: Mixed strategy equilibria of Bach or Stravinsky

	B	S
B	2,1	0,0
S	0,0	1,2

The game has two Nash equilibria, (B,B) and (S,S). Now consider mixed strategy equilibria (α^1, α^2) in which at least one of the strategies is not pure. If one player's mixed strategy is pure, the other player's optimal strategy is pure, so in any non-pure equilibrium both players assign positive probability to both of their actions.

For both actions to be optimal for player 1 we need the expected payoffs to these actions, given player 2's mixed strategy, to be equal. Thus we need $2\alpha^2(B) = \alpha^2(S)$, so that $\alpha^2(B) = \frac{1}{3}$ and $\alpha^2(S) = \frac{2}{3}$. Similarly $\alpha^1(B) = \frac{2}{3}$ and $\alpha^1(S) = \frac{1}{3}$.

Hence the game has three mixed strategy equilibria, two that are pure and one that is not. In the non-pure equilibrium the probability of the players' meeting is $\frac{4}{9}$ and each player's expected payoff is $\frac{2}{3}$, less than the payoff from his worst pure equilibrium.

An interpretation of the non-pure equilibrium is that in each population two-thirds of individuals choose the action corresponding to their favorite outcome and one-third compromise.

We end the discussion of mixed strategies with a somewhat more complicated economic example.

Example 15.15: War of attrition

Two players compete for an indivisible object whose value is 1 for each player. Time is discrete, starting at period 0. In each period, each player can either give up or fight. The game ends when a player gives up, in which case the object is obtained by the other player. If both players give up in the same period, no one gets the object. For each period that passes before a player gives up, he incurs the cost $c \in (0,1)$. If player 1 plans to give up in period t and player 2 plans to do so in period s, with $s > t$, then player 2 gets the object in period $t+1$, incurring the cost $(t+1)c$, and player 1 incurs the cost tc.

We model the situation as a strategic game in which a player's action specifies the period in which he plans to give up. We have $N = \{1,2\}$ and, for $i = 1, 2$, $A^i = \{0,1,2,3,\dots\}$ and

$$u^i(t^i, t^j) = \begin{cases} -t^i c & \text{if } t^i \le t^j \\ 1 - (t^j + 1)c & \text{if } t^i > t^j. \end{cases}$$

First consider pure Nash equilibria. For any action pair (t^1, t^2) in which $t^1 > 0$ and $t^2 > 0$, the player who gives up first (or either player, if $t^1 = t^2$) can increase his payoff by deviating to give up immediately. Thus any pure Nash equilibrium has the form $(0, t^2)$ or $(t^1, 0)$. In any equilibrium, t^i is large enough that $c(t^i + 1) \ge 1$, so that player j's payoff from giving up immediately, 0, is at least $1 - (t^i + 1)c$, his payoff from waiting until period $t^i + 1$.

Let (α, α) be a symmetric mixed strategy equilibrium. (We leave the asymmetric mixed strategy equilibria for you to investigate.)

Step 1 *The set of periods to which α assigns positive probability has no holes: there are no numbers t_1 and t_2 with $t_1 < t_2$ for which $\alpha(t_1) = 0$ and $\alpha(t_2) > 0$.*

Proof. Suppose $\alpha(t_1) = 0$ and $\alpha(t_2) > 0$. Then there is a period t such that $\alpha(t) = 0$ and $\alpha(t+1) > 0$. We show that the action $t+1$ is not a best response to α. If the other player plans to give up before t, then t and $t+1$ yield the same payoff. If the other player plans to give up at $t+1$ or later, which happens with positive probability given that $\alpha(t+1) > 0$, then the player saves c by deviating from $t+1$ to t.   ◁

Step 2 *We have $\alpha(t) > 0$ for all t.*

Proof. Suppose, to the contrary, that T is the last period with $\alpha(T) > 0$. Then T is not a best response to α since $T+1$ yields a higher expected payoff. The two actions yield the same outcome except when the other player plans to give up at period T, an event with positive probability $\alpha(T)$. Therefore the expected payoff of $T+1$ exceeds that of T by $\alpha(T)(1 - c)$, which is positive given our assumption that $c < 1$.   ◁

Step 3 *For every value of t we have $\alpha(t) = c(1 - c)^t$.*

Proof. From the previous steps, a player's expected payoff to T and $T+1$ is the same for every period T. The following table gives player i's payoffs to these actions for each possible action t_j of player j.

	$t_i = T$	$t_i = T+1$
$t_j < T$	$1-(t_j+1)c$	$1-(t_j+1)c$
$t_j = T$	$-Tc$	$1-(T+1)c$
$t_j > T$	$-Tc$	$-(T+1)c$

The expected payoffs of player i from T and $T+1$ must be equal, given the mixed strategy α of player j, so that the difference between his expected payoffs must be 0:

$$\alpha(T)\big(1-(T+1)c-(-Tc)\big)+\left(1-\sum_{t=0}^{T}\alpha(t)\right)\big(-(T+1)c-(-Tc)\big)=0$$

or

$$\alpha(T)-c\left(1-\sum_{t=0}^{T-1}\alpha(t)\right)=0.$$

Thus for all T, conditional on not conceding before period T, the strategy α concedes at T with probability c, so that $\alpha(T)=c(1-c)^T$. ◁

15.8 Interpreting Nash equilibrium

The concept of Nash equilibrium has several interpretations. In this book we interpret an equilibrium to be a stable norm of behavior, or a convention. A Nash equilibrium is a profile of modes of behavior that is known to all players and is stable against the possibility that one of them will realize that his action is not optimal for him given the other players' behavior. Thus, for example, the equilibrium (Y, Y) in the coordination game represents the convention that the players meet at Y; the equilibrium (F, N) in Bach or Stravinsky represents the norm that player 1 (perhaps the younger player) always insists on meeting at his favorite concert whereas player 2 (the older player) yields; and the game matching pennies has no stable norm.

In a related interpretation, we imagine a collection of populations, one for each player. Whenever the game is played, one individual is drawn randomly from each population i to play the role of player i in the game. Each individual bases his decision on his beliefs about the other players' actions. In equilibrium these beliefs are correct and the action of each player in each population is optimal given the common expectation of the individuals in the population about the behavior of the individuals in the other populations.

As discussed in Section 15.7, this interpretation is appealing in the context of mixed strategy equilibrium. In that case, the individuals in each population may differ in their behavior. All individuals are anonymous, so that no individual obtains information about the action chosen by any specific individual. But every individual holds correct beliefs about the distribution of behavior in each of the other populations. A Nash equilibrium is a steady state in which every individual's belief about the action chosen by the individuals in each population is correct and any action assigned positive probability is optimal given the equilibrium distribution of actions in the other populations. Thus, for example, the mixed strategy equilibrium in matching pennies represents a steady state in which half of each population of individuals chooses each action.

Nash equilibrium is sometimes viewed as the outcome of a reasoning process by each player or as the outcome of an evolutionary process. In this book, we do not discuss these ideas; we focus on Nash equilibrium as a norm of behavior or as a steady state in the interaction between populations of individuals that frequently interact.

15.9 Correlated equilibrium

We have discussed some interpretations of mixed strategy equilibrium. We now briefly discuss an equilibrium concept that springs from another interpretation of mixed strategy equilibrium: each player bases his action on the realization of some private information that is known only to him, does not affect his preferences, and is independent of the information on which the other players base their actions.

Consider the game Bach or Stravinsky, reproduced here.

	B	S
B	2,1	0,0
S	0,0	1,2

Suppose that each player independently wakes up in a good mood with probability $\frac{1}{3}$ and in a bad mood with probability $\frac{2}{3}$. Then the mixed strategy equilibrium can be thought of as the result of each player's choosing the action he likes least (S for player 1, B for player 2) if and only if he wakes up in a good mood.

We generalize this idea by assuming that the signals on which the players base their actions may be correlated. Suppose, for example, that the weather has three equally likely states, x (rainy), y (cloudy), and z (clear), and

> player 1 is in a bad mood in $\{x, y\}$ and in a good mood in z
>
> player 2 is in a bad mood in $\{y, z\}$ and in a good mood in x.

Assume that each player knows only his own mood, not the other player's mood. Suppose that each player chooses his less favored action when his mood is good and his favored action when his mood is bad. Over time he accumulates information about the other player's behavior conditional on his mood. Then player 1 concludes that if he is in a bad mood, player 2 chooses B and S with equal probabilities. Given these beliefs she optimally chooses B, yielding expected payoff 1, which is greater than his expected payoff of choosing S, namely $\frac{1}{2}$. When he is in a good mood, he concludes that player 2 chooses S, making his choice of S optimal. Analogously, player 2's plan is optimal whatever he observes. Thus this behavior is an equilibrium in the sense that for each player, each signal he can receive, and the statistics about the other player's behavior given his signal, a player does not want to revise his rule of behavior.

Generalizing this idea leads to the following definition.

Definition 15.8: Correlated equilibrium of strategic game

Let $G = \langle N, (A^i)_{i \in N}, (u^i)_{i \in N} \rangle$ be a strategic game for which the set A^i of actions of each player i is finite. A candidate for a correlated equilibrium is a tuple $(\Omega, \mu, (P^i)_{i \in N}, (s^i)_{i \in N})$ for which

- Ω is a finite set (of *states*)

- μ is a probability measure on Ω

- for each player $i \in N$, P^i is a partition of Ω (*i*'s *information partition*: if the state is $\omega \in \Omega$ then i is informed of the cell of P^i that includes ω)

- for each player $i \in N$, s^i is a function that assigns an action in A^i to each state in Ω such that the same action is assigned to all states in the same cell of P^i.

The tuple $(\Omega, \mu, (P^i), (s^i))$ is a *correlated equilibrium* if for every $\omega \in \Omega$ and each player i, the action $s^i(\omega)$ is a best response for i to the distribution of a^{-i} given the cell in P^i that contains ω.

Consider again the game Bach or Stravinsky. The correlated equilibrium that we have discussed in which the set of states is $\{x, y, z\}$ yields the distribution of outcomes that assigns equal probabilities to the three outcomes (B, B), (B, S), and (S, B):

	B	S
B	$\frac{1}{3}$	$\frac{1}{3}$
S	0	$\frac{1}{3}$

This distribution can be obtained also by another correlated equilibrium, defined as follows.

- The set of states is the set of outcomes, $\{(B, B), (B, S), (S, B), (S, S)\}$.

- The probability measure on this set assigns probability $\frac{1}{3}$ to each of the three states (B, B), (B, S), and (S, S).

- Player 1's information partition is $\{\{(B, B), (B, S)\}, \{(S, B), (S, S)\}\}$ and player 2's is $\{\{(B, B), (S, B)\}, \{(B, S), (S, S)\}\}$.

- Player 1's strategy in state (X, Y) chooses X and player 2's strategy chooses Y.

In this equilibrium, a state can be interpreted as the profile of actions recommended by nature, with each player being informed only of the action he is recommended to take.

The construction of this correlated equilibrium illustrates a general result: for every correlated equilibrium there is another correlated equilibrium with the same distribution of outcomes in which the set of states is the set of outcomes in the game.

Definition 15.9: Standard correlated equilibrium

Let $G = \langle N, (A^i)_{i \in N}, (u^i)_{i \in N} \rangle$ be a strategic game. A *standard correlated equilibrium* is a correlated equilibrium $(\Omega, \mu, (P^i)_{i \in N}, (s^i)_{i \in N})$ in which

- the set Ω of states is the set of outcomes (action profiles), $A = \times_{i \in N} A^i$

- the information partition P^i of each player i is the collection of all sets $\{(x^j)_{j \in N} : x^i = a^i\}$ for $a^i \in A^i$

- the strategy s^i of each player i is defined by $s^i((x^j)_{j \in N}) = x^i$.

The next proposition implies that if we are interested only in the distribution of outcomes in correlated equilibria then we can limit attention to standard correlated equilibria.

Proposition 15.4: Correlated and standard correlated equilibrium

For any correlated equilibrium there is a standard correlated equilibrium that induces the same distribution of outcomes.

Proof

Let $(\Omega, \mu, (P^i), (s^i))$ be a correlated equilibrium. For each player i let Q^i be the partition of Ω for which for each action $a^i \in A^i$ for which $s^i(\omega) = a^i$ for some $\omega \in \Omega$, there is a cell in Q^i that is the union of the cells in P^i to which

s^i assigns a^i. Then $(\Omega, \mu, (Q^i), (s^i))$ is a correlated equilibrium. The reason is a basic property of expected utility: if a^i is optimal given a set of cells in P^i then it is optimal also given the union of the set of cells.

To define the associated standard correlated equilibrium we need only specify the probability measure μ^* over the set of states, which is the set A of outcomes of the game. We define $\mu^*((a^i)_{i \in N}) = \mu(\{\omega \in \Omega : s^i(\omega) = a^i \text{ for all } i \in N\}$. In this standard correlated equilibrium a player's signal is the action he is supposed to take. Given that he is supposed to choose a^i, his belief about the other players' actions is the same as it is in $(\Omega, \mu, (Q^i), (s^i))$ when he plays a^i, and is thus optimal.

Finally, every mixed strategy equilibrium can be described also as a correlated equilibrium. For example, the game Bach or Stravinsky has a mixed strategy equilibrium (α^1, α^2) for which $\alpha^1(B) = \alpha^2(S) = \frac{2}{3}$. The behavior presented by this equilibrium is obtained also by a standard correlated equilibrium with $\mu(X, Y) = \alpha^1(X)\alpha^2(Y)$ (see the table).

	B	S
B	$\frac{2}{9}$	$\frac{4}{9}$
S	$\frac{1}{9}$	$\frac{2}{9}$

Given μ, whatever recommendation player 1 receives, he believes that player 2 chooses B and S with probabilities $\alpha^2(B)$ and $\alpha^2(S)$, so that both actions are optimal for him given his beliefs. Similarly for player 2.

More generally, if $(\alpha^i)_{i \in N}$ is a mixed strategy equilibrium of G then in the standard correlated equilibrium defined by $\mu((a^i)_{i \in N}) = \prod_{i \in N} \alpha^i(a^i)$, the players' choices are independent and each player's distribution of choices is the same as her choice in the mixed strategy equilibrium.

15.10 *S*(1) equilibrium

We end the chapter with a discussion of another solution concept for finite strategic games. By doing so we wish to emphasize that Nash equilibrium, with or without mixed strategies, is not the only possible solution concept for strategic games.

At the heart of the concept of an $S(1)$ equilibrium lies an assumption about the procedure a player uses to decide the action to take when he is not familiar with the consequences of the possible actions. Imagine a large society in which each individual has to decide between two actions, L and R. Suppose that we know that an individual's experience from the action L is with equal probabilities

Very good or *Bad* and his experience from the action R is with equal probabilities *Good* or *Very bad*. The outcome is uncertain, so different individuals may have different experiences from using the actions. A new individual who arrives into the society does not have any idea about the virtues of the two alternatives, so he consults one individual who chose L and one who chose R. He compares their experiences and chooses accordingly: if either (*i*) the individual who chose L had a *Very good* experience or (*ii*) this individual had a *Bad* experience and the individual who chose R had a *Very bad* experience, then he chooses L, and otherwise he chooses R. Thus as observers we will find that a newcomer to the society chooses L with probability $\frac{3}{4}$ and R with probability $\frac{1}{4}$.

Let us turn back to games. We consider only two-player symmetric games. Such a game is characterized by a set Y of actions and a payoff function $u :$ $Y \times Y \to \mathbb{R}$, with the interpretation that $u(a,b)$ is a player's payoff if he chooses a and the other player chooses b. For any action a and any mixed strategy σ (interpreted as a distribution of actions in the population), define $L(a,\sigma)$ to be the lottery that yields $u(a,b)$ with probability $\sigma(b)$ for each action b. We imagine that a player who enters the society samples each action once himself, or, for each possible action, asks an individual who chose that action about his experience. This information leads him to associate a payoff with each action, and he chooses the action with the highest payoff. Thus he selects the action a whenever $L(a,\sigma)$ yields a higher payoff than do all lotteries $L(x,\sigma)$ for $x \in Y \setminus \{a\}$. If more than one lottery yields the highest payoff, he chooses each of the tied actions with equal probabilities. Denote the probability that he chooses a by $W(a,\sigma)$. We define an $S(1)$ *equilibrium* to be a mixed strategy σ for which the probability $W(a,\sigma)$ is equal to $\sigma(a)$ for all $a \in Y$.

Definition 15.10: $S(1)$ **equilibrium**

Let $G = \langle \{1,2\}, (A^i)_{i \in N}, (u^i)_{i \in N} \rangle$ with $A^1 = A^2 = Y$ and, for all $a \in Y$ and $b \in Y$, $u^1(a,b) = u(a,b)$ and $u^2(a,b) = u(b,a)$, be a two-player symmetric strategic game. An $S(1)$ *equilibrium* of G is a mixed strategy σ for which the probability $W(a,\sigma)$ is equal to $\sigma(a)$ for all $a \in Y$.

Thus an $S(1)$ equilibrium is a stable distribution of play in the population: the distribution of the actions chosen by new entrants is equal to the equilibrium distribution.

Obviously, every strict symmetric Nash equilibrium, where all players choose some action a^*, is an $S(1)$ equilibrium: when he samples a^*, a new individual has a better experience than he does when he samples any other action, given that the other player chooses a^*.

Every finite symmetric strategic game has an $S(1)$ equilibrium. The proof of this result is above the level of this book, but we present it for readers who are familiar with Brouwer's fixed point theorem.

Proposition 15.5: Existence of $S(1)$ equilibrium

Every symmetric finite strategic game has an $S(1)$ equilibrium.

Proof

Assume that $Y = \{a_1, \ldots, a_K\}$ and let Δ be the set of all probability distributions over Y. The set Δ can be identified with the set of all K-vectors of nonnegative numbers that sum to 1, and is convex and compact. Define the function $F : \Delta \to \Delta$ by $F(\sigma) = (W(a_k, \sigma))_{k=1\ldots K}$. This function is continuous and so by Brouwer's fixed point theorem has at least one fixed point, namely a point σ^* for which $F(\sigma^*) = \sigma^*$. Any fixed point of F is an $S(1)$ equilibrium.

The next example demonstrates that the notion of $S(1)$ equilibrium, unlike that of mixed strategy equilibrium, depends only on the players' ordinal preferences over the set of action profiles.

Example 15.16: $S(1)$ equilibrium in simple game

Consider the following symmetric strategic game for $M > 3$.

	a	b
a	2	M
b	3	0

The game has no pure symmetric Nash equilibrium and has one symmetric mixed strategy equilibrium, (α, α) with $\alpha(a) = M/(M+1)$. This equilibrium depends on the value of M.

To calculate the $S(1)$ equilibrium note that a player concludes that a is the better action if (*i*) the other player chooses a when he samples a (payoff 2) and b when she samples b (payoff 0) or (*ii*) the other player chooses b when she samples a (payoff M). Thus for σ to be an $S(1)$ equilibrium we need $p = p(1-p) + (1-p)$, where $p = \sigma(a)$. This equation has a unique solution $p^* = (\sqrt{5} - 1)/2 \approx 0.62$. Thus independently of M, as long as $M > 3$, the game has a unique $S(1)$ equilibrium, in which a is chosen with probability p^*.

The next example demonstrates that unlike a mixed strategy Nash equilibrium, an $S(1)$ equilibrium may assign positive probability to an action that is strictly dominated in the sense that another action yields a higher payoff regardless of the other player's action.

Example 15.17: Dominated action in support of $S(1)$ equilibrium

Consider the following game.

	a	b	c
a	2	5	8
b	1	4	7
c	0	3	6

A story behind this game is that each of two players holds 2 indivisible units that are worth 1 to him and 3 to the other player. Each player has to decide how many units he gives voluntarily to the other player: none (a), one (b), or two (c). Thus, for example, if a player keeps his two units and gets one unit from the other player his payoff is $2 \cdot 1 + 1 \cdot 3 = 5$.

The action a strictly dominates the other two, and the game has a unique Nash equilibrium, in which each player chooses a. To calculate the $S(1)$ equilibria, let $(\alpha, \beta, \gamma) = (\sigma(a), \sigma(b), \sigma(c))$. Then an $S(1)$ equilibrium is characterized by the following set of equations:

$$\alpha = \alpha^3 + \beta(1-\gamma)^2 + \gamma$$
$$\beta = \beta\alpha(1-\gamma) + \gamma(1-\gamma)$$
$$\alpha + \beta + \gamma = 1.$$

This set of equations has two solutions, $(\alpha, \beta, \gamma) = (1,0,0)$ and $(\alpha, \beta, \gamma) \approx (0.52, 0.28, 0.20)$. The first solution corresponds to the (strict) Nash equilibrium. The other solution assigns positive probabilities to b and c, even though these actions are strictly dominated.

If an action in a game is duplicated, the analysis of the Nash equilibria of the game is unaffected. The same is not true for the $S(1)$ equilibria, as the following example shows.

Example 15.18: Duplication of actions affects $S(1)$ equilibria

Consider the following games.

	a	b
a	1	4
b	3	2

	a_1	a_2	b
a_1	1	1	4
a_2	1	1	4
b	3	3	2

In the game on the right, the actions a_1 and a_2 are duplicates of a. The only $S(1)$ equilibrium of the game on the left assigns probability $\frac{1}{2}$ to each action. Denote by β the probability assigned to b. In an $S(1)$ equilibrium of the game on the right, $\beta = (1-\beta)^2$, which has a single solution, $\beta \approx 0.38$.

More generally, if the action a is replicated m times then the only $S(1)$ equilibrium assigns to b the probability β that is the solution of the equation $\beta = (1-\beta)^m$. As m increases without bound, this probability goes to 0. Thus, duplicating strategies has a significant affect on the $S(1)$ equilibrium.

Problems

Examples of games

1. *Centipede game.* Two players, 1 and 2, alternate turns in being able to stop interacting or to continue doing so. Player 1 starts the game. Initially each player has 0 in his account. Any decision by a player to continue reduces the player's account by 1 and adds 2 to the other player's account. After 100 actions to continue, the game stops. Thus, each player has at most 50 opportunities to stop the game. Each player wants the amount in his account at the end of the game to be as large as possible.

   Model this situation as a strategic game and show that the game has a unique Nash equilibrium.

2. *Demand game.* Two players can allocate ten indivisible desirable identical objects among themselves. Find the Nash equilibria of the following two games.

   a. The players simultaneously submit demands, members of $\{0, 1, \ldots, 10\}$. If the sum of the demands is at most 10, each player gets what he demands. Otherwise both get 0.

   b. As in part *a*, except that if the sum of the demands exceeds 10, then (*i*) if the demands differ then the player who demands less gets his demand and the other player gets the rest, and (*ii*) if the demands are the same then each player gets 5.

3. *War of attrition.* Two individuals, 1 and 2, compete for an object. Individual *i*'s valuation of the object is v^i for $i = 1, 2$. Time is a continuous variable that starts at 0 and continues forever. The object is assigned to one of the individuals once the other one gives up. If both of them give up at the same

time, the object is divided equally (half the object is worth $\frac{1}{2}v^i$ to i). As long as neither individual gives up, each individual loses 1 unit of payoff per unit of time.

Model the situation as a strategic game and show that in every Nash equilibrium the game ends immediately.

4. *Extended Prisoner's dilemma.* Each of n tenants in a large building has to decide whether to keep his property clean, C, or not, D. Assume that each player's preferences can be represented by a payoff function in which he loses $B > 0$ if he keeps his property clean and loses $L > 0$ for every other tenant who chooses D. Model the situation as a strategic game and find the Nash equilibria for any parameters $n \geq 2$, B, and L.

5. *Guessing two-thirds of the average.* Each of n players has to name a member of $\{1, \ldots, 100\}$. A player gets a prize if the number he names is the integer closest to two-thirds of the average number named by all players (or one of the two closest integers, if two integers are equally close). Notice that it is possible that nobody gets a prize or that several players get prizes.

Model the situation as a strategic game and find its Nash equilibria.

6. *Cheap talk.* Two players are about to play Bach or Stravinsky (BoS, Example 15.3). Before doing so, player 1 sends one of the following messages to player 2: "I will choose B", or "I will choose S". Construct a strategic game in which an action of player 1 is a combination of the message to send and an action in BoS (a total of four possible actions) and an action for player 2 is a specification of the action in BoS to take for each possible message of player 1 (a total of four possible actions). Assume that both players care only about the payoff in BoS (not about the content of the message). Find the Nash equilibria of this game.

Economic games

7. *War.* Two players, 1 and 2, fight over a single indivisible object worth $V > 0$ to each of them. Each player invests in becoming more powerful; denote by e^i, a nonnegative number, the investment of player i. Given investments (e^1, e^2), player i's probability $p^i(e^1, e^2)$ of winning the object is $e^i/(e^i + e^j)$ if $e^1 + e^2 > 0$, and $\frac{1}{2}$ if $e^1 = e^2 = 0$. The preferences of each player i are represented by the payoff function $p^i(e^1, e^2)V - e^i$.

Model the situation as a strategic game, show that in all Nash equilibria the two players choose the same investment, and characterize this investment level.

8. *All-pay auction.* An all-pay auction is a sealed-bid auction in which every bidder (not only the winner) pays his bid. Assume that there are two players, and that if their bids are the same each gets half of his value of the object.

   Model the situation as a strategic game and show that it does not have a Nash equilibrium.

9. *Another version of the location game.* Consider a variant of the location game in which the two players are candidates for a post and the set of positions is the interval $[0,1]$. A population of voters has favorite positions distributed uniformly over this interval; each voter endorses the candidate whose position is closer to his favorite position. (The fraction of citizens with favorite positions equidistant from the candidates' positions is zero, so we can ignore these citizens.) A candidate cares only about whether he receives more, the same number, or fewer votes than the other candidate.

   Model the situation as a strategic game and show that it has a unique Nash equilibrium.

10. *Nash demand game.* Two players bargain over one divisible unit of a good. Each player submits a demand, a number in $[0,1]$. For the pair of demands (t^1, t^2), the probability that agreement is reached is $g(t^1 + t^2) \in [0,1]$, where g is differentiable, nonincreasing, positive when the sum of the demands is less than 1, and 0 when the sum of the demand exceeds 1. If agreement is reached on (t^1, t^2) then player i $(= 1, 2)$ gets t^i and his utility is $\alpha^i t^i$, with $\alpha^i > 0$. Each player maximizes his expected utility.

    a. Model the situation as a strategic game and show that in any Nash equilibrium the two players make the same demand.

    b. For any $\varepsilon > 0$, let G_ε be a game with $g_\varepsilon(t^1 + t^2) = 1$ if $t^1 + t^2 \le 1 - \varepsilon$. What can you say about the limit of the Nash equilibria of G_ε as $\varepsilon \to 0$?

11. *Contribution game.* Two players contribute to a joint project. The payoff function of player i has the form $v^i(c^1 + c^2) - c^i$, where c^i is i's contribution and v^i is an increasing, differentiable, and concave function satisfying $v^i(0) = 0$. Assume that for each player i there is a number $x^i > 0$ for which $(v^i)'(x^i) = 1$ (so that $(v^i)'(0) > 1$ and hence each player optimally contributes a positive amount if the other player contributes zero). Finally assume that player 2 is interested in the project more than player 1 in the sense that $(v^2)'(x) > (v^1)'(x)$ for all x.

    Model the situation as a strategic game and show that in any Nash equilibrium only player 2's contribution is positive.

Strictly competitive games

12. max min *versus* min max. Show that in any two-player strategic game the maximum payoff a player can guarantee for himself is at most the minimum payoff that the other player can inflict on his.

13. *Comparative statics.* Consider two games G_1 and G_2 that differ only in that one of the payoffs for player 1 is higher in G_1 than it is in G_2.

    a. Show that if the games are strictly competitive then for any Nash equilibria of G_1 and G_2, player 1's payoff in the equilibrium of G_1 is at least as high as his payoff in the equilibrium of G_2.

    b. Give an example to show that the same is not necessarily true for games that are not strictly competitive.

Kantian equilibrium

14. *Kantian equilibrium.* Find the Kantian equilibrium (Section 15.6) for the price-setting duopoly in Example 15.11 with no production costs.

Mixed strategy equilibrium

15. *Mixed strategy equilibrium.* Find the mixed strategy equilibria of the following game.

	L	M	R
T	2,2	0,3	2,2
B	3,0	1,1	2,2

16. *Hawk or dove.* A population of individuals is frequently matched in pairs to fight over an object worth 1. Each individual can choose either Hawk (H) or Dove (D). If one individual chooses H and the other chooses D then the first individual gets the object. If both choose D then the object is split equally between the individuals. If both choose H then neither of them gets the object and each player i suffers a loss of $c^i > 0$. The situation is modeled by the following strategic game.

	H	D
H	$-c^1,-c^2$	1,0
D	0,1	0.5,0.5

The game has two Nash equilibria, (H,D) and (D,H). Prove that it has only one other mixed strategy equilibrium. Show that the higher is a player's loss when both players choose H the higher is his payoff in this equilibrium.

17. *Attack and defend.* Army 1 has one missile, which it can use to attack one of three targets of army 2. The significance of the three targets is given by the numbers $v(1) > v(2) > v(3) > 0$. The missile hits a target only if it is not protected by an anti-missile battery. Army 2 has one such battery. Army 1 has to decide which target to attack and army 2 has to decide which target to defend. If target t is hit then army 1's payoff is $v(t)$ and army 2's payoff is $-v(t)$; if no target is hit, each army's payoff is zero.

    a. Model this situation as a strategic game.

    b. Show that in any mixed strategy equilibrium, army 1 attacks both target 1 and target 2 with positive probability.

    c. Show that if $v(3) \leq v(2)v(1)/(v(1) + v(2))$ then the game has an equilibrium in which target 3 is not attacked and not defended.

18. *A committee.* The three members of a committee disagree about the best option. Members 1 and 2 favor option A, whereas member 3 favors option B. Each member decides whether to attend a meeting; if he attends, he votes for his favorite option. The option chosen is the one that receives a majority of the votes. If the vote is a tie (including the case in which nobody attends the meeting), each option is chosen with probability $\frac{1}{2}$. Each player's payoff depends on whether he attends the meeting and whether the outcome is the one he favors, as given in the following table.

	favored	not
participate	$1 - c$	$-c$
not	1	0

Assume that $c < \frac{1}{2}$. Find the mixed strategy equilibria of the strategic game that models this situation in which players 1 and 2 (who both favor A) use the same strategy. Show that in such a mixed strategy equilibrium, A may be chosen with probability less than 1 and study how the equilibrium expected payoffs depend on c.

19. *O'Neill's game.* Each of two players chooses one of four cards labeled 2, 3, 4, and J. Player 1 wins if

    • the players choose different numbered cards (2, 3, or 4) or

    • both players choose J,

and otherwise player 2 wins. Model the situation as a strategic game and find the mixed strategy equilibria of the game.

20. *All-pay auction.* An item worth 10 is offered in an all-pay auction. Two players participate in the auction. Each player submits a monetary bid that is an integer between 0 and 10 and pays that amount regardless of the other player's bid. If one player's bid is higher than the other's, he receives the item. If the players' bids are the same, neither player receives the item. The players are risk neutral.

   a. Show that the game has no Nash equilibrium in pure strategies.

   b. Prove that the expected payoff for each player in any symmetric mixed strategy equilibrium is 0.

   c. Characterize the symmetric mixed strategy equilibria.

   d. Find an asymmetric mixed strategy equilibrium.

Correlated equilibrium

21. *Aumann's game.* Consider the following game.

	A	B
A	6,6	2,7
B	7,2	0,0

   Show that the game has a correlated equilibrium with a payoff profile that is not a convex combination of the payoff profiles of the three Nash equilibria (with and without mixed strategies).

22. *Convexity of the set of payoff vectors.* Show that the set of correlated equilibrium payoff profiles is convex. That is, if there are correlated equilibria that yield the payoff profiles $(u^i)_{i \in N}$ and $(v^i)_{i \in N}$ then for every $\lambda \in [0,1]$ there is also a correlated equilibrium with payoff profile $(\lambda u^i + (1-\lambda)v^i)_{i \in N}$.

S(1) equilibrium

23. *S(1) equilibrium of a 2 × 2 game.* Consider a symmetric two-player game in which the set of actions is $\{a,b\}$. Assume that a strictly dominates b: $u(a,x) > u(b,x)$ for $x = a$, b. Show that the only S(1) equilibrium of the game is its unique Nash equilibrium.

24. *S(1) equilibrium in price-setting duopoly.* Each of two sellers holds an indivisible unit of a good. Each seller chooses one of the K possible prices $p_1,\ldots,p_K$ with $0 < p_1 < \cdots < p_K$. The seller whose price is lower obtains a payoff equal to his price and the other seller obtains a payoff of 0. If the prices

are the same, each seller's payoff is half of the common price. Assume that $p_{k-1} > \frac{1}{2}p_k$ for all $k > 1$. Show that the game has a unique $S(1)$ equilibrium.

25. *S(2) equilibrium.* The concept of $S(2)$ equilibrium is a variant of $S(1)$ equilibrium in which each player samples each action twice, rather than once, and chooses the action for which the average payoff for his two samples is highest. Compare the $S(1)$ and $S(2)$ equilibria of the following symmetric game.

	a	*b*
a	2	5
b	3	0

Notes

The model of a strategic game was developed by Borel (1921) and von Neumann (1928). The notion of Nash equilibrium is due to Nash (1950). (Cournot 1838, Chapter 7 is a precursor.)

Proposition 15.2 is a simple example of a result of Topkis (1979). The theory of strictly competitive games was developed by von Neumann and Morgenstern (1944). The notion of Kantian equilibrium is due to Roemer (2010). The notion of a mixed strategy was developed by Borel (1921, 1924, 1927). The notion of correlated equilibrium is due to Aumann (1974). Section 15.10, on $S(1)$ equilibrium, follows Osborne and Rubinstein (1998).

The Traveler's Dilemma (Example 15.1) is due to Basu (1994). The Prisoner's dilemma (Example 15.2) seems to have been first studied, in 1950, by Melvin Dresher and Merrill Flood (see Flood 1958/59). The game-theoretic study of auctions (Examples 15.6 and 15.7) was initiated by Vickrey (1961). The location game (Example 15.8) is due to Hotelling (1929). The model of quantity-setting producers (Example 15.10) is due to Cournot (1838) and the model of price-setting producers (Example 15.11) is named for Bertrand (1883). The war of attrition (Example 15.15) is due to Maynard Smith (1974).

The centipede game (Problem 1) is due to Rosenthal (1981), the game in Problem 5 is taken from Moulin (1986, 72), and the game in Problem 19 is due to O'Neill (1987). The game in Problem 21 is taken from Aumann (1974); it is the game he uses to demonstrate the concept of correlated equilibrium.

16 Extensive games

A market is currently served by a single incumbent. A competitor is considering entering the market. The incumbent wants to remain alone in the market and thus wishes to deter the competitor from entering. If the competitor enters, the incumbent can start a price war or can act cooperatively. A price war is the worst outcome for both parties; cooperative behavior by the incumbent is best for the competitor, and for the incumbent is better than a price war but worse than the competitor's staying out of the market.

We can model this situation as a strategic game. The competitor (player 1) decides whether to enter the market (*In*) or not (*Out*). If the competitor enters, the incumbent (player 2) decides whether to *Fight* the competitor or to *Cooperate* with it. The following table shows the game.

	Fight	*Cooperate*
In	0,0	2,2
Out	1,5	1,5

The game has two pure Nash equilibria, (*In, Cooperate*) and (*Out, Fight*). In the second equilibrium the incumbent plans to fight the competitor if he enters, a decision that deters the competitor from entering.

The formulation of the situation as this strategic game makes sense if the incumbent can decide initially to fight a competitor who enters the market and cannot reconsider this decision if the competitor does in fact enter. If the incumbent can reconsider his decision, the analysis is less reasonable: after the competitor enters, the incumbent is better off being cooperative than waging a price war. In this case, a model in which the timing of the decisions is described explicitly is more suitable for analyzing the situation. One such model is illustrated in Figure 16.1. Play starts at the initial node, indicated in the figure by a small circle. The label above this node indicates the player whose move starts the game (player 1, the competitor). The branches emanating from the node, labeled *In* and *Out*, represent the actions available to the competitor at the start of the game. If he chooses *Out*, the game is over. If he chooses *In*, player 2, the incumbent, chooses between *Cooperate* and *Fight*. The payoffs at the endpoints represent the players' preferences: player 1 (whose payoff is listed first in each pair) prefers (*In, Cooperate*) to *Out* to (*In, Fight*), and player 2 prefers *Out* to (*In, Cooperate*) to (*In, Fight*).

Chapter of *Models in Microeconomic Theory* by Martin J. Osborne and Ariel Rubinstein. Version 2023.5.30 (h).
© 2023 Martin J. Osborne and Ariel Rubinstein CC BY-NC-ND 4.0. https://doi.org/10.11647/OBP.0362.16

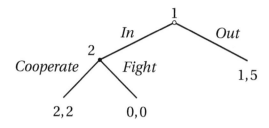

Figure 16.1 The entry game described in the introduction to the chapter.

We refer to each sequence of actions as a history. In Figure 16.1 there are five histories. The initial node represents the null history: no action has yet been chosen. The node shown by a small disk represents the history (*In*). Each of the three other histories, (*In, Cooperate*), (*In, Fight*), and (*Out*), leads to an endpoint of the game. We refer to these histories as terminal, and to the other histories, after which a player has to choose an action, as nonterminal.

16.1   Extensive games and subgame perfect equilibrium

An extensive game is specified by a set of players, a set of possible histories, a player function, which assigns a player to each nonterminal history, and the players' preferences over the terminal histories. We focus on games in which every history is finite.

Definition 16.1: Finite horizon extensive game

A (*finite horizon*) *extensive game* $\langle N, H, P, (\succsim^i)_{i \in N} \rangle$ has the following components.

Players
   A set of players $N = \{1, \ldots, n\}$.

Histories
   A set H of *histories*, each of which is a finite sequence of *actions*. The empty history, $\varnothing$, is in H, and if $(a_1, a_2, \ldots, a_t) \in H$ then also $(a_1, a_2, \ldots, a_{t-1}) \in H$.

   A history $h \in H$ is *terminal* if there is no x such that $(h, x) \in H$. The set of terminal histories is denoted Z. (We use the notation $(h, a_1, \ldots, a_t)$ for the history that starts with the history h and continues with the actions $a_1, \ldots, a_t$).

Player function
   A function $P \colon H \setminus Z \to N$, the *player function*, which assigns a player to each nonterminal history (the player who moves after the history).

Preferences

For each player $i \in N$, a preference relation $\succsim^i$ over Z.

We interpret this model as capturing a situation in which every player, when choosing an action, knows all actions previously chosen. For this reason, the model is usually called an extensive game *with perfect information*. A more general model, which we do not discuss, allows the players to be imperfectly informed about the actions previously chosen.

The example in the introduction, represented in Figure 16.1, is the extensive game $\langle N, H, P, (\succsim^i)_{i \in N} \rangle$ in which

- $N = \{1, 2\}$

- $H = \{\varnothing, (Out), (In), (In, Cooperate), (In, Fight)\}$ (with $Z = \{(Out), (In, Cooperate), (In, Fight)\}$)

- $P(\varnothing) = 1$ and $P(In) = 2$

- $(In, Cooperate) \succ^1 (Out) \succ^1 (In, Fight)$ and $(Out) \succ^2 (In, Cooperate) \succ^2 (In, Fight)$.

Notice that we use the notation $P(In)$ instead of $P((In))$; later we similarly write $P(a_1, \ldots, a_t)$ instead of $P((a_1, \ldots, a_t))$.

A key concept in the analysis of an extensive game is that of a strategy. A player's strategy is a specification of an action for every history after which the player has to move.

Definition 16.2: Strategy in extensive game

A *strategy* of player $i \in N$ in the extensive game $\langle N, H, P, (\succsim^i)_{i \in N} \rangle$ is a function that assigns to every history $h \in H \setminus Z$ for which $P(h) = i$ an action in $\{x : (h, x) \in H\}$, the set of actions available to him after h.

A key word in this definition is "every": a player's strategy specifies the action he chooses for *every* history after which he moves, even histories that do not occur if he follows his strategy. For example, in the game in Figure 16.2, one strategy of player 1 is s^1 with $s^1(\varnothing) = A$ and $s^1(B, G) = I$. This strategy specifies the action of player 1 after the history (B, G) although this history does not occur if player 1 uses s^1 and hence chooses A at the start of the game. Thus the notion of a strategy does not correspond to the notion of a strategy in everyday language. We discuss this issue further in Section 16.2.

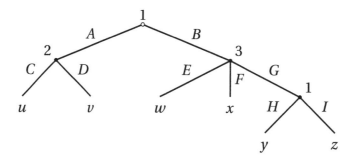

Figure 16.2 An example of an extensive game.

Each strategy profile generates a unique terminal history $(a_1 \ldots, a_T)$ as the players carry out their strategies. The first component of this history, a_1, is the action $s^{P(\varnothing)}(\varnothing)$ specified by the strategy $s^{P(\varnothing)}$ of player $P(\varnothing)$, who moves at the start of the game. This action determines the player who moves next, $P((a_1))$; his strategy $s^{P(a_1)}$ determines the next action, $a_2 = s^{P(a_1)}(a_1)$, and so forth.

Definition 16.3: Terminal history generated by strategy profile

Let s be a strategy profile for the extensive game $\langle N, H, P, (\succsim^i)_{i \in N} \rangle$. The *terminal history generated by* s is $(a_1, \ldots, a_T)$ where $a_1 = s^{P(\varnothing)}(\varnothing)$ and $a_{t+1} = s^{P(a_1,\ldots,a_t)}(a_1, \ldots, a_t)$ for $t = 1, \ldots, T-1$.

The main solution concept we use for extensive games is subgame perfect equilibrium. Before defining this notion, we define a Nash equilibrium of an extensive game: a strategy profile with the property that no player can induce a more desirable outcome for himself by deviating to a different strategy, given the other players' strategies.

Definition 16.4: Nash equilibrium of extensive game

Let $\Gamma = \langle N, H, P, (\succsim^i)_{i \in N} \rangle$ be an extensive game. A strategy profile s is a *Nash equilibrium* of Γ if for every player $i \in N$ we have

$$z(s) \succsim^i z(s^{-i}, r^i) \text{ for every strategy } r^i \text{ of player } i,$$

where, for any strategy profile σ, $z(\sigma)$ is the terminal history generated by σ.

The entry game, given in Figure 16.1, has two Nash equilibria: (*In, Cooperate*) and (*Out, Fight*). The latter strategy pair is a Nash equilibrium because given the incumbent's strategy *Fight*, the strategy *Out* is optimal for the competitor, and given the competitor's strategy *Out*, the strategy *Fight* is optimal for the incumbent. In fact, if the competitor chooses *Out*, then any strategy for the incumbent is optimal.

The non-optimality of *Fight* for the incumbent if the competitor chooses *In* does not interfere with the status of (*Out, Fight*) as a Nash equilibrium: the notion of Nash equilibrium considers the optimality of a player's strategy only at the start of the game, before any actions have been taken.

The notion of subgame perfect equilibrium, by contrast, requires that each player's strategy is optimal, given the other players' strategies, after every possible history, whether or not the history occurs if the players follow their strategies. To define this notion, we first define, for any strategy profile s and nonterminal history h, the outcome (terminal history) that is reached if h occurs and then the players choose the actions specified by s.

Definition 16.5: Terminal history extending history

Let s be a strategy profile for the extensive game $\langle N, H, P, (\succsim^i)_{i \in N} \rangle$ and let h be a nonterminal history. The *terminal history extending h generated by s*, denoted $z(h, s)$, is $(h, a_1, \ldots, a_T)$ where $a_1 = s^{P(h)}(h)$ and $a_{t+1} = s^{P(h, a_1, \ldots, a_t)}(h, a_1, \ldots, a_t)$ for $t = 1, \ldots, T-1$.

In the game in Figure 16.2, for example, if $h = B$ and the players' strategies specify $s^1(\varnothing) = A$, $s^1(B, G) = H$, $s^2(A) = C$, and $s^3(B) = G$, then the terminal history extending h generated by s is (B, G, H).

Definition 16.6: Subgame perfect equilibrium of extensive game

Let $\Gamma = \langle N, H, P, (\succsim^i)_{i \in N} \rangle$ be an extensive game. A strategy profile $s = (s^i)_{i \in N}$ is a *subgame perfect equilibrium* of Γ if for every player $i \in N$ and every nonterminal history h for which $P(h) = i$ we have

$$z(h, s) \succsim^i z(h, (s^{-i}, r^i)) \text{ for every strategy } r^i \text{ of player } i,$$

where, for any history h and strategy profile σ, $z(h, \sigma)$ is the terminal history extending h generated by σ.

The difference between this definition and that of a Nash equilibrium is the phrase "and every nonterminal history h for which $P(h) = i$". The notion of Nash equilibrium requires that each player's strategy is optimal at the beginning of the game (given the other players' strategies) whereas the notion of subgame perfect equilibrium requires that it is optimal after every history (given the other players' strategies), even ones that are not consistent with the strategy profile.

Every subgame perfect equilibrium is a Nash equilibrium, but some Nash equilibria are not subgame perfect equilibria. In a subgame perfect equilibrium of the entry game (Figure 16.1), the incumbent's strategy must specify *Cooperate* after the history *In*, because the incumbent prefers the terminal history (*In, Cooperate*) to the terminal history (*In, Fight*). Given this strategy of the incumbent, the competitor's best strategy is *In*. The Nash equilibrium (*Out, Fight*) is not a subgame perfect equilibrium because *Fight* is not optimal for the incumbent after the history *In*.

Example 16.1: Ultimatum game

Two players have to agree how to allocate two indivisible units of a good between themselves. If they do not agree then each of them gets nothing. They use the take-it-or-leave-it protocol: Player 1 proposes one of the three partitions of the two units, which player 2 either accepts or rejects. Each player cares only about the number of units of the good he gets (the more the better) and not about the number of units the other player gets.

Denote by (x^1, x^2) the proposal in which i gets x^i, with $x^1 + x^2 = 2$. The situation is modeled by the following extensive game. At the start of the game (the null history, $\varnothing$), player 1 makes one of the three proposals, $(2,0)$, $(1,1)$, and $(0,2)$, and after each of these proposals player 2 either agrees (Y) or disagrees (N).

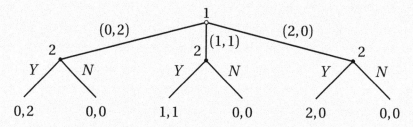

Player 1 has three strategies and player 2 has eight. Each of player 2's strategies specifies his reaction to each possible proposal of player 1; examples are (Y, Y, Y), in which he accepts all proposals, and (Y, N, N), in which he accepts the proposal $(0,2)$ and rejects the two other proposals.

The game has several Nash equilibria. In particular, for *any* allocation the game has a Nash equilibrium with that outcome: player 1 proposes the allocation and player 2 accepts that allocation and rejects the other two. The strategy pair $((2,0),(N,N,N))$ is also a Nash equilibrium, which yields disagreement.

Consider the Nash equilibrium $((0,2),(Y,N,N))$. Player 2's strategy accepts only the offer $(0,2)$, which gives him both units. However, his threat to reject $(1,1)$ is not credible, because if player 1 proposes that allocation, player 2 prefers to accept it and get one unit than to reject it and get nothing.

In any subgame perfect equilibrium, player 2's action after every proposal of player 1 must be optimal, so that he accepts the proposals $(0,2)$ and $(1,1)$. He is indifferent between accepting and rejecting the proposal $(2,0)$, so either action is possible in a subgame perfect equilibrium. Thus the only strategies of player 2 consistent with subgame perfect equilibrium are (Y,Y,Y) and (Y,Y,N). Player 1 optimally proposes $(2,0)$ if player 2 uses the first strategy, and $(1,1)$ if he uses the second strategy. Hence the game has two subgame perfect equilibria, $((2,0),(Y,Y,Y))$ and $((1,1),(Y,Y,N))$.

If there are K units of the good to allocate, rather than two, then also the game has two subgame perfect equilibria, $((K,0),(Y,\dots,Y))$ and $((K-1,1),(Y,\dots,Y,N))$. In the first equilibrium player 1 proposes that he gets all K units and player 2 agrees to all proposals. In the second equilibrium player 2 plans to reject only the proposal that gives him no units and player 1 proposes that player 2 gets exactly one unit.

Example 16.2: Centipede game

Two players, 1 and 2, alternately have the opportunity to stop their interaction, starting with player 1; each player has T opportunities to do so. Whenever a player chooses to continue (C), he loses \$1 and the other player gains \$2. Each player aims to maximize the amount of money he has at the end of the game.

This situation may be modeled as an extensive game in which the set of histories consists of $2T$ nonterminal histories of the form $C_t = (C,\dots,C)$, where $t \in \{0,\dots,2T-1\}$ is the number of occurrences of C ($C_0 = \emptyset$, the null history), and $T+1$ terminal histories, C_{2T} (both players always choose C) and $S_t = (C,\dots,C,S)$ for $t \in \{0,\dots,2T-1\}$, where t is the number of occurrences of C (the players choose C in the first t periods and then one of them chooses S).

After the history C_t, player 1 moves if t is even (including 0) and player 2 moves if t is odd. Each player's payoff is calculated by starting at 0, subtracting 1 whenever the player chooses C, and adding 2 whenever the other player chooses C. The diagram on the next page shows the game for $T=3$. (The shape of the tree is the reason for the name "centipede".)

Any pair of strategies in which each player plans to stop the game at the first opportunity is a Nash equilibrium. Given player 2's plan, player 1 can

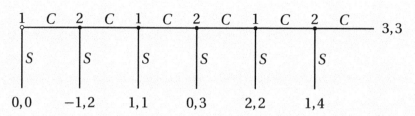

only lose by changing his strategy, and given that player 1 intends to stop the game immediately, player 2 is indifferent between all his strategies.

In fact, we now show that in every Nash equilibrium player 1 stops the game immediately. That is, the only terminal history generated by a Nash equilibrium is S_0. For any pair of strategies that generates the terminal history S_t with $t \geq 1$, the player who moves after the history C_{t-1} can increase his payoff by changing his strategy to one that stops after this history, saving him the loss of continuing at this history. The terminal history C_{2T} occurs only if each player uses the strategy in which he plays C at every opportunity, in which case player 2 can increase his payoff by deviating to the strategy of stopping only at C_{2T-1}.

Although the outcome of every Nash equilibrium is S_0, the game has many Nash equilibria. In every equilibrium player 1 chooses S at the start of the game and player 2 chooses S after the history (C), but after longer histories each player's strategy may choose either C or S.

However, the game has a unique subgame perfect equilibrium, in which each player chooses S whenever he moves. The argument is by induction, starting at the end of the game: after the history C_{2T-1}, player 2 optimally stops the game, and if the player who moves after the history C_t for $t \geq 1$ stops the game, then the player who moves after C_{t-1} optimally does so.

When people play the game in experiments, they tend not to stop it immediately. There seem to be two reasons for the divergence from equilibrium. First, many people appear to be embarrassed by stopping the game to gain \$1 while causing the other player to lose \$2 when there is an opportunity for a large mutual gain. Second, people seem to continue at least for a while because they are not sure of their opponent's strategic reasoning, and given the potential gain they are ready to sacrifice \$1 to check his intentions.

16.2   What is a strategy?

Consider player 1's strategy (S, C, C) in the centipede game with $T = 3$. According to this strategy, player 1 plans to stop the game immediately, but plans to continue at his later moves (after the histories (C,C) and (C,C,C,C)). To be a complete plan of action, player 1's strategy has to specify a response to every possible action of player 2. But a strategy in an extensive game does more than that. Under the strategy (S,C,C) player 1 plans to stop the game immediately, but specifies also his action in the event he has a second opportunity to stop the game, an opportunity that does not occur if he follows his own strategy and stops the game immediately. That is, the strategy specifies plans after contingencies that are inconsistent with the strategy.

In this respect the notion of a strategy in an extensive game does not correspond to a plan of action, which naturally includes actions only after histories consistent with the plan. In the centipede game with $T = 3$, player 1 has four natural plans of action: always continue, and stop at the tth opportunity for $t = 1$, 2, and 3.

Why do we define a strategy more elaborately than a plan of action? When player 2 plans his action after the history (C) he needs to think about what will happen if he does not stop the game. That is, he needs to think about the action player 1 will take after the history (C,C). The second component of player 1's strategy (S,C,C), which specifies an action after the history (C,C), can be thought of as player 2's belief about the action that player 1 will take after (C,C) if player 1 does not stop the game. Thus a pair of strategies in the centipede game, and in other extensive games in which players move more than once, is more than a pair of plans of action; it embodies also an analysis of the game that contains the beliefs of the players about what would happen after any history.

16.3 Backward induction

Backward induction is a procedure for selecting strategy profiles in an extensive game. It is based on the assumption that whenever a player moves and has a clear conjecture about what will happen subsequently, he chooses an action that leads to his highest payoff. The procedure starts by considering histories that are one action away from being terminal, and then works back one step at a time to the start of the game.

To describe the procedure, we first define the diameter of a history h to be the number of steps remaining until the end of the game in the longest history that starts with h.

> **Definition 16.7: Diameter of history**
>
> The *diameter* of the history h in an extensive game is the largest number K for which there are actions $a_1, \ldots, a_K$ such that $(h, a_1, \ldots, a_K)$ is a history.

Note that the diameter of a history is zero if and only if the history is terminal, and the diameter of the null history is the number of actions in the longest history in the game.

The backward induction procedure starts by specifying the action chosen by each player who moves after a history with diameter 1, and then works back in steps to the start of the game. As it does so, it associates with every history h the terminal history $z(h)$ that occurs if the game reaches h and then the players take the actions specified in the previous steps.

In the first step we define $z(h) = h$ for every terminal history h.

In the second step we consider histories with diameter 1. Let h be such a history, so that one action remains to be taken after h, by player $P(h)$. (In the game in Figure 16.3, the two such histories are A and (B, G), with $P(A) = 3$ and $P(B, G) = 1$.) For every action a of $P(h)$ after h, the history (h, a) has diameter 0 (i.e. it is terminal), and hence $z(h, a)$ is defined from the first step (it is equal to (h, a)). From among these actions, let $a = a^*(h)$ be one that maximizes $P(h)$'s payoff over all terminal histories $z(h, a)$, and set $s^{P(h)}(h) = a^*(h)$. Note that if there is more than one such action, we select one of them arbitrarily. (In the game in Figure 16.3, C is such an action for the history (A), and both H and I are such actions for the history (B, G). Either of these actions can be chosen at this step.) Define $z(h) = z(h, a^*(h))$, the terminal history that occurs if the game reaches h and then player $P(h)$ chooses $a^*(h)$.

The procedure continues working backwards until the start of the game. After step k, for every history h with diameter at most k an action for the player who moves after h is defined, together with the resulting terminal history $z(h)$, so that at step $k+1$, for every history with diameter $k+1$, we can find an optimal action for the player who moves after this history. At the end of the process, a strategy for each player in the game is defined.

> **Procedure: Backward induction**
>
> The *backward induction procedure* for an extensive game $\langle N, H, P, (\succsim^i)_{i\in N}\rangle$ generates a strategy profile s as follows. For any history $h \in H$, denote the diameter of h by $d(h)$.
>
> **Initialization**
> For each history h with $d(h) = 0$ (that is, each terminal history), let $z(h) = h$.
>
> **Inductive step**
> Assume that the terminal history $z(h)$ is defined for all $h \in H$ with $d(h) \in \{0, \ldots, k\}$ and $s^{P(h)}(h)$ is defined for all $h \in H$ with $d(h) \in \{1, \ldots, k\}$, where $k < d(\varnothing)$. For each history h with $d(h) = k+1$, let $a^*(h)$ be an action a that is best according to $P(h)$'s preferences over terminal histories $z(h, a)$, and set $s^{P(h)}(h) = a^*(h)$ and $z(h) = z(h, a^*(h))$.

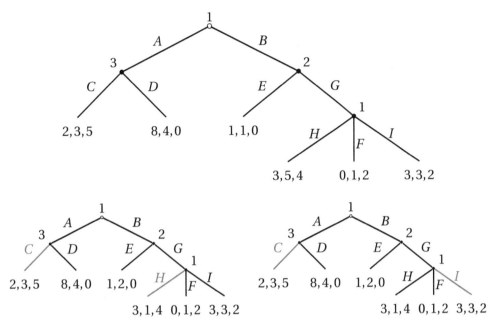

Step 1: Choosing optimal actions for the player who moves after each history with diameter 1. The action C is optimal after the history (A). Both H and I are optimal after the history (B,G). The diagrams show the resulting two possible outcomes of the step.

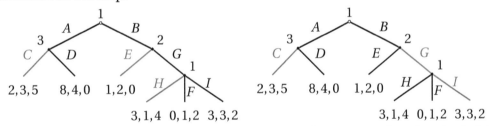

Step 2: Choosing optimal actions for the player who moves after the single history with diameter 2.

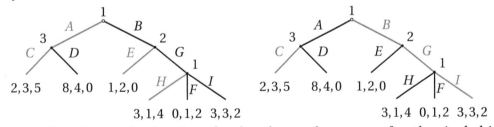

Step 3: Choosing optimal actions for the player who moves after the single history with diameter 3 (the initial history).

Figure 16.3 An example of backward induction. For this game, the procedure selects one of two strategy profiles, which yield one of the two terminal histories (A,C) and (B,G,I).

We say that the strategy profile s *is generated by backward induction* if for some choice of an optimal action after each history, this procedure generates s.

The procedure is well-defined only if an optimal action exists whenever the procedure calls for such an action. In particular it is well-defined for any game with a finite number of histories. If the number of actions after some history is not finite, an optimal action may not exist, in which case the procedure is not well-defined.

We now show that any strategy profile generated by the backward induction procedure is a subgame perfect equilibrium. To do so, we first give an alternative characterization of a subgame perfect equilibrium of an extensive game.

Recall that a strategy profile s is a subgame perfect equilibrium if after no history h does any player have a strategy that leads to a terminal history he prefers to the terminal history generated by s after h. In particular, for any history, the player who moves cannot induce an outcome better for him by changing only his action after that history, *keeping the remainder of his strategy fixed*. We say that a strategy profile with this property satisfies the one-deviation property.

Definition 16.8: One-deviation property of strategy profile

Let $\Gamma = \langle N, H, P, (\succsim^i)_{i \in N} \rangle$ be an extensive game. A strategy profile s for Γ satisfies the *one-deviation property* if for every player $i \in N$ and every nonterminal history $h \in H \setminus Z$ for which $P(h) = i$ we have

$$z(h, s) \succsim^i z(h, (s^{-i}, r^i)) \text{ for every strategy } r^i \text{ of player } i$$
$$\text{that differs from } s^i \text{ only in the action it specifies after } h.$$

A profile of strategies that is a subgame perfect equilibrium satisfies the one-deviation property. The reason is that a subgame perfect equilibrium requires, for any history and any player, that the player's strategy is optimal at that history among all strategies, whereas the one deviation property requires the optimality to hold only among the strategies that differ in the action planned after that history.

We now show that the converse is true: any strategy profile satisfying the one-deviation property is a subgame perfect equilibrium. To illustrate the argument suppose, to the contrary, that the strategy profile s satisfies the one-deviation property, generating the payoff u^i for some player i, but that after some history h at which i moves, i can obtain the payoff $v^i > u^i$ by changing the action specified by his strategy at both h, from say a to a', and at some history h' that extends h,

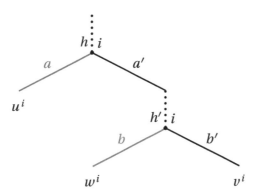

Figure 16.4 An illustration of the argument that a strategy profile that satisfies the one-deviation property is a subgame perfect equilibrium.

from say b to b' (given the other players' strategies). (See Figure 16.4.) Because s satisfies the one-deviation property, the payoff s generates for i starting at h' (after i changes his action only at h), say w^i, is at most u^i. But then $v^i > w^i$ and hence at h' player i can induce a higher payoff than w^i by changing only his action at h' from b to b' holding the rest of his strategy fixed, contradicting the assumption that s satisfies the one-deviation property.

Proposition 16.1: One-deviation property and SPE

For an extensive game (in which every terminal history is finite) a strategy profile satisfies the one-deviation property if and only if it is a subgame perfect equilibrium.

Proof

As we explained earlier, if a strategy profile is a subgame perfect equilibrium then it satisfies the one-deviation property.

Now let s be a strategy profile that satisfies the one-deviation property. Assume, contrary to the claim, that s is not a subgame perfect equilibrium. Then for some player i there is a history h with $P(h) = i$ and at least one strategy of player i that differs from s^i only for histories that start with h and generates a terminal history that i prefers to $z(h,s)$ (the terminal history extending h generated by s). Among these strategies let r^i be one for which the number of histories after which the action it specifies differs from the action that s^i specifies is minimal. Then $z(h,(s^{-i},r^i)) \succ^i z(h,s)$. Let h^* be a longest history for which $r^i(h^*) \neq s^i(h^*)$ and let q^i differ from r^i only in that $q^i(h^*) = s^i(h^*)$, so that q^i and s^i are identical after any history that extends h^* and q^i differs from s^i after fewer histories than does r^i. By the one-deviation property $z(h^*,(s^{-i},q^i)) \succsim^i z(h^*,(s^{-i},r^i))$. Therefore

$$z(h,(s^{-i},q^i)) = z(h^*,(s^{-i},q^i)) \succsim^i z(h^*,(s^{-i},r^i)) = z(h,(s^{-i},r^i)) \succ^i z(h,s),$$

contradicting the definition of r^i.

Note that the proof uses the assumption that all histories are finite, and indeed if not all histories are finite, a strategy profile may satisfy the one deviation property and not be a subgame perfect equilibrium (see Problem 9).

In many games, this result greatly simplifies the verification that a strategy profile is a subgame perfect equilibrium, because it says that we need to check only whether, for each history, the player who moves can increase his payoff by switching to a different action after that history.

We now show that any strategy profile generated by the procedure of backward induction is a subgame perfect equilibrium, by arguing that it satisfies the one-deviation property.

Proposition 16.2: Backward induction and SPE

For an extensive game (in which every terminal history is finite), a strategy profile is generated by the backward induction procedure if and only if it is a subgame perfect equilibrium.

Proof

A strategy profile generated by the backward induction procedure by construction satisfies the one-deviation property. Thus by Proposition 16.1 it is a subgame perfect equilibrium.

Conversely, if a strategy profile is a subgame perfect equilibrium then it satisfies the one-deviation property, and hence is generated by the backward induction procedure where at each step we choose the actions given by the strategy profile.

An immediate implication of this result is that every extensive game with a finite number of histories has a subgame perfect equilibrium, because for every such game the backward induction procedure is well-defined.

Proposition 16.3: Existence of SPE in finite game

Every extensive game with a finite number of histories has a subgame perfect equilibrium.

Chess is an example of a finite extensive game. In the game, two players move alternately. The terminal histories are of three types: player 1 wins, player 2 wins, and the players draw. Each player prefers to win than to draw than to lose. The game is finite because once a position is repeated three times, a draw is declared. Although the number of histories is finite, it is huge, and currently no computer can carry out the backward induction procedure for the game. However, we know from Proposition 16.3 that chess has a subgame perfect equilibrium. Modeled as a strategic game, chess is strictly competitive, so we know also (Proposition 15.3) that the payoffs in all Nash equilibria are the same and the Nash equilibrium strategies are maxmin strategies: either one of the players has a strategy that guarantees he wins, or each player has a strategy that guarantees the outcome is at least a draw.

Ticktacktoe is another example of a finite extensive game that is strictly competitive. For ticktacktoe, we know that each player can guarantee a draw. Chess is more interesting than ticktacktoe because whether a player can guarantee a win or a draw in chess is not known; the outcome of a play of chess depends on the player's cognitive abilities more than the outcome of a play of ticktacktoe. Models of bounded rationality, which we do not discuss in this book, attempt to explore the implications of such differences in ability.

16.4   Bargaining

This section presents several models of bargaining, and in doing so illustrates how an extensive game may be used to analyze an economic situation. Bargaining is a typical economic situation, as it involves a mixture of common and conflicting interests. The parties have a common interest in reaching an agreement, but differ in their evaluations of the possible agreements. Bargaining models are key components of economic models of markets in which exchange occurs through pairwise matches and the terms of exchange are negotiated. These market models differ from the market models presented in Part II of the book in that the individuals do not perceive prices as given.

For simplicity we confine ourselves to the case in which two parties, 1 and 2, bargain over the partition of a desirable pie of size 1. The set of possible agreements is

$$X = \{(x^1, x^2) : x^1 + x^2 = 1 \text{ and } x^i \geq 0 \text{ for } i = 1, 2\}.$$

The outcome of bargaining is either one of these agreements or disagreement. We assume that the players care only about the agreement they reach and possibly the time at which they reach it, not about the path of the negotiations that precede agreement. In particular, a player does not suffer if he agrees to an offer that is worse than one he previously rejected. Further, we assume that each party regards a failure to reach an agreement as equivalent to obtaining none of the pie.

We study several models of bargaining. They differ in the specification of the order of moves and the options available to each player whenever he moves. As we will see, the details of the bargaining procedure critically affect the outcome of bargaining.

16.4.1 Take it or leave it (ultimatum game)

Player 1 proposes a division of the pie (a member of X), which player 2 then either accepts or rejects. (Example 16.1 is a version of this game in which the set of possible agreements is finite.)

Definition 16.9: Ultimatum game

The *ultimatum game* is the extensive game $\langle\{1,2\}, H, P, (\succsim^i)_{i\in\{1,2\}}\rangle$ with the following components.

Histories
 The set H of histories consists of

- $\varnothing$ (the initial history)
- (x) for any $x \in X$ (player 1 makes the proposal x)
- (x, Y) for any $x \in X$ (player 1 makes the proposal x, which player 2 accepts)
- (x, N) for any $x \in X$ (player 1 makes the proposal x, which player 2 rejects).

Player function
 $P(\varnothing) = 1$ (player 1 moves at the start of the game) and $P(x) = 2$ for all $x \in X$ (player 2 moves after player 1 makes a proposal).

Preferences
 The preference relation $\succsim^i$ of each player i is represented by the payoff function u^i with $u^i(x, Y) = x^i$ and $u^i(x, N) = 0$ for all $x \in X$.

The game is illustrated in Figure 16.5. Note that this diagram (unlike the diagrams of previous games) does not show all the histories. It represents player 1's set of (infinitely many) actions by a shaded triangle, and shows only one of his actions, x, and the actions available to player 2 after the history (x).

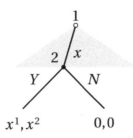

Figure 16.5 An illustration of the ultimatum game.

Player 1's set of strategies in the ultimatum game is X, and each strategy of player 2 is a function that for each $x \in X$ specifies either Y or N. The game has a unique subgame perfect equilibrium, in which player 1 proposes that he gets the entire pie and player 2 accepts all proposals.

Proposition 16.4: SPE of ultimatum game

The ultimatum game has a unique subgame perfect equilibrium, in which player 1 proposes $(1,0)$ and player 2 accepts all proposals.

Proof

The strategy pair is a subgame perfect equilibrium: given that player 2 accepts all proposals, the proposal $(1,0)$ is optimal for player 1, and after any proposal, acceptance (Y) is optimal for player 2.

Now let s be a subgame perfect equilibrium. The only optimal response of player 2 to a proposal x with $x^2 > 0$ is acceptance, so $s^2(x) = Y$ for any x with $x^2 > 0$. Thus if $s^1(\varnothing) = (1 - \varepsilon, \varepsilon)$ with $\varepsilon > 0$ (which player 2 accepts), then player 1 can do better by proposing $(1 - \frac{1}{2}\varepsilon, \frac{1}{2}\varepsilon)$, which player 2 also accepts. Hence $s^1(\varnothing) = (1,0)$. Finally, $s^2(1,0) = Y$ because if player 2 rejects $(1,0)$ then player 1 gets 0 and can do better by making any other proposal, which player 2 accepts.

Notice that after the proposal $(1,0)$, player 2 is indifferent between Y and N. Nevertheless, the game has only one subgame perfect equilibrium, in which player 2 accepts $(1,0)$. In contrast, in Example 16.1, where the number of possible agreements is finite, the game has also a subgame perfect equilibrium in which player 2 rejects the proposal $(1,0)$.

A long history of experiments has demonstrated that the unique subgame perfect equilibrium is inconsistent with human behavior. For example, a population of 19,000 students from around the world similar to the readership of this book have responded to a question on http://arielrubinstein.org/gt

asking them to imagine they have to divide $100 between themselves and another person. The most common proposal, chosen by about 50% of subjects, is the division ($50, $50). Only about 11% choose to offer the other person $0 or $1, as in the subgame perfect equilibrium.

Rather than necessarily calling into question the concept of subgame perfect equilibrium, these results point to the unrealistic nature of the players' preferences in the game. First, some people have preferences for fairness, which lead them to most prefer an equal division of the pie. Second, many people are insulted by low offers, and hence reject them. When players' preferences involve such considerations, the (modified) game may have a subgame perfect equilibrium in which the proposer receives significantly less than the entire pie.

16.4.2 Finite horizon with alternating offers

Now assume that after player 2 rejects player 1's offer, he can make a counteroffer, which player 1 can accept or reject, and that the players can continue to alternate proposals in this way for up to T periods. If the offer made in period T is rejected, the game ends with disagreement.

Definition 16.10: Finite-horizon bargaining game with alternating offers

A *finite-horizon bargaining game with alternating offers* is an extensive game $\langle \{1,2\}, H, P, (\succsim^i)_{i \in \{1,2\}} \rangle$ with the following components.

Histories

The set H of histories consists, for some positive integer T, of

- $\varnothing$ (the initial history)

- $(x_1, N, x_2, N, \ldots, x_t)$ for any $x_1, \ldots, x_t \in X$ and $1 \leq t \leq T$ (proposals through period $t - 1$ are rejected, and the proposal in period t is x_t)

- $(x_1, N, x_2, N, \ldots, x_t, N)$ for any $x_1, \ldots, x_t \in X$ and $1 \leq t \leq T$ (proposals through period t are rejected)

- $(x_1, N, x_2, N, \ldots, x_{t-1}, N, x_t, Y)$ for any $x_1, \ldots, x_t \in X$ and $1 \leq t \leq T$ (proposals through period $t - 1$ are rejected, and the proposal in period t is accepted).

Player function

Let $i_\tau = 1$ if τ is odd and $i_\tau = 2$ if τ is even. Then

- $P(\varnothing) = 1$ (player 1 makes the first proposal)

- $P(x_1, N, x_2, N, \ldots, x_t) = i_{t+1}$ for $t = 1, \ldots, T$ (player i_{t+1} responds to the offer made by i_t)

- $P(x_1, N, x_2, N, \ldots, x_t, N) = i_{t+1}$ for $t = 1, \ldots, T-1$ (player i_{t+1} makes the proposal at the beginning of period $t+1$).

Preferences

The preference relation $\succcurlyeq^i$ of each player i is represented by the payoff function u^i with $u^i(x_1, N, x_2, N, \ldots, x_t, Y) = x_t^i$ and $u^i(x_1, N, x_2, N, \ldots, x_T, N) = 0$.

We show that in this game all the bargaining power belongs to the player who makes the proposal in the last period: in every subgame perfect equilibrium this player receives the whole pie.

Proposition 16.5: SPE of finite-horizon game with alternating offers

In every subgame perfect equilibrium of a finite-horizon bargaining game with alternating offers, the payoff of the player who makes a proposal in the last period is 1 and the payoff of the other player is 0.

Proof

Let i be the player who proposes in period T, let j be the other player, and let $e(i)$ be the partition in which i gets the whole pie. The game has a subgame perfect equilibrium in which player i proposes $e(i)$ whenever he makes a proposal and accepts only $e(i)$ whenever he responds to a proposal, and player j always proposes $e(i)$ and accepts all proposals.

The game has many subgame perfect equilibria but all of them end with i getting all the pie. Let s be a subgame perfect equilibrium. Consider a history $h = (x_1, N, x_2, N, \ldots, x_{T-1}, N)$ in which $T-1$ proposals are made and rejected. The argument in the proof of Proposition 16.4 implies that $s^i(h) = e(i)$ and that player j accepts any proposal of player i in period T.

Now if i does not get the whole pie in the outcome of s, he can deviate profitably to the strategy r^i in which he rejects any proposal in any period and always proposes $e(i)$. The outcome of the pair of strategies r^i and s^j is agreement on $e(i)$ in period T at the latest.

16.4.3 Infinite horizon with one-sided offers

The result in the previous section demonstrates the significance of the existence of a final period in which a proposal can be made. We now study a model in which no such final period exists: the players believe that after any rejection there will be another opportunity to agree. For now, we assume that only player 1 makes proposals. Since we do not limit the number of bargaining periods, we need to use a natural extension of the model of an extensive game in which terminal histories can be infinite.

Definition 16.11: Infinite-horizon bargaining game with one-sided offers

The *infinite-horizon bargaining game with one-sided offers* is the extensive game $\langle\{1,2\}, H, P, (\succsim^i)_{i\in\{1,2\}}\rangle$ with the following components.

Histories
The set H of histories consists of

- $\varnothing$ (the initial history)

- $(x_1, N, x_2, N, \ldots, x_{t-1}, N, x_t)$ for any $x_1, \ldots, x_t \in X$ and $t \geq 1$ (proposals through period $t-1$ are rejected, and player 1 proposes x_t in period t)

- $(x_1, N, x_2, N, \ldots, x_t, N)$ for any $x_1, \ldots, x_t \in X$ and $t \geq 1$ (proposals through period t are rejected)

- $(x_1, N, x_2, N, \ldots, x_{t-1}, N, x_t, Y)$ for any $x_1, \ldots, x_t \in X$ and $t \geq 1$ (proposals through period $t-1$ are rejected, and player 1's proposal in period t is accepted).

- $(x_1, N, x_2, N, \ldots, x_t, N, \ldots)$ for any infinite sequence of proposals $x_1, \ldots, x_t, \ldots$ (all proposals are rejected).

Player function
$P(\varnothing) = P(x_1, N, x_2, N, \ldots, x_t, N) = 1$ and $P(x_1, N, x_2, N, \ldots, x_t) = 2$.

Preferences
The preference relation $\succsim^i$ of each player i is represented by the payoff function u^i with

$$u^i(x_1, N, x_2, N, \ldots, x_t, Y) = x_t^i \text{ and } u^i(x_1, N, x_2, N, \ldots, x_t, N, \ldots) = 0.$$

In this game, every partition of the pie is the outcome of some subgame perfect equilibrium. In fact, for every partition of the pie, the game has a subgame perfect equilibrium in which agreement is reached immediately on that partition. Thus when the horizon is infinite, the fact that only player 1 makes offers does not give him more bargaining power than player 2.

Proposition 16.6: SPE of infinite-horizon game with one-sided offers

For every partition $x_* \in X$, the infinite-horizon bargaining game with one-sided offers has a subgame perfect equilibrium in which the outcome is immediate agreement on x_*. The game has also a subgame perfect equilibrium in which the players never reach agreement.

Proof

We first show that the following strategy pair is a subgame perfect equilibrium in which the players reach agreement in period 1 on x_*.

Player 1
Always propose x_*.

Player 2
Accept an offer y if and only if $y^2 \geq x_*^2$.

After the initial history or any history ending with rejection, player 1 can do no better than follow his strategy, because player 2 never accepts less than x_*^2. After any history ending with an offer y for which $y^2 < x_*^2$, player 2 can do no better than follow his strategy, because if he rejects the proposal then player 1 subsequently continues to propose x_*. After any history ending with an offer y for which $y^2 \geq x_*^2$, player 2 can do no better than follow his strategy and accept the proposal, because player 1 never proposes that player 2 gets more than x_*^2. Thus the strategy pair is a subgame perfect equilibrium.

We now show that the following strategy pair is a subgame perfect equilibrium in which the players never reach agreement.

Player 1
After the initial history and any history in which all proposals are $(1,0)$, propose $(1,0)$. After any other history, propose $(0,1)$.

Player 2
After any history in which all proposals are $(1,0)$, reject the proposal. After any other history, accept the proposal only if it is $(0,1)$.

Consider first player 1. After each history, if player 1 follows his strategy the outcome is either agreement on $(0,1)$ or disagreement, both of which yield the payoff 0. Any change in player 1's strategy after any history also generates disagreement or agreement on $(0,1)$, and thus does not make him better off.

Now consider player 2. After a history in which player 1 has proposed only $(1, 0)$, player 2's following his strategy leads to the players' never reaching agreement, and any change in his strategy leads either to the same outcome or to agreement on $(1, 0)$, which is no better for him. After a history in which player 1 has proposed a partition different from $(1, 0)$, player 2's following his strategy leads to his favorite agreement, $(0, 1)$.

The equilibrium in which the players never reach agreement may be interpreted as follows. Initially, player 2 expects player 1 to insist on getting the whole pie and he plans to reject such a proposal. When player 1 makes any other proposal, player 2 interprets the move as a sign of weakness on the part of player 1 and expects player 1 to yield and offer him the whole pie. This interpretation of an attempt by player 1 to reach an agreement by offering player 2 a positive amount of the pie deters player 1 from doing so.

16.4.4   Infinite horizon with one-sided offers and discounting

We now modify the model in the previous section by assuming that each player prefers to receive pie earlier than later. Specifically, we assume that the payoff of each player i at a terminal history in which agreement on x is reached at time t is $(\delta^i)^t x^i$, where $\delta^i \in (0, 1)$.

Definition 16.12: Infinite-horizon bargaining game with one-sided offers and discounting

An *infinite-horizon bargaining game with one-sided offers and discounting* is an extensive game that differs from an infinite-horizon bargaining game with one-sided offers only in that the payoff of player i to an agreement on x in period t is $(\delta^i)^t x^i$ for $i = 1, 2$, where $\delta^i \in (0, 1)$. For notational economy we write $\delta^1 = \alpha$ and $\delta^2 = \beta$.

The first strategy pair in the proof of Proposition 16.6, in which player 1 always proposes x_* and player 2 accepts only proposals in which he receives at least x_*^2, is not a subgame perfect equilibrium of this game unless $x_*^2 = 0$. If $x_*^2 > 0$, consider the history in which at the beginning of the game player 1 proposes $(x_*^1 + \varepsilon, x_*^2 - \varepsilon)$ with $\varepsilon > 0$ small enough that $x_*^2 - \varepsilon > \beta x_*^2$. Given player 1's strategy, player 2's strategy (which in particular rejects the proposal) gives him x_*^2 at a later period; accepting $x_*^2 - \varepsilon$ is better for player 2.

We now show that the introduction of discounting makes a huge difference to the set of subgame perfect equilibria: it restores the bargaining power of the player who makes all offers, even if player 2's discount factor is close to 1.

> **Proposition 16.7: SPE of infinite-horizon game with one-sided offers and discounting**
>
> For any values of the discount factors α and β, an infinite-horizon bargaining game with one-sided offers and discounting has a unique subgame perfect equilibrium, in which player 1 gets all the pie immediately.

> **Proof**
>
> First note that the strategy pair in which player 1 always proposes $(1,0)$ and player 2 accepts all proposals is a subgame perfect equilibrium.
>
> Now let M be the supremum of player 2's payoffs over all subgame perfect equilibria. Consider a history (x) (player 1 proposes x). If player 2 rejects x, the remainder of the game is identical to the whole game. Thus in any subgame perfect equilibrium any strategy that rejects x yields player 2 at most M with one period of delay. Hence in a subgame perfect equilibrium player 2 accepts x if $x^2 > \beta M$. So the infimum of player 1's payoffs over all subgame perfect equilibria is at least $1 - \beta M$. Therefore the supremum of player 2's payoffs M does not exceed βM, which is possible only if $M = 0$ (given $\beta < 1$).
>
> Given that player 2's payoff in every subgame perfect equilibrium is 0, he accepts all offers x in which $x^2 > 0$. Player 1's payoff in every subgame perfect equilibrium is 1 because for any strategy pair in which his payoff is $u < 1$ he can deviate and propose $(u + \varepsilon, 1 - u - \varepsilon)$ with $\varepsilon < 1 - u$, which player 2 accepts. Thus in any subgame perfect equilibrium player 1 offers $(1,0)$ and player 2 accepts all offers.

16.4.5 Infinite horizon with alternating offers and discounting

Finally consider a model in which the horizon is infinite, the players alternate offers, and payoffs obtained after period 1 are discounted.

> **Definition 16.13: Infinite-horizon bargaining game with alternating offers and discounting**
>
> An *infinite-horizon bargaining game with alternating offers and discounting* is an extensive game $\langle \{1,2\}, H, P, (\succsim^i)_{i \in \{1,2\}} \rangle$ with the following components, where $i_t = 1$ if t is odd and $i_t = 2$ if t is even.
>
> **Histories**
>   The set H of histories consists of

- ∅ (the initial history)

- $(x_1, N, x_2, N, \ldots, x_t)$ for any $x_1, \ldots, x_t \in X$ and $t \geq 1$ (proposals through period $t - 1$ are rejected, and the proposal in period t is x_t)

- $(x_1, N, x_2, N, \ldots, x_t, N)$ for any $x_1, \ldots, x_t \in X$ and $t \geq 1$ (proposals through period t are rejected)

- $(x_1, N, x_2, N, \ldots, x_{t-1}, N, x_t, Y)$ for any $x_1, \ldots, x_t \in X$ and $t \geq 1$ (proposals through period $t - 1$ are rejected and the proposal in period t is accepted)

- $(x_1, N, x_2, N, \ldots, x_t, N, \ldots)$ for any infinite sequence of proposals $x_1, \ldots, x_t, \ldots$ (all proposals are rejected).

Player function

The player function is defined as follows

- $P(\varnothing) = 1$ (player 1 makes the first proposal)

- $P(x_1, N, x_2, N, \ldots, x_t) = i_{t+1}$ for $t \geq 1$ (player i_{t+1} responds to the offer made by i_t)

- $P(x_1, N, x_2, N, \ldots, x_t, N) = i_{t+1}$ for $t \geq 1$ (player i_{t+1} makes the proposal at the beginning of period $t + 1$).

Preferences

The preference relation $\succsim^i$ of each player i is represented by the payoff function u^i with $u^i(x_1, N, x_2, N, \ldots, x_t, Y) = (\delta^i)^t x_t^i$ for $t \geq 1$ and $u^i(x_1, N, x_2, N, \ldots, x_t, N, \ldots) = 0$ for $i = 1, 2$, where $\delta^i \in (0, 1)$. For notational economy we write $\delta^1 = \alpha$ and $\delta^2 = \beta$.

Giving player 2 the opportunity to make offers restores his bargaining power. We now show that the game has a unique subgame perfect equilibrium, in which the players' payoffs depend on their discount factors.

Proposition 16.8: SPE of infinite-horizon game with alternating offers and discounting

An infinite-horizon bargaining game with alternating offers and discounting has a unique subgame perfect equilibrium, in which

- player 1 always proposes x_* and accepts a proposal x if and only if $x^1 \geq y_*^1$

- player 2 always proposes y_* and accepts a proposal y if and only if $y^2 \geq x_*^2$

where

$$x_* = \left(\frac{1-\beta}{1-\alpha\beta}, \frac{\beta(1-\alpha)}{1-\alpha\beta} \right) \quad \text{and} \quad y_* = \left(\frac{\alpha(1-\beta)}{1-\alpha\beta}, \frac{1-\alpha}{1-\alpha\beta} \right).$$

Proof

Note that the pair of proposals x_* and y_* is the unique solution of the pair of equations $\alpha x^1 = y^1$ and $\beta y^2 = x^2$.

Step 1 *The strategy pair is a subgame perfect equilibrium.*

Proof. First consider a history after which player 1 makes a proposal. If player 1 follows his strategy, he proposes x_*, which player 2 accepts, resulting in player 1's getting x_*^1 immediately. Given player 2's strategy, player 1 can, by changing his strategy, either obtain an agreement not better than x_* in a later period or induce perpetual disagreement. Thus he has no profitable deviation.

Now consider a history after which player 1 responds to a proposal y.

If $y^1 \geq y_*^1$, player 1's strategy calls for him to accept the proposal, resulting in his getting y^1 immediately. If he deviates (and in particular rejects the proposal), then the outcome is not better for him than getting x_* at least one period later. Thus any deviation generates for him a payoff of at most $\alpha x_*^1 = y_*^1 \leq y^1$, so that he is not better off deviating from his strategy.

If $y_1 < y_*^1$, player 1's strategy calls for him to reject the proposal, in which case he proposes x_*, which player 2 accepts, resulting in x_* one period later. Any deviation leads him to either accept the proposal or to obtain offers not better than x_* at least one period later. Given $\alpha x_*^1 = y_*^1$, he is thus not better off accepting the proposal.

The argument for player 2 is similar. ◁

Step 2 *No other strategy pair is a subgame perfect equilibrium.*

Proof. Let G^i be the game following a history after which player i makes a proposal. (All such games are identical.) Let M^i be the supremum of player i's payoffs in subgame perfect equilibria of G^i and let m^i be the infimum of these payoffs.

We first argue that $m^2 \geq 1 - \alpha M^1$. If player 1 rejects player 2's initial proposal in G^2, play continues to G^1, in which player 1's payoff is at most M^1. Thus in any subgame perfect equilibrium player 1 optimally accepts any proposal that gives him more than αM^1, so that player 2's payoff in any equilibrium of G^2 is not less than $1 - \alpha M^1$. Hence $m^2 \geq 1 - \alpha M^1$.

We now argue that $M^1 \leq 1 - \beta m^2$. If player 2 rejects player 1's initial proposal in G^1, play continues to G^2, in which player 2's payoff is at least m^2. Thus player 2 optimally rejects any proposal that gives him less than βm^2, so that in no subgame perfect equilibrium of G^1 is player 1's payoff higher than $1 - \beta m^2$. Hence $M^1 \leq 1 - \beta m^2$.

These two inequalities imply that $1 - \alpha M^1 \leq m^2 \leq (1 - M^1)/\beta$ and hence $M^1 \leq (1 - \beta)/(1 - \alpha\beta) = x_*^1$. By Step 1, $M^1 \geq x_*^1$. Thus $M^1 = x_*^1$. Since $1 - \alpha x_*^1 = (1 - x_*^1)/\beta = y_*^2$ we have $m^2 = y_*^2$.

Repeating these arguments with the roles of players 1 and 2 reversed yields $M^2 = y_*^2$ and $m^1 = x_*^1$, so that in every subgame perfect equilibrium of G^1 the payoff of player 1 is x_*^1 and in every subgame perfect equilibrium of G^2 the payoff of player 2 is y_*^2.

Now, in G^1 player 2, by rejecting player 1's proposal, can get at least $\beta y_*^2 = x_*^2$. Thus in every subgame perfect equilibrium of G^1 his payoff is x_*^2. Payoffs of x_*^1 for player 1 and x_*^2 for player 2 are possible only if agreement is reached immediately on x_*, so that in every subgame perfect equilibrium of G^1 player 1 proposes x_* and player 2 accepts this proposal. Similarly, in every subgame perfect equilibrium of G^2 player 2 proposes y^* and player 1 accepts this proposal. Thus the strategy pair given in the proposition is the only subgame perfect equilibrium of the game.   ◁

Notice that as a player values future payoffs more (becomes more patient), given the discount factor of the other player, the share of the pie that he receives increases. As his discount factor approaches 1, his equilibrium share approaches 1, regardless of the other player 2's (given) discount factor.

If the players are equally patient, with $\alpha = \beta = \delta$, the equilibrium payoff of player 1 is $1/(1 + \delta)$ and that of player 2 is $\delta/(1 + \delta)$. Thus the fact that player 1 makes the first proposal confers on him an advantage, but one that diminishes as both players become more patient. When δ is close to 1, the equilibrium payoff of each player is close to $\frac{1}{2}$. That is, when the players are equally patient and value future payoffs almost as much as they value current payoffs, the unique subgame perfect equilibrium involves an almost equal split of the pie.

In the subgame perfect equilibrium, agreement is reached immediately. In Problem 11 you are asked to analyze the game with different preferences: the payoff of each player i for an agreement on x in period t is $x^i - c^i t$ for some c^1, $c^2 > 0$ (rather than $(\delta^i)^t x^i$). When $c^1 \neq c^2$ this game also has a unique subgame perfect equilibrium in which agreement is reached immediately. However, as you are asked to show in Problem 12b, when $c^1 = c^2$ the game has subgame perfect equilibria in which agreement is reached after a delay.

16.5 Repeated games

We end the chapter with an introduction to the family of repeated games. In a repeated game, the same set of players engages repeatedly in a fixed strategic game. We model a repeated game using an extension of the notion of an extensive game that allows players to move simultaneously, and apply to the model the solution concepts of Nash equilibrium and subgame perfect equilibrium.

To motivate the main idea, consider the Prisoner's dilemma. In this game, the pair of actions (C, C), which we can think of as a cooperative outcome, is not a Nash equilibrium. But if the players repeatedly play the game, the outcome in which (C, C) occurs in every period may be a Nash equilibrium. If each player plans to choose C as long as the other player does so, and plans to switch to D for long enough to erase the other player's one-period gain if he ever deviates to D, then neither player has an incentive to deviate from his plan.

We distinguish between repeated games with a finite horizon and those with an infinite horizon. As for bargaining games, the distinction reflects two types of long term interaction. A game with a finite horizon fits a situation where the players are fully aware of the last period; one with an infinite horizon captures a situation in which every player believes that after each period there will be another one.

To analyze a repeated game, we need to specify the players' preferences over sequences of action profiles. We derive these preferences from payoff functions that represent the players' preferences in the underlying strategic game. For convenience, *in the remainder of this section we refer to a tuple $\langle N, \{A^i\}_{i \in N}, \{u^i\}_{i \in N}\rangle$, where N is a set of players, for each player $i \in N$ the set A^i is the set of actions of player i, and for each $i \in N$ the function $u^i : A \to \mathbb{R}$ represents player i's preferences over the set A of outcomes, simply as a strategic game.*

A key concept in the analysis of the repeated games derived from a strategic game $G = \langle N, \{A^i\}_{i \in N}, \{u^i\}_{i \in N}\rangle$ is the profile $(v^i(G))_{i \in N}$ of numbers given by

$$v^i(G) = \min_{a^{-i} \in A^{-i}} \max_{a^i \in A^i} u^i(a^i, a^{-i}) \quad \text{for all } i \in N. \tag{16.1}$$

The number $v^i(G)$ is the lowest payoff in G that the other players can inflict on player i. That is, (*i*) whatever the other players do, player i can respond by obtaining at least $v^i(G)$ and (*ii*) there is a list of actions for $N \setminus \{i\}$, which we denote by $p(i)$, that guarantees that i's payoff is no higher than $v^i(G)$. A profile $(w^i)_{i\in N}$ of numbers is *individually rational* if $w^i \geq v^i(G)$ for all $i \in N$. Note that if a is a Nash equilibrium of G then $u^i(a) \geq v^i(G)$ for every player i.

16.5.1 Finitely repeated games

We start with the definition of the game in which for some positive integer T the strategic game G is played in each period $t = 1, \ldots, T$. In this game, in every period t each player is fully informed about the action chosen by each player in the previous $t - 1$ periods, and each player's payoff is the sum of his payoffs in G in the T periods.

Definition 16.14: Finitely repeated game

Let $G = \langle N, \{A^i\}_{i\in N}, \{u^i\}_{i\in N}\rangle$ be a strategic game and let T be a positive integer. The *T-period repeated game of G* is the tuple $\langle G, T, H, P, (\succeq^i)_{i\in N}\rangle$ where

Histories

H consists of $\varnothing$ (the initial history) and all sequences $(a_1, \ldots, a_t)$ for $t = 1, \ldots, T$ and $a_k \in A = \times_{i\in N} A^i$ for $k = 1, \ldots, t$ (the outcomes in the first t plays of the game)

Player function

P is a function that assigns to each nonterminal history h (that is, member of H with length less than T) the set N (all players move after every nonterminal history)

Preferences

for each $i \in N$, $\succeq^i$ is a preference relation over the terminal histories (player i's preferences over sequences $(a_1, \ldots, a_T)$ of outcomes of G) that is represented by the function $\sum_{t=1}^{T} u^i(a_t)$.

A strategy for player i in a T-period repeated game is a function that attaches to each nonterminal history an action in A^i. Given a profile $(s^i)_{i\in N}$ of strategies, the outcome $O((s^i)_{i\in N})$ of the game is the terminal history $(a_t)_{t=1,\ldots,T}$ with $a_1^i = s^i(\varnothing)$ and $a_t^i = s^i(a_1, \ldots, a_{t-1})$ for all $i \in N$ and $t = 2, \ldots, T$. A Nash equilibrium is a strategy profile for which no player can increase his payoff by changing his strategy. A subgame perfect equilibrium is a strategy profile $(s^i)_{i\in N}$ for which there is no history h and player i such that by changing his strategy after histories that extend h, player i can induce a terminal history that extends h that he prefers to the one that extends h generated by $(s^i)_{i\in N}$.

We first show that for a strategic game that has a unique Nash equilibrium, like the Prisoner's dilemma, repetition does not lead to any new outcomes in a subgame perfect equilibrium.

Proposition 16.9: SPE of finitely repeated game of game with unique Nash equilibrium

Let G be a strategic game and let T be a positive integer. If G has a unique Nash equilibrium $(a^i_*)_{i \in N}$ then the T-period repeated game of G has a unique subgame perfect equilibrium $(s^i_*)_{i \in N}$, with $s^i_*(h) = a^i_*$ for every history h and every player i.

Proof

The strategy profile $(s^i_*)_{i \in N}$ is a subgame perfect equilibrium because a deviation by any player in any period does not increase the player's payoff in the period and has no effect on the other players' future actions.

To show that there is no other subgame perfect equilibrium, let $(s^i)_{i \in N}$ be a subgame perfect equilibrium and let h be a longest history after which the outcome $(b^i)_{i \in N}$ of G generated by $(s^i)_{i \in N}$ is not $(a^i_*)_{i \in N}$. Given that $(b^i)_{i \in N}$ is not a Nash equilibrium of G, some player j can increase his payoff by deviating from b^j. This deviation does not affect the outcome in any future period because these outcomes occur after histories longer than h and hence are all equal to $(a^i_*)_{i \in N}$. Thus j's deviation increases his payoff.

For the T-period repeated game of the Prisoner's dilemma, the outcome in which D is chosen by each player in each period is not merely the only subgame perfect equilibrium outcome, but is also the only Nash equilibrium outcome. To see why, let (s^1, s^2) be a Nash equilibrium and let t be the last period for which the outcome $O_t(s^1, s^2) \neq (D, D)$. Suppose that according to s^i, player i chooses C after the history $h = (O_1(s^1, s^2), \ldots, O_{t-1}(s^1, s^2))$. Then by deviating to D in period t following the history h and continuing to play D from period $t+1$ on, player i increases the sum of his payoffs.

This argument can be extended to the T-period repeated game of any strategic game G that has a unique Nash equilibrium (a^i_*) and the payoff of each player i in this equilibrium is the number $v^i(G)$ defined in (16.1). Let (s^i) be a Nash equilibrium of the repeated game. Suppose that t is the last period for which the outcome of (s^i) is not (a^i_*) and denote the action profile chosen in this period by x_t. Let b^i be an action of player i for which $u^i(b^i, x_t^{-i}) > u^i(x_t)$. Then the strategy of player i that differs from s^i in that it chooses b^i after $O_{t-1}((s^i)_{i \in N})$

and in each subsequent period chooses an action that yields i a payoff of at least $v^i(G)$, given the other players' actions, increases the sum of his payoffs.

Contrast this observation with the analysis of the following strategic game G.

	C	D	E
C	6,6	0,7	0,0
D	7,0	1,1	0,0
E	0,0	0,0	−1,−1

This game has a unique Nash equilibrium (D, D), but each player's payoff in this equilibrium, which is 1, is greater than $v^i(G)$, which is 0. For $T \geq 2$, the T-period repeated game of G has a Nash equilibrium for which the outcome is not a constant repetition of the Nash equilibrium of G. In one such equilibrium, each player's strategy selects C after any history up to period $T - 1$, with two exceptions: (i) after the history in which the outcome is (C, C) in periods $1, \ldots, T - 1$ it selects D, and (ii) after any history in which the other player chose D in some period before T, it selects E. The outcome of this strategy pair is (C, C) in periods 1 through $T - 1$ and (D, D) in period T. The strategy pair is a Nash equilibrium: deviating in the last period is not profitable; deviating in an earlier period increases a player's payoff by 1 in that period, but induces the other player to choose E in every subsequent period, reducing the player's payoff by at least 1 in each of those periods.

More generally, let G be a strategic game with a unique Nash equilibrium a_* for which $u^i(a_*) > v^i(G)$ for each player i. Let a be an action profile in G for which $u^i(a) > u^i(a_*)$ for each player i. Then for some number K and any number $T > K$, the T-period repeated game of G has a Nash equilibrium in which the outcome has two phases: each player i chooses a^i through period $T - K$ and then a^i_*. If a single player, say j, deviates in the first phase, every other player i subsequently chooses the action $p^i(j)$, where $p(j)$ is a solution of (16.1) (that is, a list of actions of the players other than j that hold j's payoff down to at most $v^j(G)$). If player j deviates from a in the first phase, he subsequently obtains a payoff of at most $v^j(G)$ in each subsequent period, so that if K is large enough his gain is offset by his loss of at least $u^j(a_*) - v^j(G)$ in each of at least K periods.

16.5.2 Infinitely repeated games with limit of the means payoffs

We now study a game in which a strategic game is played in each of an infinite sequence of periods, 1, 2, 3, ... As for a finitely repeated game, each player is fully informed in each period of the sequence of action profiles chosen in the previous periods. There are several ways of specifying the players' payoffs in the infinitely-repeated game. We focus on a criterion called the limit of the means: each player assesses a sequence of payoffs by the limit, as $T \to \infty$, of the mean of these payoffs in the first T periods. Thus, for example, the payoff in the repeated game for the sequence of payoffs $0, 0, 0, \ldots, 0, 1, 3, 1, 3, \ldots$ in which 0 occurs a finite number of times and subsequently the payoff alternates between 1 and 3 is 2.

Definition 16.15: Infinitely repeated game with limit of means payoffs

Let $G = \langle N, \{A^i\}_{i\in N}, \{u^i\}_{i\in N} \rangle$ be a strategic game. The *infinitely repeated game of G* is the tuple $\langle G, H, P, (\succsim^i)_{i\in N} \rangle$ where

Histories
H consists of $\varnothing$ (the initial history) and all finite and infinite sequences of members of $A = \times_{i\in N} A^i$ (the infinite sequences are the terminal histories)

Player function
P is a function that assigns to each nonterminal history (that is, any finite sequence of members of A) the set N (all players move after every nonterminal history)

Preferences
for each $i \in N$, $\succsim^i$ is a preference relation over infinite sequences $(a_t)_{t=1}^\infty$ of members of A (player i's preferences over the set of terminal histories) that is represented by the function $\lim_{T\to\infty} \sum_{t=1}^T u^i(a_t)/T$.

This definition glosses over one issue: the limit of the means is not well defined for every sequence of numbers (even for sequences in which all the numbers are 0 or 1). However, the definition suffices for our purposes because we restrict attention to strategy profiles that yield streams of outcomes of the type $(b_1, \ldots, b_K, c_1, \ldots, c_L, c_1, \ldots, c_L, \ldots)$, in which there is an initial block of finite length (which is possibly empty) followed by a perpetual repetition of a sequence $(c_1, \ldots, c_L)$. The limit of the means payoff for player i for such a sequence is the average of i's payoff in $(c_1, \ldots, c_L)$, namely $\sum_{t=1}^L u^i(c_t)/L$. If you are especially interested in repeated games, we suggest Osborne and Rubinstein (1994, Chapter 8) for a detailed description of strategies that are executed by finite automata. A profile of such strategies induces such an outcome in a repeated game.

If the payoff of any player j in the repeated game is less than $v^j(G)$ (see (16.1)) then he can deviate to a strategy that guarantees him at least $v^i(G)$ in every period, so that in every Nash equilibrium of the repeated game his payoff is at least $v^j(G)$.

The next result shows that the unending repetition of any finite sequence of outcomes that yields every player i an average payoff greater than $v^i(G)$ is the outcome of some subgame perfect equilibrium of the repeated game. In particular, the infinite repetition of the Prisoner's dilemma

$$\begin{array}{c|c|c|}
 & C & D \\
\hline
C & 3,3 & 0,4 \\
\hline
D & 4,0 & 1,1 \\
\hline
\end{array}$$

has subgame perfect equilibria in which the payoff profiles are, for example, $(3,3)$ ((C,C) in every period), $(2,2)$ (alternating between (C,D) and (D,C)), and $(\frac{11}{4},\frac{7}{4})$ (cycling through $(C,C),(C,C),(D,C),(D,D)$).

Proposition 16.10: SPE of infinitely repeated game with limit of means payoffs

Let G be a strategic game and let $c_1,\dots,c_L$ be outcomes of G with $w^i = \sum_{t=1}^{L} u^i(c_t)/L > v^i(G)$ for all $i \in N$, where $v^i(G)$ is given in (16.1). Then the infinitely repeated game of G has a subgame perfect equilibrium for which the outcome is an unending repetition of $(c_1,\dots,c_L)$.

Proof

Recall that $v^i(G) = \min_{a^{-i}} \max_{a^i} u^i(a^i, a^{-i})$ and $p(i)$ is a combination of actions for the players other than i that guarantees that i's payoff in G is no more than $v^i(G)$.

To construct a subgame perfect equilibrium of the infinitely repeated game, think of the players as being in one of $n+1$ phases. In the phase *Regular*, the players choose their actions so that the outcome consists of repetitions of the sequence $(c_1,\dots,c_L)$. At the end of every L periods in this phase, the players conduct a review. If no player or more than one player has deviated, they stay in the phase and start the sequence again. If exactly one player i has deviated, the players move to a phase P^i in which all of them other than i punish player i by choosing $p(i)$ for T^i periods, where T^i is large enough that player i's average payoff over the $L + T^i$ periods is less than w^i. This is possible because $w^i > v^i(G)$ and whatever player i does when he is punished he cannot obtain a payoff higher than $v^i(G)$. At the end of the T^i periods all players move back to the *Regular* phase.

To see that this profile of strategies is a subgame perfect equilibrium, consider any history h. For this profile of strategies, the average payoff of each player' i following h is exactly w^i (the players return to the *Regular* phase if they leave it). Whatever alternative strategy a player i uses, his stream of payoffs is a sequence consisting of blocks each with an average payoff of at most w^i. Thus, the limit of his average payoffs does not exceed w^i.

Problems

1. *Trust game.* Player 1 starts with $10. He has to decide how much to keep and how much to transfer to player 2. Player 2 triples the amount of money he gets from player 1 and then decides how much, from that total amount, to transfer to player 1. Assume that each player is interested only in the amount of money he has at the end of the process.

   Model the situation as an extensive game and find its subgame perfect equilibria.

   Does the game have a Nash equilibrium outcome that is not a subgame perfect equilibrium outcome?

   What are the subgame perfect equilibria of the game in which the process is repeated three times?

2. *Multiple subgame perfect equilibria.* Construct an extensive game with two players that has two subgame perfect equilibria, one better for both players than the other.

3. *Nash equilibrium and subgame perfect equilibrium.* Construct an extensive game with two players that has a unique subgame perfect equilibrium and a Nash equilibrium that both players prefer to the subgame perfect equilibrium.

4. *Comparative statics.* Construct two extensive games that differ only in the payoff of one player, say player 1, regarding one outcome, such that each game has a unique subgame perfect equilibrium and the subgame perfect equilibrium payoff of player 1 is lower in the game in which his payoff is higher.

5. *Auction.* Two potential buyers compete for an indivisible item worth $12. Buyer 1 has $9 and buyer 2 has $6. The seller will not accept any offer less than $3.

   The buyers take turns bidding, starting with buyer 1. All bids are whole dollars and cannot exceed $12. A player can bid more than the amount of cash he holds, but if he wins he is punished severely, an outcome worse for him than any other. When one of the bidders does not raise the bid, the auction is over and the other player gets the item for the amount of his last bid.

   a. Show that in all subgame perfect equilibria of the extensive game that models this situation player 1 gets the item.

    b. Show that the game has a subgame perfect equilibrium in which the item is sold for $3.

    c. Show that the game has a subgame perfect equilibrium in which the item is sold for $8.

6. *Solomon's mechanism.* An object belongs to one of two people, each of whom claims ownership. The value of the object is H to the owner and L to the other individual, where $H > L > 0$. King Solomon orders the two people to play the following game. Randomly, the people are assigned to be player 1 and player 2. Player 1 starts and has to declare either *mine* or *his*. If he says *his*, the game is over and player 2 gets the object. If he says *mine*, player 2 has to say either *his*, in which case the object is given to player 1, or *mine*, in which case player 2 gets the object and pays M to King Solomon, with $H > M > L$, and player 1 pays a small amount $\varepsilon > 0$ to King Solomon.

Explain why the outcome of this procedure is that the owner gets the object without paying anything.

7. *Communication.* Consider a group of n people, with $n \geq 3$, living in separate locations, who need to share information that is received initially only by player 1. Assume that the information is beneficial only if all the players receive it. (The group may be a number of related families, the information may be instructions on how to get to a family gathering, and the gathering may be a success only if everyone attends.) When a player receives the information, he is informed of the path the information took. He then decides whether to pass the information to one of the players who has not yet received it. If every player receives the information, then every player who passed it on receives a payoff of $1 - c$, where $c \in (0, 1)$, and the single player who got it last receives a payoff of 1. Otherwise, every player receives a payoff of $-c$ if he passed on the information and 0 otherwise.

    a. Draw the game tree for the case of $n = 3$.

    b. Characterize the subgame perfect equilibria of the game for each value of n.

8. *Race.* Two players, 1 and 2, start at distances A and B steps from a target. The player who reaches the target first gets a prize of P (and the other player gets no prize). The players alternate turns, starting with player 1. On his turn, a player can stay where he is, at a cost of 0, advance one step, at a cost of 2, or advance two steps, at a cost of 4.5. If for two successive turns both players stay where they are then the game ends (and neither player receives a prize).

Each player aims to maximize his net gain (prize, if any, minus cost). For any values of A, B, and P with $6 \le P \le 8$, find the unique subgame perfect equilibrium of the extensive game that models this situation.

9. *One-deviation property.* Show that a strategy pair that satisfies the one-deviation property is not necessarily a subgame perfect equilibrium of a game that does not have a finite horizon by contemplating the one-player game illustrated below. In each period 1, 2, ... the player can *stop* or *continue*. If in any period he chooses *stop* then the game ends and his payoff is 0, whereas if he chooses *continue* he has another opportunity to *stop*. If he never chooses *stop* then his payoff is 1.

10. *Implementation.* You are a mediator in a case in which two neighbors cannot agree how to split the $100 cost of hiring a gardener for their common property. Denote by v^i the value of hiring the gardener for neighbor i. Each neighbor knows both v^1 and v^2.

Your aim is to ensure that the gardener is hired if the sum of the neighbors' values is greater than $100 and is not hired if the sum is less than $100.

You suggest that the neighbors participate in the following procedure. First neighbor 1 names an amount. Neighbor 2 observes this amount and names an amount himself. (Each amount can be any nonnegative number.) If the sum of the amounts is less than $100, the gardener is not hired. If the sum exceeds $100, the gardener is hired and each neighbor pays the gardener the amount he named.

a. Show that for any values of v^1 and v^2, the outcome of the subgame perfect equilibrium of the game that models this procedure is that the gardener is hired if $v^1 + v^2 > 100$ and is not hired if $v^1 + v^2 < 100$.

b. Suppose that the neighbors are asked to report amounts simultaneously and the gardener is hired if and only if the sum of the reports is at least 100. Show that if $100 < v^1 + v^2 < 200$ and $v^i \le 100$ for $i = 1, 2$ then the strategic game that models the procedure has a Nash equilibrium in which the gardener is not hired.

Bargaining

11. *Alternating offers with fixed bargaining costs.* Analyze the variant of the
    infinite-horizon bargaining game with alternating offers and discounting in
    which each player i values an amount x received in period t by $x - c^i t$ (rather
    than $(\delta^i)^t x$). (That is, he bears a fixed cost of c^i for each period that passes
    before agreement is reached.) Assume that $0 < c^1 < c^2$. Show that the game
    has a unique subgame perfect equilibrium and in this equilibrium player 1
    gets the entire pie.

12. *Alternating offers with equal fixed costs.* Consider the variant of the game in
    Problem 11 in which $c^1 = c^2 = c$.

    a. Show that each partition in which player 1 gets at least c is an outcome
       of a subgame perfect equilibrium.

    b. Show that if $c \leq \frac{1}{3}$ then the game has a subgame perfect equilibrium in
       which agreement is not reached in period 1.

13. *Alternating offers with a discrete set of agreements.*

    Two indivisible items, each valued at \$1, are to be split between two bar-
    gainers if they agree how to share them. Assume that they use the infinite-
    horizon alternating offers procedure to reach agreement and that they have
    the same discount factor δ, with $\frac{1}{2} < \delta < 1$.

    a. Show that for any positive integer K, the game has a subgame perfect
       equilibrium in which the players reach agreement only in period K.

    b. Is it possible that in a subgame perfect equilibrium the players never
       reach agreement?

    c. What are the subgame perfect equilibria if $0 < \delta < \frac{1}{2}$?

Repeated games

14. *Infinitely repeated game with the overtaking criterion.* Recall that the limit
    of the means criterion is not sensitive to the payoffs in a finite number of
    periods. The overtaking criterion is more sensitive. We say that an individ-
    ual prefers the sequence of payoffs (x_t) to the sequence (y_t) if there exists
    $\varepsilon > 0$ such that eventually (for all T larger than some T^*) we have $\sum_{t=1}^{T} x_t - \sum_{t=1}^{T} y_t > \varepsilon$.

    a. Compare the following sequences by the limit of the means and over-
       taking criteria: $a = (4,1,3,1,3,\dots)$, $b = (3,1,3,1,\dots)$, $c = (2,2,\dots)$, and
       $d = (10,-10,10,-10,\dots)$.

b. Consider the following game G.

	C	D
C	6,6	1,0
D	7,4	2,0

Why is the strategy pair described in the proof of Proposition 16.10 with the outcome (C, C) in every period not a subgame perfect equilibrium of the infinitely repeated game with the overtaking criterion?

c. Suggest a subgame perfect equilibrium of the repeated game of G with the overtaking criterion for which the outcome is (C, C) in every period.

15. *Infinitely repeated game of exchange of favors.* Consider the following variant G of Bach or Stravinsky in which player 1 prefers to coordinate on B, player 2 prefers to coordinate on S, and if they do not coordinate then each player prefers to choose her favorite action.

	B	S
B	7,2	4,4
S	0,0	2,7

Consider the infinitely repeated game of G (with limit of the means payoffs).

a. Construct a subgame perfect equilibrium of the repeated game in which the outcome alternates between (B, B) and (S, S).

b. The players consider a partition of the week into days on which the players choose the action pair (B, B) and days on which they choose the action pair (S, S). Which combinations of the seven days can be an outcome of a subgame perfect equilibrium of the repeated game?

Notes

The notion of an extensive game originated with von Neumann and Morgenstern (1944); Kuhn (1950, 1953) suggested the model we describe. The notion of subgame perfect equilibrium is due to Selten (1965). Proposition 16.3 is due to Kuhn (1953).

The centipede game (Example 16.2) is due to Rosenthal (1981). Proposition 16.8 is due to Rubinstein (1982).

The idea that cooperative outcomes may be sustained in equilibria of repeated games is due to Nash (see Flood 1958/59, note 11 on page 16) and was elaborated by Luce and Raiffa (1957) (pages 97–105 and Appendix 8) and Shubik (1959) (Chapter 10, especially page 226). The result on finitely repeated games discussed at the end of Section 16.5.1 is due to Benoît and Krishna (1987). Proposition 16.10 was established by Robert J. Aumann and Lloyd S. Shapley and by Ariel Rubinstein in the mid 1970's; see Aumann and Shapley (1994) and Rubinstein (1977).

The game in Problem 6 is taken from Glazer and Ma (1989). The game in Problem 8 is a simplification due to Vijay Krishna of the model in Harris and Vickers (1985). Repeated games with the overtaking criterion (Problem 14) are studied by Rubinstein (1979).

IV Topics

17 Mechanism design

The models in Parts II and III analyze the behavior of individuals given a specific structure for their interaction. In this chapter, we turn this methodology on its head. That is, we seek a set of rules for the interaction between the individuals that generates specific outcomes. Analyses of this type are called "mechanism design". This field is huge; we demonstrate some of the basic ideas through a simple model.

17.1 Deciding on a public project

A community of individuals has to decide whether to carry out a joint project. For example, the inhabitants of a city consider building a new subway, or the tenants in a neighborhood consider adding a bench to their community garden. The action to be taken is public in the sense that all individuals are affected by it. The community can either undertake the project or not.

> **Definition 17.1: Public project problem**
>
> A *public project problem* $\langle N, D \rangle$ consists of a set $N = \{1, \ldots, n\}$ of individuals and a set $D = \{0, 1\}$ of public decisions (1 means a project is executed and 0 means it is not).

The individuals may differ in their attitudes to the project: some may support it and some may oppose it. We look for mechanisms that balance these interests. The mechanism is allowed to require the agents to make and receive payments, which are used to induce a desirable outcome. The presence of payments means that the individuals' preferences have to be defined not on the set D but on pairs of the type (d, t) where d is the public decision and t is the transfer (positive, zero, or negative) to the individual.

Each individual i is characterized by a number v^i, which may be positive or negative, with the interpretation that he is indifferent between (*i*) the project's not being carried out and his not making or receiving any payment and (*ii*) the project's being carried out and his paying v^i (when $v^i > 0$) or receiving $-v^i$ (when $v^i < 0$). Thus if $v^i > 0$ then i benefits from the project and is willing to pay up to v^i to have it realized; if $v^i < 0$ then i is hurt by the project and is willing to

Chapter of *Models in Microeconomic Theory* by Martin J. Osborne and Ariel Rubinstein. Version 2023.5.30 (h).
© 2023 Martin J. Osborne and Ariel Rubinstein CC BY-NC-ND 4.0. https://doi.org/10.11647/OBP.0362.17

pay up to $-v^i$ to stop its being realized. If $v^i = 0$ then i is indifferent between the project's being executed and not. Note that the interests of an individual depend only on his own valuation of the project.

Definition 17.2: Valuation profile

A *valuation profile* $(v^i)_{i \in N}$ for a public project problem $\langle N, D \rangle$ consists of a number v^i for each individual $i \in N$. The number v^i determines i's preferences over pairs (d, t^i) consisting of a public decision $d \in D$ and a number t^i, the amount of money transferred to (if $t^i > 0$) or from (if $t^i < 0$) individual i. Specifically, the preferences of each individual $i \in N$ over pairs (d, t^i) with $d \in D$ and $t^i \in \mathbb{R}$ are represented by the utility function

$$\begin{cases} v^i + t^i & \text{if } d = 1 \\ t^i & \text{if } d = 0. \end{cases}$$

17.2   Strategy-proof mechanisms

We assume that the valuation v^i of each individual i is known only to him. So if the community wants to base its decision on these valuations, it needs to query the individuals. A direct mechanism with transfers asks each individual to report a number and interprets this number as his valuation. The mechanism then specifies the public decision and the monetary transfers to or from the individuals, as a function of their reports.

Definition 17.3: Direct mechanism with transfers

For a public project problem $\langle N, D \rangle$, a *direct mechanism with transfers* is a collection $(\delta, \tau^1, \ldots, \tau^n)$ of functions that assign to each profile $(x^1, \ldots, x^n)$ of numbers (the individuals' reports) a public decision $\delta(x^1, \ldots, x^n) \in D$ and a monetary transfer $\tau^i(x^1, \ldots, x^n)$ for each $i \in N$.

Each individual can report any number he wishes, so we need to consider the possibility that individuals may benefit from reporting numbers different from their valuations. Intuitively, an individual may benefit from exaggerating his valuation of the project positively if he supports it and negatively if he opposes it. We say that a mechanism is strategy-proof if every individual, whatever his valuation, optimally reports this valuation, regardless of the other individuals' reports. That is, given any reports of the other individuals, no individual can do better than reporting his valuation.

Definition 17.4: Strategy-proof mechanism

For a public project problem $\langle N, D \rangle$, a direct mechanism with transfers $(\delta, \tau^1, \ldots, \tau^n)$ is *strategy-proof* if for every valuation profile $(v^i)_{i \in N}$, every individual $i \in N$, every list $(x^1, \ldots, x^{i-1}, x^{i+1}, \ldots, x^n)$ of numbers (reports of the other individuals), and every number z^i (report of i) we have

$$\delta(x^1, \ldots, v^i, \ldots, x^n)v^i + \tau^i(x^1, \ldots, v^i, \ldots, x^n)$$
$$\geq \delta(x^1, \ldots, z^i, \ldots, x^n)v^i + \tau^i(x^1, \ldots, z^i, \ldots, x^n).$$

That is, i optimally reports his valuation, whatever it is, regardless of the other individuals' reports.

Notice that the definition does not require that an individual's true valuation is the only optimal report for him regardless of the other individuals' reports.

An example of a strategy-proof mechanism is majority rule.

Example 17.1: Majority rule

Majority rule is the direct mechanism in which the project is executed if and only if a majority of individuals report a positive number, and no monetary transfers are made. That is,

$$\delta(x^1, \ldots, x^n) = 1 \text{ if and only if } |\{i \in N : x^i > 0\}| > n/2$$

and $\tau^i(x^1, \ldots, x^n) = 0$ for all $i \in N$ and for all profiles $(x^1, \ldots, x^n)$.

This mechanism is strategy-proof. Take an individual with a positive valuation. His changing his report from one positive number to another has no effect on the outcome. His switching from a positive report to a nonpositive one might affect the outcome, but if it does so then it changes the outcome from one in which the project is carried out to one in which the project is not carried out. Such a change makes the individual worse off (given that his valuation is positive). Thus for any reports of the other individuals, an individual with a positive valuation can do no better than report that valuation. A similar argument applies to an individual with a negative valuation.

Although the majority rule mechanism is strategy-proof, the condition it uses to determine whether the project is carried out has the disadvantage that it ignores the magnitudes of the individuals' valuations. If, for example, a few individuals would benefit hugely from the project and the remaining majority of individuals would be made slightly worse off, then majority rule leads to the project's not being carried out.

An alternative mechanism, which takes into account the magnitudes of the individuals' valuations, carries out the project if the sum of the reported valuations is positive and, like majority rule, makes no monetary transfers. This mechanism, however, is not strategy-proof.

Example 17.2: Summing reports

Consider the direct mechanism in which the project is executed if and only if the sum of the individuals' reports is positive, and no monetary transfers are made. That is,

$$\delta(x^1,\ldots,x^n)=1 \text{ if and only if } \sum_{j\in N} x^j > 0$$

and $\tau^i(x^1,\ldots,x^n)=0$ for all $i \in N$ and for all profiles $(x^1,\ldots,x^n)$.

This mechanism is not strategy-proof. Consider an individual whose valuation is positive. If, when he reports his valuation, the sum of all reports is negative, so that the project is not carried out, then he is better off reporting a number high enough that the project is carried out.

We now describe a variant of the mechanism in this example that adds monetary transfers in such a way that the resulting mechanism is strategy-proof.

17.3 Vickrey-Clarke-Groves mechanism

The Vickrey-Clarke-Groves (VCG) mechanism is a direct mechanism with transfers that executes the project if and only if the sum of the individuals' valuations is positive. The transfers in the mechanism are designed to make it strategy-proof: no individual benefits by reporting a number different from his true valuation. All transfers are nonpositive: under some circumstances an individual pays a penalty.

Suppose that, given the other individuals' reports, individual i's report is pivotal in the sense that given all the reports the project is executed, but in the absence of i's report it would not be. That is, the sum of all the reports is positive, but the sum of the reports of the individuals other than i is nonpositive. Then the monetary transfer for individual i in the VCG mechanism is equal to the sum of the other individuals' reports: i pays a penalty for causing the project to be executed when the other individuals' reports point to non-execution.

Now suppose that i's report is pivotal in the other direction: given all the reports the project is not executed, but in the absence of i's report it would be. (In particular, i's report is negative.) Then the monetary transfer for individual i is the negative of the sum of the other individuals' reports. That is, i pays a penalty for causing the project not to be executed when the other individuals' reports point to execution.

Individual i pays a penalty only if his report makes a difference to the outcome. The penalty does not change when his report changes as long as the change does not affect the sign of the sum of the reports. If i's report is not pivotal in either sense, he pays no penalty.

Definition 17.5: VCG mechanism

For a public project problem $\langle N, D \rangle$, the *VCG mechanism* is the direct mechanism with transfers $(\delta, \tau^1, \ldots, \tau^n)$ defined by

$$\delta(x^1, \ldots, x^n) = 1 \text{ if and only if } \sum_{j \in N} x^j > 0$$

and

$$\tau^i(x^1, \ldots, x^n) = \begin{cases} \sum_{j \in N \setminus \{i\}} x^j & \text{if } \sum_{j \in N \setminus \{i\}} x^j \leq 0 \text{ and } \sum_{j \in N} x^j > 0 \\ -\sum_{j \in N \setminus \{i\}} x^j & \text{if } \sum_{j \in N \setminus \{i\}} x^j > 0 \text{ and } \sum_{j \in N} x^j \leq 0 \\ 0 & \text{otherwise.} \end{cases}$$

Notice that for some profiles of reports, the operator of the mechanism receives a positive amount of money from the individuals. It can be shown that for no strategy-proof direct mechanism do the transfers sum to zero for all possible profiles of reports (see Problem 1).

Here is a numerical example that illustrates the VCG mechanism.

Example 17.3: VCG mechanism

Consider the public project problem with $n = 5$. The following table shows the decision and transfers specified by the VCG mechanism for four profiles of reports.

x^1	x^2	x^3	x^4	x^5	δ	τ^1	τ^2	τ^3	τ^4	τ^5
5	−1	−1	−1	−1	1	−4	0	0	0	0
−5	1	1	1	1	0	−4	0	0	0	0
−7	1	1	3	4	1	0	0	0	−1	−2
−5	2	2	2	2	1	0	0	0	0	0

Proposition 17.1: VCG mechanism is strategy-proof

For any public project problem the VCG mechanism is strategy-proof.

Proof

Let $\langle N, D \rangle$ be a public project problem and let $(\delta, \tau^1, \ldots, \tau^n)$ be the VCG mechanism for this problem. Let $(v^i)_{i \in N}$ be a valuation profile.

Consider an individual $i \in N$ with $v^i > 0$, let $(x^1, \ldots, x^{i-1}, x^{i+1}, \ldots, x^n)$ be the reports of the other individuals, and let S be the sum of these other reports.

If $S > 0$ then if i reports v^i, the project is executed ($\delta(x^1, \ldots, x^n) = 1$) and his transfer is 0 ($\tau^i(x^1, \ldots, x^n) = 0$). Thus his utility is v^i. No outcome is better for him.

If $-v^i < S \leq 0$ then if i reports v^i or any other number greater than $-S$ the project is executed and his transfer is S, so that his utility is $S + v^i > 0$. If instead he reports a number at most $-S$ the project is not executed and his transfer is 0, so that his utility is only 0.

If $S \leq -v^i \leq 0$ then if i reports v^i or any other number at most $-S$ the project is not executed and his transfer is 0, so that his utility is 0. If instead he reports a number greater than $-S$ the project is executed and his transfer is S, so that his utility is $v^i + S \leq 0$.

Similar arguments apply if $v^i \leq 0$.

We conclude that for any reports of the other individuals and any valuation v^i, i's reporting v^i is not worse than his reporting any other number.

Discussion The VCG mechanism specifies that the project is carried out if and only if the sum of the individuals' valuations is positive. It is fairly simple, and relies only on the fact that no individual, regardless of his beliefs about the other individuals' reports, has any reason not to truthfully report his valuation. However, the following points diminish its appeal.

1. The outcome of the mechanism may require some individuals to make payments even if the project is not executed. For example, if the valuation profile is $(-5, 1, 1, 1, 1)$, then the project is not carried out and individual 1 makes a payment of 4. People may regard the requirement to pay money if the project is not carried out as unacceptable.

2. The mechanism is not very transparent; it takes time or experience to be persuaded that reporting one's valuation is indeed optimal independent of the other individuals' reports.

3. The payments are not distributed back to the individuals. If we change the mechanism so that the total payments collected are returned to the individuals then an individual's reporting his valuation is no longer necessarily

optimal for him regardless of the other individuals' reports. Consider, for example, a problem with two individuals, and assume that the total amount paid is distributed equally between the individuals. Suppose that $v^1 = 1$ and individual 2 reports 10. If individual 1 reports 1 the project is carried out and individual 1's utility is 1 (no payment is made). If individual 1 reports -8, however, the project is also carried out and individual 2 makes a payment of 8, half of which goes to individual 1, so that his utility is $1 + 4 = 5$. Thus individual 1 is better off reporting -8 than reporting his valuation of 1.

4. Using the sign of the sum of the valuations as the criterion for carrying out the project is not necessarily desirable, especially in a society in which the individuals differ widely in their wealths. Suppose that two individuals benefit slightly from the project, but due to their high wealth have valuations of 100 each. The other 99 individuals are hurt significantly by the project but are impoverished and have valuations of only -1. In this case the criterion requires that the project is carried out, even though it may seem unjust. The VCG mechanism not only requires that it is carried out but also that the wealthy make no payments. Their *willingness* to pay is enough to require the project to be carried out.

Problems

1. *Balanced budget.* A direct mechanism with transfers is *balanced* if, for all profiles of reports, the sum of the transfers is 0. A result that we do not prove states that there exists no strategy-proof balanced direct mechanism with transfers that carries out the project if and only if the sum of the valuations is positive. To illustrate this result, consider a public project problem with two individuals and assume that each individual's valuation is 4, -1, or -5.

   a. Find the outcome specified by the VCG mechanism for each report profile under the assumption that each individual is restricted to report only one of the three possible valuations, and verify that the mechanism is strategy-proof.

   b. Show that there exists no strategy-proof *balanced* direct mechanism with transfers for which the project is carried out only if the sum of the valuations is positive and the transfers are symmetric in the sense that the transfer for individual 1 when he reports x and individual 2 reports y is the same as the transfer for individual 2 when he reports x and individual 1 reports y.

2. *Vickrey auction.* One unit of a good is to be transferred to one of the individuals $1, \ldots, n$. Each individual i's valuation of the good is a nonnegative number v^i. Consider the following direct mechanism with transfers. Each individual reports a nonnegative number; the good is transferred to the individual, the *winner*, who reports the highest number. (In case of a tie, the good is transferred to the individual with the smallest index i among the individuals reporting the highest number.) The winner makes a payment equal to the highest of the other individuals' reports. (Thus if the reports are distinct, the winner's payment is the second highest report.) The winner's utility is his valuation minus his payment, and the utility of every other individual is 0. We can interpret this mechanism as a second-price auction, in which individuals submit bids and the good is transferred to the individual with the highest bid, who pays only the second highest bid (see Example 15.7).

   a. Show that the mechanism is strategy-proof.

   b. Explain why the direct mechanism with transfers that differs from the above only in that the winner makes a payment equal to his report is not strategy-proof.

3. *A project with a cost.* A group of n individuals has to decide whether to execute a project that costs C. If the project is executed, each individual pays $c = C/n$ to cover the costs. Individual i's utility from (α, t^i) is $\alpha(v^i - c) + t^i$ where α is 1 if the project is carried out and 0 if it is not, and t^i is a transfer.

   Design a VCG-like mechanism for this situation that is strategy-proof.

Notes

The idea behind the VCG mechanism is due to Clarke (1971) and Groves (1973), and has its origins in Vickrey (1961). Proposition 17.1 is established in Groves and Loeb (1975). The auction in Problem 2 was first studied by Vickrey (1961).

18 Matching

Consider the following problem. Some individuals in a society are X's and others are Y's. Every individual of each type has to be matched with one and only one individual of the other type. For example, managers have to be matched with assistants, or pilots have to be matched with copilots. Each X has preferences over the Y's and each Y has preferences over the X's. Every individual prefers to be matched than to remain unmatched. We look for matching methods that result in sensible outcomes given any preferences.

18.1 The matching problem

We denote the set of X's by X and the set of Y's by Y and assume that they have the same number of members. Each $x \in X$ has a preference relation over the set Y and each $y \in Y$ has a preference relation over the set X. We assume that all preferences are strict (no individual is indifferent between any two options).

Definition 18.1: Society and preference profile

A *society* (X, Y) consists of finite sets X and Y (of individuals) with the same number of members. A *preference profile* $(\succ^i)_{i \in X \cup Y}$ for the society (X, Y) consists of a strict preference relation $\succ^i$ over Y for each $i \in X$ and a strict preference relation $\succ^i$ over X for each $i \in Y$.

A matching describes the pairs that are formed. Its definition captures the assumption that each individual has to be matched with exactly one individual of the other type.

Definition 18.2: Matching

A *matching* for a society (X, Y) is a one-to-one function from X to Y. For a matching μ and $x \in X$ we refer to $(x, \mu(x))$ as a *match*.

We discuss matching methods, which map preference profiles into matchings. That is, a matching method specifies, for each preference profile, who is matched with whom.

Chapter of *Models in Microeconomic Theory* by Martin J. Osborne and Ariel Rubinstein. Version 2023.5.30 (h).
© 2023 Martin J. Osborne and Ariel Rubinstein CC BY-NC-ND 4.0.   https://doi.org/10.11647/OBP.0362.18

Definition 18.3: Matching method

A *matching method* for a society is a function that assigns a matching to each preference profile for the society.

The following example treats one side (the Y's), like the houses in the models of Chapter 8, and takes into account only the preferences of the X's.

Example 18.1: Serial dictatorship

The X's, in a pre-determined order, choose Y's, as in the serial dictatorship procedure. Each X chooses from the Y's who were not chosen by previous X's. This procedure always results in a matching, and thus defines a matching method.

Here are two more examples of matching methods.

Example 18.2: Minimizing aggregate rank

For any pair (x, y) consisting of an X and a Y, let $n_x(y)$ be y's rank in x's preferences and let $n_y(x)$ be x's rank in y's preferences. Attach to each pair (x, y) a number $I(x, y) = \alpha(n_x(y), n_y(x))$, where α is a function increasing in both its arguments (for example $\alpha(n_1, n_2) = n_1 + n_2$). The number $\alpha(n_x(y), n_y(x))$ is a measure of the dissatisfaction of individuals x and y with their match. The matching method chooses the matching that minimizes the sum of $I(x, y)$ over all pairs (x, y) (or one such matching if more than one exists).

Example 18.3: Iterative selection of the best match

Start by choosing a pair for which the value of $I(x, y)$ defined in Example 18.2 is minimal over all pairs (x, y). Remove the members of the chosen pair from X and Y and choose a pair for which the value of $I(x, y)$ is minimal over the smaller sets. Continue iteratively in the same way.

18.2   Gale-Shapley algorithm

We now consider a matching method that has an interesting description and some attractive properties. The algorithm that defines it has two versions, one in which the X's initiate matches, and one in which the Y's do so. We describe the former.

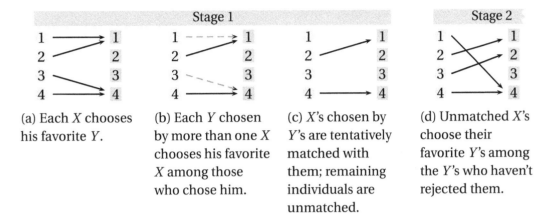

(a) Each X chooses his favorite Y.

(b) Each Y chosen by more than one X chooses his favorite X among those who chose him.

(c) X's chosen by Y's are tentatively matched with them; remaining individuals are unmatched.

(d) Unmatched X's choose their favorite Y's among the Y's who haven't rejected them.

Figure 18.1 An example of the first stages of the Gale-Shapley matching method. The X's are indicated by a green background and the Y's by an orange background.

The algorithm proceeds in a series of stages. At the end of each stage, some pairs are tentatively matched; at the end of the procedure, the existing tentative matches become final.

Stage 1

Each X chooses his favorite Y. If every Y is chosen by exactly one X then the algorithm ends with that matching. If some Y is chosen by more than one X, then every such Y chooses his favorite X from among those who chose him and is tentatively matched with this X. He rejects the other X's who chose him. All X's who were not chosen by a Y are left unmatched. (See Figure 18.1 for an illustration of the start of the algorithm in the case that 1 is the favorite of 1 and 2 and 4 is the second best of 1; 4 is the favorite of 3 and 4 and 2 is the second best of 3; and 1 prefers 2 to 1 and 4 prefers 4 to 3.)

Stage $t+1$ for $t \geq 1$

At the start of stage $t + 1$, tentative matches exist from stage t, and some individuals are unmatched. Each unmatched X chooses his favorite Y among those who have not rejected him in the past. Some of the Y's thus chosen may already be tentatively matched with X's. (In the example in Figure 18.1, that is the case in Stage 2 for 4.) Each Y chooses his favorite X from the set consisting of the X with whom he was tentatively matched at the end of stage t and the unmatched X's who chose him, resulting in new tentative matches.

Stopping rule

The process ends when every X is tentatively matched with a Y, in which case the tentative matches become final.

The following definition specifies the algorithm formally, but if you find the previous description clear you may not need to refer to it.

Procedure: Gale-Shapley algorithm

Given a society (X, Y), the *Gale-Shapley algorithm for (X, Y) in which X's initiate matches,* denoted GS^X, has as input a preference profile $(\succsim^i)_{i \in X \cup Y}$ for (X, Y) and generates a sequence $(g_t, R_t)_{t=0,1,\ldots}$ where

- $g_t : X \to Y \cup \{unmatched\}$ is a function such that no two X's are mapped to the same Y

- R_t is a function from X to subsets of Y.

A pair (g_t, R_t) is the state of the algorithm at the end of stage t. If $g_t(x) \in Y$ then $g_t(x)$ is the Y with whom x is tentatively matched and $R_t(x)$ is the set of all Y's who rejected x through stage t.

Definition of (g_0, R_0)

Every X is *unmatched* and every set $R_0(x)$ is empty:

$$g_0(x) = unmatched \quad \text{for all } x \in X$$
$$R_0(x) = \varnothing \quad \text{for all } x \in X.$$

Definition of (g_{t+1}, R_{t+1}) **given** (g_t, R_t)

For each $y \in Y$ let

$$A_{t+1}(y) = \{x \in X : y \text{ is best in } Y \setminus R_t(x) \text{ according to } \succsim^x\}.$$

That is, $A_{t+1}(y)$ is the set of the X's who choose y in stage $t+1$. (Note that if $g_t(x) = y$ then $x \in A_{t+1}(y)$.)

Now

$$g_{t+1}(x) = \begin{cases} y & \text{if } x \text{ is best in } A_{t+1}(y) \text{ according to } \succsim^y \\ unmatched & \text{otherwise} \end{cases}$$

and

$$R_{t+1}(x) = \begin{cases} R_t(x) & \text{if } g_{t+1}(x) \in Y \\ R_t(x) \cup \{y \in Y : x \in A_{t+1}(y)\} & \text{if } g_{t+1}(x) = unmatched. \end{cases}$$

Thus $R_{t+1}(x)$ is equal to $R_t(x)$ unless x is rejected at stage t by some $y \in Y$, in which case that y (and only him) is added to $R_t(x)$.

Stopping rule

The process ends at stage T if $g_T(x) \in Y$ for all $x \in X$.

The description of the algorithm talks of individuals choosing matches. But that language should not be taken literally. We use it simply to describe the algorithm attractively (as we did for serial dictatorship). The Gale-Shapley algorithm simply defines a function that attaches a matching to every preference profile. Soon we prove that the algorithm indeed always ends with a matching, but first we give an example.

Example 18.4

Consider the society with four X's and four Y's and the following preference profiles, where X's are shown in green and Y's in orange.

1:	$1 \succ 4 \succ 2 \succ 3$	1:	$3 \succ 1 \succ 2 \succ 4$
2:	$2 \succ 3 \succ 1 \succ 4$	2:	$3 \succ 2 \succ 4 \succ 1$
3:	$4 \succ 2 \succ 3 \succ 1$	3:	$4 \succ 3 \succ 2 \succ 1$
4:	$4 \succ 3 \succ 1 \succ 2$	4:	$1 \succ 4 \succ 3 \succ 2$

X's initiate matches   We first apply GS^X (where X's initiate matches) to this preference profile.

Stage 1: 1 chooses 1, 2 chooses 2, and both 3 and 4 choose 4. 4 prefers 4 to 3 and thus rejects 3 and keeps 4. That is, $g_1(1) = 1$, $g_1(2) = 2$, $g_1(3) = $ *unmatched*, and $g_1(4) = 4$, and $R_1(1) = \varnothing$, $R_1(2) = \varnothing$, $R_1(3) = \{4\}$, and $R_1(4) = \varnothing$.

Stage 2: 3 chooses 2, who is tentatively matched with 2. 2 prefers 3 to 2 and so rejects 2. That is, $g_2(1) = 1$, $g_2(2) = $ *unmatched*, $g_2(3) = 2$, and $g_2(4) = 4$, and $R_2(1) = \varnothing$, $R_2(2) = \{2\}$, $R_2(3) = \{4\}$, and $R_2(4) = \varnothing$.

Stage 3: 2 chooses 3. Every Y is now matched with a unique X, and the process ends. We have $g_3(1) = 1$, $g_3(2) = 3$, $g_3(3) = 2$ and $g_4(4) = 4$.

Y's initiate matches   Now we apply GS^Y to the profile.

Stage 1: 1 and 2 choose 3, 3 chooses 4, and 4 chooses 1. 3 prefers 2 to 1 and so rejects 1.

```
1          1
2          2
3          3
4          4
```

Stage 2: 1 chooses 1, who prefers 1 to 4 and so rejects 4.

```
1          1
2          2
3          3
4          4
```

Stage 3: 4 chooses 4, who prefers 4 to 3 and so rejects 3.

```
1          1
2          2
3          3
4          4
```

Stage 4: 3 chooses 3, who prefers 2 to 3 and so rejects 3.

```
1          1
2          2
3          3
4          4
```

Stage 5: 3 chooses 2. Every X is now matched with a unique Y, and the process ends.

```
1          1
2          2
3          3
4          4
```

Note that the matchings in these two examples are the same. But don't jump to conclusions: for many preference profiles the matchings generated by GS^X and GS^Y differ.

We now show that for every profile of preferences the algorithm is well defined and eventually terminates in a matching.

Proposition 18.1: Gale-Shapley algorithm yields a matching

For any society and any preference profile for the society, the Gale-Shapley algorithm is well defined and generates a matching.

> **Proof**
>
> We consider the algorithm GS^X, in which X's initiate matches. The argument for GS^Y is analogous.
>
> We first show that the algorithm is always well defined. That is, we argue that for no preference profile does GS^X have a stage t at which some $x \in X$ has been rejected by all Y's (that is, $R_t(x) = Y$). Note that when a Y rejects an X, he remains tentatively matched with some other X. Thus if some $x \in X$ has been rejected after stage t by every Y, then every Y is tentatively matched with an X. But the number of members of X is the same as the number of members of Y, so it must be that x is tentatively matched (that is $g_t(x) \in Y$), and in particular has not been rejected by $g_t(x)$, a contradiction.
>
> We now show that the algorithm terminates. At each stage at which the algorithm continues, at least one X is rejected. Thus if the algorithm did not stop, we would reach a stage at which one of the X's would have been rejected by every Y, which we have shown is not possible.
>
> Finally, the algorithm terminates when no X is unmatched, so that the outcome is a matching.

18.3   Gale-Shapley algorithm and stability

We now consider properties of the matching generated by the Gale-Shapley algorithm. We classify a matching as unstable if there are two individuals who prefer to be matched with each other than with the individuals with whom they are matched. That is, matching μ is unstable if for some $x \in X$ and $y \in Y$ with $y \neq \mu(x)$, x prefers y to $\mu(x)$ (the Y with whom x is matched) and y prefers x to $\mu^{-1}(y)$ (the X with whom y is matched). In this case both x and y want to break the matches assigned by μ and match with each other. A matching is stable if no such pair exists.

> **Definition 18.4: Stable matching**
>
> For a society (X, Y) and preference profile $(\succeq^i)_{i \in X \cup Y}$, a matching μ is *stable* if there is no pair $(x, y) \in X \times Y$ such that $y \succ^x \mu(x)$ and $x \succ^y \mu^{-1}(y)$.

To illustrate the concept of stable matching we give an example showing that the serial dictatorship algorithm, in which the members of X sequentially choose members of Y from those who were not chosen previously, may generate an unstable match.

Example 18.5

Consider a society $(\{1,2,3\},\{1,2,3\})$ with the following preferences.

$$
\begin{array}{ll}
\text{1:} \quad 1 \succ 2 \succ 3 & \qquad \text{1:} \quad 2 \succ 3 \succ 1 \\
\text{2:} \quad 1 \succ 2 \succ 3 & \qquad \text{2:} \quad 3 \succ 2 \succ 1 \\
\text{3:} \quad 1 \succ 2 \succ 3 & \qquad \text{3:} \quad 1 \succ 3 \succ 2
\end{array}
$$

Apply the serial dictatorship algorithm in which the X's choose Y's in the order 1, 2, 3. The algorithm yields the matching in which each $i \in X$ is matched to $i \in Y$. This matching is unstable because $2 \in X$ and $1 \in Y$ both prefer each other to the individual with whom they are matched.

We now show that the Gale-Shapley algorithm generates a stable matching.

Proposition 18.2: Gale-Shapley algorithm yields a stable matching

For any society and any preference profile for the society, the Gale-Shapley algorithm generates a stable matching.

Proof

Consider a society (X, Y) and preference profile $(\succeq^i)_{i \in X \cup Y}$. Denote by μ the matching generated by the algorithm GS^X. Assume that for $x \in X$ and $y \in Y$, individual x prefers y to $\mu(x)$ $(y \succ^x \mu(x))$. Then at some stage before x chose $\mu(x)$, he must have chosen y and have been rejected by him in favor of another X. Subsequently, y rejects an X only in favor of a preferred X. Thus it follows that y prefers $\mu^{-1}(y)$, the X with whom he is eventually matched, to x. We conclude that no pair prefers each other to the individual with whom he is assigned by μ, so that μ is stable.

Many matchings may be stable. The GS^X algorithm finds one stable matching and GS^Y finds another, possibly the same and possibly not. Is it better to be on the side that initiates matches? Is any stable matching better for one of the X's than the matching generated by GS^X? The next result answers these questions: for each $x \in X$ the matching generated by GS^X is at least as good for x as any other stable matching, and in particular is at least as good as the matching generated by GS^Y.

Proposition 18.3: GS^X algorithm yields best stable matching for X's

For any society and any preference profile for the society, no stable matching is better for any X than the matching generated by the GS^X algorithm.

Proof

Let μ be the (stable) matching generated by GS^X for the society (X, Y) and preference profile $(\succcurlyeq^i)_{i \in X \cup Y}$. Suppose that ψ is another stable matching and $\psi(x) \succ^x \mu(x)$ for some $x \in X$. Let X^* be the set of all $x \in X$ for whom $\psi(x) \succ^x \mu(x)$. For each $x \in X^*$ denote by $t(x)$ the stage in the GS^X algorithm at which x chooses $\psi(x)$ and is rejected by him. Let $x_0 \in X^*$ for whom $t(x_0)$ is minimal among the $x \in X^*$. Let $y_0 = \psi(x_0)$ and let $x_1 \in X$ be the individual y_0 chose when he rejected x_0 in the GS^X algorithm. That is, at stage $t(x_0)$ individuals x_0 and x_1 choose y_0, who rejects x_0 in favor of x_1 ($x_1 \succ^{y_0} x_0$). Let $\psi(x_1) = y_1$.

$$
\begin{array}{c}
\qquad\qquad t(x_0) \\
x_0 \dashrightarrow y_0 = \psi(x_0) \\
x_1 \cdots\cdots\cdots\cdots\cdots\cdots\cdots\longrightarrow y_1 = \psi(x_1)
\end{array}
$$

If $y_0 \succ^{x_1} y_1$ then each member of the pair (x_1, y_0) prefers the other member to the individual assigned him by ψ, contradicting the stability of ψ. Therefore $y_1 \succ^{x_1} y_0$. But then in the GS^X algorithm x_1 must choose y_1 and be rejected before stage $t(x_0)$, so that $t(x_1) < t(x_0)$, contradicting the minimality of $t(x_0)$.

We complement this result with the observation that for each Y no stable matching is worse than the matching generated by the GS^X algorithm.

Proposition 18.4: GS^X algorithm yields worst stable matching for Y's

For any society and any preference profile for the society, no stable matching is worse for any Y than the matching generated by the GS^X algorithm.

Proof

Consider a society (X, Y) and suppose that for the preference profile $(\succcurlyeq^i)_{i \in X \cup Y}$ the algorithm GS^X leads to the (stable) matching μ. Suppose another stable matching ψ is worse for some $y \in Y$: $x_2 = \psi^{-1}(y) \prec^y \mu^{-1}(y) = x_1$. Let $y_1 = \psi(x_1)$.

$$
\begin{array}{cc}
\mu & \psi \\
\hline
y \longleftrightarrow x_1 & y \longleftrightarrow x_2 \\
& y_1 \longleftrightarrow x_1
\end{array}
$$

By Proposition 18.3, $y = \mu(x_1) \succ^{x_1} \psi(x_1) = y_1$. Given $x_1 \succ^y \psi^{-1}(y) = x_2$, x_1 and y prefer each other to the individuals with whom they are matched in ψ, contrary to the assumption that ψ is stable.

Problems

1. *Stable matching and Pareto stability.*

   a. Show that any stable matching is Pareto stable. That is, for no preference profile is another matching (stable or not) better for one individual and not worse for every other.

   b. Give an example of a Pareto stable matching that is not stable.

2. *Pareto stability for the X's.* Show that the outcome of the GS^X algorithm is weakly Pareto stable for the X's. That is, no other matching is better for every X.

3. *All X's have the same preferences.* Assume that all X's have the same preferences over the Y's.

   a. How many stages does the GS^X algorithm take?

   b. Which serial dictatorship procedure yields the same final matching as the GS^X procedure?

   c. Show that in this case GS^X and GS^Y lead to the same matching.

4. *Matching with unequal groups.* Group A has m members and group B has n members, with $m < n$. Each individual has strict preferences over the members of the other group. Let GS^A be the Gale-Shapley algorithm in which the A's initiate the matches and let GS^B be the algorithm in which the B's initiate the matches.

   a. Show that if $m = 1$ then GS^A and GS^B yield the same matching.

   b. Explain why GS^A and GS^B do not necessarily yield the same matching if $m = 2$.

   c. Show that in both GS^A and GS^B every individual in A is matched with one of his m most preferred members of B.

5. *Clubs.* Assume that $3n$ students have to be allocated to three programs, each with capacity n. Each student has strict preferences over the set of programs and each of the programs has strict preferences over the students. Describe an algorithm similar to the Gale-Shapley algorithm, define a notion of stability, and show that for any preference profile your algorithm ends with a stable matching.

6. *Manipulation.* The Gale-Shapley algorithm is not strategy-proof and thus is not immune to manipulation. Specifically, if each individual is asked to

report preferences and the GS^X algorithm is run using the reported preferences, then for some preference profiles some individual is better off, according to his true preferences, if he reports preferences different from his true preferences.

To see this possibility, consider the following preference profile for a society with three X's and three Y's.

1:	$1 \succ 2 \succ 3$	1:	$2 \succ 1 \succ 3$
2:	$2 \succ 1 \succ 3$	2:	$1 \succ 2 \succ 3$
3:	$1 \succ 2 \succ 3$	3:	$1 \succ 2 \succ 3$

Show that 1 can benefit by reporting preferences different from his true preferences.

7. *The roommate problem.* A society contains $2n$ individuals. The individuals have to be partitioned into pairs. Each individual has a (strict) preference over the other individuals. An assignment μ is a one-to-one function from the set of individuals to itself such that if $\mu(i) = j$ then $\mu(j) = i$. An assignment is stable if for no pair of individuals does each individual prefer the other member of the pair to his assigned partner. Construct an example of a preference profile (with four individuals) for which no assignment is stable.

Notes

The chapter is based on Gale and Shapley (1962).

19 Socialism

Consider a society in which each individual can produce the same consumption good, like food, using a single input, like land. Each individual is characterized by his productivity. The higher an individual's productivity, the more output he produces with any given amount of the input.

An economic system can be thought of as a rule that specifies the output produced by the entire society and the allocation of this output among the individuals as a function of the individuals' productivities. Should individuals with high productivity get more output than ones with low productivity? Should two individuals with the same productivity receive the same amount of output? Should an increase in an individual's productivity result in his receiving more output? The design of an economic system requires an answer to such questions.

The approach in this chapter (like those in Chapters 3 and 20) is axiomatic. The central result specifies conditions capturing efficiency and fairness that are satisfied only by an economic system that resembles the socialist ideal.

19.1 Model

A society contains n individuals, denoted $1,\ldots,n$. A fixed amount of a single good, referred to as input (like land), is available for division among the individuals. For convenience, we take this amount to be 1. Each individual uses input to produce output, which we refer to as wealth. Each individual i is characterized by his productivity $\lambda^i \geq 0$; using an amount α^i of the input, he produces the amount $\alpha^i \lambda^i$ of wealth.

Definition 19.1: Society and productivity profile

A *society* consists of a set of *individuals* $N = \{1,\ldots,n\}$ and a total amount of *input* available, which we assume to be 1.

A *productivity profile* is a vector $(\lambda^1,\ldots,\lambda^n)$ of nonnegative numbers. For any nonnegative number α^i, individual i transforms the amount α^i of input into the amount $\alpha^i \lambda^i$ of *wealth*.

Note that in this formulation an individual does not choose how much effort to exert. If he is assigned α^i of the input then he produces $\alpha^i \lambda^i$ of wealth independently of the share of the output he gets.

Chapter of *Models in Microeconomic Theory* by Martin J. Osborne and Ariel Rubinstein. Version 2023.5.30 (h).
© 2023 Martin J. Osborne and Ariel Rubinstein CC BY-NC-ND 4.0.   https://doi.org/10.11647/OBP.0362.19

A distribution of the input is a vector $(\alpha^1, \ldots, \alpha^n)$ of nonnegative numbers with sum 1: $\sum_{i=1}^{n} \alpha^i = 1$. If each individual i is assigned the amount α^i of the input, then the total wealth of the society is $\sum_{i=1}^{n} \alpha^i \lambda^i$, which has to be divided among the individuals.

Definition 19.2: Feasible wealth profile

For any productivity profile $(\lambda^1, \ldots, \lambda^n)$, a profile $(w^1, \ldots, w^n)$ of nonnegative numbers is a *feasible wealth profile* if for some profile $(\alpha^1, \ldots, \alpha^n)$ of nonnegative numbers with $\sum_{i=1}^{n} \alpha^i = 1$ we have $\sum_{i=1}^{n} w^i = \sum_{i=1}^{n} \alpha^i \lambda^i$.

We model an economic system as a rule that specifies for each productivity profile a feasible wealth profile. Note that this notion of an economic system does not specify the amount of wealth each individual produces; the same wealth profile may be achieved by different distributions of the input among the individuals.

Definition 19.3: Economic system

An *economic system* is a function F that assigns to every productivity profile $(\lambda^1, \ldots, \lambda^n)$ a feasible wealth profile $F(\lambda^1, \ldots, \lambda^n)$.

If $F(\lambda^1, \ldots, \lambda^n) = (w^1, \ldots, w^n)$ then we write $F^i(\lambda^1, \ldots, \lambda^n) = w^i$, the wealth assigned to individual i by the rule F given the productivity profile $(\lambda^1, \ldots, \lambda^n)$. Notice that an economic system is a *rule* that specifies how wealth is distributed for *every* possible productivity profile, not only for a specific profile. (The following analogy might help you. When we talk about the rule for converting Celsius to Fahrenheit we specify the formula $F = 32 + 1.6C$ and not simply that 0 Celsius is equivalent to 32 Fahrenheit.)

Although this formalization of an economic system specifies only the total wealth produced and its distribution among the individuals, the rationale for some of the examples we discuss subsequently involves principles for the allocation of the input among the individuals and the dependence of the individuals' outputs on the wealth distribution.

Regarding the distribution of the input, one leading principle is that it should maximize the total wealth, which occurs if all the input is assigned to the individuals with the highest productivity. (If no two individuals have the same productivity, that means that all the input is assigned to the most productive individual.) Another leading principle is that the input should be distributed equally among all individuals, which is typically inefficient.

Regarding the distribution of wealth, one leading principle is that we allow each individual to keep the amount he produces. At the other extreme, the total amount of wealth produced is distributed equally among the individuals. If we combine each of these two rules with each of the two rules for assigning input discussed in the previous paragraph, we get the following four examples of economic systems.

Example 19.1: Equality of input, no redistribution

The input is divided equally among the individuals and each individual receives the wealth he produces. That is, for any productivity profile $(\lambda^1,\ldots,\lambda^n)$ we have $F^i(\lambda^1,\ldots,\lambda^n)=\lambda^i/n$ for each individual i.

Example 19.2: Input to most productive, no redistribution

The input is divided equally among the individuals with the highest productivity and each individual receives the wealth he produces. That is, for any productivity profile $(\lambda^1,\ldots,\lambda^n)$ we have

$$
F^i(\lambda^1,\ldots,\lambda^n)=\begin{cases} \dfrac{\lambda^i}{|\{j \in N : \lambda^j \geq \lambda^k \text{ for all } k \in N\}|} & \text{if } \lambda^i \geq \lambda^k \text{ for all } k \in N \\[2ex] 0 & \text{otherwise.} \end{cases}
$$

Example 19.3: Equality of input, equality of wealth

The input is divided equally among the individuals and the total wealth is also divided equally among the individuals. That is, for any productivity profile $(\lambda^1,\ldots,\lambda^n)$ we have $F^i(\lambda^1,\ldots,\lambda^n)=\sum_{j=1}^{n}\lambda^j/n^2$ for each individual i.

The last of the four combinations of input and wealth allocation rules assigns the input to the most productive individuals and divides the resulting wealth equally among all individuals. It is one possible formalization of the socialist principle "from each according to his ability, to each according to his needs" (Marx 1971, Section I.3) in the case that every individual has the same needs.

Example 19.4: Input to most productive, equality of wealth (socialism)

The input is divided equally among the individuals with the highest productivity and the wealth is divided equally among all individuals. That is, for any productivity profile $(\lambda^1,\ldots,\lambda^n)$ we have $F^i(\lambda^1,\ldots,\lambda^n)=\max\{\lambda^1,\ldots,\lambda^n\}/n$ for each individual i.

Of the many other possible economic systems, we mention two.

Example 19.5: One worker, one beneficiary

For some individuals j_1 and j_2, individual j_1 is assigned all the input and individual j_2 gets all the wealth. That is, for any productivity profile $(\lambda^1, \ldots, \lambda^n)$ we have

$$F^i(\lambda^1, \ldots, \lambda^n) = \begin{cases} \lambda^{j_1} & \text{if } i = j_2 \\ 0 & \text{otherwise.} \end{cases}$$

This economic system can be thought of as a reflection of an extreme power relation in which one individual is a master and the other is a slave.

Example 19.6: Input to most productive, wealth relative to productivity

The input is divided equally among the individuals with the highest productivity and each individual receives an amount of wealth proportional to his productivity. That is, for any productivity profile $(\lambda^1, \ldots, \lambda^n)$ we have $F^i(\lambda^1, \ldots, \lambda^n) = \max\{\lambda^1, \ldots, \lambda^n\} \lambda^i / \sum_{j=1}^{n} \lambda^j$ for each individual i.

19.2   Properties of economic systems

Here are some properties that an economic system might satisfy. The first property is similar to Pareto stability.

Efficiency   An economic system is efficient if, for every productivity profile, no feasible wealth profile different from the one generated by the system is better for some individuals and not worse for any individual.

Definition 19.4: Efficient economic system

An economic system F is *efficient* if for every productivity profile $(\lambda^1, \ldots, \lambda^n)$ there is no feasible wealth profile $(w^1, \ldots, w^n)$ for which $w^i \geq F^i(\lambda^1, \ldots, \lambda^n)$ for all $i = 1, \ldots, n$, with at least one strict inequality.

An economic system is efficient if and only if, for every productivity profile, the sum of the wealths the system assigns to the individuals is equal to the maximum total wealth that can be produced. The maximum total wealth is produced only if the input is distributed among the individuals with the highest productivity, so among the examples in the previous section, only the economic systems in Examples 19.2, 19.4, and 19.6 are efficient. An economic system is not efficient if for at least one profile the total production is not maximal. To illustrate, Example 19.5 with $n=2$, $i_1=1$, and $i_2=2$ is not efficient since $F(2,3)=(0,2)$ with total wealth 2, which is less than the potential maximum of 3.

Symmetry   An economic system is symmetric if for any productivity profile in which two individuals have the same productivity, they are assigned the same wealth.

Definition 19.5: Symmetric economic system

An economic system F is *symmetric* if for any individuals i and j and any productivity profile $(\lambda^1,\dots,\lambda^n)$,

$$\lambda^i = \lambda^j \quad\Rightarrow\quad F^i(\lambda^1,\dots,\lambda^n) = F^j(\lambda^1,\dots,\lambda^n).$$

Note that this property does not constrain the wealths assigned by the economic system to productivity profiles in which all individuals' productivities differ. The property is satisfied by all the examples of economic systems in the previous section except Example 19.5 (one worker, one beneficiary).

Relative monotonicity   An economic system is *relatively monotonic* if whenever individual i has higher productivity than j, the amount of wealth assigned to i is at least as high as the amount assigned to j.

Definition 19.6: Relatively monotonic economic system

An economic system F is *relatively monotonic* if for every productivity profile $(\lambda^1,\dots,\lambda^n)$,

$$\lambda^i \geq \lambda^j \quad\Rightarrow\quad F^i(\lambda^1,\dots,\lambda^n) \geq F^j(\lambda^1,\dots,\lambda^n).$$

All the examples in the previous section except Example 19.5 (one worker, one beneficiary) satisfy this property.

The properties we have defined, efficiency, symmetry, and relative monotonicity, require that for each productivity profile, the wealths assigned by the economic system satisfy certain conditions. The properties we now define have a different logical structure: they impose conditions on the relation between the wealth distributions assigned by the economic system to *different* productivity profiles.

Anonymity An economic system is anonymous if it does not discriminate among individuals on the basis of their names. (It may still discriminate among individuals according to their productivity.) Recall that a permutation of the set of individuals N is a one-to-one function from N to N. For example, there are six permutations of $N = \{1,2,3\}$; one of them is the function σ defined by $\sigma(1) = 3$, $\sigma(2) = 2$, and $\sigma(3) = 1$.

Consider a productivity profile $(\lambda^1,\dots,\lambda^n)$. Given a permutation σ of N, we consider the new productivity profile in which each individual $\sigma(i)$ has the productivity of individual i in $(\lambda^1,\dots,\lambda^n)$. That is, we consider the productivity profile $(\hat{\lambda}^1,\dots,\hat{\lambda}^n)$ where $\hat{\lambda}^{\sigma(i)} = \lambda^i$. The anonymity condition requires that the wealth of $\sigma(i)$ for the new productivity profile is the same as the wealth of i in the original profile: $F^{\sigma(i)}(\hat{\lambda}^1,\dots,\hat{\lambda}^n) = F^i(\lambda^1,\dots,\lambda^n)$. For example, consider the productivity profile $(7,3,13)$ and the permutation σ with $\sigma(1) = 3$, $\sigma(2) = 1$, and $\sigma(3) = 2$. Then $F^2(3,13,7) = F^3(7,3,13)$.

> **Definition 19.7: Anonymous economic system**
>
> An economic system F is *anonymous* if for all productivity profiles $(\lambda^1,\dots,\lambda^n)$ and $(\hat{\lambda}^1,\dots,\hat{\lambda}^n)$ for which there is a permutation σ of N such that $\hat{\lambda}^{\sigma(i)} = \lambda^i$ for all i, we have
>
> $$F^{\sigma(i)}(\hat{\lambda}^1,\dots,\hat{\lambda}^n) = F^i(\lambda^1,\dots,\lambda^n) \text{ for all } i = 1,\dots,n.$$

All the examples in the previous section except Example 19.5 (one worker, one beneficiary) satisfy this property.

If an economic system is anonymous then it is symmetric (Problem 1a). But anonymity is stronger than symmetry. Symmetry relates only to the way that the economic system assigns wealth to a productivity profile in which some individuals have the same productivity. Anonymity requires also consistency in the wealths assigned for pairs of productivity profiles that are permutations of each other. Suppose, for example, that $N = \{1,2\}$ and consider the economic system that for any productivity profile (λ^1,λ^2) with $\lambda^1 = \lambda^2$ assigns each individual i the wealth $\frac{1}{2}\lambda^i$ and for any other productivity profile assigns individual 1 the wealth $\max\{\lambda^1,\lambda^2\}$ and individual 2 the wealth 0. This economic system is symmetric but not anonymous.

Monotonicity in own productivity An economic system is monotone in own productivity if, when an individual's productivity increases, his wealth does not decrease. Notice the difference between this property and relative monotonicity, which requires that if one individual's productivity is at least as high as another's then his wealth is also at least as high.

> **Definition 19.8: Monotonicity in own productivity**
>
> An economic system F is *monotone in own productivity* if for every productivity profile $(\lambda^1, \ldots, \lambda^n)$, every individual i, and every number $\Delta > 0$, we have $F^i(\lambda^1, \ldots, \lambda^i + \Delta, \ldots, \lambda^n) \geq F^i(\lambda^1, \ldots, \lambda^i, \ldots, \lambda^n)$.

All the examples in the previous section satisfy this property. The economic system in which the input is divided equally among the individuals with the lowest productivity and each individual receives the wealth he produces does not satisfy the property since, for example, $F^1(2,3) = 2 > 0 = F^1(5,3)$. If an economic system is monotone in own productivity and symmetric then it is relatively monotonic (Problem 1b).

Monotonicity in others' productivities An economic system is monotone in others' productivities if any increase in the productivity of one individual does not hurt another individual.

> **Definition 19.9: Monotonicity in others' productivities**
>
> An economic system F is *monotone in others' productivities* if for every productivity profile $(\lambda^1, \ldots, \lambda^n)$, any two individuals i and j, and every number $\Delta > 0$, we have $F^j(\lambda^1, \ldots, \lambda^i + \Delta, \ldots, \lambda^n) \geq F^j(\lambda^1, \ldots, \lambda^i, \ldots, \lambda^n)$.

All examples in the previous section except Examples 19.2 (input to most productive, no redistribution) and 19.6 (input to most productive, wealth relative to productivity) satisfy this property. To see that Example 19.2 does not satisfy the property, notice, for example, that $F^1(3,2) = 3 > 0 = F^1(3,4)$.

19.3 Characterization of socialism

We now show that socialism is the only economic system that satisfies four of the properties defined in the previous section.

> **Proposition 19.1: Characterization of socialist economic system**
>
> The only economic system that is efficient, symmetric, monotone in own productivity, and monotone in others' productivities is socialism, according to which all wealth is produced by the individuals with the highest productivity and the total wealth is divided equally among all individuals.

Proof

Problem 1c asks you to verify that the socialist economic system satisfies the four properties. We now show that it is the only economic system that does so.

Let F be an economic system satisfying the four properties. We first show that for every productivity profile $(\lambda^1, \ldots, \lambda^n)$ and every individual j, the wealth $F^j(\lambda^1, \ldots, \lambda^n)$ assigned by F to j is at most M/n, where $M = \max\{\lambda^1, \ldots, \lambda^n\}$. Suppose to the contrary that for some productivity profile $(\lambda^1, \ldots, \lambda^n)$, we have $F^i(\lambda^1, \ldots, \lambda^n) > M/n$ for some individual i. Given that $M \geq \lambda^j$ for every individual j, the repeated application of the monotonicity of F in others' productivities yields

$$F^i(M, \ldots, M, \lambda^i, M, \ldots, M) \geq F^i(\lambda^1, \ldots, \lambda^n).$$

Now use the monotonicity of F in own productivity to conclude that

$$F^i(M, \ldots, M) \geq F^i(\lambda^1, \ldots, \lambda^n).$$

Let $F^i(M, \ldots, M) = H$. By symmetry, $F^j(M, \ldots, M) = H$ for every individual j. But $F^i(\lambda^1, \ldots, \lambda^n) > M/n$, so $H > M/n$, and hence the wealth distribution $(H, \ldots, H)$ is not feasible. Thus $F^i(\lambda^1, \ldots, \lambda^n) \leq M/n$ for every individual i.

By efficiency, the input is distributed among the individuals with the highest productivity, so that for every productivity profile $(\lambda^1, \ldots, \lambda^n)$ we have $\sum_{i=1}^n F^i(\lambda^1, \ldots, \lambda^n) = M$ and hence $F^i(\lambda^1, \ldots, \lambda^n) = M/n$ for every individual i.

We close the chapter by showing that the four properties are independent in the sense that none of them is implied by the other three. For each property we find an economic system that does not satisfy that property but satisfies the other three. Thus all four properties are required to reach the conclusion of Proposition 19.1.

Proposition 19.2: Independence of properties

The properties of efficiency, symmetry, monotonicity in own productivity, and monotonicity in others' productivities are independent. That is, for each property there is an economic system that does not satisfy that property but satisfies the other three.

Proof

Efficiency

The economic system defined by $F^i(\lambda^1,\ldots,\lambda^n) = \min\{\lambda^1,\ldots,\lambda^n\}/n$ satisfies all axioms but efficiency. (For any productivity profile $(\lambda^1,\ldots,\lambda^n)$ that is not constant, $(w,\ldots,w)$ with $w = \max\{\lambda^1,\ldots,\lambda^n\}/n$ is a feasible wealth profile, and $w > \min\{\lambda^1,\ldots,\lambda^n\}/n = F^i(\lambda^1,\ldots,\lambda^n)$.)

Symmetry

The economic system defined by $F^1(\lambda^1,\ldots,\lambda^n) = \max\{\lambda^1,\ldots,\lambda^n\}$ and $F^i(\lambda^1,\ldots,\lambda^n) = 0$ for $i \neq 1$ for every productivity profile $(\lambda^1,\ldots,\lambda^n)$ (all wealth goes to individual 1) satisfies all the axioms except symmetry.

Monotonicity in own productivity

The economic system according to which the individuals with the *lowest* productivity share $\max\{\lambda^1,\ldots,\lambda^n\}$ equally and the wealth of every other individual is zero satisfies all the axioms except monotonicity in own productivity. (If the productivity of an individual increases from $\min\{\lambda^1,\ldots,\lambda^n\}$ to a larger number, the wealth assigned to him decreases to zero.)

Monotonicity in others' productivities

The economic system according to which the individuals with the *highest* productivity share $\max\{\lambda^1,\ldots,\lambda^n\}$ equally and the wealth of every other individual is zero satisfies all the axioms except monotonicity in others' productivities. (If the productivity of an individual i increases from less than $\max\{\lambda^1,\ldots,\lambda^n\}$ to more than this number, the wealth of every individual whose productivity was formerly $\max\{\lambda^1,\ldots,\lambda^n\}$ decreases to zero.)

Comments

This chapter is not an argument for or against socialism. Its main aim is to demonstrate that some economists are interested in economic systems with a centralized component and consider fairness to be a criterion by which a system should be judged. The main result shows that a system we label "socialism" is characterized by four properties. Of course other economic systems are characterized by other sets of properties. Those characterizations can help us normatively evaluate economic systems.

In the model the distribution of output depends only on the profile of productivities. No other factors are taken into account; in particular, information about the individuals' needs is ignored. The model also does not touch upon the issue of incentives, which is central to most economic models. Each individual produces an output proportional to his productivity even if he does not obtain the output.

Problems

1. *Relations between properties.* Show the following results.

   a. Anonymity implies symmetry.

   b. For $n = 2$, find an economic system that satisfies monotonicity in own productivity and symmetry but not relative monotonicity.

   c. The socialist economic system satisfies the properties of efficiency, symmetry, monotonicity in own productivity, and monotonicity in others' productivities.

2. *Input and wealth to most productive.* Consider the economic system F in which the input is divided equally among the individuals with the highest productivity and the wealth is divided equally among these individuals.

   a. Show that F satisfies the following *strong monotonicity in own productivity* property. For any productivity profile $(\lambda^1, \ldots, \lambda^n)$ and any number $\Delta > 0$,

$$F^i(\lambda^1, \ldots, \lambda^n) > 0 \quad \Rightarrow \quad F^i(\lambda^1, \ldots, \lambda^i + \Delta, \ldots, \lambda^n) > F^i(\lambda^1, \ldots, \lambda^n).$$

   b. Show that F is not the only economic system that satisfies strong monotonicity in own productivity, symmetry, and efficiency.

3. *Shapley value.* Consider economic systems that are efficient and symmetric and satisfy the following two conditions.

   Zero contribution
   For every productivity profile $(\lambda^1, \ldots, \lambda^n)$ with $\lambda^i = 0$, we have $F^i(\lambda^1, \ldots, \lambda^n) = 0$.

   Marginal contribution
   Let $(\lambda^1, \ldots, \lambda^n)$ be a profile and S be a subset of the most productive individuals (those with productivity $\max\{\lambda^1, \ldots, \lambda^n\}$). Suppose that the productivity profile $\mu = (\mu^1, \ldots, \mu^n)$ is obtained from the profile $(\lambda^1, \ldots, \lambda^n)$ by adding $\delta > 0$ to the productivity of each member of S. Then the wealth of each individual $j \in S$ is $F^i(\lambda^1, \ldots, \lambda^n)$ plus the wealth he would receive

if the productivity of every individual in S were δ and the productivity of every other individual were 0. Formally, if

$$(\mu^1,\ldots,\mu^n)=(\lambda^1,\ldots,\lambda^n)+(\Delta^1,\ldots,\Delta^n)$$

where (i) $\Delta^i \in \{0,\delta\}$ and (ii) if $\Delta^i > 0$ then $\lambda^i = \max\{\lambda^1,\ldots,\lambda^n\}$, then

$$F^i(\mu^1,\ldots,\mu^n)= F^i(\lambda^1,\ldots,\lambda^n)+ F^i(\Delta^1,\ldots,\Delta^n).$$

(Thus, for example, $F^1(8,8,7,6,4)= F^1(7,7,7,6,4)+ F^1(1,1,0,0,0)$.)

a. For such an economic system F find the wealths assigned when $n = 2$ and the productivity profile is $(1,3)$.

b. For such an economic system F, find the wealths assigned when $n = 4$ and the productivity profile is $(1,3,6,10)$.

c. Imagine that the four individuals with productivity profile $(1,3,6,10)$ arrive on the scene one after the other in one of the 24 possible orders. Consider the marginal contribution of each individual: the increase in the wealth that can be produced due to his arrival. For example, if the order in which the individuals arrive is $(1,3,2,4)$ then the marginal contribution of individual 1 is 1, that of individual 3 is $6 - 1 = 5$, that of individual 2 is zero (because individual 3, with productivity 6, has already arrived), and that of agent 4 is $10 - 6 = 4$.

   Show that the averages of the marginal contributions are exactly the wealths you found in the previous part. For example, individual 1 makes a positive contribution, and that contribution is 1, only if he is the first in the list. He is first in a quarter of the orders, so the average of his marginal contributions is $\frac{1}{4}$.

d. For each of the four properties (efficiency, symmetry, zero contribution, and marginal contribution) find an economic system that does not satisfy the property but satisfies the other three.

Notes

This chapter is inspired by the work of John Roemer (for example Roemer 1986).

20 Aggregating preferences

When we discuss public decisions, we often talk about the preferences of a group of people, like a nation, a class, or a family. We do so even though the members of the group have different preferences; we say that "the group prefers one option to another" even though the meaning of such a statement is unclear. In this chapter we discuss one model of the aggregation of individuals' preferences into a social preference relation.

20.1 Social preferences

Society consists of a set of individuals, each of whom has preferences over a set of social alternatives X, which is fixed throughout our discussion. The information we have about each individual's preferences is purely ordinal, in the sense that it tells us only that the individual prefers one alternative to another, or regards two alternatives as indifferent. In particular, it does not specify the intensity of an individual's preferences. On the basis of the information, we cannot say, for example, that an individual "prefers a to b more than he prefers c to d" or that "individual i prefers a to b more than individual j prefers b to a".

We want to aggregate the individuals' preferences into a social preference. A voting procedure is sometimes used to do so. An example is the method used in the Eurovision song contest. In this case X is the set of songs performed in the contest. Each country submits an ordered list of the members of X that expresses its preference ordering (which itself is an aggregation of the orderings of the listeners in that country). The countries' rankings are aggregated by assigning points to the songs according to their positions in each country's ranking (12 for the top song, 10 for the second, 8, 7, ..., 1 for the next 8 songs, and 0 for all others) and then summing the points across countries to give the European ranking. This method is a special case of a family of aggregation methods called scoring rules, which we define later.

Majority rule is a simpler, and natural, principle for determining a social preference. According to this rule, the society prefers alternative a to alternative b if a majority of individuals prefer a to b. A major difficulty with this rule is that when X contains more than two alternatives, the resulting binary relation may not be transitive, so that it is not a preference relation. Recall the Condorcet paradox

Chapter of *Models in Microeconomic Theory* by Martin J. Osborne and Ariel Rubinstein. Version 2023.5.30 (h).

discussed in Chapter 1. A society contains three individuals, 1, 2, and 3, and three social alternatives, a, b, and c. The individuals' preferences are given in the following table, where each column lists the alternatives in the order of one individual's preferences.

1	2	3
a	b	c
b	c	a
c	a	b

Individuals 1 and 3, a majority, prefer a to b, individuals 1 and 2 prefer b to c, and individuals 2 and 3 prefer c to a. Thus the binary relation $\succeq$ defined by majority rule satisfies $a \succ b \succ c \succ a$, and hence is not transitive.

20.2 Preference aggregation functions

The central concept in this chapter is a preference aggregation function (PAF), which maps the preferences of the individuals in a society into a single "social" preference relation. A PAF is usually called a social welfare function. We avoid this term because the concept is not related to the individuals' welfare in the everyday sense of that word.

> **Definition 20.1: Society**
>
> A *society* consists of a finite set N (the set of *individuals*) and a finite set X (the set of *alternatives*).

We assume that every individual in N has a preference relation over X. For simplicity we assume that each of these preference relations is strict (no individual is indifferent between any two alternatives). A profile of preferences specifies a (strict) preference relation for every individual.

The domain of a PAF is the set of all preference profiles. That is, we do not impose any restrictions on the set of preference profiles. Problem 2 illustrates the significance of this assumption. To each preference profile, a PAF assigns a single preference relation. We do not assume that this preference relation is strict: the social preference may have indifferences.

> **Definition 20.2: Preference aggregation function**
>
> A *preference aggregation function* (PAF) for a society $\langle N, X \rangle$ is a function that assigns a ("social") preference relation over X to every profile of strict preference relations over X.

Note that a preference aggregation function is not a single preference relation. Rather, it is a rule for aggregating the individuals' preference relations into a single preference relation. Here are a few examples.

Example 20.1: Counting favorites

The alternative x is ranked above y if the number of individuals for whom x is the best alternative is greater than the number of individuals for whom y is the best alternative. Formally, for any preference profile $(\succsim^i)_{i\in N}$, the social preference relation $\succsim$ is defined by

$$x \succsim y \text{ if } |\{i \in N : x \succsim^i a \text{ for all } a \in X\}| \geq |\{i \in N : y \succsim^i a \text{ for all } a \in X\}|.$$

(Note that every alternative that is not any individual's favorite is indifferent to any other such alternative in the social preferences, and is ranked below all other alternatives.)

Example 20.2: Scoring rules

Given a preference relation $\succsim^i$, the *position* $K(\succsim^i, x)$ of alternative x in $\succsim^i$ is the number of alternatives that are at least as good as x according to $\succsim^i$: $K(\succsim^i, x) = |\{a \in X : a \succsim^i x\}|$. Thus the position of the best alternative according to $\succsim^i$ is 1, the position of the second-ranked alternative is 2, and so on. A scoring rule is characterized by a function p that gives the number of points $p(k)$ credited to an alternative for being ranked in each position k. Assume $p(1) \geq \cdots \geq p(|X|)$. Alternatives are compared according to the sum of the points they accumulate across the individuals' preferences. Precisely, the scoring rule defined by p maps the preference profile $(\succsim^i)_{i\in N}$ into the social preference relation $\succsim$ defined by

$$x \succsim y \text{ if } \sum_{i\in N} p(K(\succsim^i, x)) \geq \sum_{i\in N} p(K(\succsim^i, y)).$$

Note that the previous example (Example 20.1) is the scoring rule for which p is given by $p(1) = 1$ and $p(k) = 0$ for all $k \geq 2$.

Example 20.3: Pairwise contests

For every pair (x, y) of distinct alternatives, say that x beats y if a majority of individuals prefer x to y, and x and y tie if the number of individuals who prefer x to y is the same as the number of individuals who prefer y to x. Assign to each alternative one point for every alternative it beats and half a point for every alternative with which it ties. Rank the alternatives by the total number of points received.

1	2	3	$\cdots$	$n-1$	n
a	b	d	$\cdots$	a	b
b	a	a	$\cdots$	d	d
c	c	b	$\cdots$	c	a
d	d	c	$\cdots$	b	c

$\Downarrow$

$b \succ c \succ a \succ d$

$\Rightarrow$

1	2	3	$\cdots$	$n-1$	n
b	a	d	$\cdots$	b	a
a	b	b	$\cdots$	d	d
c	c	a	$\cdots$	c	b
d	d	c	$\cdots$	a	c

$\Downarrow$

$a \succ c \succ b \succ d$

Figure 20.1 An illustration of the neutrality property. Each column shows the preference ordering of the individual whose name heads the column, from best at the top to worst at the bottom. When the alternatives a and b are interchanged in every individual's preferences, they are interchanged also in the social preferences.

The last two examples are extreme.

Example 20.4: External preferences

The social preference relation is some fixed given preference relation regardless of the individuals' preferences. That is, for some preference relation $\succeq^*$ we have $x \succeq y$ if and only if $x \succeq^* y$.

Example 20.5: Dictatorship

The social preference relation coincides with the preference relation of one of the individuals, called the dictator. That is, for some individual i^* we have $x \succeq y$ if and only if $x \succeq^{i^*} y$.

20.3   Properties of preference aggregation functions

How do we evaluate a preference aggregation function? We proceed by specifying properties that seem appealing, and then look for preference aggregation functions that satisfy them.

Neutrality   A PAF is neutral if it treats the alternatives symmetrically. That is, for any preference profile, if we interchange the positions of any pair of alternatives in every individual's preference relation then the PAF responds to the change by interchanging the positions of these alternatives in the social preference relation. The property is illustrated in Figure 20.1.

1	2	3	$\cdots$	$n-1$	n
a	b	d	$\cdots$	a	b
b	a	a	$\cdots$	d	d
c	c	b	$\cdots$	c	a
d	d	c	$\cdots$	b	c

$$\Downarrow$$
$$b \succ c \succ a \succ d$$

$\Rightarrow$

1	2	3	$\cdots$	$n-1$	n
d	b	a	$\cdots$	a	b
a	a	b	$\cdots$	d	d
b	c	c	$\cdots$	c	a
c	d	d	$\cdots$	b	c

$$\Downarrow$$
$$b \succ c \succ a \succ d$$

Figure 20.2 An illustration of the anonymity property. When the preferences of two individuals are interchanged, the social preferences remain the same.

Definition 20.3: Neutrality

A preference aggregation function F for a society $\langle N, X \rangle$ is *neutral* if for any profiles $(\succcurlyeq^i)_{i \in N}$ and $(\trianglerighteq^i)_{i \in N}$ of preference relations over X such that for some alternatives x and y the preference relation $\trianglerighteq^i$ for each $i \in N$ is obtained from $\succcurlyeq^i$ by interchanging the positions of x and y, then the social preference relation $F((\trianglerighteq^i)_{i \in N})$ is obtained from $F((\succcurlyeq^i)_{i \in N})$ by interchanging the positions of x and y as well.

For $X = \{a, b\}$, an example of a PAF that is not neutral is the one that ranks a above b only if at least $\frac{2}{3}$ of the individuals prefer a to b. All the examples in the previous section except Example 20.4 (external preferences) are neutral.

Anonymity A PAF is anonymous if it does not discriminate between individuals. Consider two profiles in which all preference relations are the same except those of i and j, which are interchanged. An anonymous PAF generates the same social preference relation for these two profiles. The property is illustrated in Figure 20.2. All the examples in the previous section except dictatorship are anonymous.

Definition 20.4: Anonymity

A preference aggregation function F for a society $\langle N, X \rangle$ is *anonymous* if whenever $(\succcurlyeq^i)_{i \in N}$ and $(\trianglerighteq^i)_{i \in N}$ are profiles of preference relations over X with $\succcurlyeq^j = \trianglerighteq^k$, $\succcurlyeq^k = \trianglerighteq^j$, and $\succcurlyeq^i = \trianglerighteq^i$ for all $i \in N \setminus \{j, k\}$, we have $F((\succcurlyeq^i)_{i \in N}) = F((\trianglerighteq^i)_{i \in N})$.

Positive responsiveness A PAF is positively responsive if whenever an alternative x rises one step in one individual's preferences and all other individuals' preferences remain the same, any alternative z that was originally ranked no higher than x in the social preferences is now ranked below x in these preferences. The examples in the previous section are positively responsive except for Example 20.4 when the external preference relation has indifferences.

Definition 20.5: Positive responsiveness

A preference aggregation function F for a society $\langle N, X \rangle$ is *positively responsive* if for any profile $(\succcurlyeq^i)_{i \in N}$ of preference relations over X and any profile $(\trianglerighteq^i)_{i \in N}$ that differs from $(\succcurlyeq^i)_{i \in N}$ only in that there exist $j \in N$, $x \in X$, and $y \in X$ such that $y \succ^j x$ and $x \rhd^j y$ (i.e. x rises one step in j's ranking), then for any $z \in X$ with $x \succcurlyeq z$ we have $x \rhd z$, where $\succcurlyeq = F((\succcurlyeq^i)_{i \in N})$ and $\trianglerighteq = F((\trianglerighteq^i)_{i \in N})$ (and $\rhd$ is the strict relation derived from $\trianglerighteq$).

Pareto A PAF satisfies the Pareto property if for any preference profile in which all individuals rank x above y the social ranking ranks x above y.

Definition 20.6: Pareto property

A preference aggregation function F for a society $\langle N, X \rangle$ satisfies the *Pareto property* if whenever $x \succ^i y$ for all $i \in N$ for a profile $(\succcurlyeq^i)_{i \in N}$ of preference relations over X we have $x \succ y$, where $\succcurlyeq = F((\succcurlyeq^i)_{i \in N})$.

A scoring rule (Example 20.2) satisfies this property if the weighting function p is decreasing (rather than merely nonincreasing). Example 20.4 (external preferences) does not satisfy the property.

Independence of irrelevant alternatives The last property we define is independence of irrelevant alternatives (IIA). This property says that the social ranking of any alternatives a relative to b depends only on the individuals' rankings of a relative to b and not on their rankings of any other alternatives or on their rankings of a or b relative to any other alternative.

Definition 20.7: Independence of irrelevant alternatives

A preference aggregation function F for a society $\langle N, X \rangle$ is *independent of irrelevant alternatives* (IIA) if for any profiles $(\succcurlyeq^i)_{i \in N}$ and $(\trianglerighteq^i)_{i \in N}$ of preference relations over X for which there are alternatives x and y with

$$x \succ^i y \text{ if and only if } x \rhd^i y \text{ for every } i$$

we have

$$x \succcurlyeq y \text{ if and only if } x \trianglerighteq y$$

where $\succeq\, =\, F((\succeq^i)_{i \in N})$ and $\trianglerighteq\, =\, F((\trianglerighteq^i)_{i \in N})$.

Dictatorship (Example 20.5) satisfies this property: the dictator's ranking of any two alternatives determines the social ranking of these alternatives. Some scoring rules (Example 20.2) do not satisfy the property. For example, consider a society with three individuals and three alternatives. Assume that the weighting function p for the scoring rule satisfies $p(1) - p(2) > 2(p(2) - p(3)) > 0$ and consider the following two preference profiles.

1	2	3
c	c	c
b	a	a
a	b	b

1	2	3
b	c	c
c	a	a
a	b	b

The relative rankings of a and b in the two profiles are the same, but the scoring rule ranks a above b for the left profile and b above a for the right profile.

20.4 Arrow's impossibility theorem

The central result of this chapter says that the only PAFs that satisfy the Pareto property and IIA are dictatorships. That is, the requirements that the social comparison of any two alternatives depends only on the individuals' binary comparisons of these two alternatives, and not on their preferences over other pairs, and that one alternative is socially preferred to another whenever there is consensus, do not leave room for real aggregation of the individuals' preferences.

Proposition 20.1: Arrow's impossibility theorem

Let $\langle N, X \rangle$ be a society for which X contains at least three alternatives. A preference aggregation function F satisfies the Pareto property and IIA if and only if it is dictatorial: there is an individual $i^* \in N$ such that for every profile $(\succeq^i)_{i \in N}$ of preference relations over X we have $x \succ y$ if and only if $x \succ^{i^*} y$, where $\succeq$ is the social preference relation $F((\succeq^i)_{i \in N})$.

Proof

If F is dictatorial then it satisfies the Pareto property and IIA. We now show the converse.

Let F be a PAF that satisfies the Pareto property and IIA. Fix $b \in X$.

Step 1 *Consider a preference profile for which b is either at the top or the bottom of each individual's ranking and let $\succeq$ be the social preferences attached to the profile by F. For such a profile, b is either the unique $\succeq$-maximal alternative or the unique $\succeq$-minimal alternative.*

Proof. Assume to the contrary that for two other alternatives a and c we have $a \succeq b \succeq c$. Consider a preference profile that is obtained from the original profile by moving c just above a for every individual who originally prefers a to c (so that it remains below b for all individuals for whom b is best), as illustrated below.

1	2	3	$\cdots$	$n-1$	n
b	b		$\cdots$	a	b
	a	a	$\cdots$		
c	c		$\cdots$	c	a
		c	$\cdots$		c
a	b		$\cdots$	b	

$\rightarrow$

1	2	3	$\cdots$	$n-1$	n
b	b		$\cdots$	c	b
	c	c	$\cdots$	a	
c	a	a	$\cdots$		c
			$\cdots$		a
a		b	$\cdots$	b	

Denote by $\unrhd$ the social preference relation that F generates for the new preference profile. By the Pareto property, $c \rhd a$. By IIA, the rankings of a and b remain unchanged, so $a \unrhd b$, and the rankings of b and c remain unchanged, so $b \unrhd c$. Thus $a \unrhd c$ by transitivity, contradicting $c \rhd a$.   ◁

Step 2 *Consider two preference profiles in which b is either at the top or the bottom of each individual's ranking and in which the set of individuals who rank b at the top is the same. Let $\succeq$ and $\unrhd$ be the social preferences attached by F to the profiles. Then either b is the unique maximal alternative for both $\succeq$ and $\unrhd$ or is the unique minimal alternative for both $\succeq$ and $\unrhd$.*

Proof. Consider one of the profiles. By Step 1, $\succeq$ either ranks b uniquely at the top or uniquely at the bottom. Suppose that it ranks it at the top. The ranking of b relative to any other alternative x is the same in both profiles and hence by IIA b and x are ranked in the same way by both $\succeq$ and $\unrhd$. Thus b is ranked at the top of $\unrhd$. If b is ranked at the bottom of $\succeq$ the argument is analogous.   ◁

Step 3 *For some individual i^*,*

i. for every preference profile for which $1,\ldots,i^*-1$ rank b at the top and $i^*,\ldots,n$ rank it at the bottom, the preference relation attached by F to the profile ranks b uniquely at the bottom *ii. for every preference profile for which $1, \ldots, i^*$ rank b at the top and $i^*+1, \ldots, n$ rank it at the bottom, the preference relation attached by F to the profile ranks b uniquely at the top.*

Proof. Take a preference profile in which b is at the bottom of all individuals' preferences. By the Pareto property, b is the unique minimal alternative for the attached social preferences. Now, for each individual in turn, starting with individual 1, move b from the bottom to the top of that individual's preferences. By Step 1, b is always either the unique maximal or unique minimal alternative in the social preferences. By the Pareto property, it is the unique maximal alternative of the attached social preferences after it moves to the top of all individuals' preferences. Thus for some individual i^* the change in his preferences moves b from the bottom to the top of the social preferences. By Step 2 the identity of i^* does not depend on the individuals' rankings of the other alternatives.   ◁

Step 4 *For all alternatives a and c different from b we have $a \succcurlyeq c$ if and only if $a \succcurlyeq^{i^*} c$.*

Proof. Assume to the contrary that for some preference profile we have $a \succ^{i^*} c$ and $c \succcurlyeq a$. Modify the profile by raising b to the top of the preferences of individuals $1, \ldots, i^*-1$, lowering it to the bottom of the preferences of individuals $i^*+1, \ldots, n$, and moving it between a and c for individual i^*, as in the following illustration.

1	2	···	i^*	···	$n-1$	n		1	2	···	i^*	···	$n-1$	n
	c			···	a	b		b	b	···			a	
b		···	a	···							c	a	···		c
a		···		···	c	c	$\rightarrow$	a		···	b	···	c	a
	a	···	c	···	b	a					···			
c	b		b	···				c	a		c	···	b	b

Denote by $\trianglerighteq$ the social preference that F attaches to the new preference profile. The relative positions of a and c are the same in the two profiles, so $c \trianglerighteq a$ by IIA. In the new profile, the individuals' rankings of a relative to b are the same as they are in any profile in which b is ranked at the top by $1, \ldots, i^* - 1$ and at the bottom by the remaining individuals, so that by Step 3 and IIA we have $a \triangleright b$. Similarly, $b \triangleright c$. Thus by transitivity $a \triangleright c$, a contradiction.   ◁

Step 4 states that i^* is the dictator regarding any two alternatives other than b. It remains to show that i^* is also the dictator regarding the comparison of b with any other alternative.

Step 5 *For every alternative a we have $a \succeq b$ if and only if $a \succ^{i^*} b$.*

Proof. Consider a preference profile for which $a \succ^{i^*} b$. Let c be an arbitrary third alternative. Modify the profile by moving c in i^*'s ranking to between b and a (if it is not already there) and raising c to the top of all the other individuals' rankings, as in the following illustration.

1	$\cdots$	i^*	$\cdots$	$n-1$	n		1	$\cdots$	i^*	$\cdots$	$n-1$	n
c			$\cdots$	a	b		c			$\cdots$	c	c
b	$\cdots$	a	$\cdots$				b	$\cdots$	a	$\cdots$	a	b
a	$\cdots$	b	$\cdots$	c	c	$\rightarrow$	a	$\cdots$	c	$\cdots$		
			$\cdots$	b	a				b	$\cdots$	b	a
		c	$\cdots$							$\cdots$		

Denote by $\unrhd$ the social preference attached by F to the new profile. By the Pareto property, $c \rhd b$. By Step 4, i^* determines the social preference between a and c, so that $a \rhd c$, and hence $a \rhd b$ by transitivity. Since the relative preferences of a and b are the same in the two profiles, we have also $a \succ b$ by IIA.   ◁

Comments

1. So far we have interpreted a PAF as a method of generating a social preference relation from the profile of the individuals' preferences. We can alternatively think of a PAF as a method for an individual to form preferences over a set of objects on the basis of several criteria. For example, an individual may base his preferences over cars on their relative price, their ranking by a car magazine, and their fuel consumption. In this context, Proposition 20.1 says that if the preference-formation process satisfies the Pareto property and the preference between any two alternatives is a function only of the way the criteria rank them, then the generated preference relation is intransitive unless it coincides with the ranking by one of the criteria.

2. Proposition 20.1 is interpreted by some as a proof of the impossibility of aggregating the preferences of the members of a group. This interpretation is incorrect. At most the result says that aggregating preferences in such a way that the social ranking of any two alternatives depends only on their

relative rankings by the individuals is not possible. This requirement can be viewed as a simplicity constraint on the aggregation process. Scoring rules with decreasing weighting functions satisfy all the properties discussed in this chapter except IIA.

3. The requirement that a PAF is defined for all possible preference profiles is very demanding. In many contexts only some preference profiles make sense. In fact, for some meaningful restrictions on the set of preference profiles, majority rule induces a transitive relation. Suppose that the alternatives are ordered along a line (from left to right on the political spectrum, for example) each individual has a favorite alternative, and each individual's ranking falls away on each side of this favorite, so that his preferences are single-peaked. In this case, majority rule induces a social preference relation (see Problem 2).

4. As we mentioned earlier, a preference aggregation function uses information only about the individuals' ordinal rankings; it does not take into account the individuals' intensities of preference and does not compare these intensities across individuals. Consider a society with two individuals and two alternatives. If one individual prefers a to b while the other prefers b to a, then a reasonable assessment of the individuals' aggregated preference would compare the degree to which individual 1 likes a better than b with the degree to which individual 2 likes b better than a. Such information is missing from the model.

20.5 Gibbard-Satterthwaite theorem

We close the chapter with another classical result, the Gibbard-Satterthwaite theorem. This result involves the concept of a social choice rule, which is related to, but different from, a preference aggregation function. Whereas a preference aggregation function assigns a preference relation to each preference profile, a social choice rule assigns an *alternative* to each preference profile, interpreted as the alternative to be chosen given the individuals' preferences.

Definition 20.8: Social choice rule

A *social choice rule* for a society $\langle N, X \rangle$ is a function that assigns a member of X (an alternative) to every profile of strict preference relations over X.

We are interested in social choice rules that satisfy two properties. The first one requires that a social choice rule selects an alternative if there is a consensus that it is the best alternative.

Definition 20.9: Unanimous social choice rule

A social choice rule f for a society $\langle N, X \rangle$ is *unanimous* if for every profile $(\succ^i)_{i \in N}$ of preference relations over X, $f((\succ^i)_{i \in N}) = x$ if x is $\succ^i$-optimal for all $i \in N$.

The second property is central to the result. Imagine that the social planner asks the individuals about their preferences. The property requires that for each individual, whatever his true preference relation, reporting this preference relation is optimal regardless of the other individuals' reports. This property, called strategy-proofness, is discussed in Chapter 17 (Definition 17.4).

Definition 20.10: Strategy-proof social choice rule

The social choice rule f for a society $\langle N, X \rangle$ is *strategy-proof* if for every individual $j \in N$ and every profile $(\succ^i)_{i \in N}$ of preference relations over X, we have $f((\succ^i)_{i \in N}) \succeq^j f((\unrhd^i)_{i \in N})$ for any preference relation $\unrhd^j$ of individual j, where $\unrhd^i = \succ^i$ for all $i \in N \setminus \{j\}$. That is, j optimally reports his true preference relation regardless of the other individuals' reports.

Which social choice rules are unanimous and strategy-proof? The striking answer is that if X contains at least three alternatives then the only such rules are dictatorships, for which there is an individual (the dictator) whose top reported alternative is always chosen. Any dictatorship is strategy-proof because the dictator cannot gain by misreporting his preferences, given that his top reported alternative is chosen, and no other individual can do better than tell the truth since the outcome is independent of his report. We now show that no other social choice rule is unanimous and strategy-proof. The following proposition has several proofs; the one we present uses Arrow's impossibility theorem.

Proposition 20.2: Gibbard-Satterthwaite theorem

For any society $\langle N, X \rangle$ for which X contains at least three alternatives, any social choice rule f that is unanimous and strategy-proof is a dictatorship: for some individual $i^* \in N$, for every profile $(\succ^i)_{i \in N}$ of preference relations over X we have $f((\succ^i)_{i \in N}) \succeq^{i^*} x$ for all $x \in X$.

Proof

Let f be a strategy-proof and unanimous social choice rule.

Step 1 *If $f((\succ^i)_{i \in N}) = x$ and $(\unrhd^i)_{i \in N}$ differs from $(\succ^i)_{i \in N}$ only in that for* *some individual j the rank of some alternative y is higher in $\unrhd^j$ than it is in $\succcurlyeq^j$, then $f((\unrhd^i)_{i\in N}) \in \{x, y\}$.*

Proof. Suppose to the contrary that $f((\unrhd^i)_{i\in N}) = z$ for some $z \notin \{x, y\}$.

If $z \succ^j x$ then f is not strategy-proof because when j's preference relation is $\succcurlyeq^j$, if every other individual i reports $\succcurlyeq^i$ then j is better off reporting $\unrhd^j$.

If $x \succ^j z$ then also $x \rhd^j z$, and f is not strategy-proof because when j's preference relation is $\unrhd^j$ and every other individual i reports $\succcurlyeq^i = \unrhd^i$ then j is better off reporting $\succcurlyeq^j$ (and obtaining the outcome x) than reporting $\unrhd^j$ (and obtaining the outcome z). $\lhd$

Step 2 *For any two alternatives x and y and any preference profile in which x and y are the top two alternatives for all individuals, the social choice rule f chooses either x or y.*

Proof. Assume that there are profiles in which x and y are the top two alternatives for every individual but some other alternative is chosen by f. Let $(\succcurlyeq^i)_{i\in N}$ be such a profile with the maximal number of individuals who rank x above y. The maximal number is not $|N|$ since by unanimity if all individuals rank x at the top then f selects x. Let $f((\succcurlyeq^i)_{i\in N}) = z$ and let j be an individual for whom $y \succ^j x$. If j reports a preference relation in which x is at the top and y is ranked second then either x or y is chosen by f, and both are better than z, contradicting the strategy-proofness of f. $\lhd$

Step 3 *If $(\succcurlyeq^i)_{i\in N}$ and $(\unrhd^i)_{i\in N}$ are two preference profiles for which x and y are the two top alternatives for every individual and $x \succ^i y$ if and only if $x \rhd^i y$ then $f((\succcurlyeq^i)_{i\in N}) = f((\unrhd^i)_{i\in N})$.*

Proof. By Step 2, $f((\succcurlyeq^i)_{i\in N}) \in \{x, y\}$. Without loss of generality assume that $f((\succcurlyeq^i)_{i\in N}) = x$. We can transform $(\succcurlyeq^i)_{i\in N}$ into $(\unrhd^i)_{i\in N}$ by a sequence of moves, at each of which we raise one alternative, other than x or y, for one individual while keeping x and y at the top for all individuals. By Step 1 the chosen alternative after each move is either the raised alternative or the alternative chosen by f before the move. By Step 2 the chosen alternative after every move is either x or y. Thus the chosen alternative after each move is x. We conclude that $f((\unrhd^i)_{i\in N}) = x$. $\lhd$

Step 4 *Given a preference profile $(\succcurlyeq^i)_{i\in N}$ define a social binary relation $\succcurlyeq$ by $x \succcurlyeq y$ if $f((\succsim^i)_{i\in N}) = x$, where for all i the preference relation $\succsim^i$ is obtained from $\succcurlyeq^i$ by moving x and y to the top in their original order. The relation $\succcurlyeq$ is complete and transitive.*

Proof. Completeness follows from Step 2. By Step 3 the relation is anti-symmetric (for no two alternatives $a \succ b$ and $b \succ a$). To verify transitivity, assume that $a \succ b \succ c \succ a$. Consider the profile $(\trianglerighteq^i)_{i \in N}$ obtained from $(\succ^i)_{i \in N}$ by moving the three alternatives to the top, preserving their order, in the preference relation of every individual. By an argument analogous to Step 2, $f((\trianglerighteq^i)_{i \in N}) \in \{a, b, c\}$. Without loss of generality let $f((\trianglerighteq^i)_{i \in N}) = a$. Now, let $(\succsim^i)_{i \in N}$ be the profile obtained from $(\trianglerighteq^i)_{i \in N}$ by downgrading b to the third position in all preferences. By Steps 1 and 2, $f((\succsim^i)_{i \in N}) = a$. For each individual the relative order of a and c in the profiles $(\succsim^i)_{i \in N}$ and $(\succ^i)_{i \in N}$ is the same and thus by Step 3 (given $c \succ a$) $f((\succsim^i)_{i \in N}) = c$, a contradiction. ◁

Step 5 *The preference aggregation function F defined in Step 4 is dictatorial.*

Proof. Step 3 implies that F satisfies IIA, and the unanimity of f implies that F satisfies the Pareto property. The existence of a dictator follows from Arrow's impossibility theorem. ◁

Step 6 *There exists an individual i^* such that $f((\succ^i)_{i \in N})$ is $\succ^{i^*}$-maximal.*

Proof. By Step 5 there is an individual i^* such that $F((\succ^i)_{i \in N}) = \succ^{i^*}$ for any preference profile $(\succ^i)_{i \in N}$. Let $f((\succ^i)_{i \in N}) = x$ and let y be another alternative. By Step 1 we have $f((\trianglerighteq^i)_{i \in N}) = x$, where $\trianglerighteq^i$ is obtained from $\succ^i$ by moving all alternatives except x and y to below these two alternatives (retaining the order of x and y). By the definition of F at Step 4, $F((\succ^i)_{i \in N})$ ranks x above y. Since i^* is the dictator $x \succ^{i^*} y$. ◁

Note that the assumption that X contains three alternatives is crucial for this proof. If X contains only two alternatives a and b, then for any K the rule that chooses the alternative a unless K individuals prefer the outcome b is strategy-proof.

Problems

1. *Two alternatives.* Let $X = \{a, b\}$ and assume, as in the body of the chapter, that each individual has strict preferences over the alternatives (he either prefers a to b or b to a). Assume that the number of individuals is odd.

   Consider the properties neutrality, anonymity, and positive responsiveness.

     a. For each of the properties give an example of a PAF not satisfying that property but satisfying the other two.

     b. Show that majority rule is the *unique* PAF satisfying all three properties.

2. *Single-peaked preferences.* Society consists of an odd number of individuals and the set X consists of three political positions. All individuals agree that one of the positions is on the left of the political spectrum, one is in the middle, and one is on the right, so we call the positions L, M, and R. Position M is not at the bottom of any individual's ranking, so that no individual has the preference $L \succ R \succ M$ or the preference $R \succ L \succ M$.

Show that for any preference profile in this restricted domain, majority rule induces a preference relation over X.

3. A. group of n individuals has to choose an alternative from a set X. Each individual has a favorite alternative. A decision method is a function F that attaches a member of X to each profile $(x_1, \ldots, x_n)$ of favorite alternatives.

     a. Define formally the property of neutrality, which requires that a decision method treats all alternatives equally. Give two different examples of decision methods that satisfy this property.

     b. Define formally the Pareto property, which requires that for any $x \in X$ a decision method chooses x if all individuals choose x. Give an example of a decision method that does not satisfy this property.

     c. Define formally the notion of a dictatorial decision method.

Say that a decision method F satisfies property I if whenever $(x_1, \ldots, x_n)$ and $(y_1, \ldots, y_n)$ satisfy the condition

- for some a the set of individuals who choose a in $(x_1, \ldots, x_n)$ is equal to the set of individuals who choose a in $(y_1, \ldots, y_n)$

then $F(x_1, \ldots, x_n) = a$ if and only if $F(y_1, \ldots, y_n) = a$.

For example, $F(a, b, c, a) = a$ if and only if $F(a, c, d, a) = a$.

     d. Show that if X contains only two alternatives and n is odd then there exists a decision method that is neutral, satisfies the Pareto property and property I, and is not dictatorial.

     e. Assume that X contains n elements and that $n \geq 3$. Show that the only methods that are neutral and satisfy property I are dictatorial.

4. *Classification.* A group N of individuals discusses a group X of objects. Each individual is associated with a partition of the objects into classes. For example, if $X = \{a, b, c\}$ then each individual is associated with one of the five possible partitions (*i*) each object is in a distinct class, (*ii*) all objects are in one class, and (*iii*) one of the objects (a, b, or c) is in its own class and the other two are in the same class. An aggregation method attaches one partition of X to each profile of partitions of X.

   a. Show that the rule that puts two objects in the same class if a majority of the individuals' partitions put them in the same class is not an aggregation method.

   b. Show that the rule that puts two objects in the same class if the partitions of all members of a certain group $G \subseteq N$ put them in the same class is an aggregation method.

5. *Ranking participants in a tournament.* A group of n players compete in a round-robin tournament. Each match ends with one of the players winning the match (a tie is not possible). A *ranking method* attaches to each possible set of results a ranking of the players (possibly with indifferences).

   Consider the following three properties of ranking methods.

   Anonymity The method treats all players equally.

   Monotonicity Let R_1 be a set of results for which the method ranks player i at least as high as player j. Let R_2 be a set of results identical to R_1 except that some player wins against i in R_1 and loses against i in R_2. Then i is ranked (strictly) above j in R_2.

   Independence The relative ranking of any two players is independent of the results for the matches in which they do not participate.

   a. A familiar method ranks players by their number of victories. Verify that this method satisfies the three properties.

   b. For each of the three properties give an example of a method that does not satisfy the property although it satisfies the other two.

6. *Median.* When the space of preferences is restricted, there exist nondictatorial strategy-proof social choice rules. Assume that the number of individuals is $2m + 1$ (for some positive integer m), $X = [0, 1]$, and each individual i has single-peaked preferences (there is $z^i \in X$ such that if $z^i < a < b$ or $b < a < z^i$ then $z^i \succ^i a \succ^i b$). Show that the social choice rule that attaches to every preference profile the median of the peaks is strategy-proof.

Notes

Proposition 20.1 is due to Arrow (1951). The proof we give is due to Geanakoplos (2005). Proposition 20.2 appears in Gibbard (1973) and Satterthwaite (1975). Problem 1 is based on May (1952) and Problem 5 is based on Rubinstein (1980).

References

Akerlof, George A. (1970), "The market for 'lemons': quality uncertainty and the market mechanism." *Quarterly Journal of Economics*, 84, 488–500, https://doi.org/10.2307/1879431. [201]

Allais, Maurice (1953), "Le comportement de l'homme rationnel devant le risque: critique des postulats et axiomes de l'école Américain." *Econometrica*, 21, 503–546. [43]

Arrow, Kenneth J. (1951), *Social choice and individual values*, first edition. Wiley, New York. [345]

Arrow, Kenneth J. (1964), "The role of securities in the optimal allocation of risk-bearing." *Review of Economic Studies*, 31, 91–96. [Translation of paper originally published in French in 1953.] [173]

Arrow, Kenneth J., and Gerard Debreu (1954), "Existence of an equilibrium for a competitive economy." *Econometrica*, 22, 265–290, http://dx.doi.org/10.2307/1907353. [155]

Aumann, Robert J. (1974), "Subjectivity and correlation in randomized strategies." *Journal of Mathematical Economics*, 1, 67–96, http://dx.doi.org/10.1016/0304-4068(74)90037-8. [255]

Aumann, Robert J., and Lloyd Shapley (1994), "Long-term competition—a game-theoretic analysis." In *Essays in game theory* (Nimrod Megiddo, ed.), 1–15, Springer-Verlag, New York. [294]

Basu, Kaushik (1994), "The Traveler's Dilemma: paradoxes of rationality in game theory." *American Economic Review (Papers and Proceedings)*, 84, 391–395. [255]

Benoît, Jean-Pierre, and Vijay Krishna (1987), "Nash equilibria of finitely repeated games." *International Journal of Game Theory*, 16, 197–204, http://dx.doi.org/10.1007/BF01756291. [294]

Bertrand, Joseph (1883), "Review of 'Théorie mathématique de la richesse sociale' by Léon Walras and 'Recherches sur les principes mathématiques de la théorie des richesses' by Augustin Cournot." *Journal des Savants*, 499–508.

[Translated by Margaret Chevaillier as 'Review by Joseph Bertrand of two books', *History of Political Economy*, 24 (1992), 646–653.] [255]

Borel, Émile (1921), "La théorie du jeu et les equations intégrales à noyau symétrique." *Comptes Rendus Hebdomadaires des Séances de l'Académie des Sciences (Paris)*, 173, 1304–1308. [Translated by Leonard J. Savage as "The theory of play and integral equations with skew symmetric kernels", *Econometrica*, 21 (1953), 97–100.] [255]

Borel, Émile (1924), *Éléments de la théorie des probabilités*, third edition. Hermann, Paris. [Pages 204–221 translated by Leonard J. Savage as "On games that involve chance and the skill of the players", *Econometrica*, 21 (1953), 101–115.] [255]

Borel, Émile (1927), "Sur les systèmes de formes linéaires à déterminant symétrique gauche et la théorie générale du jeu." *Comptes Rendus Hebdomadaires des Séances de l'Académie des Sciences (Paris)*, 184, 52–54. [Translated by Leonard J. Savage as "On systems of linear forms of skew symmetric determinant and the general theory of play", *Econometrica*, 21 (1953), 116–117.] [255]

Chernoff, Herman (1954), "Rational selection of decision functions." *Econometrica*, 22, 422–443. [29]

Clarke, Edward H. (1971), "Multipart pricing of public goods." *Public Choice*, 11, 17–33. [304]

Cournot, Antoine A. (1838), *Recherches sur les principes mathématiques de la théorie des richesses*. Hachette, Paris. [Translated by Nathaniel T. Bacon as *Researches into the mathematical principles of the theory of wealth*, Macmillan, New York, 1897.] [255]

Davidson, Donald, J. C. C. McKinsey, and Patrick Suppes (1955), "Outlines of a formal theory of value, I." *Philosophy of Science*, 22, 140–160, https://doi.org/10.1086/287412. [29]

Debreu, Gerard (1954), "Representation of a preference ordering by a numerical function." In *Decision processes* (Robert M. Thrall, Clyde H. Coombs, and Robert L. Davis, eds.), chapter 11, 159–165, Wiley, New York. [15, 56]

Debreu, Gerard (1959), *Theory of value*. Yale University Press, New Haven. [155]

Edgeworth, Francis Y. (1881), *Mathematical psychics*. Kegan Paul, London. [155]

Flood, Merrill M. (1958/59), "Some experimental games." *Management Science*, 5, 5–26. [255, 293]

Frisch, Ragnar (1957), "Sur un problème d'économie pure." *Metroeconomica*, 9, 79–111, https://doi.org/10.1111/j.1467-999X.1957.tb00651.x. [Republication of 1926 work.] [15]

Gale, David, and Lloyd S. Shapley (1962), "College admissions and the stability of marriage." *American Mathematical Monthly*, 69, 9–15, https://doi.org/10.4169/amer.math.monthly.120.05.386. [315]

Geanakoplos, John (2005), "Three brief proofs of Arrow's impossibility theorem." *Economic Theory*, 26, 211–215, https://doi.org/10.1007/s00199-004-0556-7. [345]

Gibbard, Allan (1973), "Manipulation of voting schemes: a general result." *Econometrica*, 41, 587–601, https://doi.org/10.2307/1914083. [345]

Glazer, Jacob, and Ching-to Albert Ma (1989), "Efficient allocation of a 'prize'—King Solomon's dilemma." *Games and Economic Behavior*, 1, 222–233, https://doi.org/10.1016/0899-8256(89)90010-9. [294]

Groves, Theodore (1973), "Incentives in teams." *Econometrica*, 41, 617–631, https://doi.org/10.2307/1914085. [304]

Groves, Theodore, and Martin Loeb (1975), "Incentives and public inputs." *Journal of Public Economics*, 4, 211–226, https://doi.org/10.1016/0047-2727(75)90001-8. [304]

Harris, Christopher, and John Vickers (1985), "Perfect equilibrium in a model of a race." *Review of Economic Studies*, 52, 193–209, https://doi.org/10.2307/2297616. [294]

Hotelling, Harold (1929), "Stability in competition." *Economic Journal*, 39, 41–57, https://doi.org/10.2307/2224214. [255]

Huber, Joel, John W. Payne, and Christopher Puto (1982), "Adding asymmetrically dominated alternatives: violations of regularity and the similarity hypothesis." *Journal of Consumer Research*, 9, 90–98, https://doi.org/10.1086/208899. [29]

Jones, Peter, and Li-Jen Jessica Hwang (2005), "Perceptions of waiting time in different service queues." [Unpublished paper.] [199]

Kagel, John H., and Dan Levin (1993), "Independent private value auctions: bidder behaviour in first-, second- and third-price auctions with varying numbers of bidders." *Economic Journal*, 103, 868–879, https://doi.org/10.2307/2234706. [225]

Kahneman, Daniel, and Amos Tversky (1984), "Choices, values, and frames." *American Psychologist*, 39, 341–350, https://doi.org/10.1037/0003-066X.39.4.341. [29]

Kuhn, Harold W. (1950), "Extensive games." *Proceedings of the National Academy of Sciences of the United States of America*, 36, 570–576. [293]

Kuhn, Harold W. (1953), "Extensive games and the problem of information." In *Contributions to the theory of games*, volume II (Harold W. Kuhn and Albert W. Tucker, eds.), 193–216, Princeton University Press, Princeton. [293]

Luce, R. Duncan, and Howard Raiffa (1957), *Games and decisions*. Wiley, New York. [20, 29, 293]

Marshall, Alfred (1895), *Principles of economics*, third edition, volume 1. Macmillan, London. [74]

Marx, Karl (1971), *Critique of the Gotha Programme*. Progress Publishers, Moscow. [Written in 1875; first published in 1890.] [319]

May, Kenneth O. (1952), "A set of independent necessary and sufficient conditions for simple majority decision." *Econometrica*, 20, 680–684, https://doi.org/10.2307/1907651. [345]

Maynard Smith, John (1974), "The theory of games and the evolution of animal conflicts." *Journal of Theoretical Biology*, 47, 209–221, https://doi.org/10.1016/0022-5193(74)90110-6. [255]

McKenzie, Lionel (1954), "On equilibrium in Graham's model of world trade and other competitive systems." *Econometrica*, 22, 147–161, https://doi.org/10.2307/1907539. [155]

McKenzie, Lionel W. (1959), "On the existence of general equilibrium for a competitive market." *Econometrica*, 27, 54–71, https://doi.org/10.2307/1907777. [155]

Moulin, Hervé (1986), *Game theory for the social sciences*, second edition. New York University Press, New York. [255]

Nash, John F. (1950), "Equilibrium points in n-person games." *Proceedings of the National Academy of Sciences of the United States of America*, 36, 48–49, `https://doi.org/10.1073/pnas.36.1.48`. [255]

O'Neill, Barry (1987), "Nonmetric test of the minimax theory of two-person zero-sum games." *Proceedings of the National Academy of Sciences of the United States of America*, 84, 2106–2109. [255]

Osborne, Martin J., and Ariel Rubinstein (1994), *A course in game theory.* MIT Press, Cambridge, Massachusetts. [287]

Osborne, Martin J., and Ariel Rubinstein (1998), "Games with procedurally rational players." *American Economic Review*, 88, 834–847. [255]

Piccione, Michele, and Ariel Rubinstein (2007), "Equilibrium in the jungle." *Economic Journal*, 117, 883–896, `https://doi.org/10.1111/j.1468-0297.2007.02072.x`. [120]

Pratt, John W. (1964), "Risk aversion in the small and in the large." *Econometrica*, 32, 122–136, `https://doi.org/10.2307/1913738`. [43]

Roemer, John E. (1986), "Equality of resources implies equality of welfare." *Quarterly Journal of Economics*, 101, 751–784, `https://doi.org/10.2307/1884177`. [327]

Roemer, John E. (2010), "Kantian equilibrium." *Scandinavian Journal of Economics*, 112, 1–24, `https://doi.org/10.1111/j.1467-9442.2009.01592.x`. [255]

Rosenthal, Robert W. (1981), "Games of perfect information, predatory pricing and the chain-store paradox." *Journal of Economic Theory*, 25, 92–100, `https://doi.org/10.1016/0022-0531(81)90018-1`. [255, 293]

Rothschild, Michael, and Joseph E. Stiglitz (1976), "Equilibrium in competitive insurance markets: an essay on the economics of imperfect information." *Quarterly Journal of Economics*, 90, 629–649, `https://doi.org/10.2307/1885326`. [213]

Rubinstein, Ariel (1977), "Equilibrium in supergames." Research Memorandum 25, Center for Research in Mathematical Economics and Game Theory, Hebrew University, Jerusalem, `https://arielrubinstein.tau.ac.il/papers/rm25.pdf`. [294]

Rubinstein, Ariel (1979), "Equilibrium in supergames with the overtaking criterion." *Journal of Economic Theory*, 21, 1–9, https://doi.org/10.1016/0022-0531(79)90002-4. [294]

Rubinstein, Ariel (1980), "Ranking the participants in a tournament." *SIAM Journal of Applied Mathematics*, 38, 108–111, https://doi.org/10.1137/0138009. [345]

Rubinstein, Ariel (1982), "Perfect equilibrium in a bargaining model." *Econometrica*, 50, 97–109, https://doi.org/10.2307/1912531. [293]

Rubinstein, Ariel (2006a), *Lecture notes in microeconomic theory*. Princeton University Press, Princeton, https://doi.org/10.2307/j.ctvcm4hb2. [15, 29, 43, 56, 74, 87]

Rubinstein, Ariel (2006b), "A sceptic's comment on the study of economics." *Economic Journal*, 116, C1–C9, https://doi.org/10.1111/j.1468-0297.2006.01071.x. [87]

Rubinstein, Ariel (2012), *Economic fables*. Open Book Publishers, Cambridge, https://doi.org/10.11647/OBP.0020. [xiii, 120, 135]

Samuelson, Paul A. (1938), "A note on the pure theory of consumer's behaviour." *Economica*, 5, 61–71, https://doi.org/10.2307/2548836. [74]

Satterthwaite, Mark A. (1975), "Strategy-proofness and Arrow's conditions: existence and correspondence theorems for voting procedures and social welfare functions." *Journal of Economic Theory*, 10, 187–217, https://doi.org/10.1016/0022-0531(75)90050-2. [345]

Selten, Reinhard (1965), "Spieltheoretische Behandlung eines Oligopolmodells mit Nachfrageträgheit." *Zeitschrift für die gesamte Staatswissenschaft*, 121, 301–324 and 667–689. [293]

Shapley, Lloyd S., and Herbert Scarf (1974), "On cores and indivisibility." *Journal of Mathematical Economics*, 1, 23–37. [135]

Shubik, Martin (1959), *Strategy and market structure*. Wiley, New York. [293]

Simon, Herbert A. (1956), "Rational choice and the structure of the environment." *Psychological Review*, 63, 129–138, https://doi.org/10.1037/h0042769. [29]

Slutsky, Eugenio (1915), "Sulla teoria del bilancio del consumatore." *Giornale degli Economisti e Rivista di Statistica*, 51, 1–26. [74]

Spence, Michael (1973), "Job market signaling." *Quarterly Journal of Economics*, 87, 355–374, https://doi.org/10.2307/1882010. [213]

Tirole, Jean (1988), *The theory of industrial organization*. MIT Press, Cambridge. [102]

Topkis, Donald M. (1979), "Equilibrium points in nonzero-sum n-person sub-modular games." *SIAM Journal on Control and Optimization*, 17, 773–787, https://doi.org/10.1137/0317054. [255]

Tversky, Amos, and Daniel Kahneman (1986), "Rational choice and the framing of decisions." *Journal of Business*, 59, S251–S278. [29]

Vickrey, William (1961), "Counterspeculation, auctions, and competitive sealed tenders." *Journal of Finance*, 16, 8–37, https://doi.org/10.1111/j.1540-6261.1961.tb02789.x. [255, 304]

von Neumann, John (1928), "Zur theorie der gesellschaftsspiele." *Mathematische Annalen*, 100, 295–320. [Translated by Sonya Bargmann as "On the theory of games of strategy" in *Contributions to the theory of games*, volume IV (Albert W. Tucker and R. Duncan Luce, eds.), 13–42, Princeton University Press, Princeton, 1959.] [255]

von Neumann, John, and Oskar Morgenstern (1944), *Theory of games and economic behavior*, first edition. Princeton University Press, Princeton. [255, 293]

von Neumann, John, and Oskar Morgenstern (1947), *Theory of games and economic behavior*, second edition. Princeton University Press, Princeton. [43]

Walras, Léon (1874), *Éléments d'économie politique pure*. Corbaz, Lausanne. [155]

Wold, Herman O. A. (1943), "A synthesis of pure demand analysis, Part II." *Skandinavisk Aktuarietidskrift*, 26, 220–263, https://doi.org/10.1080/03461238.1943.10404737. [15]

Zahavi, Amotz (1975), "Mate selection—a selection for a handicap." *Journal of Theoretical Biology*, 53, 205–214, https://doi.org/10.1016/0022-5193(75)90111-3. [213]

Index

Definition   Proposition   Procedure   Example   Problem

Definition Proposition Procedure Example Problem

Definition   Proposition   Procedure   Example   Problem

Definition   Proposition   Procedure   Example   Problem

THE PUBLISHING TEAM

Alessandra Tosi was the managing editor for this book.

Adèle Kreager and James Hobson proofread the book.

Martin J. Osborne created the cover image and designed the front cover.

The book was typeset by the authors, who are greatly indebted to Donald Knuth (TeX), Leslie Lamport (LaTeX), Timothy van Zandt (PSTricks), Thomas F. Sturm (tcolorbox), and others for creating superlative software and generously making it freely available. The text font is 12pt Utopia.

Luca Baffa provided quality control and archived the external links.

Cameron Craig created the paperback, hardback, and pdf editions.